Eisenhower and the Cold War Economy

Eisenhower and the
Cold War Economy

WILLIAM M. MCCLENAHAN JR.

and

WILLIAM H. BECKER

The Johns Hopkins University Press
Baltimore

All rights reserved. Published 2011
Printed in the United States of America on acid-free paper
2 4 6 8 9 7 5 3 1

The Johns Hopkins University Press
2715 North Charles Street
Baltimore, Maryland 21218-4363
www.press.jhu.edu

Library of Congress Cataloging-in-Publication Data

McClenahan, William M.
Eisenhower and the Cold War economy / William M. McClenahan, Jr.,
and William H. Becker.
p. cm.
Includes bibliographical references and index.
ISBN-13: 978-1-4214-0265-9 (hardcover : alk. paper)
ISBN-10: 1-4214-0265-3 (hardcover : alk. paper)
1. United States—Economic policy—1945–1960.   2. United
States—Politics and government—1953–1961.   3. Cold War—
Economic aspects—United States.   4. National security—Economic
aspects—United States.   5. Eisenhower, Dwight D. (Dwight David),
1890–1969.   I. Becker, William H.   II. Title.
HC106.5.M326 2011
330.973'0921—dc22   2011009951

A catalog record for this book is available from the British Library.

*Special discounts are available for bulk purchases of this book. For more
information, please contact Special Sales at 410-516-6936 or
specialsales@press.jhu.edu.*

The Johns Hopkins University Press uses environmentally friendly
book materials, including recycled text paper that is composed of
at least 30 percent post-consumer waste, whenever possible.

To the memory of Raymond J. Saulnier

Contents

Preface   *ix*

Prologue: Preparing for the Presidency   1

PART 1   MACRO-LEVEL ECONOMIC POLICIES

1 Setting a Consistent Course, 1953–1956   23

2 Economic Policy in Good Times, 1955–1957   53

3 Narrowing the Course, 1957–1961   81

PART 2   MICROECONOMIC POLICIES

4 Agriculture: A Tough Battle   113

5 A Coalescing Antitrust Policy   152

6 Foreign Economic Policy   183

Epilogue: The Eisenhower Legacy   225

Acknowledgments   *235*
Abbreviations   *237*
Notes   *239*
Essay on Primary Sources   *293*
Index   *295*

Preface

Our book challenges what many people think they know about the Eisenhower administration: that for eight years the White House was focused on military and foreign policy, while in domestic affairs it produced a "middle way" between what New Dealers and conservative Republicans advocated. This latter portrayal is not so much inaccurate as insufficient in characterizing Eisenhower's domestic policies, especially his approach to the economy. Few writing about the Eisenhower presidency devote much attention to his economic policies. What our detailed study demonstrates is that during Eisenhower's tenure in the White House, economic policy was second only to national security in the president's mind. Indeed, at times it is inaccurate to suggest that one was subordinate to the other. Eisenhower believed the economy's structure and performance to be inextricably connected to how the United States needed to respond to the changed international and domestic circumstances it faced in the post–World War II world. Prosecuting the Cold War, he thought, posed a profound dilemma. How was the United States to engage in that struggle without undermining American political democracy *and* a market economy? Preserving the American way of life was, to Eisenhower, the preeminent objective of the Cold War. To achieve that goal required sustained attention to military, security, and diplomatic policy. But it also required a sharp focus on economic policy, the subject of this book.

We believe that it's a good time to take a fresh look at Eisenhower and the making of economic policy in the 1950s. The United States in the first decades of the twenty-first century faces major changes in both the national and the international economy, as Eisenhower did in the mid-twentieth century. Of course, the American and world economies of the 1950s were quite different from those of the twenty-first century, and so Eisenhower and his presidency must be taken on their own terms. After all of the economic changes in the last two generations, however, policymakers and interested members of the public today may still learn from the Eisenhower approach to policy.

Eisenhower offers an attractive example of how to cope with broad domestic and international change. He struggled to apply traditional financial principles to the economic policies of a government profoundly altered by the Depression of the 1930s, World War II, and the Cold War. His thinking was essentially conservative in ways often neglected or forgotten in current political discourse. Eisenhower emphasized personal self-reliance and a limited role for government in economic affairs. He also believed in gradual change and rejected sharp or radical alterations in government policies (e.g., on taxes and Social Security). Nevertheless, he tied his commitment to gradualism to an appreciation for the long term. Thus, Eisenhower could be pragmatic in short-term matters, something necessary in view of the constraints under which he had to operate. That is, he could be flexible within the parameters of his conservatism. This served him well in addressing, with varying degrees of success, the changes in international and domestic policy and economic environments in the 1950s and the legacy of policies and institutions created to meet the challenges of the Great Depression and World War II.

For political observers more generally concerned about the direction of public policy making, Eisenhower has much to offer, too. Few presidents were more skeptical of the distortions that partisanship could bring to government policy. Likewise, no president in the twentieth century understood the growth of bureaucracy better than did Eisenhower. His economic policy was informed by a keen understanding of the workings of large organizations, gained from a career in the army, high-level command during World War II, and an important role at the Pentagon in the Truman years. He feared that growing ties between public and private business bureaucracies imperiled the American way of life, especially as the Pentagon developed close relations with Congress and those who supplied the military. Early on, he saw the danger that policy making could be captured by a nexus of well-organized private interests, a compliant Congress, and a federal establishment bent on self-preservation and enhanced missions.

His military career also influenced his approach to economic policy in other ways. With no formal training in economics, he nevertheless embraced the economist's zeal for the optimal use of scarce resources. Because of his long experience as a military planner, he recognized that policy objectives should always be in line with available resources. So as president he sought to balance foreign policy goals with the resources available for their achievement.

Prior experience also made Eisenhower a shrewd, flexible, but principled leader. He recognized that the international and domestic circumstances of the postwar world were significantly different from those faced by his three immediate predecessors, Herbert Hoover, Franklin D. Roosevelt, and Harry S. Truman. Because of the Cold War the new occupant of the White House inherited an open-ended, extremely costly, long-term commitment to international engagement and a federal government grown large because of the Depression of the 1930s, a global war, and the beginnings of the Cold War. But these realities were not static. Soviet Cold War strategy changed after the death of Stalin, soon after Eisenhower was inaugurated. And a younger, more mobile, and ultimately more prosperous American citizenry had enhanced expectations of government. What did not change were the narrow interests of partisan politicians and the intractability of well-entrenched bureaucracies. Eisenhower appreciated the dynamic and static realities of the unique new world he faced overseas and at home, and he brought a holistic rather than an ad hoc approach to the making of policy, especially economic policy. This has not been a general characteristic common to most of those who followed him in the White House.

To achieve his goals of fighting the Cold War while preserving the American way of life, he had to address four interrelated challenges. How to pay for the prosecution of the Cold War was his most important and persistent challenge. Second was how to shape a Republican economic policy that adhered to traditional party commitments to restrain budgets, limit taxes, keep inflation low, and reduce the deficit, while recognizing new foreign and domestic demands on the United States. Third was how to modify policies inherited from the New Deal and the Fair Deal, many that Eisenhower believed irrational and, indeed, harmful. Fourth was how to work with new instruments of government policy-making authority—in particular, the Council of Economic Advisers and the newly independent Federal Reserve Bank—to meet Congress's mandate articulated in the Employment Act of 1946 essentially to avoid a repeat of the Depression of the 1930s.

Eisenhower successfully met many of the challenges he faced. Full success with others frankly eluded him. He had more difficulty with microeconomic policies than macroeconomic. His attempts to reform farm price support polices and the subsidies they bestowed ran into a firestorm of opposition. Well-entrenched farming interests in both political parties succeeded in protecting many aspects of what Eisenhower wanted to change. Foreign economic policy found the administration altering its initial goal of eliminating government-sponsored foreign aid and unreservedly promoting freer trade. Because of Soviet inroads in the developing world and the growth of leftist movements there and elsewhere, the United States continued foreign economic and military assistance. Trade policy required compromises, too. The administration tried to manage the growth of aggressively marketed Japanese exports to the United States, integrate Japan into the world trading system, and continue the forward momentum of trade liberalization.

In important respects, Eisenhower's macroeconomic policies met with greater success. Certainly that was the case when compared to the previous administration and those that followed in the 1960s and 1970s. This was particularly true in Eisenhower's dogged efforts to restrain inflation. Between 1953 and 1961, economic growth rates were slightly lower than over the period 1946–53, but inflation was dramatically lower. By the end of his term in 1961, few residual inflationary expectations existed in the American economy. Economic growth rates also were higher in the 1960s and 1970s than in the 1950s, but inflation was dramatically higher after 1965, reaching unprecedented peacetime levels at the end of the 1970s.

Eisenhower also succeeded in reducing the growth of federal spending. In 1929, federal purchases of goods and services represented little more than 1 percent of the nation's gross national product (GNP), while state and local governments' were little more than 7 percent. Subsequently, the Great Depression of the 1930s, World War II, and the Cold War changed the role of the federal government in the economy. In 1950, because of an increase in the ranks of federal employees, the scale of bureaucracy, and the number of departments to support new domestic programs and foreign responsibilities the federal purchase of goods and services had increased to almost 7 percent of GNP. When Eisenhower took office in 1953, it soared to 16 percent because of the Korean War and a contemporaneous Cold War strategic buildup. Direct costs of the Korean War ended soon after Eisenhower became president, but thereafter he carried on a determined campaign to control spending and the growth of government. By the end of his second term he had done much to flatten the steep trajectory of military spending on Cold War weaponry and forces that had been authorized during a sharp acceleration in Truman's last years as president. During his two terms, Eisenhower's policies led to dramatic declines in defense spending, increased fiscal restraint, and generally low inflation. Because of economic growth, by 1960 federal government purchases of goods and services declined to just 10.4 percent of GNP, a percentage that remained relatively constant through the late 1970s. Continued economic growth, of course, contributed to that outcome. But Eisenhower had stabilized and then reduced the growth of the federal government vis-à-vis a growing national economy and state and local government in the era before transfer payments (Social Security, Medicare, and Medicaid) came to dominate national expenditures during the 1970s.[1]

In doing so, Eisenhower succeeded in balancing three budgets (fiscal 1956, 1957, and 1960), although the surpluses produced were not large enough to substantially reduce the long-term public debt of the United States in the 1950s. Eisenhower understood that deficits would be needed during recessions and that the goal of macroeconomic policy was to approximately balance the budget over the business cycle. Compared to the experience of the United States over the last thirty years, the budget deficits that the Eisenhower administration ran were modest. Even the $12.4 billion deficit that deeply disappointed Eisenhower in fiscal 1959 was only about 2.4 percent of GNP—a fraction of today's figure.

These accomplishments support revisionist historians' positive views of the Eisenhower administration. Over recent decades his reputation among serious students of the presidency has continued to rise, as more of the president's papers have been opened to researchers. We do not question the revisionist view that has contributed to the change in Eisenhower's standing among presidents. In fact, Eisenhower's handling of economic policy adds to what the revisionists have had to say about Eisenhower. They have put to rest notions that the president was passive, politically inept, and dominated by powerful associates such as George M. Humphrey and John Foster Dulles. Instead, Eisenhower appears much more informed, determined, and indeed visionary than he was given credit for in the 1950s and immediately thereafter. His record in economic policy compares favorably to that of those who have occupied the White House since 1961.

Nevertheless, such studies do not present the full scope of what Eisenhower hoped to achieve with his economic policies. Some revisionist scholars have focused on the growing prosperity during the Eisenhower years. Their works recognize that in making federal economic policy Eisenhower was an active and effective executive. Books by John W. Sloan, Iwan Morgan, and Gerard Clarfield, for example, credit the president with skillfully addressing monetary and fiscal policy and the larger issue of military reorganization and spending.[2] These authors, however, have not appreciated how the administration had to navigate in new—often quite difficult and challenging—international and domestic policy environments. Their works do not portray Eisenhower's economic policy as an essential part of the administration's approach to the Cold War. And certainly the general public has little understanding of the issues involved in economic policy making in the 1950s; the challenges the administration faced in addressing these new situations; and what its responses were.[3]

In writing about the Eisenhower years, others focus on the president as an exemplar of "Modern Republicanism." It's true that, especially during the 1956 presidential election, he talked much of Modern Republicanism.[4] According to this characterization, the administration represented a "middle way" between the antigovernment sentiments of the Hoover-Taft wing of the Republican Party and the "statist" inclinations of the Democrats' New Deal and Fair Deal. Eisenhower accepted various aspects of the New Deal, including Social Security and the agencies created in the 1930s to regulate the banking, finance, communications, transportation, and energy industries. Over time the administration also supported an expansion of the federal role in education, road building, and limited increases in expenditures for education, urban renewal, and conservation.

On balance, though, we conclude that the president's "liberal" tendencies were outweighed by his more traditional "conservative" predilections. This became particularly obvious in the second term, although Eisenhower's commitment to conservative fiscal policies—balanced budgets, tight money, reduced public debt, and low inflation—were obvious throughout his eight years in the White House. What's important about Eisenhower is not that he accepted some liberal programs or not that he was about to fight an all-out campaign against the New Deal and Fair Deal programs. It's that he thought that he could restrain the growth of government by adherence to traditional conservative precepts of fiscal management and by reigning in and reducing the budgets for major government bureaucracies.

We organize our account as follows. In the prologue we discuss Eisenhower's ideas and the experiences in his youth and his military career that shaped his views not only about the economy and management but also about American life and its institutions. We also consider the context in which the Eisenhower administration had to operate. The policies followed by his predecessor and the way in which Truman used government institutions responsible for economic policy created the political and policy realities faced by the new Eisenhower administration upon taking office.

The remainder of the book is divided into two parts. In each chapter we orient the discussion about various macro- and microeconomic policy issues to focus on Eisenhower's ideas about and goals for the economy. Part 1 addresses macroeconomic policy: issues having to do with fiscal and monetary policy. We also consider some aspects of debt management as well as the balance of payments. Chapters 1, 2, and 3 examine how Eisenhower created an organizational structure to make economic policy, how he dealt with recessions and a boom, and how fiscal considerations shaped his strategic response to the Cold War. In part 2, chapters 4, 5, and 6 deal with microeconomic policy, in alphabetical order: agriculture, antitrust, and foreign economic policy. Of course, these were not the only economic issues that the administration faced—there were significant, even dramatic, changes in transportation, energy, and labor relations policies.

In selecting the microeconomic policies we cover, often neglected in writings about the administration, we highlight subjects that Eisenhower himself and his closest advisers paid attention to. Eisenhower saw foreign economic policy as of great importance, in large part because it had direct Cold War policy ramifications. Foreign economic policy exemplified how the president's market-oriented goals fared against the realities of a changing international economy and new directions in the Cold War. But the other two policies also received considerable presidential attention. Agricultural exports and their prices had foreign policy ramifications among allies and in the developing world. But spending on domestic agricultural subsidies (price supports) dwarfed all other spending, after expenditures on defense and interest on the national debt. Eisenhower hoped expenditures for agriculture could be reduced by introducing more market-based discipline to policies inherited from Roosevelt and Truman.

Antitrust was significant because Eisenhower was initially concerned that under Roosevelt and Truman it had become a tool to gain partisan advantage. Eventually, after careful study, the administration discounted the importance of partisanship in the application of the antitrust laws. Far more important was that the administration's policy coalesced around new statutes and initiatives. As such it was largely able to reduce uncertainty about the application of the antitrust laws to the new Cold War economy. In the epilogue, we give perspective to the Eisenhower experience in federal economic policy, addressing what of the 1950s may be of relevance to those making policy half a century later and what Eisenhower contributed to a "conservative" understanding of what economic policy might be.

Eisenhower and the Cold War Economy

PROLOGUE

Preparing for the Presidency

Eisenhower took office in January 1953 in a transformed world of international and domestic politics. He had spent much of the previous seven years advising President Harry S. Truman and his administration on how the military should adjust to a new international environment. As a result, Eisenhower became deeply engaged in contemplating the new realities brought about by the Great Depression, World War II, and the Cold War. His professional experiences as an army officer during the interwar period, the war itself, and the postwar Truman administration shaped his thinking about important issues, including the economy.[1] Obviously, Eisenhower had played a major role as a military leader in World War II as Supreme Allied Commander, Europe. He understood well the momentous changes that the conflict had brought about in warfare, diplomacy, and the United States' international role. But the emergence of the Cold War called for fresh thinking about the country's enlarged role in the world and the implications for the mission of the American military, its organization, resulting costs, and impact on American economic life.

During the post–World War II period, Eisenhower developed distinct ideas about the interrelationship between Cold War strategy and the economy. The ideas he formed in these years served as the basis for his approach to economic policy during his presidency. For most of the Truman era Eisenhower had served as a high-level army officer. He worked directly with the president to reorganize the military and prepare it operationally and strategically to meet the needs of the Cold War. So, during the Truman administration, Eisenhower had the opportunity to observe firsthand the strategic, political, and budget problems the president encountered in developing a Cold War strategy. Because of Eisenhower's status as one of the two best-known war heroes of the era (Douglas MacArthur was the other) his opinions on military and strategic issues were closely followed by the press. His high profile encouraged speculation, indeed even before the end of the war, that he might seek the presidency. Truman, on more than one occasion, privately encouraged him to consider running for president. He was not alone. At first, Eisenhower dismissed such talk. By 1948, however, his interest had been stoked. Over the next four years, a combination of ambition, sense of duty, and growing unhappiness with Truman's policies, especially spending on the military that grew out of Truman's approach to the Cold War and the Korean War, led Eisenhower to seek the Republican presidential nomination in 1952. He feared that leaders like Truman, war hero General Douglas MacArthur, and Republican senator Robert A. Taft, a major voice in the Republican Party, were not up to addressing the country's defense and economic problems.[2] Eisenhower believed that national security and national economic solvency were mutually dependent. In his eyes, failure to understand that linkage disqualified a person for high-level responsibilities.[3]

EISENHOWER, THE POST–WORLD WAR II MILITARY, AND THE COLD WAR

Eisenhower served as army chief of staff (1945–48), informal head of the Joint Chiefs of Staff (1949), and NATO Supreme Allied Commander, Europe (1950–52). Truman appointed Eisenhower to each of these positions. He had close access to the president and had the opportunity to follow closely many of the problems Truman faced. Eisenhower's focus was on military matters, but these impinged on many of the other major contentious issues of the time, including economic policy. He was deeply involved in one of the central debates of the Truman administration over Cold War strategy and how to pay for it. This was to be a dominant issue in the Eisenhower administration, too. In view of his experience, Eisenhower was a powerful voice in the debates over the future organization and financing of the armed services. Even during his two years (1948–50) as president of Columbia University, Eisenhower remained heavily engaged with these issues, traveling numerous times from New York to confer at the White House and Pentagon.

During each of his postwar appointments Eisenhower was deeply enmeshed in the often sharp debates over reorganizing and financing the military establishment to cope with the Cold War. From these experiences, Eisenhower developed strong views about how tightly entwined Cold War strategy was to the country's abilities to fund the military. Integral to the arguments over organization were contests among the armed services over their missions and funding, and growing concerns of the economic consequences of increased spending on defense. To address these problems, Eisenhower became a leading proponent of integrating the armed services (army, navy, marines, and army air corps) into a unified command structure. He believed such integration was the only cost-effective way to develop and implement Cold War strategy. Once the air force achieved independent status in 1947, he became even more strongly wedded to the need for unification in the interest of developing and carrying out a coherent, affordable national strategy.

Eisenhower's experience during World War II had convinced him of the value of a unified command within the major theaters of the war. Indeed, in his estimation, unified theater commands produced the teamwork that made victory possible. As supreme commander of the Allied forces in the European Theater, he had joined American and British forces together into a single command. If the military leadership of two countries could work jointly for a common cause, he refused to accept that the individual services of the American military could not do the same. He rejected notions—common to the British in World War II and to leaders of the US Navy in the late 1940s—that the individual services could work best through a loose, consensus-based organizational structure.[4]

So, he carried into the debates over Cold War strategy his conviction that ground, naval, and air power had to be deployed in concert. The advent of nuclear weapons and long-range bombers reinforced his views about the necessity of integrated forces. A joint military command appealed to Eisenhower for economic reasons, too. He anticipated savings by minimizing duplication of equipment and overlapping missions.[5] But more importantly, a unified approach to the assignment of missions, the development of strategy, and the allocation of resources would remove the source of the intense rivalries among the services over funding that, in his view, led to serious inefficiencies and redundancies.[6]

Eisenhower's commitment to a combined approach to service missions had developed years before in the late 1920s and early 1930s. His disdain for the parochial interests of each service first grew during these years, as he witnessed an unseemly scramble for scarce resources between the army and the navy. His ideas crystallized during an important stint he had in the office of the secretary of the army.

At the end of 1929, Secretary of War Patrick J. Hurley brought Eisenhower to the War Department to work on planning for industrial mobilization in a possible future war. During the 1920s, Hurley, as assistant secretary, had focused on industrial planning, only to be frustrated by a lack of interest in the Harding and Coolidge administrations, both intent on cutting back the military. President Hoover, however, had different ideas. Deeply interested in organizational questions and the need for long-term planning, he appointed Hurley secretary of the army. Hurley used the opportunity to begin serious work on industrial war planning. Eisenhower, as the leader of the investigative team, produced a detailed plan for industrial mobilization in a future conflict. In taking the lead on researching and then writing the Industrial Mobilization Plan (IMP), Eisenhower visited numerous military installations and many of the factories that supplied the large variety of goods the American military would need to fight a major war. He met with and got to know many army officers, industrial leaders, and government officials.[7]

Eisenhower premised the IMP report on ideas he wrote about while at the Army War College in 1927–28. During his time there, he became convinced that the advantage in future wars would go to countries that had thoroughly planned for industrial production, access to raw materials, and adequate reserves of manpower. He believed that, because of new technologies, American adversaries would be able to move quickly. Failure to speedily mobilize our forces and industry, Eisenhower concluded, might lead to defeat, since economic organization, as much as if not more than brilliant tactics, led to victory. To achieve a high level of speed would require cooperation among the federal government, industry, labor, and the military. This was especially true for the armed forces, which had strong traditions and many leaders with deep commitments to their particular service.[8]

Eisenhower's IMP study also led him to another conclusion. Congress was a serious part of the problem that the military faced in planning for future wars. There was little congressional interest in long-run planning and funding of the military. The resulting feast-or-famine approach to budgeting exacerbated the rivalries between the army and navy. Congress had generously funded the military during World War I. After the conflict, though, spending on the armed forces collapsed. Things only worsened during the country's economic hard times in the 1930s, and reduced military spending set off another intense struggle between the army and navy for available resources.[9] As the situation in Europe became more ominous after 1937, Congress ramped up military spending. But increasing resources, as with a scarcity, also led to bitter interservice struggles. Matters intensified as Congress provided increased funds for the army air corps. Since the 1920s the well-known general Billy Mitchell and his supporters proselytized for an independent American air force. That did not happen until the National Defense Act of 1947. But even while a part of the army, the air corps developed a sense of a distinct mission and of independence. Meanwhile, the navy also sought funding for air power to support its missions. Once the United States entered World War II, Congress spent lavishly on the military establishment, and both the army and navy obtained generous funding for air power.[10]

Eisenhower's work on the IMP further raised his professional profile. He had already gained attention because he graduated first in his class from the Command and Staff School in 1925–26. An appointment to the American Battle Monuments Commission, from 1926 to 1929, suggested that junior officer Eisenhower was a "comer," since General John J. Pershing himself selected men to work for him and the commission. Eisenhower took a leave to study during the 1927–28 term at the War College. On his return to the commission, he went to France to help edit a guide to French battlefields. Living in Paris, Eisenhower and his wife found living there very expensive. Eisenhower also observed at close range the bitter battles within the French military, concluding that they could be very destructive.[11]

In any event, during the 1930s leaders of the US Army took notice of the IMP and Eisenhower's thoughtful approach to meshing new technologies, traditional organizations, and available resources.[12] The attention he received led to his appointment as chief military adviser in 1933–35, to army chief of staff, Douglas MacArthur. Following that assignment, he served as an assistant to MacArthur from 1935 to 1939, when he went to the Philippines to advise its government on building defenses.[13]

He returned to the United States in January 1940 in hopes of commanding troops in preparation for a war that he was sure was coming. For a brief time he had his wish. From February until November 1940, he served as executive officer of the 15th Infantry and commander of the 1st Battalion at Fort Lewis, Washington. What followed, though, were chief of staff appointments at Fort Lewis and at the Third Army in San Antonio, Texas. Days after Pearl Harbor, army chief of staff George C. Marshall called him to the Department of War in Washington, where for four months he worked in the War Plans and then in the Operations Division. Initially, Marshall had selected Eisenhower to help plan for the war in the Pacific precisely because he was one of the few people in the military who had studied industrial mobilization. As Eisenhower worked closely with Marshall, the general developed a great appreciation of the younger man's administrative and organization skills. In April 1942, Marshall appointed him assistant chief of the Operations Division, where he became, in effect, Marshall's chief planner. And then in May, Marshall sent Eisenhower to London. He headed a commission in which he became the architect of cooperation with the British, which led in June 1942 to his appointment as the commanding general of US Army forces in Europe. In November 1942, he commanded the Allied invasion of North Africa. During the following summer and fall he was in command of the invasion of Italy. His achievements led to his appointment as the supreme commander of the Allied Expeditionary Forces in December 1943. His responsibility was to plan and implement "Operation Overlord," which led to the successful invasion of Normandy on June 6, 1944, and ultimately, after months of hard battle, to the unconditional surrender of Nazi Germany on May 7, 1945. Following the war, he was appointed commander of the US occupation in Germany.[14]

In November 1945, Truman made Eisenhower army chief of staff, and his responsibilities changed drastically from the assignments during the war that had propelled him to the heights of military responsibility and fame. Spending problems reappeared again once the war ended, as Congress sharply cut back military funds from $45 billion (fiscal 1946) to $14.4 billion (fiscal 1947). Rapid cuts in appropriations revived the contest for scarce resources that Eisenhower had witnessed in the 1920s and 1930s. He believed that a seesaw approach to spending had to end. The United States' postwar responsibilities demanded planning on strategy and spending for the long haul. As with the creation of a unified command structure, orderly, predictable budgeting was imperative. He first made his views public soon after he became chief of staff in testimony in December 1945 at congressional hearings called to consider military reorganization.[15]

In the debates in Congress and the Pentagon, Eisenhower harked back to a standard practice in military planning. Strategy had to reflect the resources available to carry it out. Questions about the relationship between strategy and assets were an essential part of planning, Eisenhower's forte throughout his military career and an issue that would deeply influence his thinking as president. During the Truman years, as Eisenhower confronted the Cold War's demands on the military, he reiterated time and again that strategy and costs were tightly bound. Because the Cold War looked to be decades long, Eisenhower fixed on the idea that strategy had to be long-term and that costs had to be contained, lest over time they overwhelm the economy. Because there never would be sufficient funds to meet what the armed services believed adequate, Eisenhower concluded that it was necessary "to set an appropriate line between desirable strength and unbearable cost."[16]

President Truman shared Eisenhower's opinions about military integration. Truman's strong views on the need for unification had developed before he

became vice president. During the war he chaired the Senate Special Committee to Investigate the National Defense Program. He concluded that both the
military and industry were wasteful and that the rivalry between the army and
navy was counterproductive.[17] As president, Truman took initiatives to force unification of the services, actions that Eisenhower supported. Weeks after the nuclear attacks on Japan in August 1945, Truman ordered the Joint Chiefs of Staff
(JCS) to come up with an integrated budget for the entire military. Up to that
point, each service had prepared its own budget. In June the navy submitted a
budget for fiscal year 1947 that called for large peacetime forces for the navy and
marines. Truman sent the navy budget to the Joint Chiefs and instructed them
to analyze it "in light of our international commitments for the postwar world,
the development of new [nuclear] weapons and the relative position of the services as a result of these factors." He wanted the services to start thinking of
themselves as part of a larger military establishment and to plan jointly.[18]

A unified budget, Truman hoped, would lead to greater cooperation, while
cutting waste and duplication. Negotiations within the JCS to create an integrated
budget failed. Generally, navy leaders continued to believe that unification of the
military services would threaten the marine corps and naval aviation. The best
that the services could do was to pull together their separate budget requests,
which they sent to the president. Truman had to decide on the allocation of resources and the size of force levels.[19]

Because of the lack of cooperation Truman chose to act on his own. On December 20, 1945, he sent a special message to Congress proposing an outline for
the unification of the military establishment. His message, and the bill based on
it, produced sharply negative reactions in Congress, especially from powerful
committee chairmen who supported the navy. Throughout 1946 the army and
navy carried on a sharp, public debate—closely covered in the press—over the
president's proposal. Navy leaders tenaciously opposed unification and strongly
defended a combat role for the marines and independent air operations.[20]

For much of 1946, Congress debated the proposed legislation based on Truman's proposal, and Eisenhower continued to hope that his views about a combined approach among the services would prevail. Once there was a common
agreement on a strategy, he thought, the mission of the various services would
be easier to define and budget for. But, in large part because of the implacable
opposition of the navy, the compromise bill that finally emerged disappointed
Eisenhower. He concluded, though, that a bill creating a weak department under
a nominally independent cabinet-level secretary of national defense was better
than nothing. He hoped that over time changes could be made to the new

department's organization and responsibilities to achieve the unity that he thought was in the national interest.[21]

Congress passed the National Defense Act of 1947 in April, and Truman signed the bill on July 26, 1947. In doing so, the act created the National Military Establishment, which included a cabinet-level secretary of national defense to preside over three independent services—army, navy, and air force.[22] Eisenhower viewed the new secretary position as inherently weak. It had no administrative authority and virtually no staff, which meant that the new secretary would find it difficult to develop independent analyses of critical issues.[23] Also troubling was the secretary's insufficient authority to develop short-term policies and long-term strategies. Finally, by creating an independent air force, battles over budgets would be more complicated, carried out among three instead of two services.[24] To make matters worse, the president continued to cut the budget for defense. The beginning of a recession in 1946 caused Truman to worry about an increased deficit and to reduce the defense budget for fiscal 1948 to $13 billion, and for the following 1949 fiscal year to $10 billion.[25]

In principle, Eisenhower did not disagree with Truman's budget cutting; he understood that federal revenues declined during the recession. Like the president, Eisenhower objected to deficits, believing that they would eventually lead to inflation. What disturbed Eisenhower about some of Truman's cuts in military spending, though, was that they were the result of partisanship, an unhappy result of the hostile stance the Republicans took toward Truman, which the president eagerly returned in kind. Further complicating the situation was that within each party there was a wing that opposed significant military spending on principle. Indeed, one of the leading figures in the Republican Party, Ohio senator Robert A. Taft, led a faction hostile to the United States' assuming a major military role in the postwar world. Taft's views were shared among some conservative Democrats as well.[26]

In the end, Eisenhower's apprehensions about the weakness of the new department were born out.[27] Initially, he was also dismayed that Truman appointed James V. Forrestal as the first secretary of national defense on September 17, 1947, when Secretary of War Robert Patterson refused to take the post. Eisenhower recognized that Forrestal was an effective manager of the Navy Department and that he had had an impressive career at the top levels of the Wall Street investment bank Dillon, Read before entering government at the beginning of the war. But as secretary of the navy since 1944, Forrestal had been a central figure in the contentious, often bitter debates between the army and the navy and had a strong hand in shaping the legislation that authorized the new, weak department.[28]

Within the first year of his tenure at Defense, Forrestal increasingly came around to Eisenhower's point of view on several issues. Indeed, he found the department unmanageable and concluded that changes were needed. Forrestal and Eisenhower, in particular, were appalled at a particularly nasty public dispute between the navy and air force over their missions in delivering nuclear weapons, which erupted in October 1948, during hearings convened by the Hoover Commission (the Commission on Organization of the Executive Branch of the Government), on amending the 1947 National Security Act.[29] This turn of events deeply disturbed Eisenhower. These interservice battles occurred while the United States faced momentous decisions over developing Cold War strategy as US-Soviet tensions escalated, culminating in the heavy-handed communist takeover of the government in Czechoslovakia in February 1948 and the initiation of an American airlift in June 1948 to counter the USSR's blockade of Berlin.[30]

Eisenhower followed the public confrontations between the air force and navy and the escalating Cold War from his new position as president of Columbia University, a post he assumed in February 1948. But he kept close to developments in the capital. During that year he traveled to Washington frequently to confer with Forrestal and the president on defense matters, especially the problems at the Pentagon. Forrestal and Truman recognized that changes had to be made in the way in which the department operated. Eisenhower used the difficulties the new secretary encountered to support amendments to the original law. Truman agreed with Eisenhower. Soon after his inauguration for a second term in January 1949, the president proposed changes much in line with what Eisenhower had suggested.[31]

Moreover, once Truman had won reelection, he wanted Eisenhower to become more directly involved in coping with the problems within the military. Since Eisenhower was not about to leave Columbia University, he only volunteered for a temporary assignment. In December 1948, as a compromise, Eisenhower agreed to act as an adviser to the president and Forrestal and to sit informally with the Joint Chiefs of Staff. The president and secretary hoped that Eisenhower would be able to encourage the chiefs to develop a common strategy and to agree on a defense budget. Beginning in February 1949, Eisenhower traveled to Washington for two days each week.[32]

In his new, informal role, Eisenhower experienced little but frustration. Wrangling continued among the services over strategy and budgets. The navy

and air force escalated their dispute over air power by again mounting independent public relations campaigns to build public support for their particular points
of view. Also, Eisenhower had difficulties in working with an increasingly troubled Forrestal. Early in 1949, the secretary was on the brink of a nervous breakdown and Eisenhower supported Truman's request for Forrestal's resignation
(effective April 1). Forrestal was subsequently hospitalized, but on May 2, 1949, he
committed suicide.[33]

Truman asked Louis Johnson to succeed him. A blunt, experienced, ambitious politician from West Virginia, Johnson proved easy to work with, not that
he and Eisenhower always agreed on issues. Johnson, for example, was willing
to accept much-reduced defense budgets—something that Eisenhower objected to.[34]

Even so, Eisenhower and Johnson had some good news in August, when Congress passed amendments to the 1947 National Security Act. On August 10, 1949,
Truman signed the law creating the Department of Defense to replace the
National Defense Establishment. In creating a full-fledged "executive department," the legislation also enhanced the powers of the secretary, making him
the principal adviser to the president on military policy. His office also gained a
deputy secretary and three assistant secretaries, one whose sole responsibility
was the budget. There was also authorization for increased staffing elsewhere in
the department. Congress mandated that the department follow uniform budgetary procedures and develop fiscal policies to be followed consistently by each
branch of the military. The legislation downgraded each service from an executive to a military department, and their secretaries would no longer serve on the
National Security Council.[35]

But there were still gaps in the legislation from Eisenhower's point of view.
In particular, the Joint Chiefs still retained a large independent staff. It could only
act when there was unanimity, and the chairman of the JCS was simply a presid-
ing officer. Congress also circumscribed the powers of the new secretary of defense over the mission of each service, and the JCS had the right to go to Congress should it disagree with department policies.[36]

Eisenhower accepted that the 1949 amended act was an improvement over
the 1947 legislation, but more still needed to be done. When Truman offered
Eisenhower the position of chairman of the Joint Chiefs of Staff, he declined. His
experience as "informal" chairman had been the source of enormous disappointment over the rancor and parochialism that marked JCS debates over defense
policy and spending. He also fretted that Truman could not get Congress to address the prospect of rekindling inflation in 1948 and of ignoring the potential

of a recession in 1949. But Eisenhower mostly objected to the continued haphazard and often politicized way in which defense spending levels were determined by Congress and the president. In fact, Johnson's acceptance of a $10 billion defense budget for fiscal 1951 convinced Eisenhower, in August 1949, that it was time to return full-time to Columbia University. After returning to New York, he nevertheless kept up ties with Secretary Johnson and others in the Pentagon. And he could easily follow the behind-the-scenes goings-on with his longtime friend Omar Bradley, whom Truman appointed chairman of the JCS.[37]

Within a few months of Truman's decision to reduce the level of military spending, Cold War developments intervened to force a radical reconsideration of defense budget priorities. In September 1949, the Soviet Union successfully tested an atomic bomb. On October 1, 1949, Mao Tse-tung proclaimed the establishment of the People's Republic of China following the victory of communist forces over those of the Chinese nationalists. Because these developments presaged a much more ominous world outlook, the president called for a special secret review of American strategy late in January 1950. The resulting National Security Council (NSC) Document Number 68, was presented to the NSC in April 1950. Its authors argued a strong case to the president that a more menacing world situation demanded rearmament and greatly increased spending on defense and foreign assistance. Truman wanted detailed proposals of programs and their costs, and the NSC convened an ad hoc committee to respond to the president's request. This led to a major planning exercise within the Department of Defense in response.[38]

In June 1950, before the exercise was completed, the North Koreans invaded South Korea and Truman responded by authorizing a "police action" under the auspices of the United Nations to repel the invasion. In September 1950, the administration accepted NSC 68 as the formal expression of American defense policy. How much such a policy would cost was not clear at the time, although among those who wrote the document, expectations were that the figure would be high.[39]

Concern that the regional conflict might turn into World War III encouraged military leaders to request an acceleration in creating a permanent force to ensure the country's long-term security. Instead of reaching this buildup in 1954, as envisioned in NSC 68, the Defense Department proposed 1952 as the year of "maximum danger." To meet the Pentagon's objectives not only would have required massive short-term increases in spending but a commitment to large future expenditures to maintain the expanded war-fighting capabilities envisioned by Truman's military advisers.[40]

Following the outbreak of hostilities in Korea, Eisenhower indicated he was ready to take on whatever task the president wanted to give him.[41] By October 1950, Eisenhower had a new assignment: Truman asked him to take on the role of NATO (North Atlantic Treaty Organization) supreme allied commander. In the wake of North Korean aggression, aided by the Soviet Union, defending Western Europe had become one of Truman's key concerns. As early as 1948, five European countries (France, Britain, Belgium, Luxembourg, and the Netherlands) joined together in the Brussels Pact to produce unified military plans. Preventing the resurgence of Germany was the initial objective. But it was becoming clearer that the threat to Western Europe was now the USSR and that other European nations would need to take part in developing a common defense. Out of these concerns, the NATO alliance emerged. Agreed to on April 4, 1949, it included in its membership—in addition to those in the Brussels Pact—Denmark, Norway, Iceland, Italy, Portugal, Canada, and the United States. The US Senate ratified the treaty on July 21, 1949. Eisenhower attacked his new NATO assignment with great energy. He saw his role at SHAPE (Supreme Headquarters Allied Powers in Europe) as promoting a fighting capability in Europe to counterbalance Soviet ambitions. Creating a joint command and a common strategy was a task that he relished. NATO's supreme allied commander shuttled among European capitals to proselytize about the dangers that the Soviet Union posed, and he periodically returned to Washington to brief the defense secretary, the JCS, and the president.[42]

While Eisenhower and the president agreed on the importance of NATO, other Truman policies alarmed him, especially the spending engendered by the Korean War and NSC 68. Indeed, Eisenhower's opposition to the hurried rearmament was a factor in his decision to run for president. For much of Truman's first term, Eisenhower believed that the president skimped on defense spending. Then, with the advent of the Korean War, the president proposed enormous increases in spending for weapons—four Forrestal supercarriers for the navy, an increase to 143 wings for the air force, and 20 divisions for the army. To Eisenhower, Truman was going from one extreme to the other, leaving the military again faced with a seesaw approach that Eisenhower believed undermined efforts to plan Cold War strategy and the spending to support it.[43]

Eisenhower worried that the vast increases in expenditure would eventually lead to serious inflation. The postwar inflation of 1946–48 truly disturbed him, by reducing spending on the military in real terms and more generally harming workers, businesses, and investors. He concluded that Truman had been stampeded into overreacting to troubling events in late 1949 and 1950. To Eisenhower's

dismay, otherwise cautious and conservative friends—men such as former secretary of the air force Stuart Symington, Defense Secretary Robert Lovett, and
Air Force Secretary Thomas Finletter—went along with the president. Only the
prospect of an immediate full-scale war with the Soviet Union, he believed,
would justify such huge expenditures. The United States needed to be strong,
but in Eisenhower's opinion the likelihood of war with the Soviet Union was not
imminent. He did not accept that a world war was any more likely with the
Soviet Union in 1950 than it had been in 1945. Russian leaders, Eisenhower
thought, could not have forgotten the devastation brought by World War II to
their homeland.[44]

Eisenhower was not alone in criticizing the president. As the Korean conflict
unfolded, Truman faced increased opposition to his defense and fiscal policies.
Funds for a long-term military expansion, based on NSC 68, would be a harder
sell than a "hot" war like Korea. The conflict in Korea, however, proved unpopular rather quickly. It was characterized by deep divisions in Congress and among
the public. There certainly was no rallying around the administration that had
occurred in World War II. Resistance to Truman's calls for further tax increases
emerged when the war did not end rapidly. Fearing inflation, the president wanted
to pay for the war as it was waged. Initially, in September 1950 Congress approved
a $5.8 billion tax increase in individual and corporate income taxes and excise
taxes.[45] Following the 1950 congressional elections—in which Democratic seats
were lost in both the House and Senate—Truman requested an excess profits
tax. Because the war in Korea was going badly, an alarmed lame duck Congress
passed the legislation, which raised corporate income taxes more than $3.5
billion.[46]

In February 1951, Truman pressed his luck again with Congress. He requested
tax increases in personal, corporate, and to a lesser extent, excise rates in order
to raise another $10 billion to fight the war, as he said, on a "pay as we go" basis.
These requests were met with widespread disapproval. Republicans proposed
cuts in domestic spending first; others in the party advocated a national sales
tax. In November 1951, nine months after the president's request, Congress approved $5.4 billion, just about half the sum originally proposed by Truman. In
little more than a year's time, Congress had raised individual and corporate income tax rates almost $15 billion, to rates near the levels of World War II. A few
months later, in January 1952, Truman asked for an additional $5 billion, but as
the New York Times said, Congress had simply "run out of gas" on tax policy.
Nothing was done, and the president had no choice but to run deficits to fund
the war. His last proposed budget for fiscal 1954, according to newspaper reports

that Eisenhower read late in January 1952, included an anticipated deficit of $14 billion.[47]

Truman also requested authority to impose wage and price controls, as inflation fears grew after the invasion of South Korea. Congress reluctantly went along with the president. Price and wage controls were no more appealing to Congress than taxes. Despite the dire situation on the ground in Korea by the end of 1950, Congress continued to be unsympathetic, and it refused to strengthen them in early 1951, as Truman requested. Indeed, the controls were weakened when Congress passed a revised Defense Production Act in 1951. The issue was largely defused after domestic American inflationary pressures substantially eased during 1952.[48]

CANDIDATE EISENHOWER'S OUTLOOK ON THE ECONOMY

From his NATO command in Europe, Eisenhower followed developments in Washington and on the Korean battlefield with growing anxiety. While he had an extremely busy schedule in his NATO post, he kept up with the struggles over budgets, taxes, and economic controls. During his brief time as president of Columbia University, he got to know donors and board members, many of whom were prominent business leaders who took an interest in the institution. Of course, he also had a wide acquaintance with military leaders, some of whom he saw personally when he returned to the United States to report to the president and officials in the Pentagon.

Commenting publicly on the Korean situation was out of the question. He and General Marshall had given their wholehearted support to Truman's strong reaction to the June 1950 North Korean invasion of the South.[49] The later battle between Truman and MacArthur put many top military figures like Eisenhower in a difficult position, at least at first. MacArthur's behavior, however, made it harder and harder to defend the general. On active duty, Eisenhower was very careful to avoid public comment about the conflict, which eventually led to the general's firing on April 11, 1951. Even writing in his diary, Eisenhower was far from direct about the protagonists. He thought that there were larger issues than the two personalities involved, even though the JCS unanimously supported Truman. MacArthur clearly disobeyed the president's instructions and risked a major war with China. Eisenhower lamented that in the world's capitals, "unworthy men either guide our destinies or are fighting bitter battles in the hope of getting an opportunity to guide our destinies."[50]

Nevertheless, MacArthur received an adulatory reception from the public and the Republican Party upon his return to the United States late in April 1951. As time went on, however, the general continued to give histrionic speeches to increasingly less than enthusiastic audiences. In addition, congressional hearings subsequently dulled his military and public reputation, and his few supporters in the Republican leadership lost what enthusiasm they had for the general's presidential ambitions. Meanwhile, Eisenhower's prospects to become the Republican presidential candidate continued to improve, although he averred that his major responsibility was his NATO command. By early 1952, however, Eisenhower moved closer and closer to active candidacy for president. He acquiesced in having his name put on the primary ballot for the March New Hampshire primary, which he won. A week later a write-in campaign in the Minnesota Republican primary brought him a substantial number of votes. Even so, he continued to move slowly, arguing that he would accept a draft but not actively seek the nomination.[51] He emphasized that he was focusing on the work still to be accomplished at NATO. Finally, at the end of May 1952, Eisenhower could no longer hope that the Republican nomination would come to him without his seeking it. He resigned from active military service and then threw himself into campaigning for the Republican presidential nomination.[52]

Contributing to Eisenhower's decision to seek the presidency was the likelihood that, if he did not run, Taft would get the Republican nomination. Earlier talk of MacArthur as a candidate had ended by 1952. MacArthur's insubordination to Truman over Korean War strategy, and his megalomania, convinced Eisenhower of his unfitness. But Eisenhower also firmly believed that Taft was not suited to the task. Taft's isolationism—he voted against NATO and refused to accept the concept of collective security—made him totally unacceptable.[53]

What clinched his thinking, though, was Truman's handling of finances during the run-up to the Korean War. Truman's apparent inability to follow a consistent policy toward military spending influenced his decision, as did the raging inflation that Eisenhower expected would follow large increases in expenditures and deficits. A vast enlargement in military spending also reinforced his conviction that the efforts to bring about a unified military establishment had failed. Patterns of spending on the various services bespoke the success each service had in enlisting congressional supporters and military contractors to support more and more spending.[54]

Taft proved to be a formidable candidate for the Republican nomination. It was his third, and surely last, try for the nomination, and he expended great energy in the campaign. Conservatives within the party strongly backed Taft. Thomas E. Dewey, the party's failed candidate in 1944 and 1948, enthusiastically promoted Eisenhower. Up until Dewey and other like-minded leaders from the eastern wing of the party convinced Eisenhower to seek the nomination, Taft appeared the obvious front-runner. Even so, the race turned out to be tight and increasingly bitter, especially at the party convention in July 1952, which opened with the candidates very close in delegates. Eisenhower's people accused Taft operatives of unfairly denying Eisenhower delegates in southern states. Ultimately, Eisenhower secured them and those of key undecided delegations to win the nomination. Taft believed that he had been cheated. He issued an obligatory statement congratulating Eisenhower and pledging his support but then took a long vacation.[55]

Eisenhower's political advisers feared that Taft and his supporters would sit out the election. In September, however, Eisenhower and Taft came together in a highly publicized meeting in which the Senator reaffirmed his support of the ticket. He was too good a Republican to have done otherwise. At these meetings at Morningside Heights in New York, Eisenhower and Taft easily agreed on most domestic issues. In addition, the candidate promised not to exclude Taft partisans from positions in his administration. Eisenhower also pledged to reduce domestic spending and stand against "creeping socialism." But it was on America's role in the world that a wide gap remained. This was only finessed, not resolved, in the statement that the candidate and his former opponent issued.[56]

Once relations with Taft were smoothed over, Eisenhower eagerly returned to campaigning. After his nomination, he put himself in the hands of Republican Party leaders who orchestrated his campaign. Eisenhower traveled widely, everywhere greeted by large enthusiastic crowds. His opponents dared not make an issue of his age, since he made more appearances and traveled more miles than his opponent, Illinois governor Adlai E. Stevenson, a man nine years his junior. Eisenhower's television and radio advertisements focused on the issues of education, inflation, and ending the war in Korea. As the campaign developed, Eisenhower also sloganeered about "Korea, Communism and Corruption." Republicans charged the Truman administration with a lack of preparation for the war in Korea. They also implied that the Democrats had not done enough to keep Soviet spies from infesting the federal government. Finally, the Republicans campaigned about corruption in the Truman administration. Eisenhower won a decisive victory, garnering 55 percent of the popular vote and 442 votes in the Electoral College. He carried every state in the union except for nine border and southern states in which Democrats continued to have a hold on politics.[57]

In preparing for the campaign, Republican strategists had arranged to have Eisenhower briefed on economic matters. While Eisenhower might not have had a deep background on some current issues, he was not a blank slate when it came to the economy. During his years in Washington in the early 1930s, he closely followed economic issues and the attempts of the Roosevelt administration to deal with the Depression. In the late 1940s he had been deeply engaged in the issue of military spending and observed at close range the contentious battles that the president had faced over budgets, taxes, spending, and deficits. So, Eisenhower came to his campaign for the presidency with distinct views about key aspects of the economic problems facing the United States.[58]

He understood from his NATO experience that the United States needed to remain engaged with the world and that such engagement would be expensive. To him the communist threat was by no means simply a matter of military intimidation but also of subversion, economic warfare, and diplomatic pressure. The USSR, he thought, would take advantage of weakness and irresolution in the West. In addition, because of the power of an authoritarian state to marshal resources, the Soviets could bring to bear great economic resources to the competition. Ultimately, he believed, the USSR would fail because of its stifling political and economic system, but in the long interim it might pose serious threats to the United States and its allies.[59]

Overall, Eisenhower recognized that the Depression, World War II, and the Cold War had forever changed American life and politics. To deter communism in Europe and Asia, Americans would have to pay taxes, maintain troops abroad, and become the arbiter of disputes among ancient rivals in Europe and Asia. But Eisenhower was also keenly aware of the threat of going too far—of spending too much on the military and, by a continuous mobilization, creating a "garrison state" that would undermine both the American political and economic systems. As his candidacy began to take shape, Eisenhower stated what would be the hallmark of his approach to economic policy as president: "Solvency and security are mutually interdependent."[60]

Even though he had the big picture in mind, running for president in 1952 forced him to clarify his thinking about various issues of economic policy. Critical as he was of Truman's handling of major issues, Eisenhower's proximity to the president in the late 1940s provided the candidate with a keen sense of the complexities that he might face. Eisenhower did not appear to be out of the mainstream of the Republican Party on most economic issues. Surely some of his appeal was that his ideas were rooted in what he learned from his modest small-town upbringing in Abilene, Kansas. He favored balanced budgets, reduced public debt, low taxes, and stable prices. Government, he thought, should limit interference in private enterprise and individual initiative. It was the responsibility of federal authorities to ensure the confidence of investors, industrialists, and workers so as not to impinge unduly on the decisions of businesses and households in making economic decisions.[61]

But this was not by any means the entirety of his approach to economic policy. He understood how much the world had changed since he left Kansas for West Point in 1911, and he had a strong sense of the cataclysmic changes brought by depression and war in the 1930s and 1940s. Over the two decades the Republican Party was out of the White House it had cultivated a robust critique of New Deal and Fair Deal policies. It included routine attacks on excessive spending and reliance on public investment, which partisans believed weakened private sector institutions and sapped individual initiative.

Yet, Eisenhower was not about to mount a full-scale attack on the New Deal, especially popular programs like Social Security. Nor did he contemplate dismantling the regulatory regime that influenced businesses in transportation, banking, finance, communications, energy, and natural resources. He did not reject the basic principles of macroeconomic policy making expressed in the Employment Act of 1946, but he did not contemplate aggressive management of routine business cycles. In 1952 few policymakers did. In addition, he understood that the United States' population had changed profoundly because of the Depression and war. It was more urban and industrial, and its growing numbers were more mobile than when he was growing up. In a much more complex society, he recognized, federal power might be necessary to help the states address problems of education and urban decay. It might also be needed to support infrastructure projects. So, Eisenhower saw his task as achieving as much of traditional party economic policy objectives as possible in this changed world.[62]

It was not going to be easy. The political environment he inherited from his predecessor emerged out of the many, often partisan, conflicts over budgets, taxes, deficits, and defense spending that Truman fought during his time in office. Eisenhower deplored the political atmosphere, which had been poisoned by years of relentless partisan bickering. This was by no means the combative Truman's fault alone. Congressional Republicans took every opportunity to fight the administration and score political points. While they desperately wanted to recapture the White House and control of Congress, much of the vociferous, deep-seated opposition to the New Deal and Fair Deal stemmed from a belief that Roosevelt and Truman had set the country on a dangerous course. It threatened the country's future by concentrating power in Washington, and in particular the

executive branch. A split within the Republican Party between its liberal eastern and conservative Midwestern wings added to the rancorous atmosphere.
Similarly, divisions in the Democratic Party between southern conservatives and
northern and western liberals also compounded the problems of congressional
politics.[63]

Public attitudes also did not help matters. Desires for new homes, automobiles, and consumer goods long postponed because of the Depression and war
created an inward-looking public not given to appeals for sacrifice and larger
purpose. Just as after World War I, the post–World War II generation hungered
for "normalcy." People had begun to chafe at high taxes, without wanting to end
many New Deal and Fair Deal programs. Eisenhower was a realist. He was not
about to attack popular programs, regardless of his personal doubts about the
growing power and intrusiveness of the federal government.[64]

Of most significance to Eisenhower, however, was the fiscal situation left by
Truman. The next administration would face the prospect of enormous budget deficits. These deficits were fueled by what Eisenhower thought was an ill-
conceived military strategy that had not taken full account of its costs and the
availability of resources to pay for it.[65]

Heightening the contentious political environment was the role the Korean
War had in the growth of the military and the willingness of policymakers to
embrace rationales for dramatically increased Cold War expenditures. In 1950,
Truman envisioned a military budget of $13 billion, but his last budget message
(fiscal 1953) estimated that maintaining the defense establishment and its long-
term security mission as laid out in NSC 68 would cost $35 to $40 billion a year,
even after the fighting stopped in Korea. These sums did not include expenditures
for overseas economic and military assistance or the costs of expanding the country's atomic energy program. In their last national security cost estimates, Truman's budget officials were estimating a figure near $60 billion per year by the
middle of the 1950s. Total expenditures might be as high as $80 billion, if the in-
ternational situation continued to deteriorate.[66] In fact, Truman's planned military
expenditures for his final fiscal 1954 (July 1953–June 1954) were over $45 billion
and, when combined with foreign aid and nuclear programs, exceeded $55 billion,
or 70 percent of a $78 billion budget. Though tax revenues were rising rapidly,
because of prosperity, the tax withholding system introduced during World War
II, and temporary tax increases to pay for the Korean War, they would not keep up
with surging expenditures. A deficit of almost $10 billion was projected.

This was the legacy of the Truman administration that Eisenhower knew he
had to address promptly once he took office. The new president settled into his

responsibilities quickly. He was no stranger to difficult issues or to the White House itself. In his first full day as president, he observed, in his diary entry for January 21, 1953: "Plenty of worries and difficult problems. But such has been my portion for a long time—the result is that this just seems (today) like a continuation of all I've been doing since July 1941—even before that."[67]

PART 1

Macro-Level
Economic Policies

CHAPTER 1

Setting a Consistent Course
1953–1956

Eisenhower came to office determined to put a clear stamp on economic policy, one that would distinguish his Republican administration from that of his Democratic predecessors. Truman's fiscal 1954 (July 1953–June 1954) budget proposal called for spending an extraordinary $78.6 billion. About 70 percent of that figure was made up of spending on defense, which included expenditures for the military, as well as nuclear programs, mutual security programs of assistance (foreign aid), and intelligence. Nothing else would be possible, Eisenhower believed, without reigning in those expenditures. Eisenhower's concerns went beyond spending on the Korean War. His experience late in the 1940s as army chief of staff, informal head of the Joint Chiefs of Staff, and NATO supreme allied commander demonstrated the urgency of dealing with defense spending. What was an appropriate level of spending to meet the needs of Cold War strategy? Answering that question first required a firm idea of Cold War objectives. Eisenhower's postwar experience had convinced him that the Truman administration had failed to align objectives and strategy with the government's available resources. Bringing about that alignment was Eisenhower's primary goal.

The president never lost sight of that issue during his eight years in office. In one form or another, balancing strategic needs against government financial capabilities dominated his thinking. Indeed, those concerns were crucial to understanding his warnings about a military-industrial complex in his farewell address delivered three days before leaving office in January 1961. But balancing strategy and spending was at the center of his efforts, especially in the first years of his time in office. He took the commanding role in the review of military spending and Cold War strategy in 1953. The result was the so-called New Look, an approach to the central issue of American foreign policy that was driven by economic as much as military and diplomatic considerations.

In addition to concern over Truman's final budget was the pressing need to address the new official responsibilities Congress mandated under the Employment Act of 1946. Its preamble stated, "It is the continuing policy and responsibility of the Federal Government to use all practicable means . . . to promote maximum employment, production, and purchasing power" (P.L. 79–304). This legislation institutionalized the government's accountability for the country's economic performance. Truman's Council of Economic Advisers, however, had not worked well. It provided the president contradictory advice and under its second chairman it became involved in political controversy.

Eisenhower's challenge was to avoid the mistakes of the previous administration. He had to establish a workable economic advisory body within the White House to adhere to the new congressional mandates while remaining true to his traditional conservative principles of balanced budgets, low taxes, reduced public debt, and minimal inflation. The president also had to work out a new relationship with the Federal Reserve, and especially its chairman. An agreement reached in 1951 with the Treasury had granted the Fed greater independence from the White House and essentially restored the Fed's ability to independently regulate monetary policy. Between 1941 and 1951 the Fed had suspended such activities, pursuant to an agreement with Treasury, so as to reduce the cost of government borrowing during and after World War II.

Within months of taking office, the president's team of economic advisers was in place, but a workable relationship with the Fed chairman took a longer period of time. In any event, the president's system of getting economic advice was soon tested by a short recession during his first year in office. Most observers at the time, if not all, credited the administration with a successful response to the recession, one important consequence of which was that Eisenhower and his closest advisers realized that there were long-standing inflationary tendencies at work in the economy; they were apparent even in the downturn in the business cycle. Eisenhower, especially during the late 1940s, had come to see inflation as one of the most serious problems of the time. He was concerned about the potential destructiveness of increasing prices on government programs, ordinary citizens, and business.

ORGANIZING ECONOMIC ADVICE

Eisenhower was the first Republican president to face the heightened responsibilities laid out in the 1946 Employment Act. As he had done in previous administrative positions, he assembled a small cadre of officials to assist him in making and carrying out economic policy. Secretary of the Treasury George M. Humphrey became one of his two most trusted advisers on economic matters, the other being Arthur F. Burns, the chairman of the Council of Economic Advisers. The treasury secretary developed a close relationship with Eisenhower and had easy access to the president. Eisenhower did not always follow Humphrey's advice, but the president did not have private sector business experience and admired the secretary's success. Humphrey was the former head of M. A. Hanna and Company, a major producer of iron ore that also controlled steel and coal interests. He had gained exposure to a range of business opinion as a leader in the Cleveland business community. While Humphrey had supported Robert A. Taft, his views were probably more influenced by his experience as a businessman and local business leader than as a partisan political supporter of the senator. In particular, Humphrey believed high taxes distorted business incentives and hindered investment. His strong opposition to increasing levels of federal spending was rooted in a belief that they led inevitably to higher taxes.[1]

Another one of Eisenhower's economic advisers was Joseph M. Dodge, who served as budget director from 1952 to 1954. He, too, was a Midwesterner and shared many of Humphrey's views, although Dodge had not been a Taft supporter. In budget policy debates, Dodge and Humphrey often found themselves on the same side. Dodge's business career was in banking—as president of Detroit Bank and Trust. After the war, Dodge headed the effort to reorganize the financial system in occupied Germany and reform the currency system under American military command in occupied Japan. The successful US policy helped tame Japan's postwar inflation, and Dodge was acclaimed for these achievements. Soon after winning the election, Eisenhower selected Dodge as his future budget director and as liaison with the outgoing Truman administration on budgetary matters.[2]

Eisenhower also relied on Minnesotan Gabriel Hauge for information about and analysis of economic matters. Hauge had done research for Republican president candidate Thomas E. Dewey during the 1948 campaign and assumed the same role during Eisenhower's first campaign. With Eisenhower's election, he became special assistant to the president for economic affairs. Hauge had a PhD in economics from Harvard and was a former editor of *Business Week*. With both an academic and journalistic background, he became heavily involved with economic issues confronting the administration, especially their political consequences. Early in Eisenhower's first term, he met weekly with the president and later had access as needed. Hauge wrote many of Eisenhower's statements and speeches on economic matters.[3]

Hauge served on the three-man committee that recommended Arthur F. Burns to Eisenhower to head the Council of Economic Advisers (CEA). Burns was one of the country's most distinguished economists. He had been a doctoral student of Wesley C. Mitchell at Columbia University and later his colleague and coauthor there. Together they had produced important works on business cycles. At the time of his appointment, Burns was president of the National Bureau of Economic Research (NBER), a private institution in Cambridge, Massachusetts, that commanded the respect of professional economists inside and outside of academia. Burns had not known Eisenhower personally, having only been introduced to him in passing during his tenure as president of Columbia University. Burns, though, had been a prominent "Democrat for Eisenhower" during the 1952 election campaign.[4]

Ultimately, the president left it to Burns to select the other two members of the CEA. In Neil Jacoby and Walter W. Stewart, Burns chose men he knew to be congenial to his own views about economic issues. Jacoby, a well-known economist, was recruited for the council from his position as dean of the business school at the University of California, Los Angeles. Stewart had long and varied experience in government. He was not an academic economist, but his substantial career in the federal bureaucracy proved valuable to Burns and the deliberations of the CEA.[5]

Burns and the president developed a close working relationship. The well-known economist became a valued adviser, providing the president with economic information, analysis, and advice. Burns appeared on the president's calendar for weekly hour-long meetings, encounters that often ran beyond the allotted time. In the early part of his tenure in the White House, according to Burns, he assumed the role of economic tutor to a willing, eager student. Eisenhower took economic issues seriously and wanted to learn more about economics. In Burns's estimation Eisenhower developed a "superb" grasp of economic analysis.[6]

When Eisenhower came to the White House, the future of the council was uncertain. The president was not convinced that it was worth saving. Truman's last chairman of the CEA, Leon Keyserling, was a highly partisan figure, so much so that the Republican Congress only provided funds for the CEA through March

31, 1953. Eisenhower seemed content to have one senior economic adviser in the White House, and Burns at first was comfortable with that arrangement. Burns thought that Truman disliked the council because its three members would report to him together, often disagreeing in front of the president. Burns could understand why Truman, or any president, would want a coherent analysis and set of policy recommendations, instead of arguments about what course of action should be taken.[7]

Nevertheless, Eisenhower asked Burns, as one of his first assignments, to prepare a report on whether to continue to fund the CEA. In writing the report, Burns changed his mind. He advised that Eisenhower retain the council and that its staff be expanded to include professional academic economists and others with long-term government experience in economic matters. Burns recommended, though, that the chairman of the council exercise administrative responsibility over the staff, be the chief spokesman for the council, and report to the president on its behalf. Eisenhower embraced the advice and appointed Burns chair, with sufficient funds to carry through on his recommendations.[8]

Burns shaped the council into an integral part of administration economic policy making. His prestige no doubt helped gain respect for the CEA. Burns, like the first chairman of the council under Truman, Edward Nourse, sought to make the CEA and its staff independent, neutral, and professional in analyzing economic issues. Burns testified reluctantly before congressional committees and insisted on appearing in executive session on issues he considered sensitive and controversial. He never criticized the president's policies and avoided taking partisan positions on economic issues when testifying. In an effort to have the administration speak with one voice, Burns took to drafting the *Economic Report of the President* (*ERP*) himself, although it appeared under the president's name. Burns worked closely with his two colleagues on the council, but he was the central figure. His goal was to avoid the partisan warfare that engulfed the council in the later years of the Truman presidency.[9]

Burns made himself and the council indispensable to the determination of economic policy. Further enhancing Burns's role was his chairmanship of the Advisory Board on Economic Growth and Stability. Late in 1953, Eisenhower appointed Burns chairman of this subcabinet entity, which included administration agencies responsible for aspects of economic policy—Treasury, Commerce, Labor, Bureau of the Budget, and the Federal Reserve. In addition, council staff convened working groups and sent representatives to other interagency assemblies. This network enabled Burns to keep abreast of economic issues within the government.[10] Moreover, Eisenhower had Burns regularly brief the cabinet on

economic developments. In his time on the council, Burns forged a close relationship with Vice President Nixon. Later, when Nixon became president, he appointed Burns chairman of the Federal Reserve (1970), where he served until
1978.

Burns's dominant role in advising the president created tensions with others
in the administration. In particular, Treasury Secretary Humphrey believed that
he should have the principal, traditional role in advising the president on fiscal
matters. Humphrey and Burns clashed on a number of issues, most notably on
the advisability of and timing of tax reductions. Close as Burns's relationship
was with Eisenhower, Humphrey also had easy access to the Oval Office. Indeed,
he also enjoyed a much closer social relationship with Eisenhower than the chairman of the CEA. Even so, the president was quite capable of viewing dispassionately the advice of his two strong-willed advisers. Helping him make up his
mind about contradictory advice was Gabriel Hauge, who served as a mediator
between the two powerful figures. On balance, Hauge probably agreed with Burns
more often than with Humphrey.[11]

Not making it into Eisenhower's inner circle of economic advisers was Charles
E. Wilson, the secretary of defense and former president of General Motors.
Eisenhower was enthusiastic about Wilson when he appointed him, hoping that
the experienced corporate executive could reign in the unwieldy department,
but Wilson disappointed the president by admitting that the Pentagon was more
difficult to bring under control than he had anticipated. Not surprisingly, the
president never developed the relationship with Wilson that he had with Humphrey. Eisenhower, of course, also had an independent basis of knowledge of
defense matters, something that could not be said of economic issues. Eisenhower, like Wilson, had succeeded in leading a large bureaucracy. In fact, the
president's management skills were probably greater than those of his defense
secretary, since the European theater in World War II presented larger and more
varied problems than the head of General Motors had ever faced.[12]

The advisers Eisenhower relied on provided him with a range of opinion on
economic matters. Humphrey offered him Treasury's perspective on economic
issues, filtered as they were through the eyes of a businessman who personally
embraced the party's fiscal orthodoxy. Burns and the CEA reflected academic
thinking about the economy and about economic issues elsewhere in the government. Dodge and his successors at the Bureau of the Budget provided the practical, day-to-day issues of budgeting. Hauge, with his New York ties, kept Wall
Street's perspective before the president.

Burns probably had the greatest influence, by dint of his expertise and attention to thinking within the executive branch. He advocated ideas of economic
policy that went beyond the fiscal orthodoxies of the Taft wing of the party. Eisenhower's chairman of the CEA hoped to develop flexible policies to prevent serious downturns in economic activity. The president ultimately accepted—at least
in principle—that in an economic trough, the government might have to cut
taxes, run deficits, ease credit, and expand public works programs. In coping with
the 1954 recession, Burns proved a key adviser to Eisenhower.[13]

TACKLING THE BUDGET

Eisenhower's principal advisers, despite their many differences, cohered quickly.
Together with the president's focused attention, they tackled the budget left by
the Truman administration and then the longer-term issue of spending on
defense. A revision of Truman's fiscal 1954 budget was due to Congress in April
1953. Within two weeks of his election, Eisenhower began to take the measure
of Truman's budget proposal. In 1952, there was little of the formal organized
transition from an outgoing to an incoming administration that developed
later. But Dodge, the designated director of the Bureau of the Budget, had been
conferring with and attending meetings of Truman officials in that office
since November 17, 1952, only days after the election. Dodge kept Eisenhower
posted on Truman's budget projections, especially in regard to the Department of Defense. Dodge briefed Eisenhower fully about the details for fiscal
1954 in December 1952, on the return trip from the president's fact-finding
mission to Korea.[14]

Truman's fiscal 1954 budget estimated spending of $78.6 billion. Expenditures
for defense, atomic energy, and mutual security (foreign aid) programs represented
70.7 percent of the estimate, that is, $55.6 billion. On the military alone, $45.4
billion was to be spent. The national debt stood at $267 billion; its congressio-
nally mandated limit, or ceiling, was $275 billion; while the gross national prod-
uct (GNP) was approximately $350 billion. Debt payments and legislated obliga-
tions for domestic programs amounted to a little more than $14 billion. Discretionary
spending was $8.6 billion. There were also unfinanced authorizations—Non-
Obligated Authorizations (NOA)—of $81 billion for defense-related contracts be-
gun in fiscal 1950. NOAs were necessary for long-term planning of military expenditures. Paying for these obligations would be the responsibility of the new
Eisenhower administration in its first two fiscal year budgets, and they would come

due at about the time that temporary tax increases to pay toward the Korean War would be ending.[15]

In his initial State of the Union message on February 2, 1953, Eisenhower announced that his first priority would be to reduce federal spending and work toward balancing the budget. His speech generated headlines by calling on federal departments to identify opportunities to cut costs. Cost-cutting proposals were due by March 1st so that the president could submit a revised fiscal 1954 budget to Congress in April. Dodge encouraged heads of government departments to cut personnel by 10 percent and to curtail construction programs. He also demanded that departments better prioritize and estimate the costs of their activities. Treasury Secretary Humphrey enthusiastically endorsed these initiatives. A few minor programs were significantly reduced or eliminated and cost savings achieved in other domestic programs.[16]

Overall, however, Eisenhower did not envision drastic cuts. He planned to spend in fiscal 1954 somewhat less than the $78.6 billion Truman had projected. In his cautious first State of the Union message, less than two weeks after the inauguration, he said of the budget, "Our goals can be clear, our start toward them can be immediate—but action must be gradual."[17] His initial target for the revised fiscal 1954 budget was approximately $70 billion. He had accepted that figure from Senator Robert Taft at a "unity" meeting in September 1952 in New York during the presidential campaign. As it turned out, estimated expenditures were reduced to $72.1 billion. Budget expenditures, however, were ultimately only $67.5 billion; tax receipts $64.4 billion; and the resulting deficit was $3.1 billion in the administrative budget, because of the Korean armistice in July 1953. The administrative (executive) budget included receipts and expenditures for budgeted items—it did not include receipts and spending on Social Security. Since receipts for that program brought in more revenues than were expended, the cash budget, which included Social Security revenues, tended to reduce deficits and increase surpluses. In emphasizing the administrative over the cash budget, administration officials anticipated enforcing greater discipline on spending.[18]

Eisenhower understood that most of the cost cutting in nondefense agencies and programs was symbolic. The real work of reducing spending, balancing the budget, and making a dent in the federal deficit would have to focus on defense spending and tax revenues. In his first message to Congress, he warned that disregard of how to pay for expanding military power would invite disaster. The president believed that less could be spent without undermining military preparedness. Truman, in his view, had been unwise to spend on security and military power without sufficient attention to the country's strategy and ability to pay for the spending authorized.[19] Eisenhower looked toward a new strategy that would properly take economic as well as military considerations into account.

Eisenhower's thinking about managing military spending was reinforced by his advisers' views. Indeed, Treasury Secretary Humphrey and Budget Director Dodge wanted more drastic cuts in defense spending than Eisenhower would countenance. Humphrey was dogmatic and voluble on the issue. Dodge was pragmatic and blunt. Following the early cost-cutting exercises directed at domestic departments, Dodge warned that the deficit would not be reduced in fiscal 1954 and would in fact increase in fiscal 1955 by $15 billion. To avoid such an outcome, he argued, military spending would have to be cut and the temporary Korean War income and excise taxes extended beyond their 1954 expiration dates.[20]

Revising Truman's proposed fiscal 1954 budget thus proved to be a difficult exercise. In large part this was a result of the continuing war in Korea. Eisenhower refused to support drastic cuts in military expenditures because of the uncertainties on the battlefield. The June 1950 North Korean attack had resulted in an emergency, accelerated military buildup, but Truman's budget requests covered much more than what were needed to repel the invasion. They reflected a consensus among foreign policy analysts, politicians, and the military that the Soviet Union had at least given its blessing to the North Korean incursion. So the war in Korea, to this way of thinking, was a prime example of newly aggressive and expansionist tendencies of the Soviet leadership, and the United States would be challenged in other areas. Since Truman and his advisers had viewed 1952 as a year of "maximum" danger, they ramped up proposed defense spending accordingly. They assumed that the Soviet Union by then would possess a hydrogen bomb (it was successfully tested in August 1953) and have the capability of delivering it.

Eisenhower, however, viewed the problem of Soviet aggressiveness differently. He had opposed Truman's decision at the time it was made in 1950 to expand military expenditures beyond what was needed for Korea, and he had not changed his mind since then. He rejected the Truman administration's thinking about the urgency of the dangers the United States faced. America, he believed, lived in a dangerous era. Defense spending needed to be based on steady considerations of preparedness balanced against the economy's ability to support expenditures for the military.[21]

After weeks of deadline-driven activity, the administration came up with a revised fiscal 1954 budget. Presented to Congress in April 1953, its projected spending on the military was $7.4 billion less than Truman had proposed. Eisenhower's proposal addressed the concerns of the budget cutters in the administration by excising $2.2 billion in already planned expenditures and cutting projected new spending by $5.2 billion. Hardest-hit in these changes was the air force, which among the military services had benefited the most in Truman's military buildup. It lost $5 billion in obligational authority (NOA), and the navy, $1.7 billion. Because of the continuing war in Korea, the army's spending authority was increased by an amount close to the cut the navy faced. There were also significant reductions in mutual security programs, that is, the military and economic assistance provided to Cold War allies. Eisenhower's fiscal 1954 proposal, as anticipated, did not produce a balanced budget. But he saw the exercise symbolically as a sharp departure from Truman's approach and as an indicator of future prudence.[22]

Not everyone was happy with the president's budget, although press reaction was positive.[23] Much to Eisenhower's dismay, Senator Taft harshly criticized it at a meeting of party leaders at the White House on April 30, 1953. His criticisms, if not his scolding tone, were soon repeated publicly. Taft insisted that the first Republican budget in two decades should be in balance. Surely, he argued, additional cuts could be made in military spending and foreign assistance. Eisenhower controlled his temper but was infuriated by Taft's hard-edged dismissal of his administration's efforts. Only Secretary Humphrey's verbal intervention prevented the president from berating Taft at the White House meeting. Humphrey defended at some length the background and details of the proposed budget. Taft, ever the partisan politician, said that he feared that the Republican Party would suffer in the 1954 congressional elections if voters concluded that Eisenhower's budget did not depart significantly from the one proposed by Truman.[24]

Eisenhower's insistence that the budget could not be cut prudently any further failed to persuade Congress. Gallingly, a Republican Congress made further reductions on a range of spending proposals, including defense. It cut $1.6 billion from new appropriations for the military and $900 million from authorizations for mutual security (foreign aid). As it turned out, at the end of fiscal 1954, the cash budget, which included revenues from Social Security, led to a considerably smaller deficit ($200 million) than what had been anticipated in the administrative budget submitted by Eisenhower.[25]

Eisenhower's goal also included structural change in the way in which the tax system worked. Because Eisenhower had better luck with Congress on taxes, more revenues became available to the government. He took a long-term view of taxation, as he had with spending. The issue needed to be handled carefully, because of the low-tax predilections of many Taft Republicans as well as conservative business leaders. Eisenhower thought that lowering taxes took second place to reducing the deficit and fighting inflation. Over the long term, he agreed that taxes needed to be lowered. In short-term budgeting, however, the president postponed cutting taxes, if doing so endangered one of his other major goals, a position Eisenhower maintained consistently throughout his eight years in office.[26]

During the 1952 campaign Eisenhower had promised tax reform once the budget was balanced. To ensure that the budget did not produce an even larger deficit, Eisenhower accepted the continuance of temporary taxes Congress had imposed to cover the expenses of the Korean War. One of these special taxes was an 11 percent short-term increase in individual income tax rates (in the higher brackets reaching over 90 percent) approved in 1951. Congress had set it to expire on January 1, 1954. Another was a temporary 5 percent increase in the corporate income tax rate (to 52 percent) slated for expiration on April 1, 1954. Eisenhower and the treasury secretary found themselves in conflict with tax-cutting enthusiasts in Congress, led by the Republican chairman of the House Ways and Means Committee, Daniel A. Reed. In February 1953, only weeks after Eisenhower's inauguration, Reed introduced legislation to remove the temporary individual income tax increases six months earlier than January 1954. The administration feared the loss of about $1.5 billion in revenue and went to the mat with Reed on the issue.[27]

Eisenhower prevailed against the Reed bill by mounting a public relations campaign. He spoke of maintaining the higher, temporary income taxes in terms of fiscal integrity and responsibility. Humphrey, despite his well-known aversion to taxes, took the administration's message to the business community. He, too, preached financial prudence as the reason to keep the tax until its scheduled expiration. Behind the scenes, the administration maneuvered against Reed among fellow Republicans. What the president advocated was not extension of the higher, temporary individual income tax rates, only letting it expire on the previously mandated date. There was no equivocation that it would be allowed to expire.[28]

Also on full display in the debate over Reed's proposal was the administration's overriding concern with inflation. Congress originally imposed the temporary individual and corporate income tax rate increases to dampen demand in the overheated economy produced by Korean War spending in 1951. But inflationary pressures soon abated in 1952, despite limited controls. Now, Reed believed that tax cutting was necessary to stimulate the economy, since he expected that Eisenhower would cut back substantially on Truman's proposed budget, especially for military spending. As Humphrey argued, though, keeping individual income tax rates was a matter of timing; allowing the individual income tax rates to expire early would increase the deficit and would also likely contribute to inflation.[29]

The next battle over taxes came in May 1953, when Eisenhower proposed a six-month extension of a 30 percent excess profits tax enacted by Congress in 1950 that targeted corporate profits beyond "normal profits"—an average of a corporation's three best profit levels for the four years 1946–49. It was set to expire on June 30, 1953. With a current corporate tax rate at 52 percent, the excess profits tax resulted in some firms paying tax rates as high as 82 percent, near the levels that prevailed during World War II. By extending the tax for six months, the administration hoped to garner about $1 billion in revenue. Political calculations were also involved in the decision to seek a six-month extension. Keeping the higher, temporary individual income tax rates until January 1954, while allowing the excess profits tax to expire, appeared to be favoring corporations (and those who received corporate dividends) over the entire spectrum of individual (personal) taxpayers.[30]

In making the case for the extension, Eisenhower took an active role in the debate. He spoke about it at news conferences and in other forums, including a speech to the Business Advisory Council. Again, Eisenhower prevailed, as Republican congressional leaders rallied to the new, popular president. Business leaders, who generally disliked the excess profits tax, accepted that the president was acting in the interest of fiscal integrity. Of course, they also knew that the tax would expire in six months. Eisenhower was quite explicit and public about that promise.[31]

Eisenhower, however, did not always prevail on taxes. While he was able to get Congress to go along with his initiatives in regard to the Korean War temporary income taxes, Eisenhower had to accept proposals made by congressional Republican leaders to reduce excise taxes. The president's victories on the war taxes— the individual income tax increases and the excess profits tax—had strained party unity. To repair the rifts coming out of these battles, Republican congressional leaders proposed significant cuts in excise taxes. Eisenhower, in principle, agreed that many of these taxes should be cut, but initially he opposed expiration or reduction of many temporary excise tax increases scheduled for April 1, 1954. His concern, though, was that the leadership would cut these taxes too drastically. After all, excise tax revenues made up almost 10 percent of the federal government's revenues in 1953. The bill that emerged from the House Ways and Means Committee cut excise taxes from 20 to 10 percent on selected luxury goods. In deference to the White House, Congress continued excise taxes on automobiles, gasoline, liquor, and tobacco. The resulting loss to anticipated revenues was about $1 billion. Eisenhower signed the bill reluctantly in January 1954.[32]

Important as these battles were, Eisenhower was also focused on the long term in the form of changes in the federal tax system. When the issue had been discussed during the Truman administration, it led to a contentious debate. As the president of the first Republican administration in twenty years, Eisenhower promptly turned to tax reform. He instructed Humphrey to have Treasury officials thoroughly review the tax code, which by 1953 was an amalgam of dozens of pieces of tax legislation enacted over the previous four decades. Eisenhower wanted the administration to take the lead in revising the code, to ensure that his priorities would be addressed. He feared that tax-cutting enthusiasts in Congress such as Chairman Reed would undermine efforts to balance the budget and reduce the deficit.[33]

Based on Treasury's study, Eisenhower outlined a proposal for tax changes in a message delivered to Congress on May 20, 1953. In proposing to reduce taxes Eisenhower had asked Treasury to estimate what level of tax cuts could be introduced without compromising the goal of balancing the budget in 1955. What Eisenhower got from the estimates was a figure of $1.4 billion. So with that very much in mind, the administration developed its proposal.[34]

The changes the president proposed rested on an idea popular in the business community. That is, underinvestment was a serious problem for American business. In contrast, many congressional Democrats believed that underconsumption was a more pressing issue. Humphrey also emphasized the need for reducing taxes on business, a position that Eisenhower accepted in principle but was willing to postpone if necessary. In any event, the proposals that emerged included changing the ways in which dividend income was taxed, accelerating depreciation on investment in new building and equipment; extending corporate tax-loss carrybacks (the ability to use recent losses to offset prior years' reported taxable income) to two from one year; allowing the write-off of current spending on R&D, reducing the penalties levied for accumulating income; and reducing the tax rates on income earned abroad.[35]

A final bill (the Revenue Act of 1954) did not emerge until March. It did not include every provision that Eisenhower had suggested. But the legislation was important to Eisenhower's goals, especially in regard to promoting private sector investment. It included a provision for accelerated depreciation of equipment and plant, which the administration considered a cornerstone of its evolving fiscal policy. The bill also contained a remission of taxes on a part of income derived from dividends, a measure clearly favorable to upper-income taxpayers, those most likely to own stocks. The reform of the tax code and its investment incentives, however, came at a high price. To address the lost revenue the administration proposed, and Congress agreed to, successive one-year extensions of the statutory corporate income tax rate at 52 percent; this rate endured for the entirety of the Eisenhower administration. It was a source of much irritation to the president and his key economic advisers, as well as Taft supporters, that a Republican administration felt compelled to continue to support such high statutory rates, which exceeded half of business profits.[36] But to Eisenhower across-the-board tax cutting was secondary to his primary economic policy goals.

DEFENSE SPENDING

Infinitely more important in clarifying the president's future budgeting task was the armistice agreement of July 27, 1953, that ended hostilities in Korea. The uncertainties of an ongoing conflict could be removed from the calculus of future military spending. That was relevant because by the summer of 1953, the National Security Council (NSC) was already deeply involved in a review of the United States' strategic posture.

Early in February 1953, Eisenhower had ordered the NSC to undertake a full review of defense policy. He premised the reexamination on the concept that spending for national security needed to be tailored to the country's capacity to pay for it. He hoped, he said at a meeting of the council, "to figure out a preparedness program . . . without bankrupting the nation." To signal the importance Eisenhower attached to what might be called the economy's capacity to "carry" military spending, he added Secretary Humphrey and Bureau of the Budget director Dodge to the NSC.[37]

Not every one of Eisenhower's economic advisers bought into the notion of the limiting relationship between military spending and the government's capacity to cover it. Gabriel Hauge, for instance, believed that the president underestimated a growing economy's ability to absorb the costs of increased military spending. He made his case privately to Humphrey.[38] Such critiques did not influence the secretary's thinking on the subject; instead, he focused on how the Pentagon was run. Throughout his tenure at Treasury, Humphrey remained a sharp critic of waste and inefficiency in the Pentagon. He prided himself on his executive abilities, and his colleagues at Treasury agreed that he was a forceful, indeed, a "great," executive. Robert Roosa, an official of the New York Federal Reserve Bank who worked closely with Treasury officials, said that Humphrey "was a bear for efficiency." Roosa also observed, however, that Humphrey was "no economist. He just didn't really understand how the big forces in the economy work together. He hadn't had to know that, in his business affairs." He was not a practiced politician either, according to Roosa. Stoking the well-developed egos of powerful members of Congress and top officials at the Pentagon was not something that Humphrey invested much, if any, time on. What mattered to the secretary was how an organization was run. A "tight ship" is "where the [administration's] example had to be shown."[39]

As a rule, Eisenhower's sentiments about defense spending tended to mirror Humphrey's.[40] Indeed, his disappointing experiences in the Pentagon during the Truman administration were not forgotten. The continuing inability of the heads of the various military services to look beyond short-term parochial interests deeply troubled Eisenhower. He once observed that no one at the Pentagon ever said to him, "Let's get rid of something." It was an old story, the president thought, for "it took the Army 50 years to get rid of horses after they became obsolete."[41]

But unbridled military spending, Eisenhower feared, was that part of the budget most likely to bust it. It was the overwhelming budget issue. Implicitly, what frightened the president and Humphrey was that defense demands would outpace economic growth and tax revenues. Overall, the two worried that the country could hobble itself economically if defense spending was not managed carefully.[42]

Truman administration officials had not been blind to the economic consequences of defense spending. Truman-era NSC documents emphasized the need to maintain a strong economy as part of the struggle with the USSR.[43] But to Humphrey such vague truisms were meaningless. How was the economy to remain strong? Humphrey clearly believed that the Truman administration was not prudent when devising expansive and expensive defense policies without taking into consideration their costs.[44] For the government to "pay its own way"— that is, avoid deficit spending—he wanted those making "major policy recommendations" to estimate the costs of carrying them out. He also suggested that there be a ten-year estimate of tax resources, to get some sense of what the government would be able to spend on defense.

Participants in the Eisenhower review had little disagreement over the premises upon which the Truman administration defined the strategic problem facing the United States. The comprehensive 1950 National Security Document 68 (NSC 68) envisioned the United States engaged in a long confrontation with the Soviet Union. Chillingly, the paper saw the struggle as one that would eventually lead to the victory of one over the other. By 1953, there was a consensus among policymakers that the United States had little choice but to oppose an expansive and aggressive USSR. The United States, according to NSC 68, confronted a conflict between the freedom enjoyed by a country with a government of laws or the tyranny imposed by the oligarchs in the Kremlin.[45] To stand up to this threat, the United States would need to increase military spending significantly and hold itself in a permanent state of readiness. The paper scoffed at the idea of half measures in the face of such a threat. Because of the Korean War, and Chinese involvement there, the Truman administration felt justified in proposing a major military buildup.[46]

Eisenhower accepted the premise of a long struggle but objected to Truman's view that the Cold War seemed to be about protecting territory. To Eisenhower, it was about protecting much more—a way of life. Such a view offered greater flexibility than a mentality based on securing particular positions. As a result, Eisenhower objected strenuously to the vast sums of money that would have to be spent on the military. Truman proposed to spend more than 15 percent of GNP on the military in his fiscal 1954 budget. Eisenhower and his closest economic advisers thought that such spending should not exceed 10 percent of GNP. Eisenhower refused to accept that, as NSC 68 stated, "budgetary considerations will need to be subordinated to the stark fact that our very independence as a nation may be at stake." Indeed, on March 25, 1953, the president wondered out loud during one of his many meetings devoted to reviewing strategy, whether "national bankruptcy or national destruction would get us first."[47]

So in the first months of the new administration, considerations of fiscal policy increasingly focused on the costs of national security policies. These discussions, begun in February, continued into October 1953, when the president signed off on a new National Security Council Paper (162/2), which became the guiding NSC document for the United States' approach to foreign and military policy in the Eisenhower years. Driving much of the discussion was the place of nuclear weapons in the American arsenal. American policy accepted the use of nuclear weapons as an option, and Eisenhower took that position. Indeed, the president thought it foolish not to consider them in the same way as other available weapons. If the Soviets invaded Western Europe, they would have to be met by force, including the nuclear option.[48]

As a result, the role that nuclear weapons would play in national security took a central place in the discussions. Their use was a major issue of strategy, but economic considerations also played a part in strategic thinking. The willingness to use nuclear weapons in a confrontation with the Soviet Union appealed to some of the participants in the debate—including the president—for reasons of economy. Stockpiling them would be less costly than training, maintaining, and deploying large numbers of conventional military forces.[49]

Unlike NSC 68, NSC 162/2 clearly stated the economic policies that would guide the administration in the achievement of national security.[50] The statement was more explicit about the importance of economic and budget policy than Truman-era NSC documents. NSC 162/2 observed that "excessive government spending leads to inflationary deficits or to repressive taxation, or to both. Persistent inflation is a barrier to long-term growth because it undermines confidence in the currency, reduces savings, and makes restrictive economic controls necessary. Repressive taxation weakens the incentives for efficiency, effort, and investment on which economic growth depends." NSC 162/2 was revolutionary because it accepted nuclear weapons as a tool of American strategy; the United States' strategic approach to the world would rest on developing and maintaining "a strong military posture, with emphasis on the capacity of inflicting massive retaliatory damage by offensive striking power." As to nuclear weapons, the paper stated, "In the event of hostilities, the United States will consider nuclear weapons to be as available for us as other munitions."[51]

In accepting the potential employment of nuclear weapons to chasten the Soviet Union, the administration hoped to settle the debate on strategy *and* spending. The policy proved controversial on both counts. Critics who saw the use of nuclear weapons as unacceptable were deeply disturbed by the administration's apparent willingness to blandish them to influence the behavior of the Soviet Union. In trying to save money on conventional military spending by threatening nuclear attacks—the New Look—the president also alienated many career military officers.[52]

Secretary of State John Foster Dulles acted as the spokesman of what became known as the administration's policy of massive retaliation. The press picked up on the phrase, originally buried in a lengthy modulated discussion of what the administration hoped to accomplish in changing Soviet behavior.[53] At first, the Soviet Union did not react forcefully to the new policy. It was in the midst of a shift of power in leadership, following the death of Joseph Stalin in March 1953. In fact, tensions between the US and USSR were relatively restrained for two years after the Soviet dictator died.

Ultimately, however, the Soviet Union responded to Eisenhower's policy of massive retaliation by accelerating its own nuclear program, focusing initially on improving the explosive power of nuclear bombs and delivery systems. At first the attention was on bombers, then intermediate range missiles, and finally intercontinental missiles. Consequently, the resulting nuclear arms race required more military spending than Eisenhower originally had anticipated, although still less than what he believed conventional arms would require.

Pressures for spending on conventional weapons and troops from within the American military were strong. Among the top level of military officers, many were skeptical from the first about Eisenhower's New Look of 1953, with its reliance on nuclear weapons. They did not accept that Eisenhower getting "more bang for the buck" would solve the strategic problems of the Cold War. The administration might have gained some public support by this facile journalistic characterization of the goals of the country's strategy. But military critics refused to accept that the United States could rely on nuclear retaliation alone to achieve its objectives in the Cold War. During the Eisenhower years, and after, pressure built within the military to recruit, train, and equip conventional (and covert) forces to fight the small wars or skirmishes in Southeast Asia and Latin America that became part of the standoff between the United States and the communist world.[54]

Partisan politics further complicated the president's approach to Cold War military strategy, as military spending became enmeshed in the give and take between the two political parties. Prominent Democrats increasingly criticized the president for not spending enough on national security. As a result, the nature of military strategy and how to pay for it did not remain an arcane debate within the Pentagon over weapons, force levels, and the missions of the armed services. Eisenhower's hopes that the New Look would solve both strategic and budgetary issues failed, as some prominent Pentagon officials openly joined congressional proponents of enlarged military spending—and the manufacturers who would benefit from military contracts—to cover forces and weapons programs left out of the New Look.

Problems in keeping the debate out of partisan politics surfaced in a major public dispute in 1955. During the annual May Day parade in Moscow, the Russians displayed a new jet-powered, long-range bomber. The plane, called the "Bison" by the US Air Force, seemed to be comparable, if indeed not superior, to the American B-52 bomber. The Bison's four large jet engines were apparently more powerful than the B-52's eight. The CIA estimated that the USSR had eleven of these planes, which could deliver nuclear weapons to the United States from airfields located in the Soviet Union.[55]

By late 1955, when the administration was putting together its fiscal 1957 defense budget, it faced a partisan-fueled confrontation. In mid-May 1955, press reports about the existence of the Bison set off a public discussion of a "bomber gap." Democrats in Congress seized on the new Soviet aircraft to highlight long-term criticisms held by what might be called the "defense wing" of the Democratic Party. Taking the lead in the criticism was Missouri senator Stuart Symington, a former secretary of the air force under Truman. He was scathing in his denunciation of Defense Secretary Wilson. The bomber gap was only the most recent manifestation, he argued, of a parsimonious approach to the country's defense. Warming to the subject, Symington warned that because of the secretary's failure, "the lights of freedom will soon be going out, all over the world."[56]

For fiscal 1957, Eisenhower proposed a defense budget of $34.9 billion in new funding. His request was below what the military had requested but $2 billion more than he had originally planned to put forward. Soon after the proposal went to Congress, the controversy over the administration's military spending heated up again. Magazines and newspapers picked up on criticisms found in the memoirs of retired Korean War commander, General Matthew Ridgway, about Secretary Wilson.[57] He accused Wilson of sacrificing the country's security for political and budgetary reasons, as Pentagon budgets failed to meet the needs that senior military officers believed were necessary to protect the country. These explosive criticisms were followed a few weeks later by the resignation of the assistant secretary of the air force for research and development, Trevor Gardner. He blasted the administration for underfunding R&D on missile development. These charges were made around the time that the press was giving attention to "nightmare" scenarios in which the USSR beat the United States in developing an intercontinental ballistic missile.[58] The resignation reinforced what Washington senator Henry "Scoop" Jackson, another Democratic hawk on defense, had been saying about the lead the USSR had over the US in developing ballistic missiles.[59]

Democrats, whether sincere or simply hoping to score some points during the presidential election year, continued to challenge the administration on its defense policies. Senator Richard Russell, chairman of the Senate Armed Services Committee, authorized a special subcommittee headed by Symington to examine the strength and effectiveness of US air power. Hearings began in April 1956 and ended three months later. Civilian Pentagon officials testified, as did research scientists and others who worked on weapons. Packing the most punch, though, were air force officers, who were generally critical of the administration's approach to air power, and criticized the administration's defense policy as inadequate. The list of witnesses included the air force chief of staff, Nathan Twining; General Earle E. Partridge, who headed the Air Defense Command and the Continental Defense Command; and General Curtis LeMay, head of the Strategic Air Command.[60]

While the hearings were sensational and drove aspects of the 1956 presidential debate, they were informational, if clearly political in nature. Of more consequence, testimony heard by the Symington subcommittee was also heard by the appropriations committees. Up to the time of proposing the fiscal 1957 defense budget in January 1956, Eisenhower had been able to prevail in determining military spending. At the Senate Appropriations Committee, General LeMay made a strong case for money for more B-52s. Much to Eisenhower's consternation, Congress ultimately added $900 million more to the air force budget than he had requested.[61]

Eisenhower was incensed at the behavior of senior officers, like Twinning and LeMay, before Congress. He railed that it was tantamount to insubordination and that they were still focused on serving the parochial interests of their services. But his anger could not mask the fact that dealing with the defense budget was going to be more difficult in the future. He faced a Congress controlled by the opposition party as well as high-ranking military officers willing to break ranks with the White House on its military spending strategy and throw in with the opposition when it served service purposes.[62]

But as the Cold War continued, and the nuclear arms race grew and intensified, the relationships among leaders in Congress, the Pentagon, and military contractors grew closer. Much as he might deplore these developments, Eisenhower continued to work on reorganizing the Department of Defense to increase civilian control and create greater unity among the services. Even so, the political aspects of defense spending, which were dependent on the growing ties between the Pentagon and members of Congress, could not be altered.[63] Nor could the president prevent the Pentagon from engaging in public relations campaigns that challenged the president's New Look policy. For the rest of Eisenhower's time in the White House, the administration fought hard to contain defense spending. Compounding the president's problem were the uncertainties of the new technologies that had become an integral part of the arms race. An advance in any number of technologies having to do with nuclear power and delivery systems might change the calculus by which the president wanted to spend money on the military. By the time Eisenhower left office, he had become deeply discouraged about what he referred to in his televised farewell address on January 17, 1961, as the powers and the dangers of the "military-industrial complex" and its corrosive impact on sound government fiscal policy.[64]

RECESSION, 1953–1954

Defense spending was not the only recurring economic challenge Eisenhower faced. Three recessions occurred during the administration's eight years in office. How to cope with, and then how to anticipate and perhaps head off, such declines were often at issue. During the first year of the administration, as Eisenhower focused on cutting Truman's last budget, bringing about a truce in the Korean War, and redefining Cold War strategy, the overall performance of the economy quickly became a problem. The administration's handling of the 1953–54 downturn invited criticism at the time and has been a source of disagreement among students of the period ever since. As Eisenhower approached the problem of the recession, he kept his basic goals in mind—budget balancing and deficit reduction. Eisenhower had come to office in a period marked by economic bright spots: low rates of unemployment and growing personal income. Inflation was low despite the war, running at about 1 percent a year. It was kept in check, in some part, by selective, highly unpopular government price controls, which remained in effect until Eisenhower ended them soon after taking office.

But shadows loomed. Soon after the election, Hauge cautioned the president that the country's economic outlook would be fine for the next six months, but after that conditions would be hard to predict. Burns, who shared Hauge's apprehensions, believed that the boom of early 1953 would not last. Eisenhower gave Burns responsibility for advising him on the recession once it became a problem. As early as July, Burns saw signs of a slowdown, and by September he alerted the cabinet that the economy was entering a recession.

In September 1953, Eisenhower began referring to Burns as his chief of staff in responding to the recession. The president asked him to make weekly reports to the cabinet on changing conditions, along with recommendations of what needed to be done. Standard indicators of an approaching recession were clear, and the administration began cautiously to respond. Burns pointed to several indicators: the stock market was declining sharply; the number of business failures was increasing; orders for durable goods were falling; and residential construction was shrinking. Other measures suggesting a slowdown included shorter workweeks, falling farm prices, and increasing inventories.[65]

While these signs clearly portended economic recession, Burns was not alarmed. He reported to the president and cabinet that the situation was not by any means critical. His view was that the slowdown was a result in part of reduced military spending and in part of a cyclical downturn. For the first three quarters of 1953, businesses accumulated inventories. In the fourth quarter, they began to liquidate them. By early 1954, the country unambiguously was in a recession. Between the end of the second quarter of 1953 and the second quarter of 1954, the GNP declined from $369.3 billion to $357.6 billion. Industrial production fell from $137 billion in July 1953 to $123 billion in March 1954. Unemployment in October 1953 was at 1.3 million; by March 1954 it had increased to 3.7 million (5.8% of the civilian workforce). These numbers were troubling, for on average during 1954, unemployment was at a rate of 5.5 percent of the civilian labor force. It peaked at slightly above 6 percent in mid-1954 and fell to approximately 4.2 percent by mid-1955 and remained at that level (or within a narrow range) until it began to rise again in mid-1957 with the next recession.[66]

Burns and many others, including the president, saw the recession as a result of the economy's transition from the heavy military spending associated with the Korean War. It also resulted, they thought, from the administration's plans to reduce military spending, as outlined in its fiscal 1954 budget. Spending on the military in calendar 1954 was projected to be $10 billion less than the year before. While the administration in 1954 could expect a $3.7 billion decline in federal taxes collected, those reductions to taxpayers alone could not offset the effect on the economy of the decline in defense spending. Helping the situation were estimates of the so-called automatic stabilizers—unemployment insurance ($2 billion paid out), agricultural price supports, Social Security payments, and reductions in withholding taxes as incomes fell. But alone they were not enough, even when combined with already scheduled tax reductions, to offset the cuts in defense expenses.[67]

The administration's response to the recession was at first limited. Burns conveyed to the cabinet his belief that the recession would be mild. But, at the president's direction, Burns took steps to prepare for worse conditions than anticipated. For example, as a precaution he assigned the CEA to study public works projects. For Republicans, who had been highly critical of Roosevelt's and Truman's spending on public works, this was not an easy step, even if, at this stage, it was little more than an exercise in identifying potential projects. Nevertheless, the president publicly did not rule out turning to public works spending, if conditions warranted. Burns, of course, held out hopes for the automatic stabilizers to make public works spending unnecessary.[68]

The scheduled expiration of the Korean War individual income tax increases and the excess profits tax at the end of 1953 was also important. In addition, selected excise taxes would be eliminated or reduced at the end of March 1954. Removing the excess profits tax allowed corporations to continue to pay dividends to the generally wealthier part of the population that owned stocks. Income tax reductions, and the willingness of consumers to use savings for purchases, contributed to keeping consumption up among the less well-off.[69] But to Burns and Eisenhower, a very significant tool in fighting the recession would be looser monetary policy. Fortunately for them, they had an ally in the head of the Federal Reserve, William McChesney Martin, who agreed with the administration's restrained approach. Martin was nominally a Democrat, initially appointed by President Truman to chair the Federal Reserve. He had had a remarkable career and was something of a phenomenon in financial circles. He became president of the New York Stock Exchange in 1936 at the age of thirty-one, called by newspapers at the time "the boy wonder of Wall Street." During the war, he worked on the Munitions Allocation Board, as a liaison between the army and Congress, and as head of the Lend-Lease program focused on providing assistance to the Soviet Union. In late 1945, Truman appointed him the chairman of the Export-Import Bank.[70] In March 1951, following a stint at the Treasury, Martin was tapped by Truman to head the Federal Reserve system. Later, Eisenhower reappointed him twice to the chairmanship; he remained in that position until 1970.[71]

Martin sympathized with Eisenhower's concerns about inflation and his determination to balance the budget. He also found the president well informed about budgetary and economic matters, so the two developed a professional and in time cordial relationship. Humphrey and Burns met regularly with Martin, and the Fed chairman was determined to develop a good working relationship with the Treasury secretary. Lower-level Treasury officials conferred with Federal Reserve staff to keep open channels between the administration and the central bank.[72]

Yet, while Martin was in sync with the administration on many issues, he was determined to establish the Fed as an independent institution. By 1953 it had only been two years since the Treasury and the Fed had worked out an agreement (the "Accord") that promised greater independence for the central bank to regulate the nation's monetary system and economic activity by ending a 1941 understanding that the Fed use monetary policy to reduce interest on government wartime debt. Martin did not want to be seen as subservient to the White House, regardless of the occupant.[73]

Martin moved decisively in the face of the 1953–54 recession. In October 1953, the Fed eased credit. Into the next spring, the bank followed what Martin called a policy of "active ease" of credit. For the most part, the Fed and the administration were in agreement. By March 1954, however, when the numbers of unemployed spiked upward to 3.3 million, Eisenhower pressed Humphrey and Secretary of

Commerce Marion Folsom to encourage Martin to ease up even more. At the time, both organized labor and the Democratic opposition in Congress criticized the administration for underestimating the seriousness of the recession, especially the rising numbers of unemployed. These critics also focused on the need to increase spending for public housing as a way to stimulate economic activity, while others promoted increased outlays for public works.[74]

Martin and the Fed were open to the administration's concerns. It was Martin's first recession, and he wanted the Fed to get its role in meeting the problem right. So, the Fed pushed a little harder on the tools it had been employing. It reduced the rediscount rate, eased reserve requirements, and made large open market purchases. The rate of interest on Treasury bills dropped from 2.11 percent in June 1953 to 0.64 percent in June 1954. Over the same twelve months, prime commercial paper went from 2.68 percent to 1.56 percent. Debt management was also a part of easing monetary policy. The Treasury worked to facilitate the availability of investment funds by shortening the terms of its offerings. Overall, the Fed's easing of monetary policy opened up about $17 billion to commercial banks for lending.[75]

These easy money policies played an important part in ending the recession, and by September 1954, there were solid indicators of an upswing in economic activity. For several months the number of new housing starts was up; industrial output in key sectors increased; and demand for credit continued to expand. Easy credit was essential in stimulating housing construction, in particular. With credit available, and interest rates declining, builders could obtain the financing needed to construct houses. Government-guaranteed mortgages through either Federal Housing Administration (FHA) or Veterans' Administration (VA) loans ensured that there was mortgage money available to buyers at attractive rates. In 1953, 408,000 new homes were insured by FHA or VA guarantees to lenders; by 1954 the number was 582,000. In 1954, 48 percent of homes were financed by government-backed mortgages; the year before it had been 39 percent.[76]

The country owed much to Burns and Martin in coping with the recession. Burns, though considered a liberal by some of Eisenhower's advisers, was highly skeptical of Keynesian theory as a means of explaining business cycles and investment.[77] Delegated with developing administration policy in fighting the recession, Burns knew as well as anyone Eisenhower's aversion to running deficits and "excessive" federal spending. He appreciated, of course, that the administration was allowing for reductions in both personal and business taxes. He also believed that the recession was a manifestation of the economy reducing its war footing and of the cuts already approved in military spending. Martin, for his part, understood that easing up on credit would be essential.[78]

Martin's loose monetary policy and the tax cuts obviously were important in ending the recession quickly. The automatic stabilizers also played a role, as they prompted continued household consumption. Corporate dividends helped in this regard, as well as the propensity of consumers to dip into savings in order to make purchases. Eisenhower believed that his studied efforts to keep business confidence up were important, too.[79]

The lessons the administration drew from the recession, however, were not necessarily going to be useful in the future. The *ERP, 1955* contained a discussion called "Lessons from Experience and Guides to the Future." In this section the report observed that "wise and early action by Government can stave off serious difficulties later." It went on to say that "monetary policy can be a powerful instrument of economic recovery, so long as the confidence of consumers and businessmen in the future remains high"; that "the automatic stabilizers, such as unemployment insurance and a tax system that is elastic with respect to national income, can be of material aid in moderating cyclical fluctuations"; and that "a minor contraction in this country need not produce a severe depression abroad."[80] This euphoric conclusion underestimated the importance of the ending of Korean War temporary income taxes. In the following recessions, taxes were going to be an important issue, especially Eisenhower's aversion to cutting them.

FIGHTING INFLATION

Once the recession was over, Eisenhower planned to return to his goals of balancing the budget, reducing the deficit, and keeping inflation low. But in 1955, and especially in 1956, fiscal policy making became more difficult, and there were indications of long-term difficulties ahead. To be sure, the budgets for fiscal 1956 and 1957 showed modest surpluses, so a key first-term goal of balancing the budget was achieved.[81] Because of a rapidly expanding economy—what many at the time described as a boom—federal tax receipts were higher than anticipated. But this positive development created its own set of fiscal policy problems. With more federal money available, pressure grew to increase federal spending in several domestic areas, most notably education. Eisenhower was not entirely opposed to limited spending in this area. The postwar period saw an increase in new family formation and the birthrate, as well as greater mobility than earlier in the century. Suburbanization created demand for new schools, as well as assistance to cities faced with a lower tax base, as more of the middle class moved to the suburbs. A better-educated population also fit the president's ideas of strengthening the public's commitment to American institutions. He thought that the administration needed to be responsive to new demands, and as a result some of his associates spoke of Eisenhower creating a new, or "Modern," Republicanism.[82] Yet spending on education and urban renewal never became a large part of the budget. Indeed, such domestic spending was virtually the same, as a percentage of the budget, in the beginning as at the end of the administration. Not surprisingly, congressional Democrats kept up criticism of the administration's limited spending on domestic programs throughout the president's two terms.

Increasing federal tax receipts had other consequences. Within the administration it led to a sharpening of the differences between Eisenhower and Humphrey. The secretary's business conservatism brought him around again and again to the need to cut taxes. Corporate taxes were high by historic standards and certainly were high compared to today. For example, even after the excess profits tax expired, statutory corporate income tax rates were 52 percent; in 2010 the figure was 34 percent. Statutory individual income tax rates were in the very top brackets—as high as 90 percent; in 2010 the maximum figure was 35 percent. Humphrey viewed the rates in the early 1950s as virtually confiscatory and made the case that they needed to be cut at every opportunity.[83] In 1955, Burns and Eisenhower rejected Humphrey's entreaties, on the ground that as the economy was expanding cutting taxes would be inflationary. Later, in 1956, when Humphrey made the same case for cutting taxes, the president opted instead to use the surplus to reduce the federal debt. Humphrey left the administration in 1957, as he apparently saw the futility of his point of view in the face of Eisenhower's overriding concerns about the deficit and inflation.[84]

Humphrey's push for lower taxes in an economic boom was not well timed. Inflation became an important public issue after the end of the recession. Late in 1954 and early in 1955, Martin began to tighten credit, as the Fed picked up on the initial signs of inflation in the economy. As the boom developed, the Fed kept tightening. Martin's emphasis on inflation stemmed from his long experience in Wall Street. He saw inflation, as did Humphrey and others, as tied to speculative behavior. He had seen speculation in assets, whether stocks, real estate, or commodities, lead to price increases and the ultimate crash of speculative booms. Crashes entailed losses and the risk of a serious economic downturn. So, he was a hawk on inflation because it represented to him so much else that might be wrong in the economy.[85]

Eisenhower approved of the Fed's policies. Inflation was a core issue in managing economic policy for the president and some of his closest advisers. Eisenhower's emphasis on the threat of inflation, however, was more focused on the federal budget than on stock market speculation. He believed that inflation hit the poor and those on fixed incomes hardest. No doubt the latter conviction had taken hold during his career in the military, where he was surrounded by retired military personnel living on fixed incomes.[86] Humphrey took a great interest in inflation, as did Arthur Burns, who after leaving the administration wrote about the subject.[87] Indeed, Humphrey and many others in the administration accepted as an article of faith that before the Accord of March 1951 the Fed's postwar role of supporting and facilitating low interest rates on Treasury securities had artificially manipulated the value of those instruments; lowered interest rates; increased liquidity; and substantially contributed to inflation. A Fed, liberated from the obligation to support low-interest-rate Treasury debt, was a formidable tool in the battle against inflation, if combined with aggressive administration fiscal policy.[88]

As we have seen, the Fed and the administration had been on the same page when it came to loosening credit during the recession. Fed officials had also cooperated with the administration early in Eisenhower's tenure. Within days of taking office, the president removed the remaining partial price controls imposed at the beginning of the Korean War. Administration officials worried about the inflationary consequences of removing these controls, in view of the previous administration's experience.[89] Between 1946 and 1948 there had been a sharp rise in inflation, after Truman vetoed legislation extending wartime price controls. Anticipating a similar response to the removal of controls early in 1953, the Fed tightened credit. When the surge in inflation failed to materialize, the Fed eased up within a few months by reducing the reserve requirements of banks.[90]

From the outset of the administration, White House officials' focus on inflation was closely linked with fiscal issues. Because Eisenhower, Humphrey, Burns, and other economic policymakers saw inflation as demand driven, their already strong interest in controlling federal spending heightened. Government funneling money into the economy was likely to increase demand and hence stimulate inflation. Fear of inflation also heightened interest in a balanced budget, which the president thought would ensure stable prices.

Fighting inflation led to a focus within the White House on the cash budget. A significant increase in Social Security taxes (0.5 percent) effective on January 1, 1954, brought in an additional $1.3 billion in annual revenues.[91] Humphrey discussed the role of the cash budget in the administration's anti-inflation program in 1955:

> As long as the government is not taking out of the economy more than it spends, the government is not increasing the money supply and thus being inflationary. So when we have a balance in the cash budget we have eliminated that inflationary pressure. We did have a cash balance between money collected from the public and money paid out by the Government last year (fiscal 1954), although we will not quite have a cash balance this year (fiscal 1955). We estimate a small cash surplus in fiscal 1956. So that the inflationary effect of deficit financing will have been almost eliminated during the entire period this Administration had been in financial control.[92]

Critics thought Eisenhower's focus on inflation was misplaced and based on faulty analysis. Perhaps the best place to see the critique fully developed was the so-called *Eckstein Report* released in late 1959. It resulted from extensive hearings of Congress's Joint Economic Committee organized by its staff director, Arthur Eckstein, and chaired by administration critic Illinois senator Paul Douglas. The report represented the evolving thinking about an "activist" or "proactive" Keynesianism that would prove influential in shaping Democratic criticism of the Eisenhower administration's economic management. Essentially, the report criticized the administration for overemphasizing the importance of demand-induced inflation. Eisenhower's critics maintained that inflation was a result of the government pursuing policies that did not fully utilize the economy's capacity, of not fully making use of its human and material resources. Inflation, the report argued, was also a result of structural problems and administered prices in key oligopolistic industries, such as steel, automobiles, and chemicals.

In retrospect, recent work of economists maintains that the president's concern about inflation does not appear to have been misplaced.[93] The 1950s experienced strong inflationary pressures. Wholesale price inflation reached its lowest level in 1955 and then began to increase rapidly. Consumer prices began accelerating in 1956.[94] Food prices were generally included in price indexes in this decade but were broken out after 1957. They declined steeply into 1956, then rose through 1958, and declined again by 1960. If one removes food prices (as is done now) from price data, there are indicators of significant inflation in the 1950s, particularly in certain concentrated industries and in services driven by demand (especially medical care). There was also a strong cost-push element to these numbers. Between 1953 and 1959 there were increases in rent, utilities, laundry services, automobile repairs, insurance, and medical and hospital services. Prices in these service areas rose much faster than the other 80 percent

INDEX, 1947-49 =100

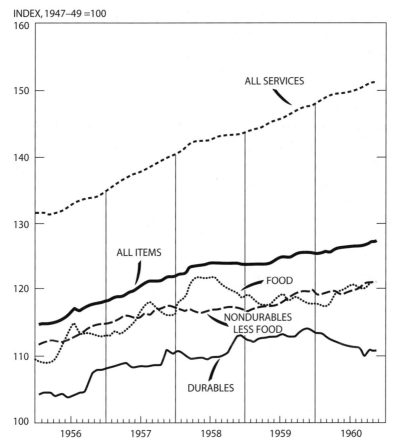

Fig. 1.1. Consumer prices. The 1960 rise in consumer prices was due largely to an advance in food prices and to the continuing increase in prices of services. Prices of durable goods fell markedly. *Source: Economic Report of the President* (Washington, DC: GPO, 1961), p. 17.

of the consumer price index. While constituting less than 20 percent of the index, these services made up 42.8 percent of the price increases between 1953 and 1959, rising 20.5 percent, while the rest of the index rose only 6.7 percent. Durable goods prices actually declined 1 percent between 1953 and 1958 and by the end of 1959 had only risen less than 1 percent above the 1953 level.[95] (See fig. 1.1.)

CONCLUSION

In his first years as president, Eisenhower showed himself to be in control of economic policy. His concerns drove the debates within the administration. He subsequently did not relent in his attention to inflation, as discussions continued over its causes and consequences for the rest of his two terms. Nor did his focus blur on the desirability of balancing the budget and reducing the federal debt. Eisenhower's record on inflation, the budget, and debt reduction was better than that of the Truman administration. Eisenhower's predecessor had to cope with great volatility resulting from reduced military spending after World War II, the end of price and wage controls, and then in 1950 the Korean War. But the record of the 1950s also compared most favorably to the administrations that followed in the 1960s and later. While the rate of economic growth was slightly higher in the Kennedy and Johnson administrations than in the 1950s, so was inflation. In the 1970s, inflation reached unprecedented levels, with serious consequences for the economy and society, as Eisenhower had feared.

CHAPTER 2

Economic Policy in Good Times
1955–1957

Good economic times challenged Eisenhower's economic policy goals almost as much as the problems of recession had. Following the recession of 1953–54, the economy did well. In particular, 1955 was the height of a boom between 1954 and 1957. In 1955, gross national product (GNP) increased, unemployment declined, and inflation remained stable.[1] Eisenhower, however, had a keen sense that he was operating in unusual times. The administration did not have recent precedent to aid in shaping what policies, if any, to pursue to keep the boom going. The hands-off policies of the 1920s, the collapse of the 1930s, and the unusual prosperity of the wartime and postwar 1940s period provided little guide to what a "modern" approach to economic policy should be during good times.

Initially, Eisenhower did not worry much about "managing" the boom. The public expected that the government would intervene in the economy when necessary, and the administration had statutory obligations under the Employment Act of 1946. Then, too, the president wanted to demonstrate that a Republican chief executive could handle economic policy. So, the president followed economic developments in the good times of the mid-1950s. He set out to ensure a climate conducive to growth and prosperity through fiscal and monetary policy, the Treasury's federal debt management abilities, the executive's authority over the terms of government-guaranteed mortgages, and bank regulators' ability to affect the levels and terms of consumer credit.

What eventually heightened Eisenhower's attention to the boom was inflation. It became an overriding concern in 1956 and 1957, as prices rose by 6 percent. Consequently, increases in real GNP (that is, the value of growth discounted by the rate of inflation) flagged for two years after 1955. Between 1955 and 1956 real GNP grew by only 2.4 percent and between 1956 and 1957 it increased only by 1.2 percent. Keeping inflation in check, in the president's estimation, was the key to promoting savings and investment. He also firmly believed that inflation had social and class implications. Indeed, he thought it harmed workers and retirees more seriously than wealthy investors. Growing concern about inflation during the boom shaped the administration's approach to policy. It influenced relations with the Federal Reserve over interest rates; Congress over taxes, spending, credit, and mortgage policies; and business and labor over prices and wages.

At first, the good economic times also had political consequences. It turned the president's attention to the future of the Republican Party. His internationalist foreign and defense policies had prevailed over the noninterventionist views of the Taft wing early in the first term. But the president and his political advisers aspired to further distance the Republican Party from Taft and the economic legacy of Hoover, which was associated with the latter's tenure as secretary of commerce during the booming 1920s, the collapse that followed in 1929 in the first year of his presidency, and his term as president during the depths of the Great Depression. Followers of the late Senator Taft, who died in 1953, distrusted an approach to politics that seemed to offer diluted versions of the Democratic Party's programs. But Eisenhower had no intention of reversing major innovations of the New Deal. A growing, more urban and mobile society invariably needed the involvement of the federal government in some form. Eisenhower hoped to direct the party toward what was called "Modern Republicanism." Thus, the administration would provide limited federal support to urgent needs in such areas as education, transportation, housing, science, and small business.

Eisenhower's new brand of Republicanism envisioned the party as prudent and business-like managers of federal programs, not proponents of their extinction. His effort drew a clear distinction between his party and the Democrats, whom he portrayed as proposing larger spending, more extensive programs, and an expanding bureaucracy to administer them. In response, Democratic leaders inside and outside Congress challenged the premises of Eisenhower's economic policy goals. During the 1956 campaign, Democratic presidential candidate Adlai Stevenson questioned the overall direction of Eisenhower's economic policies. Out of these debates emerged a focus on sustainable economic growth, a subject that would dominate economic policy in both the Democratic and Republican administrations through the 1960s and 1970s.

These debates had little effect on the president's thinking, whatever their future influence. Instead, early in Eisenhower's second term, a divisive battle over the proposed budget for fiscal 1958 served as a moment of truth for the president. He worried that his efforts to restrain spending were insufficient and concluded that his energy would have to be even more concentrated on preventing inflation than before. Increasing pressure for more spending and a large deficit had to be restrained, no matter the cost to other goals, including the creation of Modern Republicanism.

THE BOOM AND THE "PROBLEM" OF PROSPERITY

Boom times prevailed between the end of the recession in 1954 and the autumn of 1957. By far the best year was 1955. After that there was a sharp slowdown in real growth—that is, after accounting for inflation. Growth slowed in 1956 and 1957, and it turned negative in the fourth quarter of 1957.[2] Unemployment averaged 5.6 percent for 1954 and just 4.4 percent for 1955. The consumer price index (CPI) was almost unchanged, as farm and food prices declined and services and manufactured goods increased. The CPI (which was at 100 in 1947–49) was at 114.3 in January 1955 and 114.7 in December 1955.[3]

Business was in good shape in almost all sectors of the economy throughout the boom period. Different sectors, though, grew more robustly than others at various times. First, in 1954–55, the growth sector was housing; then in 1955–56 it was consumer durables, particularly automobiles; finally, during 1956–57 there was a boom in capital goods expenditures, induced in part by increased spending on rising and projected defense expenditures.[4]

Initially, demographic changes, especially new "household formation," fueled the boom. Disposable personal income increased 3.8 percent a year between 1947 and 1957, adjusted for inflation. New family formation increased during and after the Korean War. In the initial and middle stage of the boom, use of credit increased dramatically, the result in part of the liberalization of credit terms. Interest rates had moved down in the recession of 1953–54, and the maximum repayment periods allowed for VA- and FHA- insured mortgages went in stages from twenty to twenty-five and then to thirty years. Down payments were reduced on FHA-insured mortgages and ultimately eliminated on VA mortgages. Federally guaranteed loans with no down payment increased from 11 percent of total purchases in 1953 to 44 percent in 1955, and thirty-year loans increased from 5 percent to 44 percent of all purchases in the same period.[5] By the time the boom in housing leveled off in May 1955, housing starts were approximately 1.7 million, 30 percent above their August 1953 level.[6] From 1956 through 1957 they declined to below 1 million, then rose to almost 1.4 million in 1958 (driven by low interest rates), and then they slowly declined through the remainder of the decade.[7]

The waning housing boom was superseded by a surge in purchases of consumer durables, especially automobiles. Financing an automobile became much easier. All controls on consumer credit (Regulation W) had been eliminated in May 1952, and a "rapid expansion of installment credit in 1955 gave rise to widespread concern."[8] Terms for new automobiles eased "to the point where 36-month maturities became rather common." Installment credit reached $29 billion by the end of 1955 and increased by $5.5 billion, or by almost one-quarter, in that year alone.[9] In 1955 cars were larger and more colorful. Sales rose from 6.1 million in 1953, to 6.6 million in 1954, and finally to 7.9 million in 1955, a level of sales not achieved again for ten years. There were also huge increases in the purchases of television sets, furniture, and household appliances. Consumer durables accounted for just 7 percent of the increase in real GNP—that is, adjusted for inflation—in 1954, but for 25 percent of the increase in real GNP in 1955.[10]

The final stage of the good times, according to Raymond J. Saulnier (who became chairman of CEA in December 1956), was a "capital goods boom of exceptional strength." Even in the trough of the recession of 1954, the utilization of manufacturing capacity was unusually high, at 80 percent, and in the next two years it increased to 88 percent, a level it would not reach again until 1965–66. Saulnier attributed the financing of this boom to a bull market in stocks, retained corporate earnings, and declining real interest rates. Spending on machinery and equipment rose 30 percent between the first quarter of 1955 and the same period in 1956.[11] Fixed business investment (durable equipment and nonresidential construction) surged in early 1955 and only began to level off in 1957. Federal outlays for goods and services dropped sharply in 1954, moderated in 1955 through mid-1956, and then began to accelerate (especially in the defense sector).[12]

Overall, the boom was dramatic but not spectacular when adjusted for inflation. It was no surprise that the big jump in corporate investment came within one year of passage of the 1954 tax legislation, which significantly liberalized depreciation for new investment. Also, a small but not insignificant amount of investment in a few industries continued to be eligible for five-year defense amortization through the end of the decade. This corporate investment, as well as the ebb and flow in defense spending, set the tone for private corporate investment during 1953–61.[13]

The last stage of the boom occurred with the increase in defense expenditures from mid-1956 into 1957. When they leveled off, according to the *Economic Report of the President (ERP)*, it was a sharp rise in exports that kept the boom going a little longer. But the *ERP* noted that these were offset to an extent by slowdowns and then declines in inventory accumulation. The *ERP* recorded that the bulk of the increase in expenditures from late 1956 into most of 1957 "was largely matched by an increase in prices," which went up 6 percent between early 1956 and the end of 1957.[14] Real value added per hour in manufacturing, however, rose only 1.9 percent between 1953 and 1957, increasing inflationary pressures.[15]

How, then, to make policy as worrisome indicators arose in credit markets and inflation increased? A review of the economic forces at work during the mid-1950s points up the complexity behind these "boom times." Contingencies driving economic performance were not lost on Eisenhower, who followed them closely with his economic advisers. The administration did not attempt to manage the boom to any great extent. Administration officials aspired to have the correct combination of monetary and fiscal policies, and by and large they believed they were on track with both. It was not by any means a hands-off approach, but neither was the administration's policy highly interventionist. Rather than seek new legislative authority, Eisenhower used the powers he had, especially in regard to consumer credit and mortgages. In addition, the president continued to resist looser fiscal policy. When budget surpluses developed, he opposed calls for tax cuts from within the administration, his party, and the Democrats. On the expenditure side, the administration attempted to hold the line against increased defense spending.[16]

One of the first issues to receive attention was consumer credit. White House officials and Federal Reserve Chairman Martin worried in 1955 that liberal credit policies were supercharging the 1955 boom. At a March 4, 1955, cabinet meeting, Secretary Humphrey remarked that the administration had to take care that the "1955 boom" did not turn into the "1956 bust." Martin obviously agreed. He moved to tighten monetary policy in 1955, although he was having difficulty in forming a consensus at the Fed about the need for restrictive policies. For its part, to take money out of the economy, the Treasury went into the long-term credit market to issue $2 billion of forty-year, 3 percent bonds and followed soon thereafter with another issue worth $800 million.[17]

To dampen demand in the housing market, Eisenhower tightened liberalized mortgage terms. Repayment schedules for FHA-guaranteed and VA-guaranteed mortgages were reduced from thirty to twenty-five years. In addition, both the FHA and the VA increased the required down payment on guaranteed loans two percentage points to 5 percent.[18] Based on authority it already possessed, the administration restricted the use of the so-called no–no–down payment mortgage loans with closing costs included in the amount financed by the loan. Eisenhower called 100 percent financing "very extraordinary—even distressing."[19] To reduce capital available for new mortgages the Federal National Mortgage Association (Fannie Mae) sold mortgages from its holdings to reduce funds available for new mortgages. Meanwhile the Federal Home Loan Bank tightened the terms of loans offered for the most part by savings and loan institutions.[20]

In addition to these measures, administration officials discussed the advisability of altering the length and rates of consumer credit. Surging automobile sales prompted the discussion. Members of the cabinet debated the merits of asking Congress for standby authority over consumer credit, but following a lengthy study by the Fed, the administration decided against requesting such authority. A White House press release of May 25, 1957, quoted from the Fed report, endorsing its observation that "the broad public interest is better served if potentially un-stabilizing credit developments are restrained by the use of general monetary measures and the application of sound public and private fiscal policies."[21]

This fairly innocuous statement masked the intensity of concern within the administration about the easy availability of mortgages and consumer credit. Cabinet discussions reveal that the administration struggled with what to do. A 1957 cabinet paper on the subject of consumer credit, circulated for discussion, provided an overview of earlier debates. It concluded that "in the past [this kind of credit] has tended to accentuate ups and downs in business." But that the "economy survived the surge of credit buying that occurred in 1955 with relatively little disturbance to growth and stability." The paper concluded, "Prima facie, this experience suggests that one should allow credit to be allocated by free market forces, within total credit volume that is held within reasonable limits by general credit restraints."[22]

While the administration came down on the side of markets determining credit, officials nevertheless used the regulatory powers at their disposal to exert pressure. Eisenhower worked behind the scenes to cope with the auto boom and its inflationary tendencies. Officials requested that federal bank examiners look closely at bank consumer credit practices. Institutions had to provide a special schedule listing the extent and terms of consumer installment lending. Saulnier later observed that he believed such action in 1955 had the desired effect of deterring banks, although it's impossible to know for certain.[23]

Related to concerns about credit markets were indicators of rising prices. This became a major concern and often animated policy deliberations. But the president was willing to work behind the scenes here, too. Privately, both Eisenhower and Humphrey attempted to influence automobile and steel executives in pricing and production decisions in 1955 and 1956.[24] But the emphasis on social responsibility to a nation caught up in a worldwide struggle against an alien ideology added urgency to Eisenhower's appeal. Even so, efforts to convince business and labor—"jawboning" as it later became known—to exercise restraint in the interest of a larger good failed. This failure was a source of great disappointment for Eisenhower.[25]

Humphrey was deeply disappointed, too. He was appalled that, in his view, most businesspeople accepted "creeping inflation." In December 1956, Humphrey wrote to Eisenhower that "there are a lot of business people who are not too thoughtful about the future so long as their current quarterly statements look good." Humphrey was responding to a memo Eisenhower had sent with a quote from Standard and Poor's 1956 quarterly report. It concluded that there was an "increasing number of executives who believe a little continuing inflation is essential to full employment."[26]

Eisenhower also used the "bully pulpit" to speak out publicly about the boom and inflation. If private entreaties to business and labor leaders were to no avail, perhaps public discussion of their role in fighting inflation might help. In doing so, the president emphasized that business and labor had, with government, a "shared responsibility" to fight inflation and ensure stable growth. In his 1957 State of the Union address, Eisenhower talked of the need to favor the long-term public interest over that of groups of private citizens who might seek short-term advantages. In particular, business and labor needed to be vigilant in keeping inflationary tendencies in check. Prices must be kept down and wage increases tied to increases in productivity. "Should we persistently fail to discipline ourselves," the president warned, "eventually there will be increasing pressure on Government to redress the failure. By that process freedom will step by step disappear. No subject on the domestic scene should more attract the concern of the friends of American working men and women and of free business enterprise than the forces that threaten a steady depreciation of the value of our money."[27]

For a Republican, Eisenhower had moved well beyond standard party orthodoxy on the efficacy of markets. Indeed, when the need for "shared responsibility" was invoked in the 1957 *ERP,* economist Milton Friedman complained. Writing to CEA chairman Saulnier, he warned, "You will not be surprised that my one really serious disagreement is with the assignment of responsibility to business and labor for restraining inflation. This seems to be not only analytically wrong, but politically dangerous. Heaven preserve us from a world of businessmen and labor leaders conducting their affairs in terms of 'social responsibility!' "[28]

It is unknown whether Saulnier ever showed Eisenhower the letter. The president, in any event, continued to press his views about the responsibility of business and labor to a society faced with a long-term threat from the Soviet Union. Elsewhere in the 1957 *ERP*, it stated, "Even more exacting [than the responsibility of government in a free economy] are the responsibilities of individuals and economic groups. Business managements should formulate and carry out their plans so as to contribute to steady economic growth. They must also recognize the broad public interest in the prices set on their products and services."[29]

In 1958, as inflation became more serious, the president reiterated his belief that business and labor had a common duty to the interests of the country in the long run. The GNP in 1957 rose by 5 percent, but Eisenhower was concerned that 80 percent of that increase was due to inflation. In submitting his annual economic report to Congress, the president laid out his concerns about the behavior of business and labor:

> Business managements must recognize that price increases that are unwarranted by costs, or that attempt to recapture investment outlays too quickly, not only lower the buying power of the dollar, but also may be self-defeating by causing a restriction of markets, lower output, and a narrowing of the return on capital investment. The leadership of labor must recognize that wage increases that go beyond over-all productivity gains are inconsistent with stable prices, that the resumption of economic growth can be slowed by wage increases that involve either higher prices or a further narrowing of the margin between prices and costs. Government, for its part, must use its powers to help keep our economy stable and to encourage sound economic growth with reasonably stable prices. . . . [The latter] can be guaranteed by a public opinion that is alert to the consequences of wrong policies and insists on policies which will yield economic growth without inflation.[30]

THE ADMINISTRATION, THE FEDERAL RESERVE, AND INFLATION

Living with the boom of the mid-1950s provided another source of concern to Eisenhower. Generally, the administration and the Federal Reserve were in agreement on the long-term need to keep inflationary pressures under control. In the short term, however, Fed chairman Martin had different ideas on how that might be achieved. From the administration's view, Martin was perhaps too stringent in raising interest rates and not careful enough in the timing of his actions.

Deliberations on interest rates were often sharply debated within the institution. The head of the New York Federal Reserve Bank had an important role to play in decision making and did not always agree with Martin. Late in 1954 Martin mounted a campaign to strengthen and centralize the power of the Fed chairman. His objective was to transfer authority over direct open market operations to the Federal Open Market Committee (FOMC) in Washington, a goal that he achieved in the summer 1956 at the expense of the power of the president of the New York Fed. The battle for bureaucratic control over direct open market operations contained within it a struggle over other Fed policy, too.[31]

Martin's decision to increase interest rates in April 1956 caused a standoff with the administration. Eisenhower approached the dispute carefully. It was essential to the administration's policy that the Fed and the White House work, if not together, at least in tandem. Eisenhower and his advisers understood that compromising Fed independence could well raise the specter of inflationary pre-Accord Fed policies, anathema to their worldview.

Nevertheless, the White House was concerned that Martin's interpretation of the sources of the inflationary threat differed from those of the president and his advisers. Martin emphasized the inflationary dangers of stock market buoyancy more than the administration did. Though some in Eisenhower's circle of advisers shared this view in part, they and Eisenhower were generally worried more about the easy availability of credit and increasing prices and wages. Martin's and the administration's concerns, of course, were not mutually exclusive. But it was the intensity of Martin's response to his fears about an overly exuberant stock market that led him to raise interest rates five times between April 1955 and August 1957. The administration feared that Martin was going too far and that he would limit the economic expansion, especially as the 1956 presidential election approached.[32]

There were other tensions with the Fed that concerned the administration. Past increases in rates created problems between the Federal Reserve and the Department of the Treasury over debt management. When the Fed tightened the discount rate late in 1955, investors stampeded out of Treasury bonds and caused a significant weakening of their prices. This came at precisely the time the Treasury was about to refund maturing notes valued at $12 billion. Investor interest in the new issue was so low that the Treasury had to approach the Fed for help. That is, it needed the Fed to reduce member bank reserve requirements, freeing up cash to purchase the new Treasury issue. This was the second time in 1955 that the Treasury sought the Fed's assistance. As earlier in May, when the Fed acceded to the Treasury's first call for help, Martin knew that acquiescing undermined his efforts to create a restrictive atmosphere. Martin and others on the FOMC were critical of the Treasury's debt management anyway, and the December 1955 request intensified their displeasure. In the end, the Fed gave in, although Martin took his time to make up his mind.[33]

As the drama over debt management played out, signs appeared that the economic expansion was slowing in late 1955 and early 1956. The hours of the manufacturing workweek stopped rising; unemployment was no longer declining; and the real GNP's rate of growth slowed in the last quarter of 1955. In addition, early in March 1956, Humphrey sounded an alarm about the increasing competitive environment in which US industry had to operate. Looking to the future, he observed that "American business was entering a period of severe competition with foreign firms under the disadvantage of higher labor costs and higher taxes in the United States."[34] Focusing more on current conditions than future prospects, Burns reported a few weeks later to the cabinet that there was a "virtual stability of industrial production, employment, individual spending power, consumer spending, and the gross national product." Burns went on to raise the question "of whether this constituted a pause in growth or the beginning of a decline."[35]

In response to these indicators, the administration reversed course on some of the measures it had adopted to moderate the expansion and contain inflation. At the end of 1955 and the beginning of 1956, the White House, on the advice of the CEA, asked the Federal Home Loan Bank Board to reduce the limits it had imposed on the borrowing of banks affiliated with the board. It also reinstituted the thirty-year term on FHA-insured and VA-guaranteed mortgages. Moreover, the administration asked Congress to speed up appropriations for planned public works projects.[36]

At the same time, Humphrey and Burns pressed Martin to lower interest rates. In January 1956 Martin reluctantly asked the FOMC to "ease up a bit," although Martin thought that the Fed should keep its foot poised on the brake, should it need to respond quickly. By the spring of 1956, Martin began again to apply the brakes. He was not certain that the economy was slipping, so he was cautious. The first tightening of interest rates was a 0.25 percent increase announced on April 13, 1956. Privately, Eisenhower was unhappy with the increase. His advisers were incensed that it might slow the economy as the presidential election approached. Eisenhower usually thought of himself as above partisan political ploys, but in fact he was not insensitive to political realities. He thought that credit was too tight. The president indicated at a cabinet meeting that he considered calling Martin to dissuade him from raising rates before the new rate was announced. But Eisenhower decided not to make the call. Such interference, he concluded, "would have constituted an overruling of the financial experts with a purely political judgment." It would not have been "in order." So Eisenhower settled for having his views conveyed by others to Martin privately.[37]

Eisenhower's refusal to press Martin on the increase did not prevent the secretary of the treasury and other administration officials from commenting. Humphrey, Burns, and Hauge in private sharply criticized the Fed's 0.25 percent increase. The three cajoled Martin to reconsider—he had told them of his intentions sometime before. But he refused to be dissuaded and went ahead. Humphrey publicly criticized Martin's move. Burns, who maintained a more professorial public persona than the plainspoken Humphrey, nevertheless called the rate increase "untimely," for the record.[38] In any event, at a news conference on April 25, 1956, almost two weeks after the rate increase, Eisenhower strongly reaffirmed the importance of keeping the Fed independent. In answering a question about making the Fed responsible to the president, Eisenhower replied, "I personally believe it would be a mistake to make it definitely and directly responsible to the political head of state."[39]

Why the difference between Eisenhower's private and public posture? Political calculations among his advisers clearly played a role, as demonstrated by the discussion at the April 20, 1956, cabinet meeting. Eisenhower shrewdly concluded that there was little to be gained politically by criticizing Martin. If the president forced the issue, Martin might have resigned to protest interference with the Fed's independence, and much would be lost in the uproar that followed. But principle clearly played a part, too. In the cabinet discussions of the issue, Burns emphasized the need to reaffirm the importance of Fed independence. Even Humphrey, the sharpest critic in the cabinet of the Fed increase, agreed that the Fed's independence was important. For his part, Eisenhower agreed in principle, although he was annoyed that Martin seemed not to understand the political ramifications of tight money.[40]

As it turned out, by the time of the election the economy was doing well. Fears that the expansion was fading at the beginning of 1956 were mistaken, and

Martin had been proved correct. Fed staff economists were predicting a growth rate of 5 percent for 1956. Their concerns about a 2.5 percent anticipated increase in consumer prices were modified somewhat by data that suggested an increase in industrial capacity. Inventories were sufficient to meet demand. The investment boom also looked like it was under control. All in all, the Fed appeared to have followed policies that avoided speculative excesses.[41]

Within the White House, views of Martin had also softened. Eisenhower, who won reelection handily in 1956, seemed to be pleased with him. He reappointed Martin to a fourteen-year term on the Fed board and a new four-year term as its chairman. Indeed, Saulnier, who took over as chairman of the CEA in December 1956, believed in retrospect that Martin had been correct to raise the discount rate in April 1956 and that the administration was wrong to oppose the move. Had the Fed raised rates even higher that year, Saulnier concluded, they might not have had to raise them so sharply in 1957.[42]

For the second term, the administration decided that it needed to improve communication between the White House and the Federal Reserve, but "improving communications" can be a bureaucratic misnomer. This is especially true when differences between powerful individuals or agencies are irreconcilable. Fundamentally, however, both Eisenhower and Martin were in agreement about major issues—they both feared inflation and wanted to keep it under control. But they had differences of emphasis on problems and policy. How to keep the two in sync about the measures adopted to fight inflation was the issue. Gabriel Hauge engineered an arrangement that allowed regular meetings between Eisenhower and Martin that included the secretary of the treasury, the chairman of the Council of Economic Advisers, and himself. These meetings began in mid-September 1957 and were listed on the president's public calendar. Transparency was a concern; neither Martin nor Eisenhower wanted the head of the Fed's visits to the White House to be misinterpreted. Congress and the press were not to see such meetings as an occasion for Eisenhower to press Martin on policy or suggest that there was a serious economic problem.[43]

Future presidents, of course, developed different relationships between the Fed and their administrations. But Eisenhower again, as in other aspects of economic policy, adopted a long-term perspective. He sacrificed the possible short-term political advantages of challenging the independence of the Fed in the interest of a longer-term goal. That is, the president believed in the independence of the Federal Reserve as a bulwark against inflation, regardless of his fleeting irritation with the Fed chairman.

BUDGETS: TAXES, SPENDING, AND SURPLUS

Eisenhower became more focused on the budget in his second term than in the first. The beginning of the second administration led to stock taking. A public battle with Congress in 1957 over the fiscal 1958 budget served as a "clarifying" experience for the president and forced him to make some hard choices about his priorities.

During the first term, Eisenhower had reduced Truman's last budget (fiscal 1954) from $78.6 billion to $64.4 billion in fiscal 1955, in part by realizing savings following the end of hostilities in the Korean War. In fiscal 1956 and 1957, the administration was able to balance the budget. Privately, the president was unhappy with the increased spending proposed in the fiscal 1958 budget. As economic growth slowed, Saulnier and Humphrey worried about a serious recession. That prospect concerned Eisenhower, too, but he came to realize early in 1957 that his goals were contradictory. His aspiration to create a Modern Republicanism— managing increasing domestic and defense needs with fiscal prudence—ran up against some unpleasant realities. In addition to a slowing economy he faced apparent growth in the strength of the Soviet Union; strong inflationary pressures; an expansion-minded bureaucracy; failure to cut costs in government agencies; the divisions within his own party over economic policy; and the increasingly partisan behavior of the congressional opposition. To tame inflation, reduce federal debt, and balance the budget—goals paramount to long-term success in the Cold War struggle—Eisenhower concluded that he had to harden his positions on military and domestic spending. Not to do so risked a country bankrupt and ridden with inflation, unable to meet the demands of defending itself and its allies in a protracted Cold War struggle.[44]

The president's commitment to conservative budget and fiscal policies would be under constant, increasing pressure during his second term. In the first years of the boom, the administration's approach to fiscal policy was to "hold the line." The budget proposed in January 1955 for fiscal 1956 called for a small reduction in overall federal spending. The following January, the budget message for fiscal 1957 included a small increase in spending. Each of these (administrative) budgets anticipated modest surpluses ($200 million in fiscal 1956 and $400 million for fiscal 1957), which were slated to reduce the federal debt.

But the budget for fiscal 1958 called for a large increase in spending and Eisenhower had a sense that he had lost some control of the budget process. If the president never lost sight of the national debt, he became increasingly focused on inflation. Indeed, by the end of 1956 and the beginning of 1957, inflation had become Eisenhower's paramount economic concern; it was running at almost 4 percent a year. Contributing to the worrisome scenario was a slowdown in productivity increases, which declined from almost 3 percent in 1955 to less than 1 percent in 1956. The CPI began to move up in April 1956, soon reaching annual increases of 3.0 to 3.5 percent in the following years. The CPI rise accelerated when agricultural prices began to increase after almost half a decade of decline. Unusually low farm prices, and ultimately food prices, had in fact masked inflationary tendencies up to that point. Prices in services and manufactured goods also had been rising for several years, and there was a growing concern about the ability of firms in major oligopolistic industries to set or administer prices, which was exacerbated by these firms' willingness to increase the wages and benefits of union workers through collective bargaining. An ominous example occurred in the steel industry, which had raised prices by 6.5 percent following settlement of a strike in July 1956 that ended with an increase in workers' wages and benefits.[45]

Not surprisingly, the January 1957 message transmitting the fiscal 1958 budget focused on inflation. Despite increased tax revenues brought about by boom times, the proposed budget did not include tax reductions. In fact, Korean War "temporary" excise and corporate income taxes scheduled to expire by previous legislation would be continued, and general rate reductions were ruled out. A projected surplus of $1.8 billion in the total $71.2 billion budget was to be applied to reducing the national debt. Eisenhower also said in his budget message that "the present situation also requires that less pressing expenditure on programs must be held back and some meritorious programs postponed."[46]

Like the president, the secretary of the treasury was unhappy with the fiscal 1958 budget. At $71.2 billion, it was larger than the three previous budgets Eisenhower had presented.[47] In addition, Humphrey argued, that the continued postponement of tax reductions, especially as an incentive for business investment, would undermine business confidence in the economy. He feared that such a loss of confidence could lead to a serious recession. A tax cut, however, would require substantial cuts in spending. Replying to a question during testimony before the Joint Economic Committee of Congress in January 1957, Humphrey estimated that a budget surplus of at least $5 billion would be necessary before taxes could be cut. To a cabinet meeting on January 9, 1957, he indicated that he thought that a 5 percent general cut in proposed spending on programs in fiscal 1958 would allow for a $4 billion cut in taxes.[48]

In getting to specific program cuts, Humphrey suggested sharp reductions in foreign aid and a 50 percent reduction in overseas troop deployments. Humphrey was a well-known critic within the administration of defense spending. He thought that such expenditures added little to capital formation and the creation of jobs, and he routinely decried waste in the Pentagon.[49]

In principle Eisenhower agreed with Humphrey that taxes should be cut. They disagreed over when the time would come. Eisenhower thought Humphrey's proposals about defense cuts too drastic. One thing that they agreed upon, though, was the tendency of departments' budgets to increase from year to year. Despite the president's efforts to restrain spending, Eisenhower believed that cabinet members failed to hold their departments in check. At the February 27, 1957, cabinet meeting, the director of the Bureau of Budget, Perceval F. Brundage, estimated that long-term program spending in the fiscal 1958 budget inevitably would lead to further spending in the future. He predicted an $80 billion budget by 1962.[50] The president hoped that the introduction of business-like methods by the corporate leaders he selected to run major departments would restrain spending. Cabinet secretaries, he feared, too easily became prisoners of the bureaucracies over which they presided. By the end of the first term he vainly entreated cabinet secretaries to distinguish between essential and desirable spending. The distinction between the two was hard to make in bureaucracies that defined success in terms of enhanced missions and the budgets to go with them.[51]

Brundage's predictions about an $80 billion budget weighed heavily on Eisenhower, as did other contrary estimates that predicted future surpluses. With conflicting estimates about spending and revenues, the president had to make tough decisions. In any event, he feared that the Democrats in control of both houses of Congress would appropriate more than his budgets called for in many programs. Liberal Democrats in Congress routinely decried as insufficient Eisenhower's limited proposed spending on education, housing, and Social Security. In addition, Eisenhower worried that defense spending would grow in part as a result of an alliance between the Pentagon and members of Congress with large defense contractors in their states or districts.[52]

To make matters worse, a rebellion was brewing within the ranks of the Republican Party. Right-wing support would be essential to build a coalition with conservative southern Democrats to hold down spending. Eisenhower, though, had alienated many of his party in Congress by promoting Modern Republicanism during the 1956 campaign and following his substantial reelection victory. His stamp on the party was to direct it to a moderate, middle-way approach to government programs, including education, housing, Social Security, and foreign assistance. Eisenhower believed that the party had to accept that the public expected the federal government to fulfill roles traditional Republicans did not find congenial.[53]

Eisenhower's talk of a new kind of Republican Party did not go over well with those still wedded to the principles of the late Senator Taft. Indeed, among these traditionalists many viewed the president's ever larger budgets as apostasy. Some members of the congressional wing of the party had lost their seats in the November 1956 election, even though the president had triumphed. It was of little comfort to them that Eisenhower appeared more popular than his party.

In his nomination acceptance speech, the president envisioned the party as more forward looking than the Democrats.[54] Throughout the 1956 election campaign Eisenhower had talked often about Modern Republicanism. Much of the president's thinking on the subject had been sharpened as a result of an ongoing dialogue he had about modern conservatism with his White House economic adviser Gabriel Hauge. The dialogue had begun in 1953, when Eisenhower and Hauge talked about the tone of political rhetoric. They agreed the administration should drop references to "creeping socialism," a favorite characterization of the New Deal by the Taft wing of the party. More substantively, Hauge said, Eisenhower often averred that "he was a conservative in fiscal matters and a liberal in matters of human concern." In 1955 Hauge gave several speeches on modern conservatism and the economy. After the first, the president praised Hauge's speech as "the most lucid and the best statement of this administration's philosophy." He added that he hoped that Hauge would not mind a little "plagiarism" by the president.[55]

With encouragement from Eisenhower, Hauge used an invitation to address the Commonwealth Club of San Francisco in October 1955 to flesh out what he and the president meant when they talked about Modern Republicanism. Hauge told Ann Whitman, the president's secretary, that he had "worked my heart out on this speech trying to make as fine a statement as I could of the President's philosophy in the field of economics." In it, he said, government had responsibility to strengthen free markets; moderate economic fluctuations to prevent swings between inflation and deflation; and "supplement the market system in those areas where it alone cannot as well provide certain essential needs."[56]

In the 1952 election campaign, Eisenhower had criticized the policies of the Truman administration, especially its record on spending and appetite for large federal programs. He did not, however, retreat from the international commitments of the Truman era. Internationalism was one—and clearly the most important—part of what Eisenhower meant by Modern Republicanism. He departed sharply from the Taft wing's skepticism about foreign involvements. But during the first term, he also supported several social programs introduced in the Roosevelt and Truman administrations. The programs that got the most attention were the expansion of Social Security and the commitment to a federal highway system. There was also increased federal participation in programs for urban renewal, government-insured mortgages, hospital construction, natural resource development, and K–12 education. The latter proved highly controversial. Not only was it likely to be costly, but it raised serious questions about the federal government becoming involved in a province historically left to the states.[57]

Personally, education had proved important to the president and his brothers, boys from "the other side of the tracks." More generally, he believed that an educated population was necessary for the struggle with the Soviet Union. In the 1956 election campaign he promised to do more for education by having the federal government support an increase in the number of classrooms, an issue that resonated in communities across the country coping with increasing school-age populations. The administration's earlier efforts on education had run into congressional opposition, when Eisenhower proposed a loan-program for the states to build new schools. The 1955 bill, named after the Health, Education, and Welfare (HEW) secretary, Oveta Culp Hobby, nevertheless failed to pass. The following year Eisenhower proposed a five-year temporary grants program, vigorously pushed by his new secretary of HEW, Marion B. Folsom. This bill failed in Congress because it included language requiring desegregation of schools receiving aid. Once reelected, the president proposed a four-year $1.3 billion grants program for school construction, as well as a $750 million federal commitment to purchase local school construction bonds offered at below-market interest rates.[58]

Eisenhower envisioned federal assistance to education as an obvious response to an immediate need. His commitment to a variety of social programs supported the latter argument. In doing so, he was able to continue to extol fiscal conservatism while trying to make the case that the Republican Party understood the demands of a fast-changing society. Yet when economic growth is taken into account, there was hardly any increase in federal spending as a percentage of GNP in the mid-1950s. Total federal spending, even in the face of increases in defense expenditures and in agriculture (after interest on the national debt, the largest source of expenditures on the domestic side of the budget), were very much the same as a percentage of GNP in fiscal 1955 and in fiscal 1958. In the former year, actual federal spending was 16.2 percent of GNP; in the latter year, federal spending was 16.1 percent of GNP.[59]

Nevertheless, Eisenhower's proposed fiscal 1958 budget became a flash point for the more traditional, conservative wing of his party. These members were not receptive to Eisenhower's talk of a modernized Republican Party. In looking at the proposed fiscal 1958 budget, they did not fixate on spending as a percentage of GNP. They looked at nominal increases and were enraged that the proposed fiscal 1958 budget had almost $7 billion more in spending than had the budget for fiscal 1957.[60]

The extent of unhappiness with Eisenhower's budget was on full display in February 1957. On the 9th of that month, 1,500 Republicans gathered in Chicago for the annual meeting of the Abraham Lincoln National Republican Club. The topic for the meeting—"Real Republicanism versus Modern Republicanism"—summed up many attendees' unhappiness with Eisenhower's plans to redirect the party. Rhetoric at the meeting was hot. One extremist referred to Eisenhower as a "stinking hypocrite." Most were more restrained and respectful, but their criticisms of the president's budget were sharp indeed. One senator, defeated in 1956, averred that the party needed to stop "flirting around with . . . Democratic Left-Wing Liberal" ideas.[61]

The battles over the fiscal 1958 budget in 1957 proved to be a turning point in Eisenhower's approach to fiscal policy. In the end, his fear of inflation outweighed his hopes for a new trajectory for the Republican Party. Modern Republicanism, based on moderate increases in spending on domestic programs proved difficult, if not impossible, to carry out. Of greater consequence, Eisenhower faced a growing alliance between the Pentagon and powerful congressional committee chairmen that made it hard for the president to hold the line on defense spending, as the battle over the USSR's new bomber the Bison had demonstrated in 1955.

Making matters more difficult for a president intent on redirecting his party was an increasingly partisan atmosphere in Congress. Democrats' modest increases to their majorities in the 1956 elections seemed to embolden them. But the Democrats, like the Republicans, were divided and therefore difficult to deal with. Whatever Eisenhower might propose by way of domestic spending was perceived per se as insufficient from the point of view of the liberal wing of the Democratic Party. Yet, conservative members, drawn heavily from the South, objected to increased federal expenditures, especially in education, which was traditionally the responsibility of the states and an area that raised the specter of increased pressure for desegregation.

The 1957 debate over the president's fiscal 1958 budget finally forced Eisenhower to make choices. He fervently believed that the US government needed to be disciplined and focused to succeed in its role in the world. Much as he did not like proposing increases in the fiscal 1958 budget, he feared that the opposition would propose even more spending. Eisenhower was determined to build support for the idea that Congress should not increase spending. On New Year's Day he invited leaders of both parties in Congress to the White House. There he sternly lectured his audience with a speech about the evils of spending and the pernicious impact of inflation. These views were echoed in the message accompanying the budget he sent Congress in January 1957.[62]

It is in this context that Eisenhower agreed to go along with a ploy devised by Secretary Humphrey that proved disastrous. Humphrey and the president were politically inept in dealing with what was, after all, their budget. According to the plan they hatched, Humphrey was to issue a letter the day the budget went to Congress imploring restraint in spending. The goal was to keep the support of conservative Republicans in Congress—despite their unhappiness with the budget—while discouraging congressional Democrats from increasing appropriations. Humphrey wanted conservatives to understand that restraint on spending was the only way a cut in taxes would be approved.

Eisenhower agreed with Humphrey that the budget was too large. But he had made promises in the campaign, especially in regard to assisting education, that he felt had to be kept. He also faced pressures from the bureaucracy on domestic programs and the Pentagon on defense spending. As to the latter, he closely followed ongoing disputes among the services over missions and finances. Even in the midst of the 1956 election campaign, as well as the Hungarian Revolution and the Suez Crisis, Eisenhower took an active part in making the Pentagon's budget. He hoped to limit defense spending to $38 billion and authorizations for future spending obligations to $38.5 billion. He demanded, for example, that the navy build a new nuclear aircraft carrier every other year instead of every year. Similarly, he wanted to limit acquisition of missiles.[63]

Eisenhower also hoped vainly to encourage governmental departments and agencies to find savings so that actual expenditures would be less than anticipated in the budget.[64] In his message accompanying the fiscal 1958 budget's transmittal to Congress, Eisenhower echoed Humphrey's themes.[65] What made Humphrey's ploy memorable was not the letter itself. It was an incautious statement that he made at the end of a news conference where his letter was discussed. He said that if spending over the long run was not kept in check the United States was headed for a depression that would "curl your hair." The press emphasized the remark, while minimizing Humphrey's point that he was talking about long-term, not immediate, prospects. Ten days later, the president defended Humphrey and admitted that he had carefully edited the secretary's letter. This made matters worse. Their political ineptness undermined the creditability of the budget that they had presented. Why should Congress take seriously a budget that the administration did not seem to believe in?[66]

Southern Democrats attacked the budget in ways that echoed the criticisms of conservative Republicans. Both had strong objections to foreign aid spending. There were also criticisms of expenditures on the military and on social programs. Perennial budget cutter Democratic senator Harry Byrd of Virginia proposed a $5 billion reduction in spending. Business groups, such as the National Association of Manufacturers, advocated cutting the budget in hopes that such savings might translate into tax reductions. These were altogether predictable positions. Likewise, leading conservative Democrats engaged in a great deal of political posturing in an effort to embarrass the administration, which was making much of the need for fiscal restraint. This was the first and only time during Eisenhower's administration that Democrats complained that the president's proposed level of spending was too high. In fact, this position caused problems for the Democratic leadership. Labor leaders, congressional liberals, and like-minded journalists criticized Democrats for supporting Eisenhower's talk of budget cutting.[67]

Congress made changes in the budget that Eisenhower did not like, and the president was forced to defend expenditures in several areas, an unwelcome position he did not enjoy. He had to accept a $2.3 billion cut in defense spending. Eisenhower knew the defense budget in detail and feared drastic cuts would undermine the country's national strategic goals. He came to accept the cuts to the army and air force budgets, but he was very unhappy about reductions in the foreign aid program, especially military assistance. Eisenhower argued to no avail that providing military assistance to other governments allowed cuts in American spending on the size of troop levels. Hostility to foreign aid was simply too strong in Congress. Ultimately, only $2.77 billion was appropriated for mutual security, that is, overseas military, economic, and technical assistance.[68]

In sum, Congress cut $4 billion from the president's proposed budget. Supporting education became entangled in a dispute over funding and apportioning assistance to the states to deal with the very real shortage of classroom space. Democrats introduced a bill in the House to provide substantially more money ($3.8 billion to be spent over six years) than Eisenhower requested. Eventually, a compromise $1.6 billion program was proposed over four years. Half the money was to be allocated to the states on the basis of their populations, the other half on the basis of demonstrable need. Eisenhower worried that allocation on the basis of population would create a permanent presence for the federal government. The president was willing to accept the need for short-term, emergency funding, but he objected to programs that would build into education policy a long-term, population-based federal commitment to schools. So, he did not press hard for the bill, although he would have signed it had it passed. It failed to gain approval by only a few votes in Congress.[69]

Congress approved an omnibus housing bill authorizing $700 million more than the president had requested and enlarging federal home loan programs. On the latter, Eisenhower threatened a veto. Republicans in Congress dissuaded him because of a slowing construction industry. He did veto a few bills—one to increase postal workers' pay. Eisenhower also vetoed rivers and harbors (public works) legislation because it was too extensive and laden with marginal projects.[70]

The contentiousness over the fiscal 1958 budget process had an impact on Eisenhower. He was not so concerned about the conservatives in the Republican Party who went overboard in criticizing his spending and his ideas about modernizing the party. Nor was it the increasing partisanship of the Democrats. He came to believe that he had to give even more attention to the budget and spending. If he did not, his larger goals of reducing the deficit and holding inflation in check would be impossible to achieve.

One who noticed the new atmosphere was Arthur Larson, the president's chief speech writer at the time. He was one of the younger men around Eisenhower who, like Hauge, was not a professional politician. Larson spent considerable time with the president on his speeches in the election campaign in 1956 and continued with the same responsibility at the beginning of the second term. Eisenhower prided himself on his excellent editing skills, and he and Larson often spent a considerable amount of time on speeches. On occasion Eisenhower also used these sessions with Larson to ruminate about people and issues.[71]

Larson was one of a few to occupy a position in which he could observe the gradual evolution of the president's thinking about major issues. Larson later observed, "If I were to select the point at which the graph of the Eisenhower Administration began to turn from moderate progressivism to conservatism, it would be about Easter 1957. . . . The gradual but unmistakable veering toward conservatism was something you could feel in the air, if you were observing the Administration at close range, although you might not be able to prove it by particular decisions and policies. To me, the most telling symptom of the change was the increasing obsession of President Eisenhower with the budget."[72]

Around this time Eisenhower appointed a new secretary of the treasury, Robert B. Anderson. In replacing the "business conservative" Humphrey,

Eisenhower found an adviser who espoused deeper, more genuinely reflective, conservative views than his first secretary. As we shall see in chapter 3, Anderson's appointment had a tremendous impact on Eisenhower's second term.

THE ECONOMIC POLICY DIVIDE BETWEEN
REPUBLICANS AND DEMOCRATS

President Eisenhower was not alone in clarifying his thinking during the boom of the mid-1950s. Battles over monetary and fiscal policy forced his Democratic opponents to be more precise and to refine their criticisms of the administration's economic policies. This was not an easy task. Democrats in Congress were divided between southern conservatives and liberals based in northern and western states. On domestic programs the conservatives often supported Eisenhower's limited approach to spending, while liberals wanted more money for education, Social Security, housing, and urban renewal. Yet, the Democrats' conservative faction was not entirely consistent about limiting federal expenditures, as its members pressed for agricultural policies that led to some of the largest increases in domestic federal spending during the Eisenhower years. Nor did either of the two party factions eschew public works spending.

Party unity showed itself most forcefully on defense spending. Invariably, congressional Democrats criticized Eisenhower's New Look policy, although a few southern Democrats in both houses of Congress focused on what they saw as wasteful and excessive Pentagon spending. But most supported increased expenditures on defense and charged that Eisenhower was risking national security in the interest of fiscal conservatism.[73]

Another issue embedded in partisanship was tax policy. Speaker of the House Sam Rayburn feared that Eisenhower and the Republicans might propose tax reductions that would steal a convenient issue upon which to attack the administration. The Speaker and Majority Leader Lyndon B. Johnson had been strong supporters of the New Deal. Rayburn, in particular, had not lost a taste for the populism that had marked his earlier career. In 1955 he proposed a modest tax cut for lower- and middle-income citizens. When Eisenhower criticized the idea as irresponsible, Rayburn shot back, "When they didn't give the little folks anything last year [1954] and gave the dividend folks theirs, that was responsibility?"[74]

For his part, Johnson supported domestic spending favored by the liberals for education, urban renewal, and Social Security. LBJ—a man anxious to make a run for the presidency—needed to portray himself as more than a regionally based politician. Ultimately though, Johnson and Rayburn were pragmatic. Johnson usually supported legislation that had made it through the gauntlet of conservative southern committee chairmen. Such bills might not have satisfied fully the party's liberal wing, but Johnson believed that the perfect was the enemy of the good. Rayburn, with none of Johnson's ambitions, also often went along with what emerged from congressional committees. He saw himself as a legislator. Like Johnson, he wanted results.[75]

Rayburn was first elected to Congress in 1912 and had been a staunch advocate of the New Deal. By the 1950s he protected its legacy by supporting the financing of public works and guarding the interests of farmers. But Rayburn's ties to leading Texas business figures in the oil, banking, and agribusiness industries influenced his votes about energy policy, labor unions, and government regulation. When in 1948 Johnson moved to the Senate from the House, he, too, heeded the views of Texas business leaders. Like Rayburn, Johnson remained true to his New Deal origins—but within limits set by the interests of his state. Johnson also owed his rise to Senate leadership to the confidence of long-serving southern committee chairmen. Generally, he did not buck their views, although Johnson served as a compromiser on civil rights issues and other liberal legislation.[76]

Not surprisingly, neither of the two Democratic congressional leaders shaped a consistent program of economic policies to challenge the administration during the first term. They were legislators, not progenitors of policy and theory. Moreover, in a practical sense, Congress had no mechanism to compel its members to think about the president's proposed budget as a whole.[77] Different aspects of the budget were parceled out to various committees for consideration. Money was authorized by various subject matter committees. Then it had to be appropriated by subcommittees of appropriations committees and full appropriation committees in both houses. In the Senate the major committees were chaired by conservative southerners who exercised considerable authority over the disposition of matters before them. Some House committees were headed by liberals, although the powerful rules and appropriations committees were not.[78]

Broad criticism of Eisenhower's record was on display during the 1956 presidential campaign. Adlai Stevenson challenged Eisenhower for a second time and talked much about foreign policy, as he had in the 1952 campaign. But by 1956, the president had an economic record to defend. Much of Stevenson's critique echoed that of congressional Democrats' complaints about domestic and defense spending. In many respects the rhetoric was standard campaign fare, but Stevenson did talk more broadly about fundamental divisions between Democrats and Republicans. In describing a vision of a "New America," he moved the debate over economic policy to general principles. What, Stevenson asked, was the United States' growing economy going to do with its abundance? How was it to distribute its wealth to meet both private and public needs? Stevenson introduced the issue of economic growth to the presidential campaign. How best to continue and stimulate economic growth and to what purposes would the fruits of such growth be put?[79]

Eisenhower's reelection, of course, was not derailed by Stevenson's criticisms of either domestic or foreign policy. But from the outset of Eisenhower's second term, Democrats began to coalesce around a more broad-based, coherent critique of administration policy. The Democrats, however, did not reach a general consensus on a new stance on economic policy until the end of the 1950s, as the 1960 presidential election approached. But the issues and rhetoric were different in Eisenhower's second term.

In Congress, criticism of the administration's macroeconomic policy emanated from the Joint Economic Committee, chaired by Illinois senator Paul H. Douglas, a former economics professor and one of the most prominent liberals in Congress. The committee had no legislative responsibility, but it served as a forum through well-publicized hearings for discussion and criticism of the administration's economic policies.[80]

Serious discussions took place before other committees, too. In June 1957, Gardiner C. Means appeared before the Senate Anti-Trust Subcommittee. Means was a former New Deal official, and the coauthor with Adolph Berle of one of the most influential studies of American capitalism in the last century, *The Modern Corporation and Private Property* (1932). His ideas commanded attention. Means's testimony in 1957 argued that big business, not big government, was the source of inflation. Instead of inflation being a result of demand, which was influenced by government fiscal and monetary policy, it came from business pricing decisions. Means maintained that prices advanced most quickly in a small group of important oligopolistic industries—rubber, automobiles, steel, and electronics—dominated by a few firms. They used their market power, Means said, to administer prices to suit their own targets for returns and profits. Prominent economists accepted Means's critique of Eisenhower's explanation for inflation. The president's advisers also were aware of the issue that Means was raising. Liberal Democrats in Congress embraced his ideas to criticize administration policy, and Means's arguments gained an important place in the critique of the administration's handling of the 1957–58 recession.[81]

In the House, liberal members sought a coherent approach to economic matters, too. In 1957, eighty Democrats from western and northern states proposed a "Liberal Manifesto" that advocated, among other things, more spending on a broader range of domestic priorities. Not one of the signatories was from the South, since the manifesto extolled the need to expand civil rights. Southern Democrats at times voted for new kinds of domestic spending, but it was from liberal members of Congress that a broader perspective on economic policies emerged and gained media attention.[82]

Yet it was from outside Democratic Party groups that sustained, elaborated critiques of administration policy at last emerged. In 1957, the Democratic National Committee (DNC) set up a Democratic Advisory Committee (DAC) to develop new policy ideas for the next presidential election. Democratic leaders in Congress saw the DAC as a threat to their authority, and so few legislators initially became involved. Those that did, though, were the members of Congress with presidential ambitions in 1960: John F. Kennedy, Hubert H. Humphrey, and Stuart Symington.[83]

The DAC moved the discussion of long-term Democratic economic policy goals several steps beyond the efforts of congressional Democrats. An economic policy advisory group of the DAC, made up of prominent academics like John Kenneth Galbraith, Seymour E. Harris, Walter Heller, and Arthur M. Schlesinger Jr., focused on economic growth. Ultimately, the debate was much influenced by Leon Keyserling, vice chairman of the DNC in 1958–59. He had been Truman's second chairman of the Council of Economic Advisers and a longtime proponent of an iconoclastic view of economic policy.

Keyserling's controversial ideas focused on how to stimulate sustained economic growth. His focus was not so much on how to divide the economic pie but on how to enlarge it. In the Truman years, he had advocated a "national prosperity budget," which would lay out national goals for employment, investment, production, and consumption. He envisioned such a budget as a logical extension of the executive branch's responsibilities as set forth in the Employment Act of 1946. These ambitious goals would cause federal spending to increase, but Keyserling believed that a fast-growing economy would provide sufficient revenues to cover the spending without increasing the federal deficit.[84]

In 1953, Keyserling became head of a Washington think tank, the Conference on Economic Progress. There he pursued a research agenda to further support his ideas. He kept his views before Democratic activists as vice chairman of Americans for Democratic Action (ADA). Later, he was able to influence the discussion of party policy as vice chairman of the DAC. Keyserling did not disagree with congressional liberals' support of increased spending on education, health, and housing. But alone, such public sector programs were not sufficient to deal with poverty, which he argued remained high during the 1950s, at more than 20 percent of the population. Only more private sector jobs at good wages would address poverty, and that would happen when the government spent more money to stimulate demand.[85]

Keyserling's ideas were controversial in the Truman era and proved no less so in the Eisenhower years. Not surprisingly, administration officials dismissed Keyserling's approach to the economy. But there were critics within the Democratic establishment, too. Harvard economist and Democratic activist John Kenneth Galbraith became a major critic of Keyserling's ideas. Galbraith emphasized how the country's wealth was being divided up—how the economic pie was being sliced. Of less concern to Galbraith was expanding production and consumption. Echoing the theme of what became his popular 1957 book, *The Affluent Society*, Galbraith argued that increased economic growth would lead to the continued misallocation of resources. Expanded growth would likely continue to encourage more private spending on consumption instead of public expenditures for public goods—schools, hospitals, parks, conservation, housing, and science.[86]

In the debate, each faulted the other's analysis. Keyserling's critics said he overestimated poverty in the 1950s. Galbraith's opponents believed that he underestimated poverty and was wrong to believe that most of the population in the 1950s could satisfy its basic needs. Galbraith's primary criticism of Keyserling, however, was that he underestimated the dangers of inflation inherent in his emphasis on spending to promote growth. Price stability, to the Harvard economist, was an essential goal of economic policy. Galbraith was not simply parroting the concerns of the administration when he focused on inflation, although he believed that budgets should be balanced during periods of prosperity. Instead, he emphasized that inflation had a negative impact on public spending, which was unlikely to increase fast enough to counter the erosion in the value of public expenditures.[87]

These differences were not resolved. In fact, as we shall see in chapter 3, neither Keyserling's nor Galbraith's take on economic policy won over the Democratic Party in the late 1950s. A compromise was reached with some of the ideas of each emerging in a major 1959 policy document, the 488-page *Eckstein Report*. Ultimately, the report shaped the Democratic Party's response to the challenges of economic policy at the end of the 1950s. Real growth—that is, growth adjusted for inflation—was emphasized as a goal in a fast-expanding economy. But the target growth rate was at the outside 4.5 percent, not the 5 percent that Keyserling believed achievable. The guarded target of the growth rate was a reflection of a genuine concern about inflation among some Democrats. Galbraith had an influence, but so did Eisenhower, who accused the Democrats of being careless in proposals for spending. Fiscal policy, as laid out in the *Eckstein Report*, was generally to be employed for stabilization, not grander goals of lowering unemployment, raising wages, and reducing poverty. Democratic Party goals came out of the battles fought with the administration in the last years of Eisenhower's second administration. It was a time when the administration focused both on fighting inflation and on struggling with two recessions, while a concern for growth became a salient Democratic issue, perhaps best encapsulated in John F. Kennedy's call in the 1960 election campaign "to get the country moving again."[88]

CONCLUSION

During the 1950s boom Eisenhower set out to create a climate for prosperity by adopting what he and his advisers thought was the right balance between fiscal and monetary policy. When necessary, the administration used the power it already had over mortgages and consumer credit, informal pressure on business and labor, and the bully pulpit to ensure an environment conducive to prosperity. Its approach was neither hands-off nor interventionist but attentive to changing conditions. The president understood that the public expected such attention, something that he thought was especially important for a Republican president to demonstrate.

When the boom of the mid-1950s led to inflation, the administration attacked the problem in several different ways. Monetary policy played a large role, and the administration worked with the Fed effectively, if not always seamlessly. Eisenhower used his executive authority to affect the availability of consumer credit and mortgage debt. He sought to persuade business and labor to limit short-term benefits in the interest of long-term goals of a stable, growing economy, one able to meet the demands of the Cold War. He pressed federal departments to exercise restraint in expanding established programs and creating new ones. The battle over the fiscal 1958 budget in early 1957 was a turning point in his presidency and led Eisenhower to much more focused attention to balancing the budget, limiting spending, and fighting inflation in his second term. Eisenhower's invigorated sense of priorities limited talk of Modern Republicanism based on increased spending for social programs. His sharp focus on spending and inflation remained, even in the face of a deep recession in 1957–58, as inflationary tendencies continued to manifest themselves.

Not to have done so, in the president's opinion, would have been reckless. Increasing debt and inflation would have undermined the country's ability to prosecute the Cold War. Resulting economic problems would have led to an increase in government power, further weakening the bulwark of a free polity and economy.

As Eisenhower focused more intently on his economic policy priorities so, too, did his Democratic opponents. During the 1956 election campaign, the Democrats engaged in a sustained critique of Eisenhower's policies. The party, though, was far from unified in these criticisms, although members of Congress and outside groups sympathetic to the party began serious discussions to take on Eisenhower's approach to economic policy. Out of these debates began to emerge a new approach that emphasized growth. These ideas ripened and formed the basis of serious economic analysis of the economy during the Eisenhower years. It became the Democrats' clarion call in the 1960 campaign.

CHAPTER 3

Narrowing the Course
1957–1961

Eisenhower addressed inflation early in his State of the Union address on January 10, 1957, days before he took the oath of office for a second time. "The principal threat," he said, "to the functioning of a free enterprise system is inflation." During his second term less and less was heard about a new Republicanism and budgetary support for domestic social programs. The president's increased emphasis on persistent inflation as a fundamental danger to the American way of life accompanied a deepening and more complex Cold War. The Hungarian Revolution in October 1956 and the Suez Crisis in summer and fall of that same year had rocked prevailing views in Washington of the behavior of the Soviet Union and of the United States' allies, Israel, Great Britain, and France.[1]

Worry about inflation guided Eisenhower's response to the two recessions (in 1957–58 and 1960–61) during the second administration. Concern about increasing levels of spending and budget deficits shaped the White House's cautious approach to combating the two downturns. Similarly, debates over military spending sharpened in the second term, as the president resisted increases in the Pentagon's budget, even in the face of public alarm over the Soviet Union's launch of Sputnik in October 1957.

For the first time unease about the strength of the dollar also heightened attention to domestic inflation. By the mid-1950s, Western Europe and Japan had fully recovered from World War II and their economies were rapidly expanding. Europeans accumulated more and more dollars, as they increased their sales of goods to the United States; the American military maintained significant military forces in Europe and Japan; American multinational corporations invested more in facilities overseas; and Americans traveled abroad in unprecedented numbers. Commitment to a sound dollar became a strong priority for the president and Treasury Secretary George M. Humphrey's successor, Robert B. Anderson. A sound dollar, they thought, was necessary in promoting a strong US economy, which in turn was essential to maintaining the strength of America's allies in the Cold War struggle.[2]

Eisenhower's narrowed policy goals contributed to a growing partisan atmosphere in Congress. Republicans suffered large losses in both the Senate and House in the 1958 congressional elections. As a result, Eisenhower's concerns about inflation and balancing the budget prompted conflict with increasingly powerful Democratic leaders. Battles over the budget became a routine aspect of the second administration's politics as Democrats refined their criticisms of the administration's economic policies. Contrary theories about the origins of inflation, its dangers, and prescriptions about how to cope with it marked many of these partisan debates, and contrasting ideas about economic policy were clarified as well. Democrats focused increasingly on the need to promote growth and seemed less concerned about inflation. Eisenhower did not discount the importance of growth, but he continued to focus on his deepest concern: persistent inflation.

THE GUARD CHANGES

When Arthur F. Burns left the administration weeks after the 1956 presidential election, he urged the president to name a successor from the Council of Economic Advisers (CEA) rather than from outside the administration. Eisenhower took the advice and appointed Raymond J. Saulnier chairman of the CEA early in December. Saulnier had served as a member of the council in 1955–56, and before that (between 1953 and 1955) he had worked with the CEA on a consulting basis.[3]

Like Burns Saulnier was a Columbia University economics professor, a respected authority on mortgage finance, but much also separated the two men. Saulnier was younger than Burns and had a very different personality. He was self-effacing and professional in his dealings with Eisenhower and did not develop the close relationship of confidant, as had the older, avuncular Burns. Certainly, Saulnier would not have presumed to fancy himself the president's tutor on economic theory. He also did not possess, as Gabriel Hauge said, Burns's "Old Testament prophet manner" that made him a favorite with congressional leaders and committee chairmen.[4]

Nevertheless, Saulnier was a well-grounded professional economist and was able to hold his own on Capitol Hill. At the White House, he enjoyed easy access to the president. Hauge, who admired Saulnier's intelligence and writing abilities, observed that he "worked smoothly with Eisenhower throughout the second term."[5] Saulnier saw himself as part of a small team of advisers to the president. He understood that the president preferred to make decisions following discussion and advice from those in this tight circle. As with Burns, Saulnier's regular meetings with the president often went beyond their allotted time, as the president and his CEA chairman discussed economic issues in depth.[6]

Unlike Burns, Saulnier did not become Eisenhower's chief economic adviser. That role fell to Robert B. Anderson, the secretary of the treasury following the departure in July 1957 of George M. Humphrey, who had resigned in May but was asked by Eisenhower to stay until Congress adjourned, to get the fiscal 1958 budget passed. Humphrey's departure marked an important divide with the Taft wing of the party. While Secretary of Agriculture Ezra Taft Benson remained throughout both terms, he had been less prominent as a Taft Republican than Humphrey. The latter had been Taft's Ohio campaign treasurer in the 1952 Republican presidential primary. Except for Benson, by the beginning of the second term most former Taft partisans had left the administration.[7]

Well before he departed, Humphrey and the president had settled on a successor. The forty-nine-year-old Anderson was no stranger to either man, and both held him in the highest regard. Indeed, Eisenhower thought so well of Anderson that he touted him privately and publicly as the kind of individual he would like to succeed him in the presidency. At another point, the president joked that "if I had a dozen more like Bob Anderson, I could run this place."[8] In some respects Anderson was more deeply conservative than Humphrey, and more theoretical and consistent in his attitudes. Humphrey was willing to shape his policies to suit political needs when necessary, but Anderson was much less concerned with partisan political issues than his predecessor, perhaps one of the reasons the new treasury secretary proved so attractive to Eisenhower.

Anderson grew up in Johnson County, Texas, south of Fort Worth. His father had maintained a store and later farmed. At the age of three, Anderson contracted polio, which destined him to a confined childhood and left him with a lifelong limp. He matured to be a serious, bookish man, given to introversion. In Washington, he avoided the city's social whirl, preferring to spend time with his family; reading was his favorite form of relaxation. His quiet demeanor and intellectualism differed from that of the outgoing, impatient, table-pounding Humphrey. Anderson easily worked across party lines, and he developed close professional relationships with two important Texas Democrats, Senate Majority Leader Lyndon B. Johnson and Speaker of the House Sam Rayburn. *Time* magazine quoted a cabinet colleague as saying, "In this Washington scramble, the most refined form of cannibalism ever devised, it's just about impossible to find anybody who has anything nasty to say about Bob Anderson."[9]

Anderson graduated from a local junior college and then taught high school for two years (Spanish, history, and mathematics) to make enough money to attend law school at the University of Texas. He graduated at the top of his class after two years and was elected to the Texas House of Representatives soon after at the age of twenty-two. Recognizing Anderson's talent, the Texas governor appointed him assistant attorney general, then state tax commissioner, and two years later head of the state unemployment commission.[10]

In 1937, Anderson left state government to become general counsel to a major Texas family business empire, the W. T. Waggoner Estate in Vernon, Texas. Sprawling over 500,000 acres, the cattle, wheat, and oil enterprise was located in six counties. Four years later in 1941, he became general manager and greatly increased the operation's profits. Anderson now began to move in elite Texas circles. He was active in local and state affairs, serving as the chairman of the Texas Board of Education. He served as deputy chairman of the Federal Reserve Bank in Dallas, and in 1949, Columbia University president Dwight Eisenhower appointed him to serve on a commission to study the utilization of manpower during World War II. The two impressed each other. A lifelong Democrat, Anderson supported Eisenhower for president in 1952. After the election, Eisenhower asked his future secretary of defense, Charles Wilson, to vet Anderson for a subcabinet job. He liked what he found and had Anderson appointed secretary of the navy. After only a little more than a year, Anderson became deputy secretary of defense, the number two position in the department. In 1955, Anderson left the administration to become president of Ventures, Limited, a Canadian holding company with substantial mining interests. When Humphrey decided to leave the administration in 1957, he and the president turned to Anderson to take his place.[11]

Another key adviser to depart the administration was Gabriel Hauge. In March 1958 he left to take a position with Manufacturers Trust Company in New York City. To some observers he was the architect of Modern Republicanism. Whether he was its architect or rather its chief spokesman, his departure signaled an important change in direction for the administration. Arthur Larson, another voice for a "progressive" party, moved on in September 1958 to head a new international law center at Duke University's law school.[12] Hauge was replaced by Don Paarlberg as special assistant to the president. A Purdue economics professor and an expert on agricultural economics, he had worked closely with Secretary of Agriculture Benson since 1953 as his chief economic adviser before moving to the White House. He organized and then coordinated the Food for Peace program.[13] Paarlberg never developed the closeness to the president enjoyed by Hauge, but he was a thoroughgoing professional, which won him the respect of his colleagues.

RECESSION, 1957–1958

Signs of an economic downturn were already appearing when Anderson took office on July 28, 1957. Ultimately, they proved to be indicators of a recession that Saulnier later dated as beginning in September 1957. Overall, the recession proved to be sharp, but short, lasting only eight months. Hardest hit were durable goods manufacturers and the lumber, mining, and textile industries. Unemployment was highest in industrial areas in the Northeast and Midwest, and in mining areas in the West, Pennsylvania, and West Virginia. Michigan suffered most of any state, with an unemployment rate of 11 percent. In large part, this was a result of a 47 percent decline in automobile production.[14]

Eisenhower and Anderson approached policy toward the recession cautiously. Data about economic conditions were ambiguous, which invited restraint. Unemployment figures—numbers that got the attention of the public and politicians—did not become ominous until late January 1958. Then, too, the president was distracted from what looked like a mild downturn in economic activity by momentous issues in the fall of 1957. First was the dramatic public confrontation with Arkansas governor Orval Faubus over school integration in Little Rock in September. In October and November, the USSR's successful launch of two earth-orbiting Sputniks touched off the wide-ranging, highly charged political debate about American defenses, technology, and science. Then, late in November, Eisenhower suffered a mild stroke that incapacitated him for several weeks.

So, with the president preoccupied with other issues and then ill, concerns about the economic slowdown initially became Saulnier's chief focus.[15] In retrospect Saulnier attributed the recession to three immediate causes. New car sales took a sharp dive, housing construction slowed, and, finally, an expansive boom in capital goods spending ended. Housing provided early signs of trouble, because it was a cyclical industry given to high activity followed by sudden reversals. In 1954, housing starts had surged to a level of 1.8 million—a number not again seen until the 1970s—but higher interest rates in 1955 and 1956 initiated a slowdown in housing. By early 1957, new house construction had fallen to about 1.2 million units—a drop of about a third.[16]

New car sales were halved between 1955 and 1958. In 1955 almost 8 million vehicles were sold, weakening future demand. During the following year auto purchases fell to below 6 million, jumped to 6.1 million in 1957, and then declined to 4.3 million in 1958. Contributing to the industry's problems was the spectacular failure of Ford Motor Company's highly advertised Edsel.[17]

Finally, the end of an expansive boom in capital goods spending added to recessionary pressures. Trouble began in 1956, with a deceleration in business planning for replacement of equipment and expansion of manufacturing facilities. The following year, not surprisingly, saw a drop in new orders for equipment. And beginning in late 1957 and into 1958, spending on new plant and equipment actually declined.[18] Federal Reserve economists also thought that the administration had contributed to the recession by cutting back on Department of Defense purchases in the first half of 1957.[19]

In the spring and summer of 1957 Saulnier faced ambiguous indicators of approaching economic trouble. Real GNP increased strongly in the first and third quarters of 1957. Also, several of the general series of data that the CEA relied on for judging likely performance in the near future were positive well into the third quarter.[20] Then, too, the Federal Reserve was not as concerned about a recession as Eisenhower's advisers. What worried Chairman Martin more was the 3.4 percent annual rate of increase in consumer prices during 1956 and the first half of 1957. As a result, the Fed maintained a tight monetary policy into fall 1957. Indeed, in August the Federal Reserve increased the discount rate one half of a point to 3.5 percent. Saulnier was concerned, however, that tight monetary policy combined with loose fiscal policy was a recipe for inflation, if federal expenditures had to be financed by borrowing. Congressional critics were apoplectic about the Fed's move, although Saulnier and the administration did not join the criticism. In retrospect, Saulnier believed that Fed policy had "had a very heavy hand in [the recession]."[21]

In October, indicators of a sharp slowdown increased. Saulnier and the administration pressed Martin, and the Fed provided a modest easing in discount rates in November, from 3.5 to 3.0 percent. At the end of December, Eisenhower had Saulnier relay to Martin that he thought the Fed had to take more serious steps. By mid-January 1958, as economic indicators continued to reflect ever more serious problems, the Fed began to act more forcefully. Within four months, by mid-April, the discount rate was reduced to 1.75 percent. Member bank capital requirements were also eased.[22]

During the second term, relations between the White House and the Federal Reserve became more formal and regular. Eisenhower instructed Saulnier at the time of his appointment that the Fed should never take action without knowing White House thinking about economic issues. He thought that at all times the Federal Reserve should know where the administration stood on major questions of economic policy.[23] So, soon after becoming chairman of the CEA, Saulnier met with Fed chairman Martin and vice chairman C. Canby Balderston. This began a pattern of biweekly meetings, usually with another member of the council attending with Saulnier. Contacts between the administration and the Federal Reserve became even closer in September 1957. At that time, Gabriel Hauge organized a group—the "little four"—to raise economic policy discussion of fiscal and monetary policy issues to the highest level by having these officials meet with the president. The small group consisted of the secretary of the treasury, chairman of the CEA, chairman of the Fed, and as an observer the president's special White House assistant for economics, that is, Hauge. At times the group also included the undersecretary of the treasury for monetary affairs.[24]

Hauge initially saw these meetings as a way to improve communications between the White House and the Federal Reserve. But they were much more. They were an effort at coordination between the administration and the Fed. Eisenhower believed, though, that the Federal Reserve had to remain independent for the sake of disciplined policy. Each side had to understand the position of the other. The president showed great restraint in the relationship with the Fed chairman, an official he could have cajoled if he had wanted to. Indeed, Martin's biographer thought that the meetings were a significant turning point in the history of economic policy making in the United States.[25] Saulnier learned, as had Burns, that the Federal Reserve Board often viewed economic conditions differently than the White House, so he believed that frank interchanges were invaluable.[26] Creating a relationship between the chief executive and the highly principled, at times prickly, head of the Federal Reserve was not the only problem that the administration had to address in the winter of 1957–58. Early in 1958, the White House faced growing criticism from the press, labor unions, and politicians (not only Democrats but some Republicans, too) that it was not dealing forcefully enough with the problems of recession.[27]

The Soviet Union's launch in October and November 1957 of its two satellites, the first human-made objects to orbit in space, added to the administration's travail. This achievement ignited a superheated debate over the state of American security, the apparent lag in the country's missile technology, and the weaknesses of science and engineering in the United States as compared to the Soviet Union. Members of Congress called for increased spending on missile research and development to counter the USSR's apparent technological and scientific lead.[28]

Eisenhower grasped the shock that the Soviet achievement sent through the body politic. But the president withstood being stampeded into what he saw as costly additions to military spending. Nevertheless, the administration had to face great public apprehension, stoked by longtime critics of the administration's defense policies. Democrats anticipated that the debate would help them in the upcoming 1958 congressional elections, an alarming prospect to Republicans. Just as the debate on the Sputniks seemed to dissipate, a further embarrassment occurred. On December 6, 1957, the United States failed to launch a navy Vanguard missile into orbit. It fizzled on its launch pad, fell over, and burned, with the whole episode carried live on network television.[29]

Administration problems had already worsened on November 25, 1957, when the president suffered what his doctors described as a mild stroke. Privately, close advisers were fearful that Eisenhower's condition was more serious than the administration was letting on. Speechwriter Arthur Larson, for example, met with the president on December 12th about drafting the upcoming State of the Union address. He came away from the meeting alarmed at the state of Eisenhower's health. Larson observed that the president "could not speak straight at all." Special Assistant Sherman Adams told him that "this man is not what he was." These fears proved exaggerated. By mid-December Eisenhower was making good progress, again attending cabinet meetings.[30]

At the end of January, Saulnier reevaluated his position on the recession.[31] The situation was more serious than he had thought in the fall and early winter. Conditions had yet to bottom out, but what changed his mind were the numbers of unemployed for January 1958. Data on the employment situation were worse than he had anticipated; there had been an increase of almost 1.2 million unemployed in January over the previous month.[32] These figures received extensive media coverage. When the numbers of unemployed moved beyond 5.1 million in January 1958, they were higher than at any point since 1941. By the time national levels of unemployment reached 7.5 percent of the workforce in April 1958, considerable anxiety followed. In comparison, during the first recession of the Eisenhower years, in 1953–54, the highest level of unemployment had only reached 6.1 percent of the workforce.[33]

For his part, as with the public's near panic over Sputnik, Eisenhower did not want to be forced into precipitous action on the recession. He and Anderson refused to embrace any grand multifaceted policy to combat the downturn. In part their position involved tactical political considerations. Eisenhower anticipated that in an election year it would be difficult to get a comprehensive recession program through Congress without battles over the provisions of proposed legislation. Greater control over specific, limited measures, he thought, would cause less damage to his efforts to reign in deficits and inflation. If the situation really deteriorated, the president was willing to do what was necessary.

As economic indicators worsened in February and March, the cabinet discussed the administration's policy options. At its February 28, 1958, meeting the cabinet directed the CEA's special assistant for public works planning (retired army general John S. Bragdon) to prepare a program of fast-starting $4.5 to $5 billion federal public works projects. Whether to submit such a program to Congress was left up to the president, that is, if and when he thought such spending might be required.[34] Cabinet discussions of public works programs were not new. They had been discussed in the face of the first unambiguous indicators of an economic downturn in the fall. In fact, at its meeting of November 15, 1957, public works planning had been the main agenda item. At that time, General Bragdon proposed two plans. A modest intermediate plan made up of "on-the-shelf projects" was his first proposal. Second was a major initiative designed to cope "with a depression of serious proportions." In the end, Eisenhower rejected both, although it directed that the CEA staff continue to study public works projects.[35]

Eisenhower wanted to reassure the public that a Republican administration could handle economic reversals. Without national confidence, he thought, there would be little room to maneuver in addressing the recession. Freedom to maneuver, though, was going to be difficult in 1958 as Congress prepared for the November elections. While the Democrats were at first slow to seize on the recession as a political issue, the startling unemployment numbers in late January 1958 provided them with a tempting political opportunity. By the end of February, congressional Democrats had decided to focus their campaign on the administration's failure to respond forcefully to Sputnik and the recession.[36]

The president presented the opposition with ammunition in a public statement he made on February 12, 1958, in which he discussed the troubling economic data but focused on positive indicators—a slight decline in unemployment—that the recession would be short.[37] In fact, Eisenhower's observations were based on a misreading of Saulnier's more nuanced advice to the president on the course and possible duration of the recession. Eisenhower's statement came under sharp attack; critics saw it as demonstrating administration complacency about the recession.

Matters were not helped when the next day the president left for a ten-day vacation at former treasury secretary Humphrey's sumptuous estate in Georgia. Even administration supporters in the press were critical of the trip. Democratic political leaders pounced on the president for his apparent lack of urgency in confronting the recession. Secretary Anderson's appearance on NBC's *Meet the Press* a few days later reinforced such perceptions. Reporters questioning him were openly skeptical of the administration's approach to the recession, especially when Anderson equivocated.[38]

Republicans in and outside the White House worried about the apparent lack of an administration plan to attack the recession. Congressional leaders feared that the party would be vulnerable on the issue in the upcoming elections. A Gallup Poll in March 1958 indicated that, by a margin of 25 percent, the public thought that Democrats were more likely to maintain prosperity than Republicans. Within the White House, Vice President Nixon echoed the refrain that a comprehensive plan was needed and proposed that the administration present a full package of programs to Congress.[39]

Saulnier and Hauge also thought that the administration needed to clarify how it planned to address the recession. Saulnier was often on the line, answering reporters' questions about Eisenhower's policy. Neither of the economic advisers was as focused on the political aspects of the situation as Nixon or congressional party leaders. But by the end of February 1958—several months into the recession—Saulnier and Hauge feared that the appearance of presidential irresolution would weaken public and business support for the administration.[40] Part of the president's reluctance to strike out boldly was his conviction that the Democrats were playing politics with the recession. A broad-based Republican plan, in Eisenhower's opinion, would only have invited partisan attacks, and administration initiatives might have led to higher levels of spending as legislation wended its way through Congress.

Majority Leader Johnson proposed a series of limited individual initiatives to cope with recessionary conditions. He had little choice, in view of the divisions within his party, and thus supported measures that might be acceptable to the two major wings of the Democratic Party. His proposals included measures to expand spending on housing, highways, reclamation, and rivers and harbors. In doing so, he wanted to embarrass Eisenhower as being slow or insensitive in the face of economic distress. Privately, politics aside, both he and Speaker Rayburn worried that hard times would lead to defaults on consumer debt, which would serve to worsen the recession. Rayburn indeed feared that growing unemployment could lead to a deep depression.[41]

Despite the partisan back and forth over what to do about the recession, Eisenhower and Anderson were confident that the experience of the 1953–54 recession provided sufficient guidance on how to proceed four years later. Each was content to rely on the automatic stabilizers—lower rates for federal withholding taxes as workers' incomes declined, Social Security payments, and unemployment compensation—to do their work. Eisenhower reiterated his thinking about the country's economic circumstances at a meeting of legislative leaders on February 25, 1958. In times of full employment, the president said, the government should be slow to start new programs. Even in a recession, like the one the country faced at the time, the government should not embrace big projects unlikely to be started until after the emergency had ended. If there were four or five projects ready to go, ones that could be helpful immediately to the economy, then he might—the key word to his thinking at the time—consider supporting them.[42]

In truth, neither the president nor his treasury secretary exhibited enthusiasm for increased public works spending. Anderson was clear on this point as early as the November 1957 cabinet discussions of new public works programs; trotting out drastic plans, he thought, might "frighten" the country.[43] Eisenhower often talked about the limits of public works spending to counter recession.[44] "I don't believe that for one second, with minor exceptions, that any additional public works to be decided upon, brought into the appropriations picture and finally built that will do anything for this present recession. Acceleration of programs already started. . . . That is the kind of thing that will bring some people to work. But to start new plans, it will be two years before they will be actually in construction."[45]

Eisenhower and Anderson were not tax cut enthusiasts, either. Nor was Federal Reserve chairman Martin. At the time, economists were not by any means unanimous about the tools needed to fight recessions. Cutting taxes to cope with a downturn was decidedly a minority view among economists in the 1950s, unless economic conditions became very serious. In fact, during the Truman administration the president had considered raising taxes to compensate for reduced revenues during the recession of 1948–49.[46]

Secretary Anderson likewise worried about the effect tax cuts would have on revenues. Further dips in tax receipts—which declined in a recession anyway—would only swell the government's deficit. If large enough, he believed, the deficit could contribute to inflationary pressures while cutting back on the capital available to private borrowers in capital markets. And deficits were becoming a serious worry as estimates of their magnitude grew during 1958. At a cabinet meeting on April 18, 1958, bureau of the budget director Maurice Stans predicted large budget deficits; the cabinet examined estimates of a deficit of $2.8 billion for fiscal 1958 (July 1957–June 1958) and an estimated $9.2 billion for fiscal 1959. These latter numbers for fiscal 1959 were raised to $12 billion at the cabinet meeting of August 1, 1958.[47] The higher figure proved more accurate.

Eisenhower shared his treasury secretary's concerns about sagging revenues, which increased their already serious doubts about the wisdom of cutting taxes. Politics also influenced their thinking because of the heightened political risks of proposing to change tax policy in a congressional election year. At a news conference on February 5, 1958, Eisenhower said that the political process involved in dealing with taxes was hopeless and that, indeed, each party's leadership feared amendments to tax bills and so stayed away from tax legislation.[48] At a meeting with legislative leaders on March 18, Anderson's comments captured his and the president's position that Republicans running for office should not emphasize tax cuts: "Hence it was all the more important to withhold comment as to any possibility of a tax cut [so as to prevent] letting any particular gimmick get well established as the thing to do."[49] Eisenhower and Anderson feared that once enacted—even if the tax cuts were designated as a temporary measure—it would be difficult to change course later and reenact the old, higher rates. Revenues, as a result, would be reduced over the long term.[50]

Within the administration Vice President Nixon was the most notable proponent of reducing taxes. In early March 1958, he talked openly about the need to consider tax cuts. Anderson, with the approval of the president, quashed such talk. In a press statement on March 12th, he said, "No decision regarding taxes has been made. Whatever decision regarding taxes is taken will be reached only when the impact of current developments on the future course of the economy has been clarified and after consulting with Congressional leaders."[51]

On the next day, March 13th, Anderson worked out a deal on tax cuts with the Democratic leadership in Congress (Johnson, Rayburn, and House Ways and Means chairman Wilbur Mills). According to the understanding, neither the congressional leadership nor the administration would advocate reducing taxes. Politics drove the agreement. Each side feared that the other might propose lower taxes and reap political benefit for being first to do so. Also, tax cutting could escalate, something the Democratic leadership and the White House wanted to avoid. If anything, the pressure from Democratic members of Congress and their labor union supporters was for more spending, not tax cuts.[52]

Yet tax cuts continued to be discussed. Former CEA chairman Burns advocated a permanent $5 billion tax reduction in a March speech at the University of Chicago. Some business groups considered the subject, with the more liberal Committee for Economic Development, a business-oriented research group, coming out in favor of it. A Rockefeller Brothers study group in March also supported a tax cut.[53] Such disagreement between the White House and major business groups was rare. Nevertheless, Eisenhower and Anderson remained deeply skeptical of tax cutting. In a letter to the president, Burns proposed broadly based reductions for individuals and businesses. He understood the president's concern that such tax cuts would increase the deficit and as a result stimulate inflation. So Burns also suggested amending the 1946 Employment Act to mandate a commitment to keeping prices level. Eisenhower responded promptly with a letter of his own. As to changing the Employment Act, the president lamented the inability to make major changes because of the "laborious and tortured channels that must be pursued in Washington in the process of translating any good idea into action that even remotely resembles the original thought." He decried the projected deficit spending for subsequent budget years and "the inflationary factors that we will likely have to combat [in the near future]." He went on to say, "A sizable tax reduction may become one of these [inflationary factors]; I have not yet been convinced of proof of its necessity. And if it is not needed at the moment then I am quite sure its future effect would be inflationary."[54]

Eisenhower remained consistent, as tax cut proponents continued to press for them. In a mid-April letter to Donald S. Kenney, a business leader and friend who wrote to support the positive psychological effect of tax cuts, the president said, "I shall hold the line as long as I possibly can. . . . I believe the recession is in the process of leveling out, [and] I am hopeful that our tax structure need not be revised."[55] Despite Eisenhower's clear reluctance to cut taxes, discussions continued. In May 1958 Eisenhower laid out his thinking again:

> Everyone in this country is, I know, concerned about taxation. We would like to achieve improvements in the tax structure. We would like to assure maximum equity in the tax burden. We would like to achieve further simplification. We would like a tax structure which least interferes with sound economic growth. The timing of such changes always poses problems. During periods of high business activity and high employment there is concern with inflationary effects. In a time like the present, with its rising government expenditures, we are particularly sensitive to tax burdens, but there is likewise great concern with the future impact of increasing current deficits.[56]

Eisenhower and Anderson did not relent on the subject of tax cuts.[57] Indeed, on May 25th, the White House worked out another understanding with Democratic congressional leaders that continued existing rates of corporate income and excise taxes. These Korean War measures, which had been extended in 1954 and 1956, would have expired at the end of June (and rates would have declined) had there not been such an agreement.[58]

By this time, Eisenhower had concluded that the recession was abating. In fact, unemployment remained persistently high during the rest of 1958. It reached its highest point—7.6 percent—in August.[59] Optimistic statements by the president about a quick end to the recession could not fail to anger those workers and businesses still facing the harsh pressures of the recession. The recession of 1957–58 exhibited sharper indicators of distress than that of 1953–54, and recovery was much slower.[60]

Eisenhower continued to take a piecemeal, gradualist approach to additional measures in supplementing so-called automatic economic stabilizers. Basically, he wanted to stimulate recovery while keeping the government's financial "house in order." His preference was for a "private enterprise rather than a 'government' campaign to provide the main strength of recovery forces."[61] But the president accommodated his cabinet secretaries and bent to party leaders when he had to. A previous slowdown in Defense Department contract awards was reversed in fall 1957 and, according to Saulnier, was having an impact by January 1958. Similarly, the administration speeded up procurement of nondefense items. Construction projects already underway were accelerated, and those already funded and planned were begun. FHA building projects were pushed ahead, as were Department of Agriculture projects for, among other things, water resource programs and rural electrification. The Department of Health, Education, and Welfare also accelerated work on projects funded and in progress, as did the Post Office. To encourage home building, the administration ended 1955 restrictions on "no–no–down payment" mortgage loans, loosened the rules on VA-guaranteed mortgages, and encouraged Fannie Mae to increase prices on mortgages it purchased in the hope of freeing up mortgage capital so that banks could issue new loans. In April 1958, Congress accepted administration requests and passed legislation modifying the interstate highway funding formula to permit larger allocations to the states essentially by borrowing from the highway trust fund, where gasoline taxes were earmarked for the interstate highway system.[62] Finally, in a measure that Saulnier thought had a great positive impact, the administration asked Congress in March 1958 to authorize federal assistance to the states so that they could lengthen the period of unemployment benefits. After considerable debate about the specific terms of the measure, Congress enacted the legislation in June 1958.[63]

Eisenhower, according to Saulnier, followed the progress of the various antirecession measures carefully. In part his attention was a result of his interest in economic policy, but it also reflected his concern that policy became an occasion for partisan controversy. While early in 1958 Eisenhower complained bitterly that "politicians have a habit of making me sick—psychically and mentally," he maneuvered when politics required him to do so. In December 1957, in response to the uproar produced by the Sputniks, the president requested a $1.2 billion supplemental defense appropriation for fiscal 1959. Funds would go toward intercontinental and intermediate-range ballistic missiles, the Strategic Air Command, and programs designed to help detect missiles. Eisenhower frankly admitted that a substantial part of the request was for the sake of public opinion, which was still abuzz about the Soviet Union's success. In spring 1958, the president also requested an additional $2 billion supplemental appropriation for defense. Ultimately, when partially enacted, these appropriations boosted defense spending $1 billion beyond what had been originally budgeted for fiscal 1959.[64]

Eisenhower's major concession to public works spending was the Rivers, Harbor and Flood Control legislation passed in April 1958, in which politics played a large role. Because the bill provided $1.7 billion for projects affecting many states, there was substantial support in Congress for the legislation, Republican leaders included. Eisenhower, however, objected to parts of the bill. Some of the items in the 1958 legislation mirrored projects in a 1956 bill that he had vetoed. He objected to the recession serving as an excuse to approve what he still found objectionable.[65]

Twenty-eight projects, costing over $350 million, had brought a veto in 1956, and they did so again in April 1958. But in his veto message he invited Congress to send him a bill that he could approve, that is, absent what he considered funding for ill-planned, dubious projects. For the most part, the revised bill met the president's criteria for public works spending, that is, projects were fully planned and ready to go or already under way.[66] Congress passed the revised legislation on July 3, 1958, and the president signed it the same day. It provided $800 million for fourteen river basin projects that had been planned and were awaiting funding.[67]

Monetary policy also played a role in dealing with the recession. When Martin became convinced of the seriousness of the recession, the Federal Reserve moved quickly. By the end of April 1958 the discount rate had been lowered to 1.75 percent, but once the Federal Reserve concluded that conditions were improving, it began to tighten the discount rate. In 1958, the Fed moved the discount rate to 2 percent in September and to 2.5 percent in November. There were three increases in 1959 in the discount rate (in March, May, and September) that increased it from 2.5 percent at the beginning of the year to 4 percent at the end. In addition, the money supply grew about 0.5 percent in 1959, as opposed to 4.0

percent in 1958.[68] Officially, recessionary conditions lasted from mid-1957 to April 1958. According to the 1959 *Economic Report of the President,* the decline was "abating by March [1958] and by May indications of a general improvement began to appear"; the recession officially ended in April.[69]

In retrospect, Eisenhower was willing to accept comparatively high rates of unemployment in the interest of preventing deficits and inflation, and the Republican Party paid a high price for Eisenhower's determination. In the elections of November 1958, the Republicans lost 48 seats in the House, and 13 seats in the Senate.[70] As a result, in both chambers Republicans were outnumbered almost 2 to 1. His party's changing political fortunes did not, however, undermine Eisenhower's views on economic issues as he entered the last two years of his term. If anything, he was as determined as ever to cope with the concerns that had defined his presidency from the beginning, the budget deficits and the corollary problem of inflation.

EISENHOWER, ANDERSON, AND INFLATION

Following the recession of 1957–58, four related concerns drove Eisenhower's increased emphasis on inflation. Bad news about the fiscal 1959 budget and the size of future budgets were one consideration. Another involved refinancing the government's debt, which became increasingly difficult as inflationary expectations rose. In addition, foreign holders of dollars began to worry about US inflation, deficits, and negative balance of payments. A strong gold-backed dollar set up in the exchange system established in 1944 at Bretton Woods was the linchpin of international trade and finance in the immediate post–World War II era. The dollar's stability, the president believed, was essential to the economic strength of the Cold War alliance against communism. Finally, the apparent resiliency of inflation, even through a sharp recession, deeply concerned Eisenhower and his economic advisers.

In August 1958, increasing budget deficit figures for fiscal 1959 (July 1958–June 1959) were becoming clearer.[71] As it turned out, federal expenditures in fiscal 1959 totaled $80.7 billion, with a $12.4 billion deficit. Defense spending in fiscal 1959 reached $41.2 billion, which was $1.4 billion more than originally estimated. Domestic spending was also considerably higher than originally anticipated, for a total of $21.1 billion, or $4.7 billion above original fiscal 1959 budget figures. Agricultural spending made up the largest part of this rise, with an increase of $2 billion. Antirecession spending accounted for $1.4 billion of the increase in spending on domestic programs.[72] Revenues also declined to $68.3

billion for fiscal 1959. High rates of unemployment in 1958 reduced income tax and Social Security tax revenues. Moreover, because corporate income taxes were collected more slowly then than now, the drastic drop in corporate profits in the recession was reflected much later in the revenue stream from corporate income taxes, which represented about one-third of total revenues.[73]

For the longer term, Bureau of the Budget director Maurice Stans estimated that the government could not anticipate a budget surplus before 1962. Stans's predictions deeply worried Eisenhower, since he believed that deficits were the most important source of inflation. Further adding to the president's gloom, Stans estimated that the cash budget deficit, which included revenues from Social Security payments, would be almost as large as the administrative deficit. Administration officials looked to the cash deficit figures as the best gauge of the inflationary impact of government operations.[74]

Eisenhower viewed the looming deficit in the second half of 1958 with alarm. At a May 23, 1958, cabinet meeting, he observed that "projected budgets had to be cut, otherwise great deficits would result, giving an inevitable push towards socialism." In preparing for the fiscal 1960 budget, he directed the Bureau of the Budget to aim to reduce expenditures below $80 billion. Budget director Stans shared the president's concerns and believed that Eisenhower needed to take drastic measures. To reduce expenditures he suggested that Eisenhower insist that only he personally authorize proposals for new domestic programs; that no new antirecession spending be approved unless the situation worsened significantly; and that public works spending be maintained at 1958 levels.[75] Tough talk about spending continued at subsequent cabinet meetings.[76] Of course, the president had been hectoring cabinet secretaries for some time to curtail spending and the growth of personnel in their departments.[77] He wanted them to contemplate long-term—that is, more than a year in the future—cuts in department expenditures. In truth this would have a limited effect, even if successful, as only about 17 percent of the budget was for domestic spending.[78]

While the deficit focused the president's attention on inflation more sharply than ever before, there were other reasons for him to be concerned about rising prices, such as refinancing the public debt. In simplest terms, investors preferred the stock market to long-term government securities in an inflationary environment. By law, Treasury could not offer long-term bonds at rates above 4.5 percent. Thus, the large fiscal 1959 deficit, and the prospect of future budget deficits, complicated the Treasury's debt management as deficits held out the prospect of growing inflation. Matters were even more troubling in 1958–59, because of the size of long-term public debt maturing over the next five years. In 1953, that figure had been $33 billion; in 1959, the amount maturing was $61 billion. In addition, approximately $80 billion of shorter-term Treasury bills were to mature in 1959; this represented about 42 percent of the government's marketable obligations. Shorter-term securities could be offered at competitive rates, but in an inflationary environment they would cost the government more in interest. Treasury also had to raise additional funds to finance the fiscal 1959 deficit.[79]

Anderson had taken advantage of lower interest rates during the recession to issue some longer-term bonds between September 1957 and June 1958. Treasury also reintroduced savings bonds for smaller investors, a program that had been discontinued after the Korean War. But once the recession abated, the Federal Reserve started raising interest rates again in August 1958. Such increases made long-term investment opportunities in corporate bonds and like instruments for private and institutional investors more attractive than long-term government bonds with the congressionally mandated 4.5 percent interest ceiling. Large deficits and indications that inflation was continuing despite the recession provided further incentives for investors to put their money in the stock market, which provided a better hedge against inflation than government bonds.[80]

The secretary also collaborated closely with Eisenhower over the international consequences of deficits and inflation, a troubling issue that arose at about the same time that Anderson struggled with refinancing the debt. International concerns about the United States' balance of payments and the fiscal situation in the United States raised questions for the first time in the postwar era about the country's ability to remain the leader in the world economy.[81] The gold-backed dollar exchange rate system created at Bretton Woods in 1944 depended on the soundness of the American currency. Because of the heavy outflows of dollars for military expenditures overseas, foreign aid, and private foreign American investment (only partially offset by large surpluses in merchandise trade and services), the United States in the 1950s ran persistent balance of payments deficits.[82] Administration officials believed that such deficits could be maintained indefinitely so long as foreigners continued to hold dollars and not seek in large numbers to convert their increasing dollar assets to gold. But if the United States was depreciating its dollar through inflationary fiscal policies, foreign holders might be less inclined to hold dollars and have US inflation "exported" to them. (See table 3.1.)

Late in 1958 Eisenhower worried that the projected budget deficit in fiscal 1959 was precisely the wrong kind of signal to send to overseas holders of dollars.[83] The president's concerns about the attitudes of foreign governments and investors were not misplaced.[84] By 1958, the United States' trading partners had

TABLE 3.1

United States Balance of Payments, 1951–60 (in millions of dollars)

Current account	1951	1952	1953	1954	1955	1956	1957	1958	1959	1960
Trade balance	2,921	2,481	1,291	2,445	2,753	4,575	6,099	3,312	988	4,687
Services & investment income, net	1,613	1,276	1,064	1,404	1,551	1,591	2,174	1,650	1,502	1,486
Balance	4,534	3,757	2,355	3,849	4,304	6,166	8,273	4,962	2,490	6,173
US government payments abroad	–4,461	–4,337	–4,590	–4,157	–5,034	–5,317	–5,739	–5,999	–5,095	–5,798
Private long-term capital, net	–783	–923	–320	–740	–674	–1,932	–2,556	–2,514	–1,743	–2,247
Private short-term capital, net	–103	–94	167	–635	–191	–528	–258	–306	–77	–1,312
US payments balance	–813	–1,597	–2,388	–1,683	–1,595	–1,611	–280	–3,857	–4,425	–3,184

Source: Harold G. Vatter, The U.S. Economy in the 1950's (New York: Norton, 1963), p. 260.

accumulated $16 billion, a sum that exceeded their trading and reserve needs. In 1950, the figure had been $7 billion. US balance of payments problems and inflationary conditions in the American economy concerned foreigners. They feared that the United States might eventually be forced to devalue its currency, which would result in losses for those with dollars or assets denominated in dollars.[85]

One response of foreign governments was increasingly to hold gold instead of dollars or convert their dollars to gold at the rate of $35 per ounce established at Bretton Woods. Gold outflows from US reserves became a real concern in 1958, as foreign holders of dollars began rapidly to convert them. Exchange of dollars for gold in 1958 amounted to $2.3 billion. In that year, US reserves totaled $23 billion, $12 billion of which was mandated by law to back American currency. At the 1958 rate of gold redemption, the United States would lose its unrestricted gold supplies in five years.[86]

Anderson heightened the president's angst upon his return from the annual meetings of the World Bank and International Monetary Fund, held in October 1958 in New Delhi. Foreign finance ministers from among the United States' most important trading partners spoke bluntly to Anderson, since they feared that the United States was caught in an inflationary spiral.[87] Anderson advised Eisenhower that the only way to maintain confidence in the dollar and prevent a gold drain was for a quick return to a balanced budget in fiscal 1960. As chairman of the National Advisory Committee on International Monetary and Financial Problems, Anderson urged American government agencies with overseas operations to tighten up on overseas expenditures.[88]

The sense of urgency increased when Western European governments accepted the full external convertibility of their currencies with the dollar after December 31, 1958. Such convertibility had been anticipated much earlier, with the creation of the International Monetary Fund in 1944. But in the early years of the postwar era, American and Western European officials agreed informally to postpone full convertibility until the European currencies had strengthened. Otherwise, there would have been a rush toward the dollar, as holders of foreign currencies would have exchanged them for a stronger US currency. As a result of full convertibility, short-term capital flows would now move in response to changes and differentials between interest rates in the United States and Europe. Such a change demanded greater attention to the impact of domestic economic policy on international financial conditions.[89]

Not surprisingly, then, the intractability of inflation, even in the face of recession, deeply troubled Eisenhower and Anderson. They were not alone in taking note of the apparent structural nature of some aspects of the inflation of the 1950s. It was a source of comment and concern among politicians, business leaders, and professional economists.[90] Eisenhower officials had first become concerned following the recession of 1953–54, when they noted the persistence of modest inflation despite the downturn.[91]

Now, during the recession of 1957–58, consumer prices increased at an annual rate of 2.6 percent; they did not begin to abate until the second half of 1958. In contrast, prices only had increased by 0.3 percent during the recession of 1953–54.[92] As it turned out, toward the end of the administration's time in office, some inflationary indicators were becoming less dire. Of course, Eisenhower and his economic advisers had no way of knowing that outcome in 1959. Indeed, 1960 inflation figures turned out better than the administration had hoped for.[93] (See fig. 1.1.)

Yet there remained ambiguity in the numbers, and hence reason for continued anxiety. Eisenhower asked Saulnier to take the lead in briefing the cabinet on the subject of persistent inflation. The CEA chairman suggested that the boom in 1954–55 led to the inflation that was still present despite the recession. He also focused on the persistence of wage pressure on production costs and, hence, prices. He observed, "We have had wage rate increases all the way through the recession." Indeed, in 1957, the increase was 12.8 percent in construction.[94] He anticipated further pressure on prices once the recession ended. His discussion of the so-called wage price spiral reflected the views of other observers of inflation in this period.[95] It was a subject very much on the president's mind, even though deficits were to him the major culprit in inflation. As he wrote to a friend, inflation clearly was the result of "badly unbalanced Federal budgets and the ever mounting wage-price spiral."[96] Coping with the spiral was not going to be easy. Saulnier believed that promoting economic growth and productivity was one way to address it, and some prominent economists were beginning to discuss measures on how to encourage growth. Nixon also showed interest, in large part as a response to the fact that Democrats were talking about it. He raised the issue at cabinet meetings and with the president.[97]

Eisenhower did not discount the importance of economic growth, but it was not his focus as a way to fight inflation. He and his advisers believed that the wage price spiral could be addressed by keeping wage increases in line with productivity improvements. That was the goal when a steel strike began on July 15, 1959. Initially, the White House preferred to avoid intervention in the strike, but it desired a settlement that would not trigger more price increases in oligopolistic industries (as was the case with autos and steel in 1955–56) and believed the

strike was a test of administration policy to keep price increases to within productivity gains. After waiting ten weeks for a resolution to the strike, the administration sought a court order in October to put the industry back to work. Negotiations resumed, and an agreement was reached in January 1960 that increased
wages 3.5 percent. Saulnier maintained that the wage settlements were in line
with productivity gains, primarily because the industry could not post price increases in the face of a sluggish economy and increased foreign competition.
Overall, according to Saulnier, the firm way in which the administration dealt
with the strike led to a settlement in a key industry that set the pace for much
smaller wage increases over the next two years.[98]

Additionally, in trying to make sense of the persistence of inflation, Anderson and others focused on the behavior of the stock market. Rapid increases in
stock prices in summer 1958, he thought, encouraged "the public feeling that [a]
great inflation is in the offing."[99] In July Fed chairman Martin had also singled
out stock market behavior as a contributor to inflationary pressures. From March
through the end of 1958, stock prices rose rapidly, increasing almost by one-third.
This was one of the reasons that the Fed began to raise discount rates as soon as
Martin believed that the recession was beginning to end. Discount rates were
raised in September and then again in November 1958.[100]

Eisenhower also focused on what Martin might have referred to as an "inflation
psychology" brought about by financial speculation.[101] Saulnier wrote to the president in August 1958 that "the most troublesome condition affecting the economy
is a wave of 'inflation psychology,' which has had a marked effect on the financial
markets." He noted that it was based on the prospect of a succession of large
budget deficits, the likelihood of wage and price boosts, and a booming automobile sector. None of these developments, Saulnier feared, could be dealt with easily by the government. Soon after he left government for the private sector, Hauge
observed that inflation psychology is "a troublesome thing and one we should
watch closely."[102]

As it turned out, the concerns of many in the administration about the persistent, and even growing, inflation pressures were overstated. By mid-1960 the
United States was again in a recession, albeit a short, shallow one. Eisenhower
and Anderson addressed this downturn as they had the one of 1957–58. Essentially, the White House again relied on the automatic economic stabilizers. This
approach worried Vice President Nixon, who was running for president and who
nervously observed the percentage of the unemployed moving upward (even if
more slowly than in the recession of 1957–58). But Eisenhower and his secretary
of the treasury believed that the earlier approach to the recession had worked

well. They were committed to allowing the automatic stabilizers to do their work again.

INFLATION AND RECESSION: BUDGETS FISCAL 1960 AND FISCAL 1961

Shaping the federal budget is the one area in which the president has direct responsibility and the opportunity, if he chooses, to become heavily involved personally. From the beginning of his administration, Eisenhower had exhibited a keen interest in budget making, and in the last two years of the second term his interest increased. Alarm over budget deficits, balance of payments problems, debt refinancing, and structural inflation drove the president's interest. Not only did these unusual circumstances focus his attention, it was also the unprecedented nature of the inflation that the United States faced in the 1950s. Economist Henry C. Wallich noted in 1958, "The U.S. has no experience with prolonged inflation. . . . [P]rice increases were not viewed by the public as a continuing process. An inflation that is expected to continue, one that everyone tries to stay ahead of, is a new phenomenon."[103]

Following Democratic victories in the November 1958 congressional elections, the president braced the administration against pressure from the enlarged Democratic majorities in the House and Senate for increased spending on defense and domestic programs. Inflationary pressures convinced Eisenhower that he would have to hold the line against increased spending, as he told Republican congressional leaders in January 1959.[104] Results of the 1958 midterm elections dissipated any illusions about substantial reductions in the budget. Eisenhower understood that he could not propose a retrenchment budget, but he was determined to resist large increases in expenditures. Ultimately, the fiscal 1960 budget included only a few modest new domestic initiatives.[105]

Not every Republican agreed with the president's approach. Most notably, Eisenhower's determination for a lean budget displeased Nixon and his supporters in the cabinet. But the vice president and his allies got nowhere with Eisenhower and the small circle of his economic advisers. Entreaties for substantial increases in social spending from Health, Education, and Welfare Secretary Arthur Fleming also failed. He still held out hopes for keeping the spirit of Modern Republicanism alive. Fleming had to settle for a concession on new legislation to provide federal assistance (through federally and state-guaranteed bonds) for school construction. In addition, the only other new programs that gained modest support from the administration were assistance for depressed areas (something the administration had first supported in 1956); grants for airport construction; and limited increases in spending for urban renewal.[106]

To hold the line on the budget Eisenhower played a shrewd political game. While Democrats had enlarged their margins in the House and the Senate, they did not have a veto-proof majority in the Senate if southern Democrats sided with Republicans. To thwart liberal Democratic proposals for increased spending in a number of domestic areas, the president secured support from about ten to twelve fiscally conservative southern Democratic senators. He also shored up the support of like-minded Republicans, many of them longtime members of the Taft wing of the party. Together these two groups allowed the White House to keep spending within limits set by, or at least acceptable to, the administration.[107]

Liberal Democrats, sensing opportunity in the 1960 presidential race, planned to make an issue of Eisenhower's vetoes of domestic spending legislation. Combined with what these Democrats saw as the administration's inadequate response to the challenges posed by Sputnik and a failure to deal forcefully with the 1957–58 recession, the vetoes would reinforce a negative view of the Republican Party and, by association, its candidate in the 1960 presidential election—Richard Nixon.[108]

Overall, the administration's fiscal 1960 budget called for reductions of about $4 billion in expenditures compared to fiscal 1959. Of course, the expectations were for higher revenues and reduced recession-related spending as the downturn ended. It also contained other unusual expenditures, which would not recur in fiscal 1960. Indeed, the largest single saving from the previous budget was a one-time $1.375 billion payment to the International Monetary Fund in fiscal 1959. Savings of $1.3 billion were also anticipated in the agriculture program and within the budget categories of commerce and housing; together these categories made up about 36 percent of domestic spending. On defense expenditures, Congress approved $40.9 billion for fiscal 1960, which was closer to Eisenhower's goal of $40 billion for defense than the Pentagon's original figure of $50 billion. Leaders of each of the three major branches of the military complained about Eisenhower's spending priorities for defense. Leading Democrats were also critical. But at a White House meeting in November 1958, the president bluntly told the Joint Chiefs that ultimately "our defense depends on our fiscal system."[109]

If the president was hard-nosed with the military, he also took an aggressive stance against congressional Democrats. He broke precedent and announced the fiscal 1960 budget in December 1958, about a month before the traditional January delivery date to Congress. Eisenhower declared that the $77 billion fiscal 1960 budget would be balanced. He also began a campaign to win public support for the balanced budget.[110] On the day the administration presented it to Congress, Eisenhower made a nationally televised address linking deficits and inflation. Failure to support his budgetary proposals would inevitably lead, he said, to "rising costs to every housewife, a falling value to every pay packet and a threat to the prosperous functioning of our economy. Every citizen, no matter where he lives or what he does, has a vital stake in preventing inflation."[111]

In other public statements early in 1959, the president continued to tie future prosperity and growth to controlling inflation. Government had to balance budgets; business had to hold down prices; labor had to make responsible wage demands; and consumers had to be careful in their purchases.[112] Lest anyone miss the president's point, administration spokesmen worked assiduously to cast the Democrats as irresponsible in their spending proposals and to portray them as the party of inflation.[113]

In the course of the partisan struggle over the fiscal 1960 budget, Eisenhower freely used the veto. He enlisted the support of Republicans in veto struggles, whether a given senator had voted for an original bill or not.[114] At times, that killed a bill; at other times, measures were rewritten—occasionally more than once—to take into account the president's demands. While the Democrats had enlarged majorities in both houses of Congress, they were not unified, and Eisenhower used the split between liberals and southern conservatives to get a budget that produced a surplus. For their part, the Democrats were not unhappy to lose fights over spending on occasion; they hoped to make an issue of presidential vetoes against popular programs in the 1960 election campaign.[115]

In preparing for his fiscal 1961 proposals, Eisenhower used the same tactics he had in getting his fiscal 1960 budget through Congress. He had more room for maneuver in preparing the fiscal 1961 budget than the one before it. Anticipating revenues of $84 billion, the administration proposed a budget for fiscal 1961 of $79.8 billion, producing a surplus of over $4 billion.[116] As a matter of general principle, Eisenhower and Anderson accepted what was called at the time "stabilizing budget policy." The idea was to balance the budget over a complete course of a business cycle. In the cycle's expansion phase, the government would accumulate surpluses (which could be used for debt reduction). By reducing public debt, capital resources would be freed up for greater private investment, which in turn would contribute to economic growth.[117] Balancing the budget over a business cycle was by no means a new idea. It had been discussed and endorsed as early as 1947 by the Committee for Economic Development, which Secretary Anderson had been affiliated with at the time.[118]

In any event, the fiscal 1961 budget provided for $1.3 billion more in domestic spending than the year before. Most of the increases were the results of earlier legislation. Much to Nixon's dismay, the administration paid scant attention to spending that might help his candidacy. The president talked of the need to look with a "jaundiced eye" at each proposed item of expenditure for the rest of fiscal 1960 and 1961.[119] As to defense spending, the budget included an increase of just $70 million, which did not keep up with inflation and so kept Pentagon programs more or less at previous levels. The one exception was in space exploration, where expenditures grew by $600 million, a 50 percent increase from 1960, in response to the continuing concern about Soviet missile advances.[120]

In debating the administration's fiscal 1961 budget proposals, the Democrats displayed greater unity than they had in the past. Helping to focus the party's attention was the analysis of Eisenhower's macroeconomic (and microeconomic) policy in the *Eckstein Report*. The report advocated the adoption of monetary and fiscal policies to achieve a 4.5 percent annual growth rate, which would allow for increased public investment in education, highways, health care, natural resources, and urban renewal. It did not advocate increased spending but rather proposed greater attention to economies in major programs such as defense and agriculture. The report also called for reform of the tax system to eliminate tax loopholes for business and the wealthy. Such savings would allow for greater investment in the programs the Democrats believed had been underfunded during the Eisenhower years.[121]

While the *Eckstein Report* provided a hard-hitting critique of Eisenhower's approach to macroeconomic policy, Eisenhower continued to prevail in most of the partisan battles over domestic spending. Political wrangling marked long, drawn-out debates over funds for education and assistance to depressed areas. Likewise, seemingly endless debates and arcane legislative maneuvering drove consideration of health care insurance for the elderly and increases in the minimum wage. No new legislation emerged to address any of these issues. The result was something of a triumph for Eisenhower, although Democrats continued to see it as only a pyrrhic victory for him. Many of the stalemated programs had substantial public support. Eisenhower's veto of a civil service pay increase, for example, was precisely the kind of "gift" Democrats had in mind, as Congress overrode the president's veto.[122]

By mid-1960 Eisenhower again had to confront a recession. It proved short-lived and relatively mild. Declines in economic activity were first confined to the durable goods manufacturing sector. While the slowdown was largely unnoticed until midyear—the Democrats did not focus on unemployment and troubled sectors during their presidential nomination convention in July—unemployment had begun to rise in the durable manufacturing sector as early as February. Unemployment became most noticeable in primary metals manufacturing and transportation equipment. Automobile manufacturers closed plants earlier than usual for annual model change retooling. Initially, modest increases in nondurable manufacturing offset these trends. In the nonmanufacturing sectors of trade, finance, services, and government employment levels held up well. By the middle of the year, except for the nonmanufacturing sectors, unemployment began to increase. In addition to durable and nondurable manufacturing, housing construction was also affected. By December 1960, the rate of unemployment nationally was 6.8 percent.[123]

To cope with the recession administration policy again relied on the automatic stabilizers. Beginning in the second quarter, the Federal Reserve adopted a policy of "active ease," which resulted in almost $1 billion of increase in the net reserve position of member banks. Chairman Martin, though, found himself constrained in lowering short-term discount rates. As these rates were eventually pushed down, American investors seeking higher short-term returns looked to foreign money markets. As a result, these movements, facilitated by the newly convertible Western European currencies, exacerbated the balance of payments problem. The changing free world economy at the end of the 1950s was creating increased constraints on macroeconomic management of the American domestic economy.[124] For its part, the administration turned to other policies employed before to cope with the recession. Measures were taken to stimulate housing construction, and federal construction projects and procurement were accelerated, as was highway construction. Eisenhower and Anderson also hoped for increases in manufacturing exports, as foreign industrial economies were operating near capacity.[125]

In the end, the short, shallow recession of 1960–61 did not become a major issue in the 1960 presidential campaign. Democrats focused on defense and civil rights issues but addressed the recession and slow growth policies indirectly by questioning how to promote economic growth in the future. Eisenhower's last *Economic Report of the President* in 1961 nevertheless was defensive about the administration's approach to the recession. In looking forward to a turnaround and an end to the economic slowdown, this last report emphasized that the administration's policies of fighting inflation and deficits promoted greater investment, which in turn led to increased productivity. "Because action to maintain stability and balance and to consolidate gains was taken in good time," the report argued, "the economy can now look forward, provided private and public policies are favorable, to a period of sound growth from a firm base."[126]

Few Democratic politicians agreed; nor did many Republicans. By the time Eisenhower left office, a full-scale debate was underway over what critics saw as the failures of the administration's handling of macroeconomic policy. The debate was a culmination of long-standing arguments about economic policy and growth put forward by Democrats trying to fashion policy, like their Republican opponents, in a new economic world. Growing awareness of rapid growth rates in Germany, France, and Japan prompted attention to growth in the United States. Sputnik also brought accelerated growth rates in the USSR into consideration, and these became part of the heated discussions of America's lag behind the Soviet Union not only in missile technology but also in economic development.[127]

In any event, the critiques of the last years of the administration looked at mistakes that critics believed hastened the arrival of the deep 1957–58 recession, in particular reduced military purchasing in 1957. Following the recession, critics also charged that the large surplus accumulated right after the recession of 1957–58 contributed to a sluggish recovery and that tight budgets and restrained spending for fiscal 1960 and 1961 helped push the economy into recession again in 1960–61.

More generally, the *Eckstein Report,* and the thinking of the "new economists"— most notably Walter Heller and Paul Samuelson—moved the earlier 1950s debate in a new direction. In the late 1950s, the new economists moved away from Leon Keyserling's theories. Heller, a University of Minnesota economist, had the opportunity to apply his ideas as President John F. Kennedy's chairman of the Council of Economic Advisers. In an appearance before the Joint Economic Committee in February 1959, Heller had laid out his critique of the Eisenhower administration's approach to macroeconomic policy. "Obsession with Federal expenditure cutbacks and early budget balance as a prerequisite to price stability is unfounded," he said. "The cost of a restrictive budgetary policy is loss of production by slowing the pace of recovery and lower investment in public education and other public services that strengthen our long run economic potential." Appearing at the same hearings, MIT's Paul Samuelson observed, "My advice is to put the major emphasis on growth of real income . . . not letting concern over price inflation dominate decisions."[128]

In retrospect there was room for criticism of the Eisenhower administration's handling of the 1957–58 recession. In particular, the government seemed willing to tolerate relatively high levels of unemployment in the recession and its aftermath. Eisenhower and Anderson also were premature in seeing a turnaround in the spring of 1958, even though manufacturing output remained below what it had been at about the same time during the recession of 1953–54. Still, looking at missteps in the 1960s and 1970s, it is difficult to criticize the president's concerns about inflation and deficits.

The new economics of the 1960s led both to inflation and to increasing deficits by the end of the 1960s. Together, with help from President Nixon, who worried little about inflation, they contributed to the "great inflation of the 1970s" and an end to the Bretton Woods system of a gold-backed dollar exchange in 1971. Much can be said in favor of freeing international capital flows in the decades that followed, but White House and congressional inattention to the international consequences of domestic economic policy is not one of the benefits of the changes that started in the 1970s. Nor is the disregard for deficit spending that accelerated in the 1980s, which has become a serious issue in the beginning of the twenty-first century. In light of what followed, Eisenhower's attentiveness to the international consequences of American domestic economic policy— enthusiastically supported by Anderson and Martin—does not seem so quaint or irrelevant. Foreign holders of dollars, both in the public and private sectors, could not fail to be reassured by Eisenhower's concern about inflation, deficits, and budgets. During the last years of his second term, he understood the connection between domestic economic policy and its impact overseas, and it dictated his policy choices.

CONCLUSION

As Eisenhower prepared to leave office, the country enjoyed a period of economic growth and price stability. The president had made a strong case for the dangers of persistent inflation, a new problem that many professional economists, politicians, businessmen, and the public had paid little attention to before. By the end of the decade Saulnier argued persuasively that inflationary expectations in the American economy had been largely subdued. The inflation rate between 1959 and 1964 was the lowest in the postwar era. The inflation that appeared ominous in the boom of the mid-1950s appeared broken.[129] Eisenhower had demonstrated that a Republican president could manage economic policy in both recession and boom. Major national security spending, while high, was about 60 percent of the budget in 1960, a significantly lower percentage than the approximately 70 percent when Eisenhower took office in 1953.[130] Informal methods of communication with the White House preserved the Fed's independence, while allowing for coordination of policy, if not always for complete agreement. The administration's record of fiscal restraint had gained the support of foreign leaders, making it easier for the United States to address its balance of payments problems in 1959–60.[131]

In part 2 we examine several cases of microeconomic policy: agriculture, antitrust, and foreign economic policy. Microeconomic policy proved, on balance, a greater challenge to the administration than macroeconomic policy. It required of the president a greater willingness to compromise on short-term and not-so-short-term objectives to achieve something larger—preserving a way of life rooted in free political institutions and a market-oriented economy during the deepening Cold War.

PART 2

Microeconomic Policies

CHAPTER 4

Agriculture

A Tough Battle

Eisenhower sought to reform federal agricultural programs to reinvigorate market incentives, which had been displaced and distorted by high, inflexible congressionally mandated price supports imposed since the early 1940s. The price supports were originally designed to spur American farm production during World War II, but their rationale largely evaporated with the advent of a very different Cold War economy. Price supports continued to exist, however, because of their political attractiveness. They delivered substantial, indirect subsidies to large producers of a limited number of important crops for which Congress mandated high support prices. Exacerbating the distortions in farm commodity and livestock markets were rapidly increasing productivity and output among the country's largest farmers, a trend that had accelerated after the late 1930s and intensified during the 1950s.

The distortions created by high, fixed price supports vexed Eisenhower. In particular, price supports proved increasingly expensive after 1951. The cost of the program soared because the federal government had to acquire and store supported commodities when market prices were below those established by government fiat. In addition, by the early 1950s export markets for American agricultural products declined rapidly because of the artificially high domestic prices created by the system. Nevertheless, the Eisenhower administration aimed to revitalize farm export markets, which still represented 20-plus percent of American agricultural production, and to dispose of some of the accumulated stored surpluses abroad. Overseas disposal of government-owned surpluses, however, had the potential to complicate foreign relations with allies and others by altering world export markets or destabilizing the domestic farm markets in other countries.

Eisenhower approached agricultural policy in much the same manner in which he tackled fiscal, monetary, and defense policy. With his personal popularity, he could afford to take a long view of how changes in farm policy would be accomplished. He did not want to radically alter policies that, in various forms, had been in place for well over a decade. As he said at a June 1954 press conference, "I am very much in favor of gradualism in everything that the Government does with respect to agriculture."[1] This was politically wise, since there was strong support in the Republican and Democratic parties for the existing price support scheme. In addition, supporters of the status quo had the advantage of making the case that the government's agricultural policy provided an attractive, albeit untested, fail-safe mechanism against a 1930s-like collapse of farm prices, which remained a vivid memory for most farmers.

THE PRICE SUPPORT SYSTEM

The incoming administration believed American agriculture was deeply troubled. The 1954 *Economic Report of the President* stated, "American agriculture has not been producing, without significant surpluses or deficits, the foods which domestic and foreign buyers want at current [supported] prices. . . . Price supports fail to reflect the important cost-reducing advances in agricultural technology."[2] White House officials thought the problems of agriculture were curable, if price support programs could be reformed so as to no longer operate as a driving force in distorting markets and incomes but rather a fail-safe floor, well below market prices, and possibly useful in the event of a sudden market and price collapse.

Since 1938, the centerpiece of American agricultural policy had been mandatory price supports for a limited group of important commodities. These were referred to as the "basic commodities": wheat, cotton, corn, tobacco, rice, peanuts, and perishables such as dairy products. Support for other commodities was "discretionary" with the US Department of Agriculture (USDA). Price supports for these basic commodities essentially guaranteed a minimum price, set annually, to farmers who participated in federal agricultural programs, if the market price fell below a set "supported" price. These support prices were established through operation of a complex federal loan program.

Each season the support price for a farm commodity was determined using a percentage of "parity," which was a ratio of the relationship of farm commodity prices to farm costs during 1909–14 (1910–14 after 1948), an era when farmer purchasing power was generally considered favorable.[3] Beginning with the Agricultural Adjustment Act (AAA) of 1938, the Department of Agriculture set this percentage by using an adjustable percentage of parity designed to balance supply and demand. The legislation allowed the USDA discretion to set support prices between 52 and 75 percent of parity based on market conditions, but loan programs became mandatory (for basic commodities) if prices fell below 52 percent of parity at the end of a crop year. Beginning in 1942, however, Congress legislated the figure for basic farm commodities (and sometimes others) at "90 percent of parity." Though initially designed to raise prices and encourage production for World War II, the practice continued through 1954.[4]

Allotments—acreage planting limitations for supported crops—were also a crucial element of the program established by the 1938 AAA. In theory, allotments would reduce production and "balance" supply and demand at the support price or above. Farmers of supported commodities who agreed (by referendum) to conditions such as allotments for the supported crop or marketing orders (USDA rules to ensure minimum prices) could obtain a nine-month "nonrecourse" loan from the federal Commodity Credit Corporation (CCC). These loans were available at the support price (loan rate), with some variations and adjustments. Allotments, however, were mandatory for certain basic commodities such as corn, cotton, rice, tobacco, and wheat—which were chronically overproduced—when supplies reached certain levels, and this discouraged farmer rejection of price support regimes.[5] The CCC took the farmer's crop as security and stored it. If the market price of the farmer's crop in CCC storage was above the support price, he could sell the crop during the duration of the CCC loan and liquidate his CCC debt. But, if market prices were below supported price levels, the farmer could choose to default on the loan and the CCC got the farmer's crop in full satisfaction of his loan debt. This nonrecourse loan feature was the key to the program.

Farmers usually defaulted when the adjusted cost of repaying the loan per unit was higher than the farmer could receive by selling his crop at market prices. Thus, when the support price for basic commodities was higher than the market price, the federal government was subsidizing the crop at higher-than-market price and it would accumulate large commodity stocks in storage—what were called "carryovers." During the Eisenhower administration, despite the president's best efforts to change the system, between a quarter and one-half of the crop of such basic commodities as corn and wheat was annually "marketed" to the CCC. Between 1952 and 1960 corn prices, which ranged between $1.00 and

$1.66 per bushel, never exceeded loan rates. Support prices exceeded market prices by between $0.06 and $0.29 a bushel, depending on the year. Wheat mirrored this: prices varied between $1.74 and $2.09, while support prices exceeded market prices by between $0.03 and $0.17 a bushel during the 1950s.[6]

As envisioned in the 1938 AAA, the operation of the system was to provide stability against wide fluctuations in the market. The goal was a so-called ever normal granary, which was supposed to protect farmers and consumers against dramatic short- to medium-term swings in farm prices, if parity percentages were set near or below market rates. During protracted periods of declining market prices, however, increased production, flat demand, and politically motivated high support prices led to a rapid increase of CCC stocks of commodities with mandated support. Storage and disposal costs increased dramatically. Such conditions prevailed between 1948 and 1954, and not surprisingly the operation of the price stabilization program proved costly to the federal government—about $2.1 billion in 1953 and $1.7 billion in 1954. Costs rose throughout the 1950s, despite Eisenhower's efforts to reduce them.[7]

Congressionally mandated high parity percentages for crops with mandatory support prevailed from immediately before World War II through 1954. After that, new legislation allowed the Eisenhower administration, albeit slowly, to begin to reduce support levels and reliance on indirect production controls, such as the allotment system of acreage restrictions and marketing orders. During a unique time like World War II, the list of supported commodities increased to over one hundred. For the most part, though, and certainly during the Truman and Eisenhower administrations, the major focus of federal support programs was on the basic commodities such as wheat, cotton, corn, and dairy products, which faced troubled markets, with sluggish demand and rapidly increasing production. Though these crops usually represented 30 percent or less of net farm income, support programs for basics and their costs were the salient feature of federal agriculture policy and the source of debate in the immediate postwar period and the 1950s. Other crops and livestock, where long-term demand and supply trends were considered more favorable were nonbasic. The 1954 *ERP* noted that "crops and livestock products accounting for about 56 percent of gross cash farm income currently receive no direct support and gain little from the support program."[8]

By the end of the Eisenhower administration only 5 basic commodities (out of over 250 agricultural commodities and products), for which price supports were mandatory, were subject to acreage controls. Overall, price supports were required for only 12 farm commodities.[9] Among the producers of basic commodities receiving CCC support, the overwhelming majority of payments went to the largest farmers. Smaller farmers were not major beneficiaries of the program. They did not have significant economies of scale. If they grew basics, the imposition of acreage controls to "balance" price support levels and demand imposed a crippling blow to their small operations by further reducing economies of scale and farm income.

Acreage controls, however, were almost from their inception unable to balance supply and demand as envisioned in the 1938 AAA. Since the 1930s, farmers had found ways of circumventing acreage controls. When they reduced the land devoted to controlled crops (in exchange for price support), it was usually the least desirable acreage they possessed, which was taken out of production. Also, enforcement of acreage restrictions was notoriously difficult, and noncompliance was significant. Thus, reductions in production through decreases in acreage were considerably less than anticipated by USDA formulas and projections. Furthermore, such schemes did not stop farmers from growing uncontrolled crops on the acreage "withdrawn" from the cultivation of controlled crops. And this tended to spread supply and demand imbalances to these crops as well. Specific quantitative controls of supported crops (volume and production limits as opposed to acreage controls) were an option under agricultural legislation but were considered even more difficult to enforce and politically unpalatable. During the 1950s Eisenhower always opposed specific, quantitative controls on output as well as restrictions on acreage as an indirect means to limit production.

Politically, reform of the price support system proved an extremely difficult task. Eisenhower's secretary of agriculture, Ezra Taft Benson, was fond of noting that "it was not the economics of agriculture that was the most difficult, it was the politics of agriculture."[10] Even though Eisenhower came into office with accumulated goodwill following his 1952 election landslide, midwestern and southern farm state politicians of both parties retained a zealous faith in 90 percent of parity for basic commodities. Eisenhower's attempts to change the system led to extensive, heated, and often bitter battles. The system delivered indirect subsidies to large, politically well-connected farmers allied with both parties in their electoral strongholds.[11] Furthermore, everyone involved in the farm policy debates conceded that 90 percent parity for basics set a floor under farm prices: though prices declined significantly between 1947 and 1955, it cushioned that decline. The Eisenhower administration and its opponents also were well aware that advocating lower and more flexible price supports to "readjust or adjust" basic commodity prices meant accelerating price decreases and lower farm income in the short term. Debate centered on how significant the declines would be. Thus, 90 percent of parity had a simple and powerful political allure for both political parties.[12] The seniority of Republican and Democrat farm state representatives and senators made change difficult, since many had long records of voting for 90 percent of parity. Even the appeals of a newly inaugurated, immensely popular president met strong resistance, or at best gained grudging acceptance.[13]

Eisenhower's chief White House economic adviser, Gabriel Hauge, recounts such resistance to change in his unpublished autobiography. Hauge recalls a 1953 encounter with one of the "deans" of the Senate Democrats, Richard Russell of Georgia, to try to get him to rethink his support of 90 percent parity:

> Russell was not even on the Agriculture Committee but he was one of the power-houses of the Senate and no change in existing farm legislation could be enacted without his consent. Because I came as an emissary of the President, the Senator agreed to see me and he sat absolutely silent as I gave him my story. When it was clear that I had finished, he said to me, "Young man, I have been in the Senate for 20 years and all this time I have been for 90 percent parity and if you think that I am about to abandon my whole previous stand on this basic issue, you misjudge me very, very badly. I don't think there's any useful purpose to be served by continuing this conversation." I tried once more, on a slightly different tack, but he just looked at me and said, "Now, didn't you hear me the first time?"[14]

LEGACIES: NEW DEAL, WORLD WAR II, AND TRUMAN FARM POLICIES

The problems of American agriculture predated the partisan battles of the Truman administration and actually began thirty years before Eisenhower took office. Though many parts of the American economy boomed in the 1920s, agriculture was not one of them. It was characterized by weak demand for basic food- and clothing-related commodities (wheat, corn, livestock, and cotton), high production and increasing productivity, falling prices, and reductions in farm populations. In the interwar years the income of people working in agriculture was less than half of those engaged in nonfarm employment. Furthermore, the number of small farms declined, as larger, more prosperous farmers, who had economies of scale, bought out their less successful neighbors. The smaller farms that remained increasingly were mired in poverty. The decline of small farms continued inexorably throughout the twentieth century century, occasionally accelerating rapidly, as in the late 1930s and early 1940s as well as during the 1950s.[15]

Farm prices collapsed dramatically after the onset of the Great Depression in 1929. A Hoover administration program to purchase surplus production was grossly undercapitalized for the task, and by the time Franklin Roosevelt became president in 1933 the farm sector was in serious crisis.[16] Initially, the 1933 Agricultural Adjustment Act sought to raise farm income through cash payments to farmers (financed by a tax on agricultural processors), price supports, and restrictions on plantings. As an emergency measure some crops and livestock were destroyed to reduce supply. After the Supreme Court declared parts of the AAA unconstitutional in early 1936, the Soil Conservation and Domestic Allotment Act of 1936 made cash payments to farmers for removing crops that depleted the soil from production. Additionally, several federal agencies purchased outright farmland deemed "unsuitable for cultivation" between 1934 and 1942.[17] Unfortunately, none of this really worked very well, and it was only the severe droughts of 1934 and 1936 that reduced farm production and stabilized agricultural prices by 1938.[18]

As discussed earlier in this chapter, price supports based on a percentage of parity and acreage restrictions to balance them were the centerpiece of the 1938 AAA. But it also authorized direct cash payments to producers of basic commodities "as funds available would permit" and continued payments to retire productive acreage. Direct cash payments to farmers were the most revolutionary part of New Deal agricultural policy. With the demise of the processing tax in 1936, their use had declined dramatically. Though such payments focused on the goal of price parity for specific commodities, many Americans opposed such direct subsidies. The price support (nonrecourse) loan system was much less overt in delivering subsidies and presented much less formidable political challenges for its defenders.[19]

Between 1938 and 1940 improving weather and the rapid acceleration of farm productivity caused surges in production and a 20 percent drop in farm prices. In response to the renewed crisis, Congress began to mandate price support levels, ignoring market-oriented USDA formulas set under the new 1938 AAA. World War II accelerated the trend. In May 1941, Congress set price supports for basic commodities at 85 percent parity. The following year it raised support prices to 90 percent parity and eventually expanded the list of supported commodities to over one hundred by the end of the fighting in 1945.[20] After 1940 large quantities of nonperishable crops—carryover stocks—began to fill CCC warehouses, where they remained. High support prices; the acceleration of farm consolidation and productivity; and the limited effectiveness of acreage controls strained the system and previewed chronic postwar problems. Only the increased consumption of the war years prevented a crisis, except in cotton. The accumulated surpluses became a war asset in the worldwide struggle.[21] Furthermore, legislation in 1942 extended the wartime regime of 90 percent of parity "until two years after the declaration of the end of hostilities," which Truman made effective on December 31, 1946.[22] Thus, wartime 90 percent parity was scheduled to end after 1948.

Just as in fiscal, inflation, and defense policies, the shifting Cold War environment and the agriculture policy battles of the Truman administration set the parameters for Eisenhower's policies.[23] Following the war there was considerable fear that the conditions of the late 1930s would reappear: abundant production would bring a return of low prices as high wartime prices and increased farmer income would accelerate the acquisition of modern machinery; foster the further consolidation of farms; and increase the use of fertilizers. Because of the possible return of a farm depression when the war ended, administrators of agricultural programs during World War II ensured that the United States would not emerge from the war with large stocks of agricultural products that ultimately would depress prices. As a result of this "bare shelf" policy, there were no large reserves of farm products and postwar prices remained high. Short supplies, in fact, proved to be a serious problem in the immediate postwar years, as the demand for farm commodities grew. Shortages also emerged overseas because of the destruction of agricultural productive capacity in both Europe and Asia during the war and the collapse of commerce and finance after hostilities ended.[24] Consequently, US food supplies were strained, leading to relatively high prices for farmers and consumers during the war and three years after.

This positive situation for farmers did not last, as overseas and domestic market conditions changed. By mid-1948 prewar conditions reappeared and farm prices began to decline. A little more than a year later, prices for agricultural commodities were 21 percent below their postwar peak. By 1949, overall farm production was 35 percent above prewar levels, and farm income dramatically dropped 15 percent below 1948. Commodities in CCC storage increased from almost nothing in early 1948 to $4.2 billion in early 1950. This sudden but not unexpected deterioration of farm prices and income had impacts on the 1948 election and farm legislation in 1948, 1949, and thereafter. Prices and farm incomes recovered briefly with the beginning of the Korean War but began a dramatic slide in late 1951 that continued unabated through 1955.[25]

By the end of World War II, farmers had become comfortable with a price support system braced by high, fixed, and relatively rigid price supports set by Congress. They associated the system with the high prices and incomes they experienced during the war. The major point of contention in the immediate postwar period focused on the issue of whether parity should be fixed at 90 percent or become part of a more flexible system of price support.[26] Sentiment also grew for a new, modernized version of the parity formula, which would reflect farm efficiencies that had grown steadily since the beginning of the century. Indeed, by 1948 there was a large group that supported more flexible price supports and modernized parity. It included Truman's secretary of agriculture, Clinton Anderson; the leadership of the Republican Party; the American Farm Bureau Federation (the largest and most influential farmer-based organization); agribusiness firms whose costs of doing business contained large agricultural inputs; and most agricultural economists.[27]

Lower and more flexible supports were also Truman's position, at least initially. But in 1948, as the Truman administration began to craft an agriculture policy for the postwar period, it underestimated the tidal wave of technological changes and farm consolidation that was creating huge leaps in American agricultural productivity and production. These increases would last into the 1960s, especially in the supported, basic commodities.[28] Farm productivity per unit increased at three times the rate of the nonfarm sector in the immediate postwar period! The downward pressure on farm prices became inexorable.[29]

All of these changes shaped the debate that led to the Agricultural Act of 1948, which extended price supports for basic commodities at 90 percent parity through 1949.[30] The legislation, however, also introduced the idea of a "market-oriented" commodity policy, which appealed to Republican leaders and their midwestern constituents, at least when prices were high, as they were in early 1948. It instituted the concept of flexible price supports for 1950 and thereafter. Prices would be supported at 75 percent of parity for a "normal" supply. So, when there was scarcity, price supports would rise above 75 percent of parity. When markets were likely to be in surplus, supports would drop below 75 percent of parity.[31] Additionally, the legislation provided for "modernized parity," which would have the effect over time of lowering the parity price for most basic commodities. The new formula was based on the relationship between farm and nonfarm prices during the most recent ten-year period, not the halcyon days of 1910–14. It was to be phased in beginning in 1950 and be limited to a 5 percent annual drop (in the ratio) until a new parity level was reached. The old formula tended to overvalue basic commodities like cotton, corn, and wheat while undervaluing livestock and livestock products.[32]

The price support provisions of the legislation became a volatile issue in the 1948 presidential election. Truman's victory proved a bitter political lesson for the Republican Party when it pulled "defeat from the jaws of victory." Dissatisfaction of many of its traditional farm electorate in the Midwest played an important part in the defeat. The experience remained a cautionary tale for the Eisenhower administration as it developed its farm policy in 1953. Dewey's defeat fueled the assumption that any farm legislation that appeared to threaten assistance to farmers was political suicide, especially in presidential elections.[33]

A new secretary of agriculture, Charles Brannan, helped make Truman's case among farmers. He succeeded Clinton Anderson, who left the administration to run for the Senate shortly before Congress passed the compromise legislation in June 1948. Brannan was an astute Democratic partisan. Republican attacks that blamed high consumer food prices on the Truman administration and criticism of CCC surplus storage expenditures gave Brannan and Truman a political opening, which they skillfully exploited. They charged that the Republicans wanted to undermine the price support system.[34] As a result of Brannan's tireless hammering at the issue in the 1948 campaign, Democrats were able to make the substantial inroads into traditional Republican, midwestern, Farm Belt strongholds that helped give control of the White House and Congress to the Democrats.

These battles over late-1940s agricultural policy shaped the parameters of later debate. Eisenhower modeled many aspects of his agricultural reform proposals on the 1948 legislation. In many respects, the subsequent 1949 legislation proposed by Secretary Brannan, who decidedly wanted to take agricultural policy in a new direction, was the antithesis of the 1948 act. Brannan's ideas influenced liberal critics of Eisenhower policy during the 1950s, Democratic approaches to agriculture policy when the party regained the White House in 1961, and agriculture legislation in the Nixon administration from 1969 to 1974. In essence, the Brannan Plan, proposed either: direct payments—an income subsidy for most farm products that were perishable or not inexpensively stored at the difference between support levels and market prices; or price supports at 90 to 100 percent of parity for the others. Both were subject to full income or price support for only the first $25,700 of farm production. The income standard would be based on a ten-year moving average beginning with the years 1938–47, rather than historic parity. *This was essentially income parity, not price parity, tied initially to a period of prosperity.* Previously, the amount of price support payments (loan proceeds) an individual could receive had not been limited and was concentrated among large farmers. Brannan argued that his proposal ensured that small and medium farms would have a long-term future in American agriculture.[35] When introduced to Congress, these proposals provoked enormous opposition and failed to pass. Direct cash payments to stabilize farm income, not prices, became a flashpoint; opponents labeled it socialism. Finally, dooming the program was its cost, estimated at $3 billion to $8 billion. Nationwide farm income was only about $20 billion.[36]

The Agriculture Act of 1949 turned into a victory for those who wanted continuation of high, fixed price supports as the best means to protect farm income. It derailed the shift to flexible supports that had been scheduled to begin in 1950 under the 1948 act. Support for basic commodities at 90 percent of parity was extended for another year, through 1950. The shift to modernized parity under the 1948 act would proceed. But Congress added other elements that dictated that for the next five years parity was to be determined by either formula, whichever generated the higher levels of price support, a principle called "dual parity."[37]

The outbreak of the Korean War in June 1950 caused further delays in implementation of the 1948 act's mandate for flexible price supports. Since USDA wanted to ensure high production during the war, Brannan administratively extended 90 percent parity for wheat, corn, and cotton, and neither acreage quotas nor marketing orders were in effect through 1952. In its renewal of the Defense Production Act in 1952, Congress extended 90 percent parity for basic commodities through 1954 and the revisions of the parity formula until the end of 1955.[38]

So when Eisenhower took office in January 1953, high fixed price supports for basic commodities had been in place for more than a decade and had become the cornerstone of bipartisan congressional farm policy. In times of national crisis, like World War II, proponents argued that the system could bring out substantial, necessary production. In other, more "normal" periods such as the late 1930s and between 1948 and 1954, the wartime system, heightened by surging farm productivity, created market-depressing volumes. As a result, crop storage in government warehouses and ultimate disposal at lower market rates incurred significant costs to the federal government. Even so, there was a widespread belief among most farmers, their bipartisan political allies in Congress, and the incoming Eisenhower administration that the recent erosion of farm prices would have been greater without high price supports and production controls.[39]

EISENHOWER TACKLES AGRICULTURAL POLICY

During the 1952 campaign, Eisenhower's advisers recommended caution on farm policy reform. After the 1948 debacle many Republicans thought it was unwise to deny farmers anything.[40] Eisenhower readily conceded that he was not well versed in the details of agriculture policy and, though he was raised in Kansas, that had been more than forty years earlier. His general view, though, was that the federal government should be less involved in farming and that government policy should be gradually realigned or adjusted to allow for more flexible (lower) price supports, fewer production restrictions, and eventually lower government costs. Such ideas had been at the core of the 1948 act, the last time agricultural policy had been addressed by a Republican Congress or in a period of rough supply-demand equilibrium.[41]

Advocacy of the flexible price supports authorized in the 1948–49 legislation, but postponed by Congress until 1954, might again provide the Democrats with an issue if the Eisenhower campaign team was not careful. Their solution was the so-called Golden Promise: a carefully couched endorsement of current 90 per-cent parity for basics, as already contained in existing legislation, through the end of 1954. In September 1952, speaking to an audience attending the National Plowing Contest in Kassom, Minnesota, Eisenhower announced, "I stand behind— and the Republican Party stands behind—the price support laws now on the books. . . . This includes the amendment to the basic Farm Act [1949] . . . to continue the price supports on basic commodities at 90 per cent of parity."[42] As president, however, he felt his statement did not limit his options for legislation effective beyond the expiration of congressional mandates at the end of 1954.[43]

Eisenhower's statement finessed the political difficulties that had gotten his party into trouble with some midwestern farmers in 1948. He carried the traditional Republican strongholds in the Midwest as well as Democratic, cotton states like Texas. Still, farm issues were not an area the new president understood in detail. Selecting a knowledgeable secretary of agriculture was important, although the man selected for the job, Ezra Taft Benson, observed that Eisenhower "knew [what] he didn't know" and "did his homework." Benson went on to say that "he observed and he listened and before the year [1953] was out he not only knew the problems, he had firm, well-reasoned convictions about how to solve them."[44]

In selecting a secretary of agriculture, Eisenhower relied heavily on his trusted brother Milton to vet candidates for the job during the preinauguration period. The younger Eisenhower had spent many years working in the USDA as director of information (1928–41) and had been president of both Kansas State University (1943–50) and Pennsylvania State University (1950–56), schools with strong agricultural programs. Ultimately, with Milton's recommendation, the president-elect settled on Benson. His name, not on the first lists of possibilities for the job, gained attention through the efforts of Ken Stern, the head of the American Institute of Cooperation, a 1,500-member group of farm cooperatives. Benson, who chaired the institute's board, had had a long career in agriculture. He came from a farming family of eleven children and spent his youth working on the Idaho farm where he had been born in 1899. After college, he received an MA in agricultural economics from Iowa State College (now Iowa State University), where his thesis focused on national marketing of farm products. He returned to the family farm and worked there for a few years before taking a job as a county extension agent in 1930 for the University of Idaho. Between 1931 and 1936, he was the executive secretary of the Idaho Cooperative Council, which he had helped found. Under Benson's leadership it succeeded in promoting the Idaho potato to worldwide prominence. In 1939 he became the executive secretary of the National Council of Farmer Cooperatives (representing 4,600 cooperatives) in Washington, DC, and held that position through 1944, representing the organization before Congress and the executive branch. During the war, he also served on the National Agricultural Advisory Committee. From 1945 to 1950 he was director of the Farm Foundation and then headed the Board of Trustees of the American Institute of Cooperation, the position he held when Eisenhower tapped him to be secretary of agriculture.[45]

For most of his life, Benson was not deeply involved in politics. Outside of his professional career in agriculture, Benson devoted himself to his Mormon faith. In 1952, he endorsed Senator Robert A. Taft—a distant cousin—but was not actively involved in the Republican primary campaign.[46] President Eisenhower was going to have to rely on Benson, since foreign and defense policies would require much of the new president's attention. Farmers, however, were an important constituency of the Republican Party, and a real opportunity existed to create policies that could be clearly distinguished from what many considered the excesses of the New Deal and Fair Deal farm programs. In addition, agricultural spending was a significant and increasingly expensive item in the federal budget, and agricultural exports had significant consequences for Cold War foreign policy.

As such, the new president embraced firm, but not inflexible views about where he wanted to take farm policy, and his goals remained quite consistent during his eight years in office. He wanted a relaxation of mandatory high price supports and less reliance on onerous schemes of indirect production restrictions, that is, acreage allotments. Lower and more flexible support prices would equate to more flexible and fewer production controls. He opposed high wartime supports that were creating more production, lower market prices, and higher government program costs. What may have been useful in an era of total war was clearly inappropriate for the new Cold War economy. Eisenhower specifically opposed direct cash subsidies for crops or more radical Brannan Plan–type income subsidies—in short, he wanted to promote market incentives for agriculture with a circumscribed minimum regulatory framework. The destruction of food as a means of regulating markets was out of the question, an approach that raised the specter of early New Deal emergency measures and more recent Truman administration embarrassments. Finally, he wanted to reduce the cost of farm support programs through lower support prices and more aggressive disposal of surpluses at home and abroad with minimum disruption of domestic markets or American foreign relations.[47]

Because Eisenhower gave his cabinet secretaries wide latitude, Benson was to take the lead in achieving what the president wanted. Eisenhower did not make decisions that were more appropriate for his cabinet secretaries to make, but he expected them to take responsibility for and to "take the heat" for their actions.[48] Thus, Benson became a lightning rod for intensifying opposition to administration farm policies during Eisenhower's eight years in office. Additionally, Eisenhower's management style prized protecting his time. He wanted differences over policy within the administration handled at levels well below that of the White House. If the issues became extremely important or his subordinates simply could not agree, the White House—and if truly necessary, the president—would intervene. Such intervention often took place after Eisenhower had undertaken a careful study and had received divergent counsel from staff analysis or cabinet debate.[49]

From their first meeting in late 1952, Eisenhower and Benson found themselves compatible. According to Benson's chief economic adviser, Don Paarlberg, they developed a warm, friendly relationship during Eisenhower's terms in office, but that relationship, like Eisenhower's with many other cabinet members, did not continue after 1961. Eisenhower called Benson "Ezry" and admired his devotion to his faith and his principled policy positions. Benson and Postmaster

General Arthur Summerfield were the only cabinet officials to remain through both presidential terms.[50]

Yet, from the first, Benson caused the White House and the president problems. Plainspoken, a devout Mormon (indeed, one of the leaders of the faith—he had been a member of the Council of Twelve of the Church of Latter Day Saints since 1948), and a man of strong conviction about agricultural matters, Benson was not comfortable with politics and the ways of Washington, despite his wartime position with the National Association of Farmer Cooperatives. He seemed particularly ill at ease with the give and take of the politically charged landscape of agriculture. Specifically, he had difficulty getting along with Congress, including Republican members from farm states, largely because of their support for 90 percent parity for basics: an issue that Benson saw in almost Manichean terms.[51] His confirmation hearings included testy exchanges with Republican senators, and not every farm state Republican voted for his confirmation. Some were suspicious of his (and Eisenhower's) commitment to 90 percent parity as only an interim policy.[52]

Eisenhower, who was often uncomfortable with political maneuvering, nevertheless realized that to accomplish anything on farm policy, or other policies for that matter, he needed to practice the art of compromise to achieve his long-term goals. Don Paarlberg recounts that on one occasion Benson told his staff about a discussion he had with Eisenhower regarding legislative strategy that had impressed the secretary. Eisenhower drew Benson a square called "the objective" and then explained and drew feints, oblique retreating, and flanking movements and gradual achievement of the objective. He told Benson, "That's the way you run a military organization and I'm convinced that that's the way you run a political enterprise. I'm thoroughly in agreement with your objective, but I don't think you'll get there fastest by driving directly toward it." Paarlberg, however, added that Benson's nature "was exactly opposed to that. He was a forthright man, and feinting and retreating and zigging and zagging were not really part of his makeup. I'm not sure the President's point really got through to the secretary, although [Benson] was impressed with it enough to tell us all about it."[53]

White House chief economic adviser Gabriel Hauge observed that Benson "was absolutely right in the position[s] he took, but there were occasions when we [the White House staff] felt his tactics were about as useful as a stone hatchet. In turn, he undoubtedly felt that we were much too pragmatic to achieve anything substantial."[54] Benson's philosophical rigidity remained a problem through both terms. In 1958, after a meeting with Republican Party leaders, Eisenhower assured Benson that, "in our efforts to improve Federal Programs affecting agriculture I have always supported you enthusiastically" and would continue to do so. But then he proceeded to chastise Benson about his apparent inflexibility and insensitivity to the concerns of the congressional Republican leadership, which was desperately trying to muster support against a veto override. Eisenhower noted that they needed to make concessions to keep the Republicans together and "sometimes in the workings of a democratic society, it is not sufficient merely to be completely right"; to make progress toward their goals, "we must have some room for maneuver, or we shall suffer for it."[55]

Public difficulties emerged early. Two weeks after taking office, on February 5, 1953, Benson issued "A General Statement on Agricultural Policy," which reflected his view about the moral imperative of needed sea changes in farm policy. It spoke of policy in terms of "How will it affect the character, morale, and well-being of our people?" He warned against the dangers of the concentrated power of big government that trapped individuals into looking to Washington to do for them what they should do themselves. "It is doubtful," the statement said, "if any man can be politically free if he depends on the state for sustenance." Like the president, Benson believed that limits on individual liberty stifled initiative and undermined character. More specifically, Benson argued that farmers should understand price supports as a way to stabilize markets for commodities from calamitous declines and not something they should see as relief for them individually. In the end, Benson conceded that the goal of agricultural policy should be "full parity prices of farm products and parity incomes for farm people. . . . [But] this objective cannot be assured by government programs alone."[56]

Personally, Benson thought that no price supports, at any level, could address the fundamental problems of farm income, which in his opinion, were caused by (1) the low productivity and high costs of many farms; (2) the high birthrate in agriculture that reinforced the tendency toward (1); (3) poor educational opportunities in many agricultural areas; and (4) lack of training and encouragement to young people to seek urban job opportunities and resistance to moving to such employment.[57] Subsequently in 1956, the Rural Development Program (RDP) was created to try to address some of these broader concerns about rural poverty, but it never received significant funding or interest from Congress during Eisenhower's term.[58]

Benson elaborated on his beliefs on the limited value of price supports about a week later in his first public speech as secretary, to the Central Livestock Association meeting in St. Paul, Minnesota. Beef producers in the audience were no doubt worried about falling prices for their product, and many, encouraged by the National Farmers Educational and Farmers Cooperative Union (the most left-leaning of the national farm organizations), were looking for price supports or other federal action. Benson bluntly told the audience that they should produce meat for the free market and not expect high price supports from the federal government.[59] Eisenhower and Benson viewed the federal government's agricultural policies as insurance against the collapse of farm prices, which could lead to larger macroeconomic problems—a not unreasonable reading of the period 1920–33 or the Depression of the 1890s, when Eisenhower was a boy in Kansas. When combined with sound fiscal and monetary policies "to stabilize the general level of prices and stabilize the general condition of industry," a flexible system of lower price support would eventually bring farm prosperity.[60] Benson condemned the operation of the current price support system and its distortions and argued that the inevitable result in the future would be a spiral of higher government costs, surpluses, lower prices, and more restrictions on acreage under cultivation to try to bring the system into balance. He was fond of stating, "The chickens are coming home to roost. They're not our chickens: but we've got to take care of them. We inherited them along with other items in our legacy [from the Democrats.]"[61]

AN EISENHOWER AGRICULTURE POLICY

Eisenhower formally presented his legislative proposals to Congress on January 11, 1954. As expected he sought greater flexibility in the price support system and hoped that a measured yet flexible approach to price supports would change the fundamental direction of federal farm policies and reduce CCC storage costs.[62] Lower price supports would clear markets and drastically reduce the need for the despised acreage controls mandated under current legislation for certain basic commodities. Nevertheless, the proposed legislation retained 90 percent of parity for basics through 1954, keeping Eisenhower's campaign promise. This was well above the current 82 percent for wheat and 79 percent for corn, with extensive acreage restrictions that USDA determined was necessary to balance supply and demand under the 1938 AAA formulas. Thus, CCC stocks still accumulated rapidly.[63]

The president hoped his cautious approach would yield political dividends. At a December 18, 1953, meeting with legislative leaders the president justified a measured approach to agricultural policy in terms of farmers' interests. A summary of the president's comments recorded that "the President was willing to further slow up the change-over [on the level and method of determining parity] proposed by the administration so as to avoid causing misplaced fear among farm-ers. He said he personally believed in a modest application of flexible supports and a modest application of acreage controls," and "he did not want to threaten the farmer with 50 percent or nothing."[64]

Eisenhower also expressed deep concern about the impact that changes in agricultural policy could have on "overall economic stability." Gradualism was the president's watchword, and this assumed even greater importance during the middle of the 1953–54 recession. He wrote, "I am confident that we can effect [a] transition to a healthier, sounder economy without generating the kind of downward spiral that has marked the great depressions of the past. . . . I am very much interested in making sure that every Department constantly bear in mind and give appropriate weight to the implications of each major decision on overall economic stability." Nothing was watched more closely during the "first Repub-lican recession since the Great Depression" than the farm situation, because of the potential political dynamite from continually falling farm prices and Ben-son's rhetorical flourishes.[65]

Under Eisenhower's proposals, after the 1954 crop year, price supports for basic commodities would gradually adjust to supply. Modernized parity (parity determined by reference to averages of costs over the previous ten years) under the 1948 and 1949 legislation would become effective beginning January 1, 1956 (also part of Eisenhower's election promise) and be phased in at 5 percent per year. Price supports for most commodities would be between 0 to 90 percent of parity, and for certain basic commodities (wheat, cotton, corn) a price floor of 75 to 90 percent of parity would be authorized for 1955 and beyond. The latter was the centerpiece of Eisenhower's program.[66]

Even these modest proposals, however, ran into serious opposition in Con-gress. Republican leaders subsequently informed the president that legislation that included a range of parity between 75 and 90 percent beginning in 1955 would never pass Congress. Eisenhower believed that he had to compromise and accepted what the leaders thought would be approved, that is, parity of between 82.5 and 90 percent for 1955 and 75 to 90 percent thereafter for basic commodi-ties, except tobacco. This change brought along the support of Farm Belt Repub-licans, acceding to the wishes of a popular Republican president, even though they favored higher supports. Still the legislation passed by only fifty-eight votes in the House, the chamber the administration considered the most difficult to deal with on farm matters, with twenty-three Republicans voting against the president's program. The margin in the Senate was five votes. It foreshadowed tougher battles ahead.[67]

The most important sections of the Agricultural Act of 1954 were the gradual two-year transition to more flexible and lower price supports for dairy products and basic commodities, except tobacco.[68] Modernized parity would finally be phased in beginning in 1956. If left to stand by Congress, these flexible lower supports would be in place for the crop year 1956, the end of Eisenhower's first term. The president and Benson saw the 1954 legislation as "not a complete and permanent solution, [but] a step towards an ultimate goal." Because of the farm product cycle and the election year Golden Promise, however, the journey began slowly. Surpluses and their attendant costs would continue to accumulate, but in theory at a much slower rate once the legislation was fully implemented.[69] The 1954 act also included provisions for setting aside reserves of $2.5 billion of CCC surpluses for foreign and domestic relief, school lunch programs, a national emergency, and other programs. These reserves were to be "insulated from normal trade channels," removing the threat of farm surpluses from current markets—an important element of Eisenhower's farm program.[70]

Eisenhower also advocated greater efforts in promoting overseas disposal of surpluses. In announcing the administration's proposed legislation in January 1954, he discussed expansion of farm markets abroad. He contemplated that surpluses could be used more frequently in foreign economic assistance and overseas relief efforts following natural disasters. But he also supported a more active program of developing overseas commercial markets for American agricultural surpluses, spearheaded by the USDA in cooperation with the State Department.[71]

Congress responded with passage of P.L. 480, on July 10, 1954. In signing the Agricultural Trade Development and Assistance Act of 1954 Eisenhower observed that the act was well suited to "providing a means whereby surplus agricultural commodities in excess of the usual marketings [*sic*] of such commodities may be sold."[72] The legislation gave the CCC more authority to dispose of the surplus overseas. It could sell surplus agricultural commodities for foreign currencies, and those balances would be spent only in the purchasing country or utilize the surplus in barter transactions to obtain essential goods needed in the United States. Surpluses could also be used for famine relief or to help cope with natural disasters in friendly countries, so long as this assistance did not disrupt normal marketing channels. The appellation "friendly governments" excluded surplus farm goods being sold to the Soviet Union or its allies.[73]

Eisenhower had great hopes for the possibilities afforded by the act to expand overseas markets for farm surpluses. Efforts to dispose of surpluses overseas, however, were filled with complexities and problems that Benson at least initially downplayed but were crucial in a Cold War environment. Foreign governments objected to what they thought were attempts to undersell their agricultural output, which raised issues under the General Agreement on Tariffs and Trade (GATT). In poorer countries, officials complained that cheap American agricultural imports would harm the poor, who often barely eked out a living on the land.[74]

Finally, the Department of State was highly skeptical of USDA's efforts. Don Paarlberg characterized the relationships between the Departments of State and Agriculture in the 1950s as quite antagonistic, with State, and its secretary John Foster Dulles, fearful that efforts to address unsound domestic farm policies, by surplus disposal, would disrupt international trade, challenging the US government's effort to promote an open international trading system. Also Benson's willingness to consider selling some surplus commodities to the Soviet Union and its allies—or to countries that would then sell the commodities to them— ran into stiff opposition from the State Department. Denying these countries American food and technology was taken to be part of the basic Cold War strategy of containment. To help alleviate the failures of Soviet agriculture weakened the objectives of that policy, at least from the Department of State's point of view.[75]

Eisenhower endorsed Benson's position that surpluses could be sold to the USSR and its allies. He looked at such sales in terms of what he referred to as "net gains." Apparently, the gain of reducing America's surplus agricultural goods outweighed the State Department's sense of a presumed loss in propping up the Soviet regime and its inefficient agriculture. But sales, as it turned out, were ultimately small.[76] Despite Benson's enthusiasm for the export program, Eisenhower soon accepted that it might somewhat ameliorate, but would not solve, the fundamental problem—that is, of an accumulating government agricultural surplus.[77]

SOIL BANK, 1955–1956

By late 1955 Eisenhower could look to limited successes. The 1954 legislation created some flexibility in setting lower price supports, but they remained above market-clearing levels and congressional resistance to further reductions seemed to be strengthening.[78] Moreover, CCC surplus carryovers and their costs were increasing rapidly and with them the cost of the entire program—a legacy of the years of high supports. CCC inventories, owned by it or subject to purchase agreements, soared from July 1952 through December 1955 from $1.5 billion to $8.7 billion.[79] Almost all of this increase was basics (wheat, corn, and cotton) and dairy products, and about one-third of all basics produced were being acquired by the CCC. A record harvest in 1955 added to the woes as price declines accelerated. The price of food grains declined almost 16 percent from December 1954 to December 1955; the prices of all farm products declined 7 percent during the same period. Almost all farm sectors were affected. Realized net farm income declined 10 percent in a single year. Nevertheless, incomes of producers of the supported basic crops steadied or rose in large part because of the massive, indirect price subsidies. Price supports and acreage restrictions for the basics were also having dramatic effects on other unsupported markets, as growers diverted restricted acreage to feed grains, which was fed to cattle and hogs. Output of all three soared, and prices dropped.[80]

Under these conditions, the price support program for basic commodities rapidly morphed into a huge budget buster. For fiscal year 1956 the Eisenhower administration had budgeted $1.3 billion, but the actual outlay was $3.9 billion, a threefold increase. Annual costs were $1.7 billion in fiscal 1954 and $3.5 billion in fiscal 1955: major sums for an administration driving toward a federal budget surplus with total expenditures of approximately $65 billion.[81]

Export of the surplus would not be a long-term solution. It might at best create a period of stasis and buy more time to get more extensive changes enacted. Agricultural exports began to rise slowly after mid-1953, but commercial exports continued to lag, since high levels of price support priced American exports out of many overseas markets. Exports rose from $2.9 billion in fiscal 1954 to $3.1 billion in 1955. Commodities aided, subsidized, bartered, or sold for foreign currency (left on the US account in the importing country) surged, however, and by fiscal 1955 accounted for 45 percent of all exports.[82] Exports continued to increase throughout the decade, but without more progress on lower supports, overseas sales were of little help. Paarlberg summarized the limited impact of the foreign program and the dilemma of disposing of CCC carryover stocks: "We sold what we could for cash. What we couldn't sell for cash we sold for credit. What we couldn't sell for dollars we sold for foreign currency. What we couldn't get money for we bartered. What we couldn't get anything for we gave away. What we couldn't export by any means we stored. And still the stocks increased."[83]

In late 1955, amid a worsening farm income and price situation, the administration looked to continue the pressure for greater price support reductions and flexibility (75% to 90% of parity for basics would become effective in 1956, if not derailed by Congress). At the same time it sought to supplement these with other approaches that might provide additional short-term and longer-term incentives for farmers to reduce production. Lowering support levels would not be left to do the job alone. Gabriel Hauge noted that many in the administration "always had to fight the fear [in Congress] that if the support floor was moved substantially downward, a bumper crop year would bring in a total collapse in farm prices and a return to the destitution of the 1930s."[84] The dismal declines in farm prices and income in 1955 seemed to reinforce such arguments and would surely have political repercussions in the 1956 election.

The president's political advisers wanted something that would work in helping farmers while being politically palatable for the upcoming election.[85] Eisenhower desired some type of farm program "during this period of restricted production by increasing payment for soil conservation practices for farmers of basic crops."[86] He believed "that some program of soil and water conservation, tied to our existing system, might result in real advantage to our farmers. Moreover, I not only believe that it could be done within reasonable costs, but that we would be investing in the long-term prosperity of the nation."[87]

In response Benson proposed what he called a "Soil Bank." It was based on ideas that had been discussed at USDA as early as 1953 and would pay farmers to retire land and "bank it," thereby reducing production and, ultimately, surpluses. Taking land out of production, of course, was not a new approach to farm problems. Acreage restrictions (allotments) were a cornerstone of the price support program for basics like wheat, cotton, and corn, going back to the AAA of 1938. Farmers could, and usually did, plant other uncontrolled crops on acreage restricted by basic commodity allotments. Now they would be asked to agree to take land out of production completely (turning it into pasture, ponds, etc.) in exchange for lease payments. The administration's plan would have long-term and short-term elements.[88]

The key part of the Soil Bank, publicly announced on January 9, 1956, was the Acreage Reserve Program (ARP). The administration anticipated that the ARP would be a short-term program (three to four years) to idle highly productive land under acreage allotment (wheat, cotton, corn, and rice). It was to be a deferred production plan designed, rather creatively, to reduce production of the supported crop and CCC carryover stocks. Farmers voluntarily participating would receive negotiable certificates for specified quantities of the commodity from CCC stocks or cash at specified rates. The administration hoped that 20–25 million acres of primarily wheat, corn, and some cotton under acreage restrictions would become fallow, rather than be converted to feed grains and livestock. Thus, the program also would relieve pressure on those markets as well.[89]

The administration designed another key element of the plan for the longer term. The Conservation Reserve Program (CRP) was to shift marginally productive agricultural land into forage, trees, and water storage under lease contracts of up to fifteen years in length. It was not meant for farmland used to grow basic crops receiving price support. Rather it was hoped that the CRP acreage voluntarily withdrawn would prevent production of crops, such as feed grains, that were burgeoning on marginal land because of acreage restrictions on basics. The administration hoped that 25 million acres would be taken out of production. Eisenhower estimated that the CRP rentals and cost sharing would cost a billion dollars over a three-year period and the ARP somewhat less. It was hoped that, all told, about 50 million acres of varying quality, or about one-eighth of American productive agricultural land, would be idled. Eisenhower suggested that, if Congress did not enact the Soil Bank, it seriously consider quantitative restrictions on basic crop production (not acreage), a drastic measure in his view.[90]

Eisenhower liked the program but soon acknowledged that it would be very expensive, somewhat more than he had initially thought. Everyone in the cabinet agreed on the "insurance" value of the program. For them, like Eisenhower, the specter of the 1920s and the Great Depression were omnipresent and something "had to be done to insure against any real disaster starting in farm country and then spreading through the whole economy . . . hence the money for the program had to be found." The Soil Bank, combined with lower and more flexible price supports, sought the same long-term goal and would be the answer to arguments for a continuation of the wartime regime of 90 percent of parity. It was hoped that it would aid in the transition to a more benign regulatory scheme of lower price supports and less onerous production controls and acreage restrictions.[91]

Congress enacted legislation establishing the Soil Bank in the Agricultural Act of 1956. But the bill that emerged included a return to 90 percent of parity for basics for one year combined with the ARP and CRP. And parity was to be dual parity, that is, in determining price supports the Department of Agriculture was to employ the modernized formula (based on data from the previous ten years) or the traditional formula, whichever produced the highest price support figure.[92] Eisenhower was particularly incensed that three midwestern Republican senators on the Agriculture Committee—Karl Mundt (SD), Milton Young (ND), and Edward Thye (MN)—voted with the Democrats for 90 percent parity and the Soil Bank. He called them "weaklings" and noted, "This is the kind of thing that makes American politics a dreary and frustrating experience for anyone who has any regard for moral and ethical standards." He thought they "acted even more reprehensively than the Democrats, because they were acting completely for themselves, since the Party is committed to direct opposition to rigid price supports." However, the bill passed the Senate by 50 to 35 and the House 237 to 181, with 27 Republicans defecting.[93]

Despite this erosion of support for his program of flexibility, Eisenhower vetoed the legislation in an election year. Privately, he called the legislation "relief for politicians," and Benson's staff called it a "monstrosity."[94] Publicly, Eisenhower argued that farm incomes had declined in every year but one between 1947 and 1954, while 90 percent parity was in effect. A return to 90 percent for basics for even one year "would put us back on the old road that proved so harmful to farmers." In his view the momentum his administration had established toward lower, more flexible supports for basics would be irretrievably lost by combining such diametrically opposed policies.[95]

In the veto message, the president described the bill as self-defeating. The Soil Bank, he said, "would provide an income incentive to farmers to reduce production temporarily so that surplus stocks might be reduced." But "the return to war-time rigid 90 percent of parity supports for the basic commodities" would invite increases in "price-depressing surpluses." He hammered at now familiar themes: support prices at 90 percent parity for farmers would not keep market prices for their goods from falling as demand changed and surpluses accumulated.[96] His message also lashed out at acreage controls, which he characterized as the inevitable bedfellow of 90 percent of parity for basic crops. Eisenhower noted that, as surpluses mounted, the government turned more and more to acreage controls. He clearly found such use of government power distasteful. Drastic reductions in acreage for basic commodities like wheat and corn had only resulted in modest reductions in production. They also led to loss of economies of scale and uneconomical farming. He reviewed other problems with acreage controls: as farmers turned to planting new, unrestricted crops on their idled land, their prices declined, which lowered income throughout the farm economy. Finally, Eisenhower believed that enforcement of acreage restrictions was difficult at best.[97]

Politically, the veto looked dangerous to nervous congressional Republicans, who pressed the president to sign the bill. Eisenhower's White House staff also strongly advised him to sign the bill because it was an election year. But Secretary Benson thought that the legislation was designed to embarrass the president and was a "political" bill. He recommended a veto. Benson reminded the president that he had once told him that what was good in principle ought to be done and "if it was right in principle in the long run it would be good politically."[98]

So, Eisenhower went on national television and radio to defend his veto. He chided Congress (narrowly controlled by the Democrats) for producing a "hodge-podge [of a bill] in which the bad provisions more than cancelled out the good." Appealing to farmers, he argued that it was their falling incomes that motivated his thinking about agriculture. While obviously trying to make some political points, Eisenhower argued that farm bills that did not address the fundamental issue of surpluses made the problems of declining prices and farm incomes worse. It was a tough argument to make, because intuitively farmers look at the short run, and they saw high price supports as a way to help them out as their incomes dropped. Eisenhower, looking at the larger context, argued that prices set without regard to the supply and demand ended up hurting farmers.[99] During negotiations prior to the legislation's passage, Benson had suggested continuing 82.5 percent of parity for basics for another year (1956) as a possible compromise. Now, in conjunction with his veto, Eisenhower did just that. By administrative action he set price supports for wheat, corn, cotton, rice, and peanuts for 1956 at levels of at least 82.5 percent of parity. USDA had already set these at levels of 75 to 81 percent of parity for 1956 crops. So, the 75 percent of parity floor of the 1954 act was postponed yet another year. Eisenhower and the severely disappointed Benson hoped that this action would benefit the administration in the coming legislative fight.[100]

Nevertheless, Midwest Republican members of Congress were dismayed at the veto. Eisenhower's continued personal popularity made overriding it out of the question. His veto, and later threats of other vetoes, now and in his second term, gave the president considerable leverage in dealing with Congress on farm issues. A subsequent attempt to override the president's veto in the House garnered less than half of the votes cast, well short of the two-thirds needed. Only twenty Republicans deserted the president this time.[101]

In a little over a month, Congress sent the president a new version of what became the Agricultural Act of 1956. Eisenhower signed it on May 24, even though he was by no means entirely pleased by all of its new provisions. Yet, the bill authorized the Soil Bank with funds for three years—$750 million for the Acreage Reserve and $450 million for the Conservation Reserve. He justified signing the legislation into law because of the Soil Bank, which in his view outweighed the negative features of the bill. The latter provisions included freezing acreage allotments for rice and cotton at 1956 levels for 1957 and 1958, which limited the government's ability to use this tool to reduce output.[102] The application of modern parity to wheat, corn, and peanuts was postponed for another year.[103] Because of the political wrangling over the legislation the act would have little impact on the 1956 planting season. Despite this, about 12 million acres were put in the ARP and much less in the CRP, but these figures increased in the following year.[104]

Concerns within the administration about the political impact of agriculture policy on the president's reelection proved to be excessive. Eisenhower handily won in 1956. He carried the Midwest farm states, although his percentage of the vote was down slightly in Iowa, Kansas, Minnesota, Oklahoma, and South Dakota from 1952. Even so, Eisenhower's personal popularity was not enough to end Democratic control of Congress. The opposition party narrowly increased its control of each chamber, with two new seats in the House (233 to 200) and one in the Senate (49 to 47).

AGRICULTURE IN THE SECOND TERM

Despite his huge election victory, agriculture policy in Eisenhower's second term continued to be characterized by limited and measured successes. Legislation allowing lower and more flexible price support was enacted in 1958, but Congress flatly rejected the president's calls for more steps in that direction afterward. Surpluses (and their costs) stabilized for a short period but then rose again to new, higher levels after 1958. The Soil Bank programs proved more expensive and less useful than anticipated. After the Democrats swept the 1958 congressional elections, Eisenhower's ability to influence farm policy was mainly negative. He could veto farm legislation that he opposed and usually have that veto sustained, but the chance of enacting his own proposals evaporated. Beginning in 1957 aggressive administrative implementation of the price support program by the USDA, within existing statutes, and vigorous promotion of more dramatic legislative changes in the program made Benson the most disliked member of the Eisenhower administration. At the end of his term, Eisenhower was frustrated with agricultural matters and mused about how simpler dealings with both sides of the aisle in Congress would have been without farm policy battles. He clearly seemed weary of the fight.[105]

At the beginning of the second term, however, the climate for agricultural regulatory reform looked better than it would later. Indeed, there might even have been reason for some optimism. In early 1956 farm prices and net income began to rise from the depressed levels of 1955. They continued to do so gradually through 1957, then spiked upward from late 1957 through mid-1958. This development was certainly a factor in Congress's willingness to legislate further flexibility in the price support program in the Agricultural Act of 1958. But these positive developments did not last. After mid-1958 farm prices resumed their decline, and real, net farm income fell to levels below the low points of 1948 and 1955. The years 1958, 1959, and 1960 provided successive record harvests, despite the fact that the acreage under cultivation was the lowest since 1916. Farm productivity continued its dramatic gains aided by generally good weather.[106]

Surpluses remained a huge problem. As always, they were concentrated largely in the basic commodities, with wheat supplies an especially serious problem by the end of the decade. Somewhat lower price supports, rising exports, and some success in taking acreage out of production under the ARP were not sufficient to address chronic problems of oversupply. Nor could supports, still above market-clearing levels, offset the effects of rising productivity and sluggish demand. At the beginning of 1959 commodities owned by the CCC under loan and purchase agreement were $9.2 billion, slightly above the prior peak levels of 1955. About 80 percent of this figure was for three basics—in order, wheat, corn, and cotton—where price supports were mandatory.

The situation was only marginally better at the end of Eisenhower's term in 1961, and the program remained very expensive. In fiscal year 1959 the administration's net budget outlay for price supports was $5.4 billion; $4.3 billion of that was for mandatory basics. The original budget estimate had been $3.2 billion. In fact, for fiscal years 1956–59, actual outlays, which were quite unpredictable, exceeded budgeted outlays in three of the four years by $2.6 billion in 1956, $1.6 billion in 1957, and $2.2 billion in 1959. Only in 1958 were the expenditures under budget, and then only by $100 million. These budget-busting figures were a source of irritation and anger to Eisenhower during his determined drive toward fiscal restraint in his second term. Budget expenditures declined some in the final year of his presidency to $4.5 billion but remained unacceptable to Eisenhower. In early 1959 Eisenhower noted that the outlays for wheat represented $7,000 for each of the nation's 1.5 million wheat farms and that 90 percent of the expenditures went to the largest 50 percent of these farms. In cotton the figures were even more skewed: $10,000 per farm for a million cotton farms. Seventy-five percent of these expenditures went to the largest fourth of the farms.[107]

Agricultural exports rose, driven by federal barter, subsidy, and restricted foreign currency sales, which represented more than 40 percent of the totals. They peaked at $4.7 billion in fiscal year 1958 and remained high—$4.5 billion in fiscal year 1960.[108] Such heavily subsidized exports stabilized surplus levels but were not successful in significantly reducing them. The late 1950s saw an upward trend in agricultural exports, which would continue and accelerate during the rest of the century.[109] Full dollar external convertibility in Western Europe after 1958 contributed to growing sales there of American agricultural products, but an overvalued postwar dollar and limited foreign currency reserves of American allies, along with restrictive trade rules of some trading partners, limited growth of commercial sales. Benson was fond of saying that "we [and the world] will have to eat our way out of this." That ultimately occurred, but from the perspective of the late 1950s the problem looked intractable.[110] Huge food aid "sales" in the mid-1960s to famine-plagued South Asia later helped reduce the surplus in the interim. Not until the end of the fixed exchange rate, Bretton Woods system in 1971 and the resulting depreciation of the dollar made American goods more attractive to foreign purchasers did commercial export markets greatly expand. The chronic surplus problem essentially disappeared as a public policy concern by 1973, reappearing only briefly and periodically thereafter.

BATTLE JOINED AGAIN, 1957–1958

Weeks after the second inaugural, Benson presented a formal paper to the cabinet on long-range agricultural policy. He thought that the respite from declining farm prices and incomes of the last year created an opening for further reforms of the price support program. Because both the disposal program and acreage controls seemed to be working better than anticipated, Benson thought it opportune to approach the chairman of the Senate Agriculture Committee, Allen J. Ellender (D-LA). The secretary wanted to lay out the problems, as he saw them, in a public letter. Benson hoped that focusing a discussion on the conceptual and practical challenges of administering agricultural policy could lead to drafting legislation with the assistance of congressional committees. Benson, however, remained totally convinced that any legislation had to greatly expand USDA discretionary powers in setting price support levels and acreage allotments, and his letter to Ellender reflected his view.[111]

Eisenhower supported the idea of a broad consideration of agricultural policy problems with the senator and his committee. He thought that soon after a presidential election, following the dissipation of the intense pressures of a political campaign, was probably a good time to address long-term problems. But the president believed that specific legislative proposals were best postponed until later. Eisenhower had no desire to provoke a sharp conflict with Congress, clearly reflecting the bruising, election-year battle over the Soil Bank. In describing problems and alternatives to Ellender—instead of proposals—the administration, however, betrayed a degree of frustration with the political fights over its agricultural policy. Its discussions reflect a certain naiveté that Ellender, those on his committee, and other opponents in Congress could be brought into some type of support for the administration's farm program by such a nonconfrontational approach. Many at the cabinet meeting, especially Secretary Humphrey, were concerned about the upward spiral in the cost of federal price support programs in the first four years and openly wondered "where they would go in the next four years." Humphrey wanted to "publish the checks that the big farmers get" and that "would blow the roof off" but agreed with Eisenhower that incremental increases in USDA discretion in setting supports and allotments would probably be the best they could achieve under the circumstances.[112]

Ellender did not use Benson's initiative as an opportunity to open a dialogue on the larger issues of farm policy. In fact, the administration may have overlooked a good opportunity. The political economy of agriculture was always more willing to look at lower, more flexible support levels in good times (i.e., 1948), and 1957 was the middle of a two-and-a-half-year period of rising prices. Politically, Eisenhower had just overwhelmingly won reelection, and the Democrats controlled Congress by only narrow margins. But both Eisenhower and the normally combative Benson declined to press major farm legislation in 1957. Further legislative initiatives in agriculture would have to wait until 1958, and by that time Congress and the administration would be more focused on national security concerns and the worst postwar recession to date.[113]

While the administration did not aggressively pursue legislation in 1957, Benson moved quickly to reduce wheat price supports early in the year, under his existing legislative and administrative authority. Wheat was rapidly becoming the most troublesome, and expensive, supported basic commodity. Benson set the support price at the statutory minimum of 75 percent of parity (the 82.5% minimum had expired at the end of 1956), and acreage allotments were put at 55 million acres nationally to try to move the market price closer to support levels. At the time, however, USDA estimated that this allotment acreage was over four times what would be necessary to meet domestic and overseas demand for wheat. But this was the minimum allowed by legislation, since Congress had frozen national allotments of wheat in 1956 in response to continued concerns about farm income levels. As a result of reduction in parity percentage, the support price for wheat fell from $2.00 to $1.78 per bushel.[114]

All hell broke loose in wheat-growing areas. Democrats loudly denounced Benson and the administration. Congressmen and senators from states where farmers were most affected were outraged. There was a bipartisan call for Eisenhower to replace Benson. In fact, thirty Republican farm state members of Congress privately asked the secretary, in the interest of the party, to resign. He refused. At a speech before the National Mechanical Corn Picking Contest in Sioux Falls, South Dakota, in fall 1957, a few angry farmers hurled eggs at the secretary as he began his speech.[115]

President Eisenhower, however, forcefully defended Benson throughout 1957. By the end of 1957, the administration was planning new farm legislation. In a meeting for Republican legislative leaders on December 4, Benson again suggested legislative changes to allow greater flexibility and lower price supports, but the administration was now trying to put a "face" on the "special interest" nature of the program as an indirect subsidy program for a few large farmers. Specifically, Benson emphasized that almost half (48 percent) of all price support payments went to wheat and cotton farmers. Overall, he observed that three-quarters of price supports ($3.3 billion) were paid to those operating large-scale farms. While basics accounted for only one-quarter of farm income, most of the support payments went to farmers of the basics. They were located in only 25 percent of the states, mostly in the cotton South. Such a focus meant, as before, a continuation of the battle with the most senior leaders of the Democratic Party.[116]

In his special message to Congress, the president rehashed the incongruities of existing agricultural policy, which he had attacked for five years: wartime price support programs were inappropriate for the Cold War and an era of surging agricultural productivity. Eisenhower, however, was able to note some progress. Farm prices were rising, and surpluses "appear to have passed their peak."[117] It wouldn't last.

The proposed legislation gave the secretary of agriculture greater authority over acreage allotments and proposed widening the range of support prices for wheat, cotton, rice, peanuts, and tobacco, from 60 to 90 percent of parity from the current 75 to 90 percent. Eisenhower wanted to give the USDA secretary authority "to increase allotments up to 50 percent above the levels determined by existing formulas" for all basics except corn, for which they would be eliminated. While it may have seemed incongruous to raise allotments of basics, the administration believed that small allotments were retarding efficiency, as in cotton, where 80 percent of the allotments were fifteen acres or less. Eisenhower echoed the refrain that allotments were a very imperfect tool to control production; were difficult to enforce; and penalized smaller farmers, who found it difficult to operate with reduced acreage. Lower support prices and higher or no allotments would be sufficient to "clear" markets, reduce expenditures, and above all, promote economic freedom.[118] The administration also wanted to extend the P.L. 480 program for a year, with an increased authorization of $1.5 billion, and expand the RDP.[119]

Significantly, Eisenhower recommended ending the Acreage Reserve initiative with the 1958 crop. The program always had been envisioned as short-term, as opposed to the Conservation Reserve, which he wanted to expand. The Acreage Reserve was proving enormously expensive because it took prime land out of use. Furthermore, the program had gotten a slow start in 1956, when about 12 million acres were banked, increasing to about 21 million acres in 1957. The program cost over $1.5 billion over its three years. While the administration claimed the program had reduced wheat production by almost "175 million bushels, cotton by 2 million bales, and corn by 220 million bushels below what it would otherwise have been," its cost in a recession year and in the shadow of a potentially huge budget deficit doomed it. In the last year of the program (1958) about 17 million acres were banked.[120] The administration proposed to expand the long-term Conservation Reserve with $450 million budgeted for 1959. In fact, this program was eventually scaled back to $375 million, because of budget concerns and perceptions that it was not efficiently addressing the core of the surplus problem. A maximum of about 29 million acres of marginal land was in the reserve, under lease, by 1960, when funding ended. Thereafter, participation declined and the last acres came out of the reserve in 1972. For the years 1957–60 the Conservation Reserve cost about $1 billion.[121]

Congress's response to Eisenhower's proposals, in an election year, was rather simple: it passed legislation "freezing" parity for basics and dairy products at 1957 levels for a year and freezing basics' allotment levels for two years. The margin in the Senate was seven votes and thirty-eight votes in the House. Many Republican farm state members of Congress in both houses voted with the Democrats. Benson remained unpopular in many farm areas, and Republican political professionals were concerned—some went so far as to say "panicked"—about discontent in rural America. In August 1957, a Democrat, William Proxmire, was elected overwhelmingly in Wisconsin in a special election called following the death of Senator Joseph McCarthy in May. Proxmire ran against Benson's policies and promoted income deficiency payments modeled after the Brannan Plan. Such proposals were becoming an increasingly popular theme with Democrats, who scored a surprise victory.[122]

Nervousness in the party notwithstanding, Eisenhower vetoed the bill in March 1958, saying he wanted a farm "thaw" not a "freeze." As before, Congress sustained the president's veto, but not before a heated meeting of Republican legislative leaders at the White House, where they aired strident criticism of Benson's administrative actions (lowering supports for wheat in 1957 and dairy products in early 1958) and his general combativeness. Eisenhower, though he wholeheartedly supported Benson's actions on the merits, later had to remind Benson of the absolute need to be flexible and less rhetorically rigid with the administration's allies in Congress, if they ever hoped to accomplish anything.[123]

Eisenhower made a brief radio and television address the evening he vetoed the bill. He objected to what he considered backsliding from changes made in 1954 and 1956. His message was blunter than on previous occasions. He summed up his opposition to the legislation: "We need less, not more governmental interference in agriculture."[124] Congress passed the compromise Agricultural Act of 1958 in August. It did not include everything that Eisenhower wanted, but he signed the bill into law because it achieved some of what he had originally proposed. Benson remarked, "The gaping hole through which the surpluses were pouring in had been shut a little more. It was still not closed. With the Congress to be elected in 1958 would rest our final hope of completing the operation."[125]

Congressional Democrats saw things differently but were willing to compromise, at least temporarily. They hoped that they would gain enough votes in the coming congressional elections to override any Eisenhower veto of farm legislation they would enact in the new session—a veto-proof majority. This was a miscalculation. The administration got its last major piece of farm reform legislation, in part because farm prices were rising rapidly for the first time in years. But, in the last two years of his term, Democrats and their Republican allies were unable to override Eisenhower vetoes of most major farm legislation, even after the Republican debacle in the 1958 congressional elections. The 1958 act lowered minimum price supports from 75 to 65 percent of parity, or 90 percent of the three-year average price, and eliminated acreage allotments for corn. A referendum would be held for corn farmers to pick between these two choices.[126] The administration hoped they would choose the latter. Price supports for feed grains became mandatory. The act ended the Acreage Reserve and set support levels for cotton and rice at 70–90 percent of parity for the 1961 crops and 65–90 percent of parity for the 1962 crops, but acreage allotments for cotton and rice were frozen.[127]

THE END OF THE BATTLE, 1959–1960

In the elections of November 1958, as expected, Democrats dramatically increased their control of both the House and Senate. Republicans lost forty-eight seats in the House (twenty-three from the Midwest) and thirteen in the Senate. Agricultural policy played a part in these results, but also the economy remained sluggish; there was continuing concern generated by Sputnik; southerners resented the use of federal troops in Little Rock to enforce desegregation; there was an unnerving confrontation with the People's Republic of China over the islands of Quemoy and Matsu in the Formosa Straights; and Sherman Adams, Eisenhower's chief of staff, resigned because he had accepted gifts from Bernard Goldfine, a party contributor.[128]

With Democratic gains in Congress, Eisenhower's last two years in office were difficult. The political atmosphere in Washington took on a tone of intensified partisanship. Congressional Democrats stepped up criticism of many aspects of administration policy, including agriculture. Ironically, the opposition to Eisenhower farm policy diverged. Liberal Democrats increasingly looked to direct product parity payments or Brannan Plan–type income support, while conservative southern Democrats and an increasing number of Farm Belt Republicans wanted higher parity percentages (90 percent) under existing CCC programs.[129] Though initially hesitant to do so, Eisenhower followed Benson's advice and proposed new farm legislation in 1959, largely because of his concerns over a growing budget deficit. Because of the possibility of unanticipated expenditures on agricultural programs, Eisenhower was willing "to do a vast amount of work to get something achieved." At a meeting with legislative leaders on December 15, 1958, the president observed that it was "paradoxical that he and others should have to spend so much time conferring on a $185 million program only to be informed that the budget would be increased $3 billion because of agricultural surpluses."[130]

As Eisenhower contemplated farm legislation, he initially saw some reason for optimism. The quest, however, became quixotic, for in late 1958 it looked as if dairy and cotton surpluses had peaked and almost liquidated. But the situation changed. The next two years saw increased production in cotton and other basics, and CCC warehouses began to fill again. Farm prices reversed their two-plus-year rise and began to fall again, never a positive environment for Congress to consider market-oriented farm legislation. By far the most serious problem was with wheat, where Benson believed that foreign disposal had accomplished as much as it could toward reducing the surplus.[131]

The administration could take some comfort in the action of corn farmers, who in late 1958 voted for a more market-oriented regime. Given a choice between (1) discontinuing acreage allotments for 1959 and subsequent crops and receiving supports at 90 percent of the average farm price over the last three years, but not less than 65 percent of parity, or (2) keep existing acreage allotments with 75 to 90 percent of parity, farmers chose the former. Price supports for most feed grains, including corn, became mandatory at these much lower levels.[132] Benson thought that the results of the referendum signaled farmers' heightened disgust with the price support and allotment system, but the markets for feed grains, much of which was used on the farms that produced it, was sufficiently distinguishable from other basics that the administration may have read too much precedential value into the corn farmers' choice.[133]

Despite the hostile political climate, the administration proposed new farm legislation to Congress in January 1959. The recent corn referendum was a model for many of its recommendations. Eisenhower pounded at old refrains and proposed that Congress enact "modern parity," based on recent market prices. The USDA secretary would have discretion to set supports and loan rates at between 75 and 90 percent of this figure. This represented a radical juxtaposition to dogged congressional support for 90 percent of historic parity. Eisenhower noted that corn growers had recently voted for program changes and cautioned that "despite the on rush . . . of science in agriculture the Congress still prefers to relate price supports to existing standards." Instead, he continued to prefer lower flexible supports not tied to arcane historical formulas (traditional parity); aggressive surplus disposal; and opposition to the growing interest in Brannan Plan–type direct cash payments and income support, which he said "would get us into greater trouble." Additionally, the president attacked the concentration of price support payments to a minority of large farmers and juxtaposed it with the lack of congressional enthusiasm for the RDP, which was designed to open up new sources of income to improve the quality of life for poorer, marginal farmers.[134]

While the president's proposal was in the House Agriculture Committee, Eisenhower and Republican legislative leaders contemplated future directions at an April 28, 1959, legislative meeting. Estimates were that, without something like Eisenhower's proposal, CCC carryover stocks and obligations would reach $12 billion by 1963—they were above $8 billion in 1959. According to budget experts, even if Eisenhower's suggestions became law, the situation might be stabilized between $9 billion and $10 billion. Because the Democrats in Congress now appeared to have the votes to determine agricultural policy, the president thought "that perhaps this was the proper time, in view of the proximity of a $12 billion investment, to make some really startling recommendations that would cut farm surpluses down to size." He stated his willingness to take any blame that might develop from a strong administration proposal at this time—even to the point of cutting supports to 50 percent in the face of the tremendous surpluses. Vice President Nixon, obviously thinking of 1960, believed this would invite severe criticism and go nowhere anyway. Nixon was right.[135]

Eisenhower also began to talk more about questions of equity concerning who received price support payments. "The President stressed several times his belief that support payments ought to be cut off as regards any one having an income of a certain amount, say $25,000," a matter of increasing interest to him since at least 1956. But, no restrictions of any substance were enacted during his administration or for that matter until the 1970s.[136] The large payments to certain individuals were an increasing source of personal irritation to Eisenhower, but he preferred to use them to highlight incongruities in existing programs, not as specific targets for reform. Of course, Congress expressed little interest in such changes, no matter how he presented them.[137] Other initiatives were not pressed. Don Paarlberg, who from 1958 to 1961 was the special assistant for economic affairs, wanted more publicity and funding for the RDP. By 1959, however, Eisenhower was becoming much less interested in programs that involved increased expenditures, even if Congress could be convinced to end its ambivalence toward the program.[138]

Basically, Congress ignored Eisenhower's legislative recommendations in 1959. It sent the president a bill that addressed wheat, the commodity most seriously in crisis. The bill authorized a 25 percent reduction in acreage with a restoration of price support levels at 90 percent of historic parity. Eisenhower vetoed the bill, observing tartly that "the bill disregards the facts of modern agriculture. The history of acreage control programs—particularly in the case of wheat— reveals that they do not control production."[139] The same day, the president vetoed a tobacco price support bill. He described it as taking a "long step backward by resurrecting 90 per cent of 'old parity' as one basis for determining the support level for tobacco." Sales of tobacco overseas faced increased competition, and Eisenhower attributed the problem to the high level of price supports. Congress tried but failed to override his vetoes.[140]

Because of the unfriendly political atmosphere and the presidential election, the administration sent no legislation to Congress in 1960. It seemed pointless. Instead, on February 9, 1960, Eisenhower sent a message to Congress that outlined "principles" that should be followed if he were to approve legislation. The president indicated that he would only sign legislation that adhered to his broad goals. His principles included a commitment to price support levels that were realistically related to production controls. Price supports should not be so high as to stimulate excessive production. He said that he would accept realistic parity percentages or levels based on recent market prices, which had been his 1959 proposal. Brannan Plan–type provisions for direct (cash) payments or income support would be unacceptable. His principles also ruled out multiple price support levels (export or domestic) because of foreign policy concerns.[141]

His message betrayed a high level of frustration with Congress. "It defies common sense," Eisenhower said, "to continue to encourage, at the cost of many millions of tax dollars, the building of ever larger excess of products that, as they accumulate, depress farm prices and endanger the future of our farmers."[142] No one really expected Congress to enact significant farm legislation for basics in 1960, and it did not. At the meeting of legislative leaders a week before he sent his message to Congress, Eisenhower ended the discussion of agricultural policy on a particularly negative note. "The discussion was closed with the President's comment that after seven years of worrying [over] the farm problems, the fight seems to get more bitter and the situation worse every year, and Sec. Benson endeavored to reassure the President that much progress had been made and the area remaining for action was steadily being narrowed."[143]

CONCLUSION

Benson was correct: progress had been made and the issues that remained had narrowed. The USDA's *History of Agricultural Price-Support and Adjustment Programs, 1933–84* observed that "early price support programs, especially those during and after World War II, relied heavily on high price support levels and controls that were mandatory after they were approved by producers of the crops affected. Since the early 1950s, the trend has been to rely more on the marketplace to set prices and voluntary programs to reduce acreage."[144] This was the goal of the stillborn 1948 act and of the Eisenhower administration that was pressed home with significant success between 1953 and 1961.

Eisenhower and his contentious USDA secretary Benson sought to establish a market-driven postwar farm policy in the difficult economic and political environment that had emerged out of the 1940s. Within a year after his administration took office, Eisenhower began what he knew would be a long-term battle to reorient price support policy for basic commodities toward the market. Congress was dominated by powerful committee chairmen and members tied to 90 percent of parity for wheat, corn, cotton, dairy, and a few other farm products that had been the source of farm "problems" for more than a decade. It was not just a partisan struggle with Democrats, though that dimension was crucial to understanding agriculture and other issues. Eisenhower also faced tremendous pressures from legislators within his own party who favored high, inflexible supports. His strategy involved compromise at crucial moments, forceful use of the presidential veto, and skillful use of Secretary Benson to "take the heat." The latter often kept Eisenhower above the political fray and preserved his reservoir of political capital. If one reads his political memoir, *Cross Fire,* the intense and ideologically driven Benson often seemed to relish his role as the "bad guy."

Furthermore, the economic environment when Eisenhower took office was not conducive to changes in the system. Slack demand both at home and overseas, coupled with surging agricultural productivity (which continued through the century, accelerating again after 1985), depressed farm prices. With high supports for basics, government surpluses piled up and their costs became a major and often unpredictable budget item. Despite real progress on price support flexibility, surplus levels increased. Wheat and cotton price supports stood at 75 percent at the end of 1960, and corn at 65 percent. The moral issues and economic costs associated with price supports incensed Eisenhower and were the cause of his intense frustration with farm issues at the end of his term.

Eventually, however, the administration's huge efforts to resuscitate and expand overseas markets for American products radically altered American agriculture and the contours of price support programs. American agricultural exports had been on a plateau since the mid-1920s and, as discussed earlier in this chapter, had declined rather dramatically in the early 1950s. The export promotion efforts of the USDA achieved some success; and more was accomplished under the foreign and domestic programs that came out of the Agricultural Trade Development and Assistance Act of 1954. World markets, however, had very limited buying power in the 1950s. A good part of the world was communist, and what was not had limited hard currency reserves or largely nonconvertible currencies. Many of the American foreign aid food programs were seen merely as ways to dump the surplus overseas at any cost. But eventually the purchasing power of overseas buyers increased. The external free convertibility of Western European currencies after 1958 was an important first step. Others followed in succeeding decades, and the developing world markets established initially by foreign aid in the 1950s subsequently became commercial customers. As early as 1955 American exports had broken out of their three-decade plateau and began a steep increase that continues today. According to USDA, by the time of the Food and Agriculture Act of 1965, "it became obvious that a more market-oriented [price support] policy was necessary to help American farmers take advantage of the rising export demands."[145] The drive for that policy began in 1954. Eisenhower knew that lower and more flexible price supports would increase American export competitiveness (and reduce surpluses) in the long term.

That is not to say that Eisenhower would have been pleased with the direction of agricultural policy after he left office, or even today. Price supports and indirect payments were the primary means to accomplish farm policy in the 1950s. Eisenhower sought a regime that would free up markets by loosening and lowering supports, the linchpin of the system in the 1940s and 1950s. Throughout his two terms he cautioned against other schemes for basic commodities, like direct payments or income subsidy ideas similar to the Brannan Plan. Both were associated with the liberal wing of the Democratic Party. During the 1960s lower price supports for basics were tied to world market prices and land diversion payments. The Democrats rapidly lost interest in mandatory controls but increasingly relied on direct payments of cash or commodities to support prices. By 1973, during the Nixon administration, surpluses of basics had finally disappeared. The Agriculture and Consumer Protection Act of 1973 further reduced the reliance of policymakers on the price support loan program that had been the bane of the Eisenhower administration. Instead the act introduced the concept of "target" prices to be used when market prices fell below target levels. "Deficiency payments" would make up the difference—direct subsidy based on crop income— echoing the Brannan Plan. Lower price support levels, however, still existed and played a role in the scheme. Sometimes this was standby only, but deficiency payments could not exceed the difference between the target price and price support loan rates, thus limiting expenditures.[146]

In variations this two-tiered system existed for more than twenty years, though numerous pieces of legislation tinkered with it to respond to short-term shifts in agricultural markets. For the most part controls were voluntary and a Conservation Reserve–program was instituted in 1985, and continues today. Finally, in 1996 Congress ended supply controls in the Federal Agriculture Improvement and Reform Act (often called the Freedom to Farm Act). New types of income support payments were instituted, and these were not tied to farmers' current production decisions. Direct income support was "decoupled" from short-term production decisions, and it replaced the old price support system. The cost of such programs remains significant. The USDA argues that "the evolution of farm policy from one based on supply controls and high price supports to one based primarily on direct Government payments has undoubtedly reduced the economic efficiencies of resource allocation and price distortions associated with farm programs."[147] Eisenhower argued against such schemes in the 1950s, while seeking lower price supports and greater flexibility in their use. It is probable that he would condemn these schemes as "giving up on (appropriately regulated) free enterprise" and "eroding the moral fiber of farmers" unless they were severely circumscribed. Nevertheless, his efforts in the 1950s changed the direction of agricultural regulation, even if the final result was not something that Eisenhower would have sought.

CHAPTER 5

A Coalescing Antitrust Policy

When Eisenhower took office in 1953, antitrust law was not one of his immediate concerns. Nevertheless, Eisenhower, his politically attuned attorney general Herbert Brownell, and others in the administration understood the importance of antitrust. On a strictly political level, traditional antitrust law and policy, based on a priori assumptions about the dangers of concentrated market power and certain types of corporate conduct, presented a potential minefield for a new "pro-business" Republican administration. Democrats routinely predicted that an Eisenhower White House would weaken or even abandon enforcement of the antitrust laws. This, of course, did not occur. Indeed, as a matter of Eisenhower's long-term Cold War goal of fostering a dynamic market economy, antitrust policy assumed a significant role.[1]

By the early 1950s many leaders of major industrial corporations were deeply concerned about what they perceived as increasing legal uncertainty and trends in recent government-initiated prosecutions and subsequent court decisions under Sections 1 and 2 of the Sherman Act. An initial goal of the incoming Eisenhower administration was to address these questions, directly and in a timely manner. But it was certainly not the only, or even the most important, White House priority.

The incoming president and his administration also wanted to reduce the partisanship and rhetoric, or at least the appearance of it, which had become associated with recent antitrust policy and enforcement. Some prominent American business executives argued in public and in private to their friends like Eisenhower that for twenty years Democratic administrations had sometimes used antitrust enforcement as a weapon against those businessmen who had vigorously opposed New Deal and Fair Deal policies. The incoming administration initially took such arguments quite seriously. Democratic partisans charged that such Republican anxieties were simply examples of unremitting hostility to antitrust. The new administration, however, moved quickly to focus on the allegations, because if antitrust policy was to support Eisenhower's ideas about a free enterprise economy, the shaping and implementation of policy could not be, or give the appearance of being, overtly political. In fact, the political rhetoric of antitrust in the 1940s and 1950s, fueled by Democratic legislators like Senators Estes Kefauver and Joseph O'Mahoney and Representative Emanuel Cellar, was intense and widely followed. Public visibility of the issue and the partisan feelings that surrounded it were probably greater during this era than they have ever been since, despite widespread public acceptance of the basic tenants of antitrust principles.

The incoming administration sought to put antitrust and the maintenance of competition in a dynamic Cold War economy on a firmer footing. The goal was to get beyond the previous two decades of fits, starts, and dramatic swings in policy and heated partisan rhetoric. The new administration aimed for a sustained period of forceful and consistent enforcement. These heightened concerns about the direction of antitrust policy and intense partisanship were coupled with a recent flourish of significant amendments to existing statutes. These changes culminated a twenty-year period of dramatic, sometimes contradictory, legislative changes. They included the, as yet untested, 1950 Cellar-Kefauver Amendment to Clayton Act merger legislation and recent (1952) amendments to the Robinson-Patman Act. The Eisenhower administration would have substantial opportunity in these and other areas to strengthen antitrust statutes, enforcement, and case law, and by the end of the decade the administration had tackled all of these antitrust issues. Its efforts largely coalesced into a consistent Cold War antitrust policy, which provided a stable framework for economic growth and business decision making.

As with its approach to agricultural policy, the White House adopted a long-term view of implementing its antitrust policy, but it moved quickly. An early step was to conduct a full-scale review of pending antitrust cases by the Department of Justice (DOJ). This analysis found no real evidence of politicization of antitrust prosecution and enforcement in the recent past. Similarly, a subsequent study of antitrust law by an independent panel, under the auspices of Attorney General Brownell, generally endorsed prior legal precedents and expressed little sympathy with the business community's concern about the direction of court cases. The administration used this study mainly as a vehicle to dampen doctrinal concerns and propose aggressive implementation of existing policy by undertaking significant case prosecutions and promoting additional legislative initiatives.

Eisenhower's personal effort in effecting change in antitrust policy was mostly indirect; potential fallout from the politically hyped antitrust rhetoric of the period encouraged him to maneuver carefully. Nevertheless, the president was convinced of the need for a vigorous but streamlined antitrust policy and serious DOJ implementation of it. Eisenhower, however, did not exercise rigid control over the DOJ, leaving day-to-day activities in the hands of senior officials.[2] Attorney General Brownell, the president's trusted political confidant, noted that

> he delegated a great deal to his cabinet officers: They were the ones, in his view, who were on the front lines, taking the blows. If they were successful, fine, if they faltered, he would get someone else. I discussed this with him on a number of occasions, and he articulated this view to me. In my own case, it meant I was given responsibility and authority in a number of controversial areas such as civil rights, *antitrust* [emphasis added] and internal security, all of which were likely to be divisive. It was wise for him to appear a bit distanced from day-to-day events to maintain his public support, which I feel is necessary for a successful presidency. Of course, he exercised control behind the scenes. There was never any doubt in the Eisenhower administration about who was in charge and who made the decisions: The president did.[3]

Overall, by 1961, the political demagoguery and the doctrinal and enforcement uncertainties that characterized many antitrust issues when Eisenhower took office had been substantially muted. Government enforcement of the Sherman Act was aggressive, and private litigation, encouraged by the administration, was for the first time becoming a major factor in antitrust enforcement. The DOJ had fashioned the Clayton Act, revised by the Cellar-Kefauver Amendment, into a significant tool for regulating merger activity. Though a substantial body of case law did not exist (the Supreme Court would not directly address the new statute until 1962), merger cases were being litigated successfully, and trends in case law were very favorable to the administration. If defendants opposed DOJ action in regard to merger and antitrust, litigation could take an inordinate time to reach a final conclusion—often a span of four years or more. So tracing the threads of any administration's "contribution" to antitrust policy requires a long-term perspective. Partisan-generated fears that the first Republican administration in twenty years would "eliminate the antitrust laws" proved unfounded, however. Indeed, Antitrust Division policies of Eisenhower's Department of Justice were aggressive, in many instances innovative, as it adopted perspectives in case litigation and enforcement tools for the first time or reinvigorated dormant past practices.[4]

THE ROOSEVELT AND TRUMAN LEGACIES, 1933–1953

The antitrust legacy from twenty years (1933–53) of Democratic presidential control could best be described as inconsistent, idiosyncratic, and ambiguous. It's not surprising that such an approach to antitrust troubled those responsible for business decision making and their Republican political allies. During the Roosevelt administration's National Recovery Administration (NRA), from 1933 to 1935, businesses were essentially permitted to cartelize under government auspices. This regime had followed a period between World War I and 1933, encompassing the tenure of three Republican presidents (1921–33) and characterized as an "era of neglect" for antitrust.[5] With the demise of the NRA in 1935, and a philosophical shift in the focus of the Roosevelt administration, antitrust enforcement surged under Thurman Arnold's tenure as head of the Antitrust Division, between 1938 and 1943. Also, during this period, major corporations faced an unwanted public spotlight resulting from explosive revelations (patent monopolies, international cartels, etc.) at the hearings of the Temporary National Economic Committee (TNEC). For almost three years, from 1938 to 1941, the TNEC investigated ninety-five industries and called over five hundred witnesses. Despite all of the drama associated with Arnold's actions and the TNEC, antitrust prosecutions declined dramatically during World War II and the early Truman administration, except for a series of cases brought against American companies participating in international cartels and against the cartels themselves.[6]

Since the mid-1930s Congress had sent mixed signals on antitrust. In 1936, in response to the increased power of chain stores, Congress enacted the Robinson-Patman Act, which if fully enforced required substantial uniformity of consumer prices in many situations, unless the seller could establish verifiable cost savings. The Miller-Tydings Act of 1937 went further and exempted price maintenance agreements (which set minimum prices) for the resale of trademark-protected, branded goods from the Sherman Act. Subsequently, in 1951, the Supreme Court held that distributors not signing price maintenance contracts with their sellers could not be covered by the provisions of the Miller-Tydings Act, allowing vertical (distributor-retailer) price fixing. Congress responded to this decision in 1952 and passed the McGuire Act. It permitted sellers to stipulate prices (not just set minimum prices) and permitted individual states to determine whether they would allow such agreements to be enforced against nonagreeing parties—so called Fair Trade laws, which remained in existence until 1975.[7] Such legislation contrasted with the Truman administration's active support of the 1950 Cellar-Kefauver Amendment to Section 7 of the Clayton Act designed to invigorate regulation of corporate mergers. The only common thread that seemed to link such diverse legislation through this period was the traditional view of antitrust promoting competition through the preservation and strengthening of smaller units of production and a bias against larger, but often more efficient, firms.[8]

The Cellar-Kefauver Amendment to the Clayton Act was the most significant antitrust merger legislation since passage of the original act in 1914. Originally, Congress had hoped the Clayton Act would preempt creation of monopolies by constraining potentially anticompetitive mergers. As passed and interpreted by the courts, however, the act had serious flaws. Because of an adverse court decision in 1926, Clayton Section 7 subsequently addressed only stock acquisitions (and only some of these) and not the acquisition of physical assets. Needless to say, corporations structured most potentially anticompetitive acquisitions to avoid the reach of the act, dramatically reducing its scope. Furthermore, Clayton's original language prohibiting stock acquisitions that "lessened competition between the acquired and acquiring company" was limited through litigation to horizontal mergers (competitors at the same level of product distribution), not vertical (different levels of product distribution) or conglomerate mergers (unrelated products or sectors). The effect of these interpretations was to preempt the government's ability to challenge most mergers, and the Clayton Act was largely stillborn.[9]

Cellar-Kefauver extended the Clayton Act's scope to include asset as well as stock acquisitions: "In any line of commerce in any section of the country, the effect of such acquisition may be substantially to lessen competition or tend to create a monopoly."[10] At the time of Eisenhower's inauguration the new legislation was untested in court and presented the incoming administration with its greatest single opportunity to reshape American antitrust law and its continuing role in postwar economic life. Other such opportunities, however, also existed.

Antitrust case law from 1940 to 1953 had developed in a manner to circumscribe some uses of the "rule of reason" that had dominated Sherman Act thinking since the *Standard Oil* decision in 1911. A little history is in order here. The Sherman Act's Section 1 contained explicit language that declared illegal "every contract, combination in the form of trust or otherwise, or conspiracy, in restraint of trade or commerce among the several states, or with foreign nations." Counterpoised to this seemingly definitive language was an older and still viable common law doctrine that in certain circumstances a showing of "reasonableness" would legitimize certain restrictions on competition, if competitive impacts were minor or other benefits were proved. Such evidence of reasonableness might be discerned from the economic context of the challenged practice or then-current economic conditions. Using rule of reason arguments in the 1920s and 1930s, a line of cases developed that allowed "tampering" with market structures to suppress "destructive" competition, often a common prescription for real or perceived economic distress. Nevertheless, courts rejected rule of reason arguments in cases involving horizontal price fixing.

After *United States v. Socony–Vacuum Oil Company* in 1940, brought by the Roosevelt administration in late 1936, the Supreme Court left no doubt that any type of horizontal agreement among competitors, even if it only had the potential to affect price structures, was "per se" illegal. Thus, evidence of reasonableness of a practice, such as "distressed conditions," procompetitive impacts, or even government encouragement, would not be considered when a court evaluated a case.[11] A leading authority on antitrust noted that "the [*Socony*] case disposed of any distinction between aggressive and defensive price fixing: It is now settled law that no amount of economic distress or depression can justify trade [voluntary] agreements to suppress price competition or indeed to 'hamper' in any way with the free working of the price mechanism."[12] For competitive firms it would be virtually impossible to insulate themselves from the antitrust laws unless by explicit statutory exemption. They could not even discuss a wide range of voluntary, collaborative arrangements that might impact price structures, even if "encouraged" to do so by government officials or under government auspices. The full impact of the decision on the American economy was not readily apparent until the end of World War II and the postwar period.

Additionally, changes had also occurred in the courts' interpretations of Section 2 of the Sherman Act, which addressed single firm monopolization. The business community believed that a spate of such decisions in cases brought by the Roosevelt and Truman administrations, starting in the 1930s and accelerating in the postwar period, had seriously narrowed the scope of permissible conduct of corporations with "monopoly power." These cases placed a cloud over what many corporate executives and their attorneys thought were legitimate activities by large, dominant firms.[13]

An authoritative Second Circuit Court of Appeals decision in *United States v. Aluminum Co. of America* (Alcoa) in 1945 seemed to most observers to define very narrowly the level of legal conduct allowed to a monopolist. Though the case was brought by the Roosevelt administration in 1937, it was only intermittently pursued because of the war. The 1945 decision conceded that the possession of monopoly power, defined in terms of a percentage of market control, was not illegal per se. It became so only when there was "an element of positive drive" that turned possession of such power into a Sherman Act Section 2 violation. Judge Learned Hand's decision opined that a monopolist might be legally safe if it was the sole survivor of a group of competitors "merely by virtue of his skill, foresight and industry." If the monopolist, however, progressively embraced each new opportunity as it occurred and "dampens the spirits of potential competitors," he might be guilty of monopolization under Sherman Section 2: "Even though seeing and taking of opportunities of expansion are matters of skill and foresight—certainly they are 'normal' and 'honestly industrial' business methods—they may yet disclose a monopolistic intent, if they are clearly exclusionary in effect." An extreme interpretation of this view would impute illegal intent to a firm with monopoly power even on account of its very efficiency, if exclusionary effects were shown to result.[14]

Less than a year later, without dissent, the Supreme Court embraced much of the *Alcoa* opinion, noting, "Neither proof of exertion of the power to exclude nor proof of actual exclusion of existing or potential competition is essential to sustain a charge of monopolization." The court, however, did not specifically endorse Hand's potentially far-reaching "embracing each new opportunity" language. Furthermore, in both cases there was other, abundant evidence of "monopolistic intent and positive drive" to support the courts' decisions.[15] Despite such factors executives at firms like General Motors, which had more than a 50 percent market share, as well as enterprises in heavily concentrated, oligopolistic industries like steel, heavy electrical equipment, and many others that dominated the immediate postwar economy were concerned. It also troubled single firms aggressively marketing patented or unique products.[16] One antitrust scholar noted that if the "mere size is no abuse" argument, as articulated in *United States v. United States Steel Corp.* (1920), remained antitrust orthodoxy, it was "well veiled."[17]

The Roosevelt and Truman administrations also brought significant cases against the cartels and cartel-like behavior of American companies overseas, especially during World War II, when domestic antitrust enforcement activity screeched to a halt. In *United States v. National Lead Company,* the Supreme Court declared illegal a series of market-sharing and patent-licensing agreements between the American defendant and foreign firms. These understandings essentially insulated National Lead from imported competition in the domestic American market and, in return, prevented it from exporting outside of the Western Hemisphere.[18]

Similarly, in *Timken Roller Bearing Company v. United States,* the Supreme Court found arrangements between an American company and European competitors a violation of Section 1 of the Sherman Act.[19] The 1951 decision actually held that arrangements between an American company and a foreign affiliate whose purpose was to restrain foreign and domestic competition violated the Sherman Act. A dissent in the case suggested that the holding of the court's majority made it questionable under the antitrust laws for any American firm to enter a foreign market through a separate affiliate or subsidiary, no matter what the effect on competition. Though flawed, the dissent, by Associate Justice Robert H. Jackson, was given wide circulation and credence at the time. It increased apprehension within the business community about what it considered the momentum of recent postwar "adverse" antitrust decisions.[20]

Despite these concerns, nothing in either decision prevented firms from establishing foreign subsidiaries or a patent owner from licensing his US or foreign patent exclusively or setting out territorial restrictions in the licenses.[21] According to Wyatt Wells, in *Antitrust and the Formation of the Postwar World*, however, these decisions and other, similar ones, "taken together . . . [the patent, cartel cases] represented perhaps the greatest victory for antitrust prosecutions since World War I. They made the participation of American firms in international cartels through patent accords, joint ventures, or Webb-Pomerene corporations illegal under most circumstances, even if the cartels in question were not directed specifically at American markets."[22] He argues that the cumulative impact of these decisions was to eventually eliminate cartels from the international scene in such high-tech fields as electrical machinery and chemicals. The international oil cartel would be the Truman administration's next target.

The Korean War resulted in budget cuts and decreased activity by the Antitrust Division, but the Truman administration left two politically sensitive antitrust cases on Eisenhower's doorstep in 1953. In 1949, under both sections of the Sherman Act and the preamendment, Section 7 of the Clayton Act, the DOJ challenged Du Pont's over 20 percent stock ownership in General Motors, which it had originally acquired in 1917–19.[23] This case, *Du Pont* (General Motors) possibly more than any other recent case, was viewed by some in the pro-Republican business community as a partisan vendetta. The other proceeding involved the intersection of the overseas activities of American multinational oil companies, evolving American Cold War foreign policy, and the American government's use of the multinationals as instruments of that policy. In June 1952 DOJ initiated a criminal grand jury investigation of the joint exploration, production, refining, pipeline, and marketing operations activities of seven major international oil companies: Standard Oil of New Jersey (SONJ), Standard Oil of California (SoCal), Standard Oil of New York (Socony), Texaco, Gulf, Royal Dutch Shell (Royal Dutch), and British Petroleum (BP). They are referred to here in any combination as the "majors." A 1950 Federal Trade Commission (FTC) report on the international oil industry concluded that "concentration in the form of jointly owned subsidiaries and affiliated companies was probably more widespread in the international petroleum industry than in any other field of enterprise."[24] It argued that the majors' control over international oil existed prior to World War II largely upon production and distribution arrangements begun in 1928 under a cartel, the "As Is" Agreement. Furthermore, it alleged that these continued after the war in various manifestations, embracing joint arrangements in exploration, production, refining, and distribution of petroleum worldwide, including newly developed sources of crude oil in the Middle East. The case, however, was largely based on an evidentiary record that was more than a decade old.[25]

Cold War tensions and a crisis in Iran quickly complicated prosecution of the case. Iran nationalized the holdings of British Petroleum in Iran in 1951. The British government owned 51 percent of BP and its exclusive Iranian petroleum concession. BP subsequently boycotted nationalized Iranian oil and threatened retaliation against any firm that dealt with what BP considered its "stolen property." Truman administration officials became unhappy with what they perceived as British inflexibility and feared that a radicalized Iran would come under the domination of the neighboring Soviet Union. It also thought that the oil supply situation in Western Europe would become critical during the crisis, unless the other majors voluntarily "coordinated" petroleum flows to rapidly expanding oil markets in Western Europe.

Joint coordination by the other majors, of course, raised antitrust concerns. Under the 1950 Defense Production Act (DPA), the president had broad allocation powers "for defense purposes" and could, after consultation with the attorney general and the FTC, exempt from the antitrust laws "those [firms] entering into voluntary agreements and programs to achieve the objectives of the act." After some prevarication Truman authorized a voluntary agreement of the American majors under the DPA, which subsequently facilitated the flow of oil to Western Europe. By 1952, the European supply crisis had subsided and the agreement terminated.[26]

The stickier problem of who would control the Iranian concession, however, remained. By October 1952 the US State Department began advocating various plans in an attempt to break the BP-Iran impasse and counter potential Soviet political advantage. Ultimately, the US government sought to involve the other six majors (and several other smaller firms) in a new Iranian concession, with a minority role for BP. Truman's DOJ opposed these discussions and plans and insisted that any such action that included American firms would have to be insulated from the antitrust laws. The majors skillfully maneuvered arguments concerning the incongruity of a criminal grand jury investigation and American interest in an independent, pro-Western Iran and a multinational (not just British) petroleum concession.

One week before leaving office Truman terminated the criminal case and determined that it should proceed as a civil matter. The actual decision whether to file a civil case, however, was gladly left to the new Eisenhower administration.[27]

EISENHOWER CONTEMPLATES ANTITRUST

The antitrust plank in the 1952 Republican Party platform said all of the correct things about the issue. It also promised to pursue "equal enforcement of the antimonopoly and unfair competition statutes and [to] simplify their administration." In an October 16, 1952, letter to the National Association of Retail Druggists, Eisenhower was more specific; the letter was typical of his commitments to antitrust on the campaign trail. He referred to the maintenance and enforcement of the antitrust laws as basic safeguards to free American enterprise and that "our laws against unfair and destructive pricing practices as well as other practices leading to monopoly must be fearless, impartially and energetically maintained and enforced. I am for such necessary rules of fair play because they preserve and strengthen free and fair competition, as opposed to monopolies, which mean the end of competition. I am for a realistic enforcement of them which they have not had during the past twenty years."[28]

Eisenhower's references to "impartial," "equal," and "realistic" enforcement were essentially code words to address the aforementioned widespread perception of many in the big business community that Democratic antitrust enforcement, especially under Truman, had been motivated by base political motives— attacking key Republican political supporters. Initiation of proceedings in the *Du Pont* (General Motors) case after the 1948 election—in June 1949—was often cited to validate such assumptions. Eisenhower occasionally echoed similar sentiments concerning past "bias" in the prior administrations' enforcement of the antitrust laws throughout his tenure in office. Brownell, Eisenhower's first attorney general, initially harbored such concerns about the Justice Department's Antitrust Division staff in 1953 but soon averred that, based on his "analysis of the cases and the on-going work of the commission [the Attorney General's National Committee to Study the Antitrust Laws], however, I became convinced of the merit of the department's efforts."[29]

The White House's course of action on antitrust policy was circumscribed in various ways by Cold War imperatives, Eisenhower's choice of cabinet members and associates from the ranks of the captains of industry, and the populist rhetoric of Democratic politicians like Senators Kefauver and O'Mahoney and Representative Cellar, all of whom advocated intensified antitrust enforcement. Nevertheless, the administration's accomplishments were significant, and by the end of the decade the outlines of modern antitrust doctrine and practice could be clearly discerned. Perhaps most notable was the dramatic decline of hyperbolic, partisan rhetoric about antitrust enforcement by the end of Eisenhower's terms.[30]

In the inner counsels of the administration, Eisenhower and his advisers were always concerned and acutely aware that their positions on antitrust legislation and enforcement might be viewed as "pro–big business and anti-consumer."[31] The president found it politically expedient to distance himself from important aspects of his antitrust policy, such as enforcement and some legislative initiatives. The attorney general's National Committee to Study the Antitrust Laws was just that—it was formed in mid-1953 under the aegis of Attorney General Brownell. Other serious studies of politically contentious issues, which began that same year, like Clarence Randall's Commission on Foreign Economic Policy (CFEP), were White House operations. When CFEP made legislative recommendations in 1954, the White House promoted them. This was generally not the case, however, with many antitrust matters, including several of the legislative proposals that had their genesis in the 1955 *Report of the Attorney General's National Committee to Study the Antitrust Laws*. Fears about political demagoguery of the administration's position vis-à-vis big business convinced Eisenhower to refrain from taking the initiative and let various members of Congress introduce piecemeal important legislative proposals regarding Robinson-Patman resale price maintenance. DOJ testified in support. Despite Eisenhower's and his cabinet's complete agreement with the committee's recommendation to repeal the Miller-Tydings and the McGuire Acts, cabinet discussion was replete with hand-wringing about being labeled probusiness. Subsequently, influential cabinet members like George Humphrey asked the essential, yet cynical question about concerns over being labeled pro–big business. At one cabinet meeting, Humphrey simply asked, "How important really is this?"[32]

Eisenhower wanted to establish separation on antitrust matters. Certainly, it went considerably further than that associated with agricultural policy and the combative Ezra Taft Benson. Legislation developed by the administration was introduced by the Department of Agriculture and, with the Revenue Act of 1954, became the centerpiece of the White House's legislative program that year. The administration was reluctant to give Democrats in Congress a convenient punching bag for pro–big business arguments, which could be made concerning legislative modification of Robinson-Patman. Antitrust legislation that conjured up the specter of big business Republicanism was not pressed. On other, perhaps more arcane but less controversial antitrust legislation, the White House took the lead or provided strong support. Administration officials openly supported increased penalties for Sherman Act violations and the creation of DOJ oversight in financial institution mergers and consolidations.

Overall, Eisenhower's decision to distance himself from much of antitrust policy and enforcement made political sense. He was to take office in the immediate aftermath of the scandal-plagued late Truman administration, which had provided embarrassing examples of conflict of interest between the administration and outside interests. While Eisenhower appointed to his cabinet seasoned corporate executives—men he hoped capable of making tough decisions about limiting bureaucratic growth—his appointments invited criticism. Critics derided his cabinet as "eight millionaires and a plumber" (the latter soon left). It included former General Motors president Charles Wilson, whose firm dominated the auto industry and had a major stake in the *Du Pont* (General Motors) case, and George Humphrey, a former mining company executive, who had close ties to the highly concentrated iron and steel industry. In addition, outside of his appointments, Eisenhower personally had numerous friends and associates who were executives in or represented firms involved in major antitrust proceedings. IBM and its president, Eisenhower's old Columbia University associate Thomas Watson Sr., were involved in a major antitrust suit filed in 1952. And a civil suit against AT&T, filed in 1949, sought divestiture of the company's Western Electric manufacturing concern, as well as restrictions on other aspects of how the phone monopoly conducted its business. Robert Lovett, Truman's former secretary of defense and Eisenhower's friend and associate who was now at Brown Brothers Harriman, subsequently lobbied the administration on behalf of AT&T.[33]

Once in office, Eisenhower could not escape the concerns of major business leaders about antitrust. These included the aforementioned broad language in the *Alcoa, Timken,* and *National Lead* decisions and the implication of pending litigation against *Du Pont* (Cellophane), a case brought in 1947 alleging that it monopolized the market in a single product—cellophane.[34] Also, as merger and acquisition activity accelerated in the prosperous mid-1950s, the business community looked to signals from the DOJ and the FTC about enforcement of amended Section 7 of the Clayton Act and the first round of court decisions under it.

THE ANTITRUST DIVISION UNDER NEW MANAGEMENT

In June 1953 Attorney General Brownell outlined the core of the new administration's antitrust policies. He emphasized (1) equality of enforcement; (2) simplification of procedures; (3) assistance to those willing to act within the law; and (4) "an uncompromising determination that there will be no slackening of effort and . . . no wholesale dismissal of pending suits." He also promised a study of the antitrust laws to determine "how the new administration might best answer the insistent public demand for review and clarification of [antitrust law]." The latter was designed to address some of the case law ambiguities and, according to Brownell's memoirs, business concern about prior "biases" of past Democratic administrations.[35]

Initially, the administration proceeded slowly. It streamlined the processing of antitrust cases, began the aforementioned study, built a consensus for legislative change in some areas, and sent signals regarding what it hoped would be a rationalized and revitalized enforcement program. The first assistant attorney general for DOJ's Antitrust Division was Stanley N. Barnes, a California state judge, with no previous experience in antitrust. He had been a political ally of Vice President Nixon and former California governor Earl Warren.[36] Noted for his speaking and "people" skills, he later conceded that he made a mistake by initially saying that he "would gladly talk with any businessman who felt that he was being wrongly sued by the previous administrations" because of the complexity of the records of the average antitrust proceeding. Subsequently, he concluded that "pretty good reasons" existed for the 144 cases pending in 1953; in fact, only 5 were dismissed.[37] The results of this review by Barnes called into question the actual extent to which the Truman administration practiced the business community's canard of biased enforcement of the antitrust laws. Brownell initially also had his suspicions but also soon abandoned them.[38]

Barnes revitalized the use of prefiling conferences in Sherman Act cases. They had been used occasionally in the 1920s but, except for criminal cases, had fallen into disuse by the 1930s.[39] In the absence of statutory requirements for premerger notification, DOJ promoted the voluntary preclearance of proposed mergers under the Clayton Act. Corporations involved in proposed acquisitions could voluntarily submit information to the Antitrust Division, which then studied the transaction's economic and legal context. If DOJ had no objections, it would inform the firms that it did not contemplate initiating legal proceedings at that time. The letter, however, typically indicated that DOJ's position was based on existing information and was not binding on successor assistant attorney generals. DOJ reserved the right to proceed. Despite these caveats, the business community thought preclearance desirable, at least for those transactions that raised potential anticompetitive issues under new Clayton Section 7. Denial of preclearance was usually the death knell of a proposed acquisition. In 1953 just seven proposed mergers were submitted to DOJ; five were cleared, one was denied, and one temporarily abandoned. For 1954, twelve mergers were submitted to DOJ for clearance; seven were cleared, five denied, and, of the latter, four were abandoned. Despite the administration's policy of delaying any major antitrust action until publication of the attorney general's committee report, Brownell and Barnes were eager to use litigation to flesh out the new standards under Cellar-Kefauver. Early on, the division was looking for a "strong case," and this may have influenced early clearance actions until 1955.[40]

Subsequently, voluntary preclearance filings increased. By mid-1957 Brownell informed Eisenhower that, to date, sixty-one mergers had been voluntarily submitted to DOJ for preclearance. DOJ cleared twenty-nine transactions: seven were voluntarily abandoned, three were withdrawn, in four transactions DOJ lacked jurisdiction, sixteen were disapproved, and two were still pending. In the sixteen cases where clearance was denied, half of the transactions were abandoned, one suit was filed, and in the other seven, according to Brownell, "our evidence, while strong enough to raise some doubts as to the legality of the transaction, was not strong enough to justify suit."[41] Outside of the voluntary preclearance program, the DOJ routinely examined, in varying detail, 2,128 corporate mergers and acquisitions through June 1957 and had filed suit in only 11 cases.[42] Such numbers seemed to belie a vigorous antitrust merger policy. In fact, most of the 2,000 "mergers and acquisitions" no doubt received little more than a cursory review. The number of top thousand corporations disappearing through mergers was relatively small during the decade—only 138. Many of these occurred through vertical or conglomerate mergers; horizontal mergers where very large firms purchased much smaller niche firms; and acquisitions in small, unconcentrated industries.[43] In the system the administration put in place, preclearance ensured an examination of major proposed mergers. Generally, the big ones were not getting away. Preclearance promoted self-policing. Firms envisioning substantial antitrust issues sought rigorous government scrutiny through preclearance to avoid subsequent lawsuits. Beginning with the 1957 *Economic Report of the President*, the administration proposed a statutory requirement of premerger notification to DOJ and FTC of certain merger and acquisition transactions. Congress, however, did not enact such requirements until the Hart-Scott-Rodino Antitrust Improvements Act of 1975.[44]

Once civil (not criminal) antitrust cases were filed, the government needed a reliable mechanism to gather information. The Civil Investigative Demand (CID), which became a cornerstone of subsequent DOJ civil antitrust litigation, did not exist in the 1950s. The 1955 attorney general's committee report recommended Congress create it. Without it DOJ was handicapped in civil investigations, because it could not compel production of documentation, except from a criminal grand jury. It was forced to rely on voluntary compliance by defendants, especially after 1958, when the Supreme Court limited use of material produced in response to criminal subpoenas in Clayton Section 7 civil actions, since unlike the Sherman Act, the Clayton Act had no criminal provisions. Despite the obvious need and the intense lobbying by the administration in 1959–60, it was never able to get a Democratic-controlled Congress to pass legislation creating CIDs. Congress ultimately authorized it in the Antitrust Civil Process Act in 1962, after Eisenhower had left office.[45]

The division's revitalization of consent decrees to settle cases was controversial, but nevertheless the administration considered it an essential part of its antitrust program. Consent decrees owed much of their popularity to Section 5 of the Clayton Act, which made final judgments, but not consent decrees, conclusive evidence of unlawful conduct in any subsequent private, treble damage civil lawsuits, which often followed on the heels of government prosecutions.[46] And the number of private cases filed in the 1940s and early 1950s had increased rapidly over earlier, very low levels, but was still substantially below numbers reached later in the 1960s and beyond. Brownell and Barnes were convinced that consent decrees saved both the division and private defendants' time and resources. Additionally, they thought consent decree mechanisms allowed DOJ to regulate firm conduct that might not come within the ambit of civil antitrust litigation—a position that subsequently caused carping in the business community. Finally, both Brownell and Barnes routinely included mechanisms in decrees to facilitate enforcement, such as periodic proof of compliance or changed market structure by a specific date. Contempt actions for noncompliance with consent decrees during Barnes's four-year tenure increased markedly.[47]

The consent decree mechanism was not an Eisenhower administration innovation. Its use, however, had significantly declined under Truman. The device received significant attention among specialists in antitrust when its use rebounded after 1953. Administration reliance on consent decrees was often criticized by Democrats and, occasionally, probusiness publications.[48] Most notable was a series of hearings conducted by Representative Emanuel Cellar's House Antitrust Subcommittee (Judiciary Committee) in 1959 and 1960. The practice had ebbed and flowed since its first use in 1906. In fact, over 90 percent of all antitrust cases settled in 1940 were by consent decree. The figure for all cases filed between 1935 and 1955 averaged 72 percent. So, although the administration's reliance on consent decrees to settle cases may have been a change from very recent patterns, it was not inconsistent with historic, long-established antitrust practices.[49]

THE ATTORNEY GENERAL'S STUDY

On July 9, 1953, Brownell appointed Barnes and S. Chesterfield Oppenheim of the University of Michigan as cochairmen of the sixty-one-member National Committee to Study the Antitrust Laws. The committee included a who's who of antitrust lawyers, academics, and economists, with the notable exception of former Roosevelt Antitrust Division head Thurman Arnold. It appears to have been politically balanced as well. Despite Eisenhower's unflattering comment to his cabinet that none of them "have to meet a payroll," it represented an excellent group to study the current state of the antitrust laws and to recommend changes. The panel was chosen to provide policy guidance and affirmation for the administration's coalescing antitrust policies. Brownell also initially sought to use the study to test the subsequently discredited hypothesis that Democratic enforcement had been, in some situations, politically motivated. Eisenhower wanted a "thoughtful and comprehensive study" but "also expressed the hope that the group would provide an important instrument to prepare the way for modernizing and strengthening our laws to preserve American enterprise against monopoly and unfair competition."[50] In his 1980 study Theodore Kovaleff noted that years later, in surveys of living members, there was near unanimous agreement that all points of view were represented on the committee.[51] That being said, it is clear that in the 1950s the antitrust bar was essentially a defendants' bar. Most lawyers who practiced antitrust represented corporate defendants in government-initiated criminal and civil cases. Private civil suits, though increasing, were still relatively rare compared to later decades and usually had very limited economic impacts.[52] But the committee's report was clearly a study of existing precedents (focusing on the previous two decades), which were generally endorsed with few criticisms. There were, however, numerous suggestions for legislative changes. One antitrust scholar, Thomas Kauper, has called the report a "remarkable exercise in consensus building," but some of the dissents to various aspects of the report at the time questioned the cumulative impact of such a conservative treatment and what they characterized as an unwillingness to address fundamental questions about the role of antitrust in the modern economy.[53] As a general matter, the endorsement of the existing status of current case law was one of the major contributions of the report. It addressed and, more importantly, it efficiently diffused, some of the more "ominous direction" arguments of the business community that existed at the time.

The committee's 1955 report largely reiterated and restated coalescing administration policy; it laid out standards for subsequent administration of the antitrust laws during Eisenhower's presidency; and made legislative recommendations. It generally endorsed the rule of reason in Sherman Act Section 1 cases, but with the caveat that "certain conduct, because of its inherent nature or effect, may more quickly be adjudicated unreasonable per se." Here it included examples that already existed, such as horizontal agreements to fix prices (*Socony*) and control production, or concerted refusals to deal.[54]

With regard to Sherman Section 2 monopolization cases, the committee thought that evidence of monopoly power was a firm's ability to "control market prices or exclude competition," but it did not believe that any predetermined percentage share of a given market should presuppose monopoly power.[55] The report also sought to address some of the more troubling aspects of recent Section 2 cases, dealing with inferred monopolistic intent, such as *Alcoa, United States v. American Tobacco Co.*, and *Du Pont* (Cellophane). It cited with approval a federal district court opinion that had been affirmed *per curium* (without opinion) by the Supreme Court in 1953 that "defendant may escape statutory liability if it bears the burden of proving that it owes its monopoly solely to superior skill, superior products, natural advantages (including accessibility to raw materials or markets), economic or technological efficiency (including scientific research, low margins of profit maintained permanently and without discrimination, or licenses conferred by, and used within, the limits of law including patents on one's own inventions, or franchises granted directly to the enterprise by a public authority)."[56] Few subsequent court cases in the 1950s raised the issue, and it gradually subsided.

Turning to the ambiguities and concerns raised by *Timken* and *National Lead*, the report rejected any blanket antitrust exemption for activities abroad. It emphasized, however, that the Sherman Act applied only to those arrangements between American firms alone or in concert with foreign firms that had substantial anticompetitive effects on domestic or foreign US commerce. Again, it diffused some of the more exaggerated fears of the business community. Finally, the report suggested expansion and extension of the antitrust exemption procedures in the Defense Production Act, which Congress ultimately rejected when it scaled back the scope of the DPA antitrust exemption in 1955.[57]

Perhaps the merger discussion of the report was its single most important section and set the tone for the administration's subsequent merger policy. Written by Assistant Attorney General Barnes, in consultation with Brownell, the report affirmed that the purpose of the 1950 Cellar-Kefauver Amendment (still untested by litigation in 1955) was to address the prior limitations of the Clayton Act in merger cases and to enable the DOJ and FTC to strike down mergers, which were beyond the reach of the Sherman Act. It sought to deal with concentrated economic power in its incipiency as mergers, rather than later as full-blown monopolies under Sherman Section 2. Barnes's draft of the merger section was essentially an explanation of and blueprint for the division's two most significant pending cases. For noncompeting firms in related markets—vertical acquisitions like the *Du Pont* (General Motors) stock case—the standard would be whether there was a reasonable probability that a merger or acquisition would foreclose a substantial share of a relevant market. For horizontal mergers (direct competitors) the report recommended a standard of "whether the competition lost as a result of the merger, may in the context of the market as a whole, constitute a substantial lessening of competition or tend to monopoly." The report gave guidelines in the form of questions for merger proponents that focused on detailed evaluations of each company and its geographic and product markets; how it sold in these markets; its respective market shares; the end uses of its products; and ease of entry into the relevant market. The last factor was especially on the minds of Barnes and the administration, since Bethlehem Steel, the nation's second largest steel producer, indicated in mid-1954 its intention to acquire Youngstown Sheet and Tube, the sixth largest, and the administration contemplated inevitable litigation under the amended Clayton Act.[58] Administration opposition to this merger became a cornerstone of its antitrust policy. Ultimately, a significant court victory defining the parameters of the Cellar-Kefauver Amendment came in late 1958. During a March 18, 1955, cabinet meeting in which the committee's report was presented, there was no dissent or even discussion of its merger policy recommendations; everyone was on board.[59]

MARKETS AND MONOPOLIZATION: THE RECORD UNDER SHERMAN 2 AND CLAYTON 7

An examination of the Eisenhower administration's litigation record in important cases indicates a strong enforcement policy, which significantly altered the nature and scope of antitrust law by the end of the 1950s. Early on, two of the major cases pending against Du Pont when Eisenhower took office in 1953 had significant impacts. One was a Sherman Section 2 monopoly case that focused on Du Pont's alleged monopolization of cellophane, which had begun in 1947. The other was the *Du Pont* (General Motors) case begun in 1949.

DOJ lost the *Du Pont* (Cellophane) case in federal district court in 1953 and at the US Supreme Court in 1956. In its decision the court determined that Du Pont had not monopolized the market in cellophane, because the relevant product market was "flexible packaging materials": cellophane possessed "reasonable interchangeability" (cross elasticity of demand) with other flexible packaging materials. With such a broad product market, Du Pont's cellophane sales were well below the threshold for a presumption of monopoly power.

The case and the court's decision opened eyes at DOJ. By widening relevant markets, a reasonable interchangeability doctrine made Sherman monopolization cases more complex and difficult to prosecute. It also had the potential to subject cases brought under the new Section 7 of the Clayton Act to similar problems. Ultimately, the Supreme Court applied this relevant product market standard when it first directly addressed market definitions under amended Section 7 of the Clayton Act in *Brown Shoe Co. v. United States* in 1962.[60] At the same time, however, the holding in the *Du Pont* (Cellophane) case had the potential to enlarge the scope of competitive markets under the Clayton Act, where competition would be adversely affected, and bring more mergers under government scrutiny. In a nutshell, Clayton merger presumptions of anticompetitive impact became an issue at much lower percentages for the surviving firm in a merger or acquisition—well below 50 percent of the relevant market. Under single-firm, Sherman 2 monopolization cases, however, monopoly power presumptions did not become an issue until market concentration exceeded 50 to 70 percent of the relevant market. DOJ's response to the potentially widening of markets in Sherman and Clayton Act cases was to make better use of economists and economic analysis to hone its market definition skills in such cases during the remainder of the decade.[61]

The Eisenhower administration had much more success with the *Du Pont* (General Motors) case under Section 2 of the Sherman Act and old Section 7 of the Clayton Act.[62] Initially, the allegations of violations of Section 7 of the Clayton Act were not the focus of either side. Even when the case reached the Supreme Court in 1956, the Clayton Act issues were not a major element of DOJ's case.[63]

In December 1954, a federal district court found for Du Pont and dismissed the case. The administration appealed to the Supreme Court, whose June 1957 decision reversed the federal district court and found for the government. The court defined the market, or "line of commerce," for Clayton Act analysis to be "automotive fabrics and finishes (paints)," because they were "distinct and peculiar from other uses." This was a different but narrower criterion for the relevant product market than the "reasonable interchangeability" criteria in the *Du Pont* (Cellophane) case. These standards for addressing issues that were at the very core of Clayton Act merger analysis were not settled by the Supreme Court until *Brown Shoe* in 1962, when it applied the "reasonable interchangeability" test to merger cases.[64] But *Du Pont* (General Motors) had potential upsides for the government.

According to Kovaleff, "The Court extended the old Section 7 tests, previously limited to horizontal acquisitions, to vertical and conglomerate acquisitions as well." The decision found that "the test of a violation is whether, at the time of suit, there is any reasonable probability that the stock acquisition may lead to a restraint of commerce or tend to create a monopoly in a line of commerce." Using this as a guide, the court found that Du Pont supplied General Motors with approximately 65 percent of the market for auto finishes in the mid-1940s and between 35 to 55 percent of its fabrics during the same period. The court found the lessening of competition in such shares of the relevant product markets significant, given General Motors' share of the auto market, which exceeded 50 percent.[65]

Implementation of the divestiture of GM stock ordered by the Supreme Court led to more litigation. But these subsequent conflicts demonstrated the administration's resolve in pressing the litigation to a satisfactory conclusion. DOJ wanted the GM stock sold and the proceeds distributed to shareholders to avoid having the GM shares retained by Du Pont family members. The problem was taxes. The Internal Revenue Service ruled that any distribution of proceeds of the sale of GM stock or stock itself by Du Pont would be taxable at the rate of dividends (20% to 91%) to Du Pont shareholders. The IRS ruling meant that sale of the stock or distribution of the GM shares as dividends would probably require the sale of all or some of GM shareholders' stock to pay taxes. This would almost certainly depress its price. In late 1959 a federal district court ruled that the tax implications made the government's share divestiture remedy punitive and unfair. The judge tried to craft a remedy that allowed Du Pont to keep its stock and allow certain holders of Du Pont stock to vote their GM shares, while Du Pont family, directors, and officers could not exercise voting rights. He believed that this "pass-through" would "sterilize" GM stock from Du Pont's control.

The judge's peculiar decision gave the Eisenhower administration another opportunity to walk away from the messy case in an election year (1960). Both GM and Du Pont stock were widely held. Instead, the DOJ appealed the case to the Supreme Court again, asking for outright divestiture and sale of GM stock by Du Pont and arguing that the tax issue was not relevant to antitrust considerations. In 1961, after Eisenhower left office, the Supreme Court reversed the district court's pass-through remedy. Eventually, Congress enacted a statute providing for phased divestiture and capital gains tax treatment of the distributions.[66]

DOJ's prosecution of the *Du Pont* (General Motors) cases helped to flesh out essential elements under the amended Clayton Act. By doing so, the administration was able to craft a strategy using Cellar-Kefauver to address the growing and diversifying "urge to merge" in the 1950s. The precise legal tests, however, remained unsettled at the Supreme Court level until *Brown Shoe* in 1962. The decade was the most active for corporate mergers since the 1920s. Between 1920 and 1929 Moody's and Standard and Poor's reported 6,818 mergers and acquisitions in manufacturing and mining. The figure for 1950–59 was 4,089, but the pace accelerated rapidly from 1954 through the end of the decade into the 1960s. Of the 1,000 largest American manufacturing firms in existence in 1951, 854 survived in September 1959. Of the 147 firms that disappeared in the nine-year period, 138 were the result of mergers, indicating a significant level of activity but also a remarkably stable environment for large American corporations during the decade.[67]

In late 1955, a young Alfred Kahn, a member of the staff of the Council of Economic Advisers discussed the acceleration of merger activity and the impact of administration policy. From a postwar low of 126 in 1949, mergers were at their highest rate in twenty-five years in 1955: 518 on an annualized basis. Kahn attributed these changes to speculative excesses of a boom and to favorable tax laws. To this must also be added a surging stock market; broad stock indices roughly tripled from early 1952 through 1959. Kahn stated that assets acquired in mergers in 1954–55 represented maybe just 10 percent of total business expenditures for new plant and equipment in the period. He argued, however, that FTC data showed "clearly that a highly disproportionate amount of acquisitions are made by corporations far above average size" and that "they [mergers] have become fashionable." He stated that large corporations had set up vice presidencies in charge of mergers and "investment and various business counseling houses have full time employees constantly seeking out merger prospects, to sell to prospective clients." He also noted that while the trends were barely perceptible, "this activity may produce an enduring change in the nature of our economy if permitted to continue. While many mergers were horizontal in nature, a far greater number represented additions to a product line, vertical diversification or geographic integration." Kahn questioned the need to grant a free hand to "conglomerate or vertically integrated giants, with far easier access to capital," for fear of creating "Ziabatsu-like giants."[68]

Becoming a little less rhetorical, Kahn believed that in the previous three years merger activity (both horizontal and vertical) was intensifying in previously relatively unconcentrated industries or businesses such as banks, shoes, food chain stores, hotels, textiles, and paper. Kahn concluded by observing that only seven suits had been brought under the amended Clayton Act as of November 1955. Only one had been settled favorably for the government by a consent decree (Minute Maid's acquisition of Snow Crop), and the others remained pending: "This is not a fair picture of their preventive activity, however. The Bethlehem–Youngstown

Steel merger has not moved forward for months; no doubt the opposition of [the DOJ] helps explain the hesitation. Several other proposed mergers have been stopped after discussions with the antitrust authorities. And undoubtedly many others have been discouraged even before this point. The greatest effectiveness of the antitrust laws must always be this hidden, preventive character."[69]

In fact, administration opposition to the Bethlehem Steel–Youngstown Sheet and Tube merger was the cornerstone of its Clayton Act enforcement policies. In mid-1954, Bethlehem (the second largest producer) expressed its intention to acquire Youngstown (the sixth largest producer). Eisenhower himself was involved in the decision to oppose the merger and use the case as a vehicle for the government to obtain a favorable decision on the scope of the amended Clayton Act.[70]

The steel firms made a formal merger announcement in December 1956. By that time Barnes had left for a judgeship on the Ninth Circuit Court of Appeals. Another California state judge, Victor Hansen, replaced him. Though most observers thought he lacked the personal appeal of Barnes, Hansen nevertheless continued to oppose the merger and actively embraced the other work of the Antitrust Division.[71] The government sought a quick decision in the Bethlehem-Youngstown merger for a variety of reasons: the need for a clear judicial statement of the scope of the amended Clayton Act because of increased merger activity; the concentrated nature of the steel industry; its importance in the administration's hope to slow inflation through "business-labor restraint" on wages and prices; and impacts on consolidation in other defense-related industries. Bethlehem argued that the merger would allow it to better compete against industry giant U.S. Steel, which controlled 30 percent of the national market. DOJ's position was that any acquisition that increased nationwide concentration in the already oligopolistic industry failed the tests of the amended Clayton Act. Since the merger would increase Bethlehem's market share from 16 to 20 percent, DOJ argued it was per se illegal.[72] Before December 1956 Bethlehem had sought voluntary premerger clearance and submitted extensive data, but DOJ denied the request. The parties agreed to expedited handling of the case because of its precedential value. At trial each party limited its stipulations to 140 pages and the trial lasted just nineteen days, despite DOJ's expanded arguments addressing vertical, as well as horizontal, aspects of the merger.[73]

In November 1958 the US District Court for the Southern District of New York made its decision. It found that the merger would lessen competition and tend to create a monopoly in the national steel market and numerous submarkets. The court issued an injunction preventing the merger. It rejected the defendant's arguments that Bethlehem competed only in the eastern and western areas of the nation and Youngstown in the Mid-Continent area. The court instead ruled that there was sufficient interregional competition that would be affected by the proposed merger. Furthermore, it held that little cross elasticity of steel products existed vis-à-vis other nonsteel products. Finally, the court expressed the fear that approval of the merger would set off a "chain-reaction" of defensive acquisitions that would increase concentration in the industry well beyond existing levels. The firms subsequently abandoned their merger plans.[74]

The *Du Pont* (General Motors) and *Bethlehem* cases firmly established the salience of the Clayton Act's anticompetitive analysis in horizontal mergers in oligopolistic industries and raised the prospect of its use in burgeoning vertical and conglomerate mergers. Also, in 1959 the government won another, similar Clayton Section 7 case, at the federal district court level in *United States v. Brown Shoe*.[75] The case had been brought in 1955 to oppose the merger of Brown and Kinney Shoes. The shoe industry was much less concentrated than steel, and the defendants had much smaller industry percentages than Bethlehem and Youngstown. Also, the consolidation of the two firms raised issues concerning both vertical and horizontal anticompetitive impacts. In both *Brown* and *Bethlehem* the trial courts found that lines of commerce broadly defined by the "reasonable interchangeability of use" (cross elasticity of demand) did not preclude separate findings of well-defined submarkets, which by themselves constituted product markets for antitrust purposes.[76] And the Supreme Court subsequently adopted this approach in *Brown Shoe* in 1962. Though these two cases had not rigidly quantified "substantial lessening of competition," they set antitrust analysis of such cases on a rigorous path that continued for at least two decades.[77] Any measurable increase in market share in horizontal mergers or foreclosure of competition in vertical mergers ensured government opposition.

SHERMAN 1 AND THE ELECTRICAL CASES

The administration was also active in other traditional areas of antitrust enforcement—price-fixing conspiracies. Near the end of its second term it initiated twenty Sherman Act Section 1 prosecutions against major American electrical equipment manufacturers. The cases, largely forgotten today, were vast in scope. Antitrust regulators had long been monitoring the industry, filing occasional actions, which were subsequently settled with little publicity since the 1940s. But in 1957, the price of heavy electrical equipment used by electrical utilities rose dramatically, and the Tennessee Valley Authority (TVA) noted a similarity of bids of most American manufacturers. When TVA solicited foreign bids, they were substantially below those of American manufacturers. A subsequent DOJ investigation revealed twenty separate price-fixing conspiracies among various manufacturers, involving thirty-two corporations (General Electric was the most common actor, being involved in all but one conspiracy) and forty-eight individual defendants. The violations were so blatant that the participants had even formulated written rules for their conduct with each other when rigging equipment bids.[78]

Assistant Attorney General Hansen left the Antitrust Division in 1959. His successor was thirty-one-year-old Robert Bicks, who remained the acting assistant attorney general for antitrust from April 1959 to the end of Eisenhower's second term. Bicks was the youngest person nominated for the position before or since. He had been one of the first members of the DOJ's "honors program" begun by Brownell in 1953 to bring highly qualified law school graduates into DOJ and enhance the attractiveness of government service. Bicks served as the executive secretary of the attorney general's committee and had been a primary assistant to Barnes and Hansen. Brownell had left the administration in 1957, replaced by William Rogers, and Bicks found his old boss representing Westinghouse, one of the conspirators in the electrical equipment settlement negotiations with DOJ.[79]

Bicks and Rogers convinced the court, in light of the egregious nature of the defendants' conduct, not to accept nolo contendere (no contest) pleas, which would have made subsequent private party (treble damage) civil antitrust suits more difficult. At this point one of the conspirator companies (Allis-Chalmers) decided to cooperate fully with the government, and the remaining defendants' resistance disintegrated. No defendant pleaded "not guilty." The court did not enter sentences and fines until the first month of the Kennedy administration. Fines totaled almost $2 million, and seven executives served short jail terms. In subsequent private litigation, over $400 million was collected by private electrical utilities in over 1,948 treble damage lawsuits. TVA and other government agencies collected over $7.5 million.[80]

Before the Eisenhower administration private lawsuits for treble damages were not common. Prior to the Electrical cases the antitrust bar, whether government or private, was small and, outside of government lawyers, very few had experience initiating suits. During the first fifty years of the Sherman Act (1890–1940) just 175 private antitrust suits were filed, and plaintiffs were successful in only 13 of these. But from 1941 through 1945, 297 private suits were filed, and 529 between 1946 and 1950. The number increased to 1,045 for the period 1951 to 1955 and 1,163 between 1956 and 1960, many of these associated with motion picture distribution. Damage awards and settlements, however, were not typically large.

Nevertheless, by the end of the decade, the transition from what had been almost exclusively a defendant's bar was well under way.

The Electrical cases were essential to this change in antitrust practice, and its transition to a more multifaceted and dynamic legal field. By encouraging private antitrust suits, the administration was able to broaden the discipline possible under the antitrust laws. The cases certainly assisted in the institutionalization of civil, treble damage lawsuits in antitrust law. Subsequent filings illustrate the depth of the change. Private cases increased to 3,598 lawsuits between 1961 and 1965, including 1,948 of the suits against electrical equipment conspiracy defendants. These treble damage civil lawsuits conclusively showed that such litigation could often have a much greater impact than government fines or remedies, especially given the relatively small Sherman Act fines during this period.[81]

Private civil antitrust activity has remained high. Indeed, these suits became a significant part of antitrust law during periods in which government actions were reduced by policy design, such as in the 1980s and the 2000s. So, unlike Clayton Act litigation, no new precedents were established for Sherman Section 1 litigation during the Eisenhower administration. Nevertheless, because of the growth of private antitrust litigation another broader, more complex variable was added to business decision making and risk evaluation.

THE OIL CARTEL CASE AND EISENHOWER'S ANTITRUST LEGACY

Despite the record of vigorous antitrust activity and precedent-setting decisions, the administration's compromise decision in the so-called oil cartel case raised questions at the time and since about its commitment to antitrust. Because of Cold War considerations, Eisenhower officials backed off action under Section 1 of the Sherman Act against the international oil industry's overseas exploration, production, transportation, refining, and marketing activities.[82]

Critics at the time and later have cited Eisenhower's handling of the "cartel" case as a prime example of how the administration willingly subsumed antitrust concerns to what it saw as Cold War imperatives. Two of the most critical works addressing the antitrust case against the major international oil companies date from the mid-1970s: John M. Blair's *Control of Oil* and, in detail, Burton Kaufman's *The Oil Cartel Case*. Even Robert Griffith's otherwise laudatory article "Dwight D. Eisenhower and the Corporate Commonwealth" finds the handling of the case the penultimate example of the administration's "low priority" for antitrust and its preference for quiet discussions with business interests. The backdrop of these works was a period of reduced Cold War tensions in the 1970s; surging oil prices (1973–74 and 1979–80); continued dominance of many aspects of the world oil business by the major international oil companies; rapidly increasing oil company profits accompanied by imperfect public understanding of the causes of domestic petroleum and petroleum products shortages; and major headline-grabbing congressional investigations.[83]

More recent studies, like Daniel Yergin's *The Prize* (1991), and especially Wyatt Wells's work, *Antitrust and the Formation of the Postwar World* (2002), have approached the matter quite differently. These studies placed the Eisenhower administration's handling of the cartel case in a clearer context of the majors' postwar international operations, international comity, and domestic American production controls in the 1950s.[84]

The maintenance of an adequate oil supply for Western Europe (and the avoidance of using Soviet oil) was a cornerstone of Eisenhower's Cold War policy.[85] In *The Oil Cartel Case,* Kaufman cites a 1957 Eisenhower letter to a friend, Dillon Anderson, who had expressed concern about Europe's growing reliance on imported oil but who deemed it unacceptable to resort to force to prevent an embargo. "I think you [Anderson] have in the analysis presented in the letter, proved that should a crisis arise threatening to cut the western world off from Mid-east oil, we would *have* [Eisenhower's italics] to use force. You specifically point out that an adequate supply of oil to Western Europe ranks almost equal in priority with an adequate supply for ourselves. . . . You prove the facts of the petroleum world are such that the west must, for self-preservation, retain access to Mid-East Oil."[86]

Middle Eastern oil quickly became crucial to Western Europe after World War II. During the 1950s, Cold War allies in Western Europe and Japan rapidly shifted from their domestic coal to significant dependence on imported oil (especially Middle Eastern oil) for their energy requirements. By 1953 Western Europe's oil imports were increasing 15 percent a year; by the end of the decade oil accounted for about one-third of European energy consumption, and about 75 percent of it came from the Middle East. The dependence on Middle Eastern oil was even greater in Japan.[87]

In pursuit of this policy, Eisenhower was constrained by the nature of the world oil business and its control by the majors. Since the 1980s, foreign governments and their national oil companies have controlled approximately 80 percent of the world's production of crude oil. Increasingly, they also control the refining of crude oil, its downstream distribution, and its retail marketing. That was not the case in the 1950s, when the majors controlled the international trade in crude oil and refined products and virtually all production and reserves in less developed countries (as well as a large share in the developed world, including the United States). A nexus of joint production, refining, and marketing agreements among these firms ensured that each knew the others' production plans. Joint control of production reduced incentives for price competition among companies while at the same time enhancing the companies' bargaining power with the governments of oil-producing countries. The majors also dominated the processing, transportation, and marketing of oil. Consequently, while Iran might seize control of production, the country found it impossible to market oil without the cooperation of the majors.[88]

Additionally, domestic US production represented 53 percent of world oil production in 1950 but had declined to 35 percent by 1960. Imports of crude oil into the United States were relatively low but rising, from about 8 percent of domestic demand in 1953 to 17 percent in 1960.[89] Much of this crude oil was imported by the majors, but by mid-decade "independent" firms were increasing their imports of oil from Canada and the Middle East.[90]

Moreover, Wyatt Wells addresses the incredible political and economic complexity of petroleum cartel issues in the fifteen years after 1945. While he concedes that joint production arrangements among the major international oil companies probably violated the antitrust laws as interpreted by American courts in the 1940s and 1950s (as had the operations of other international cartels that had faced antitrust discipline), he believes that "it is hard to blame the Truman and Eisenhower administrations for ignoring these violations. Many of the oil concessions in the Middle East like Iran (after 1953), Iraq and Kuwait emerged from tortuous [multiparty] international negotiations, and all the concessions reflected careful attempts to balance the interest of companies and producing nations." In the early 1950s most of the oil exported from Venezuela, Iran, Iraq, Kuwait, and Saudi Arabia was destined for Europe and Japan, not the United States. Though the Department of Justice could prove, and the majors conceded, that these operations "affected" the commerce of the United States for purposes of acquiring jurisdiction for antitrust litigation, Wells argues, "Washington had no moral right to reorganize this trade without reference to the desires of all these nations." And in the 1950s, unlike in recent decades, antitrust was a peculiarly American institution, enforced in the United States periodically at best. Other nations looked upon the United States' intermittent penchant for vigorous antitrust activity with curiosity or disdain, and generally with little desire to emulate it.[91]

Wells also faults the view of the DOJ, which ignored the fact that the United States itself "did not tolerate a free market in oil." The Texas Railroad Commission restricted output and coordinated its scheme with other producing states, through federal legislation and coordinating agreements. Such actions stabilized domestic prices and, because of the continued relative importance of Texas (and the United States) in world production, had a stabilizing impact on the world trade in petroleum in the immediate postwar period. Finally, Wells argues that the scale of the operational tasks confronting the majors in Third World venues often justified cooperation. "These nationals usually had very little in the way of modern infrastructure. The seven sisters [the majors] not only had to drill wells and build pipelines, expensive operations in and of themselves, but also had to construct ports, roads and towns and to train a workforce. Cooperation allowed companies to spread these huge costs among themselves, making manageable tasks that might daunt a single firm."[92]

To be sure, the antitrust law of the 1940s and 1950s would seem to indicate that an action against the oil cartel was a logical extension of prior international cartel cases. But because of the circumstances of the industry, world markets, and Truman's and Eisenhower's central assumptions that an opportunistic Soviet Union was pressing the Cold War in Asia and the Middle East, both administrations and their two successors stepped back from vigorous pursuit of the case.

Even before the overthrow of Iran's Mohammad Mosaddeq in August 1953, the Eisenhower administration had moved to limit the scope of the antitrust action against the majors. Following the Truman administration's lead, Eisenhower's DOJ refiled the case as a civil matter in April 1953. It limited the litigation to those firms headquartered and doing business in the United States—SONJ, Socony, Gulf, Texaco, and SoCal—and excluded BP, Royal Dutch, and Aramco (the Texaco, SoCal, SONJ, and Socony joint venture in Saudi Arabia). The British government had limited the information that BP could provide, and the Dutch government forbade Royal Dutch from providing any information at all. Even against majors headquartered in the United States, without the mechanism of a civil investigative demand, DOJ's ability to get information in a civil case was very limited. Much of its evidence related to the operation of the "As Is" Agreement prior to World War II and was more than a decade old.[93]

In August 1953 an American-engineered coup returned the shah to power in Iran, and the new government needed oil revenue. BP, however, remained exceedingly unpopular in Iran. US officials wanted to resolve the impasse, so to help strengthen the new Iranian government and raise revenue, the United States proposed negotiating a new concession that would reduce BP's ownership to 40 percent while increasing the position of the American majors and Royal

Dutch. The American majors, however, had assurances of ample supplies from other Middle East sources and were reluctant to see greater Iranian production come onto the world market. Moreover, the administration was asking them to enter into a joint production and distribution agreement to promote American foreign policy goals while at the same time similar agreements were a focal point of DOJ's antitrust litigation. Subsequently, the majors sought an antitrust "clearance" from DOJ as a prerequisite to their participation in the proposed new Iranian consortium. The National Security Council made a finding that the participation of American majors in the proposed Iranian consortium was necessary as a matter of national security and that the Department of State should take the lead in negotiation of the matter with instructions only to consult "from time to time during negotiation with the Attorney General on legal aspects of the case."[94]

As a result, by early 1954 DOJ was under intense pressure to approve American participation (exploration, production, and refining) in the consortium. It did so in January 1954 but required that each company market its own share of Iranian-produced oil independently of the other members. Iranian oil production restarted in October 1954. As a practical matter this agreement and DOJ's acquiescence severely compromised that portion of the antitrust case that sought to terminate the majors' joint ventures in exploration, production, and refining of oil. Thus, the case proceeded largely, but not exclusively, as a challenge to the joint international marketing and price fixing of the American majors overseas.[95] Kaufman argues that the Iranian precedent hung over the case as it continued in this more limited form. In settlement negotiations both the Eisenhower and later Kennedy administrations would raise the prospect of revisiting the joint production and refining issues in an effort to force the majors to a settlement. The threat was rather hollow, and the defendants knew it. In 1955 Attorney General Brownell had ruled out seeking restrictions on future joint Middle Eastern production and refining ventures as inconsistent with the Iranian consortium decision.[96]

Eisenhower's DOJ settled the case with SONJ and Gulf in November 1960, and a consent decree was entered in both cases. Subsequently, Texaco settled in 1963, but the case against SoCal and Socony was dismissed in 1968 without any consent decree being entered. With certain exceptions, the SONJ settlement prohibited joint marketing with other majors and provided for the breakup of the SONJ-Socony international joint marketing venture Stanvac, as well as a division of Stanvac's other assets. Socony agreed with SONJ to break up Stanvac but did not enter into a consent decree settling the lawsuit. The settlements enjoined agreements and combinations between each defendant and "any of its competi-

tors to fix prices, divide markets, or regulate production of foreign oil." Each decree also specified that combinations involving each defendant (except for joint-
production and refining ventures) "were also prohibited from allocating or limiting
production of crude oil in any foreign country and from limiting United States'
imports and exports of crude oil and petroleum products."[97]

The Gulf decree was identical, but it did not include marketing restrictions,
because Gulf had no joint marketing subsidiary. It did, however, provide that
some of Gulf's large Kuwaiti production be sold to independent firms.[98] When
Texaco settled in 1963, it was along these same lines. Texaco also promised to
vote its 50 percent ownership (with SoCal) of the Eastern Hemisphere joint operation, Caltex, consistent with its settlement with the government and to cooperate with the government in trying to bring about the dissolution of Caltex.
SoCal opposed the latter but finally consented to the dissolution of Caltex in Europe later in the decade.[99]

Changes in the postwar world market for oil were instrumental in the
willingness of SONJ, Gulf, and ultimately Texaco to settle. By the late 1950s the
world was awash in oil, and many of the majors felt that they would have more
to gain if they reduced their commitments to some, but not all, of their joint operations with other majors. Conversely, firms with weaker crude oil and distribution positions in some areas, like SoCal, opposed any settlement. Furthermore,
the increased participation of independent oil companies in the international
petroleum business was gradually weakening the commanding positions of
the majors. Beginning with the negotiation of the new Iranian consortium and
through the cartel case settlements, the Eisenhower administration had promoted
such participation by independents. These factors contributed to the settlement
of the cartel case, but there was no question that the consent decrees provided
real anticompetitive benefits worldwide and domestically, even as American policy limited crude oil imports.[100] However, the joint exploration and production,
and some of the distribution, activities of the majors overseas (especially in the
Middle East) remained intact at the end of the decade simply because the administration considered it crucial to Cold War security.

Attorney General Brownell summarized DOJ's circumscribed view of the
proposed settlement in 1957: "The consent decree does not prohibit SONJ from
participating with other oil companies in exploration abroad. Any incidental
effect on foreign commerce involved in such operations is indirect and more
than counter-balanced by the national security, foreign relations, and foreign
trade advantages to the United States."[101] In his memoirs, Brownell claims the
case proceeded to settlement as Truman had envisioned it.[102] While Wells was

sympathetic to the administration's position, he acknowledged the obvious: the market-sharing prohibitions of the consent decrees "dismantled some of the cartel accords that had survived from the 1930s, but they did not affect production arrangements, which was the nexus of the cartel's [slowly eroding] power."[103]

CONCLUSION

Possibly the greatest compliment to the administration's antitrust policy was what was not included in the December 1959 *Eckstein Report*. Antitrust was barely mentioned in the liberal Democrats' otherwise detailed and withering attack on Eisenhower administration macroeconomic, microeconomic, and foreign economic policies, a foreshadowing of their party's economic platform in the 1960 presidential campaign. Out of its 488 pages, only 9 pages are devoted to "Public Policy and Market Power" (antitrust). Furthermore, much of that simply discussed antitrust's impact on labor organizations and called for more consultative mechanisms in the executive branch on changes in wages and prices. The report dutifully called for more funding for DOJ's Antitrust Division and an enhancement of its power to subpoena records in civil cases (CIDs). It reiterated the call in the attorney general's committee report for further examination of possible action against situations in oligopolistic industries where power was exercised without overt agreement by price leadership. But the report blamed the courts (not DOJ regulators) for a lack of understanding "of the wider economic implications of size as a factor in market power," though it noted recent contrary trends such as the *Bethlehem-Youngstown* case.[104] The Eisenhower administration's antitrust policy was spared a partisan attack, and as a general matter the level of partisan rhetoric about antitrust declined by the end of the decade, a trend that continued thereafter.

Eisenhower saw antitrust policy as crucial to a strong market-based economy necessary for the United States to successfully engage in a protracted Cold War struggle with the Soviet Union. At times (as in the oil cartel case) these policies were subordinated to more salient Cold War imperatives. The administration, however, was able to reduce the partisan posturing of antitrust issues; eliminate much doctrinal uncertainty; win substantial court victories; and smooth out variations in enforcement, while streamlining and amplifying it at the same time.[105]

CHAPTER 6

Foreign Economic Policy

When Eisenhower took office in January 1953, he set specific goals for American foreign economic policy: reinforcing the US commitment to liberal trade policies, which had slipped during the second Truman administration; increasing American private investment overseas; and promoting free currency convertibility of Cold War allies in Western Europe and Japan. If these policies were successful, he believed, expenditures for foreign military and economic assistance (foreign aid, broadly defined) could be reduced rapidly. Even if success was not quick in coming, Eisenhower anticipated that foreign aid, especially foreign economic assistance, could be scaled back significantly.

Expenditures for the European Recovery Program, or Marshall Plan, were already in a steep decline by 1953. Economic aid to Europe, either European Recovery Program or later Mutual Security Act assistance, had declined from its postwar peak in 1949 of $3.7 billion to about $1.0 billion in 1953. The Marshall Plan was deemed a success at the time, but the new administration viewed its reliance on large grants of economic aid as a necessary, temporary expediency not as a blueprint for a permanent aid policy. Furthermore, the nature of the United States' program had changed remarkably in just a few years because of the rapid decline of Marshall Plan economic aid to Western Europe and the militarization of the Cold War. Mutual Security Act military aid expenditures had surged since 1950 from about $0.5 billion to more than $4.5 billion in 1953. Very few areas outside Europe were recipients of foreign economic assistance grants, and the amounts were low, just $0.3 billion in 1952 and $0.4 billion in 1953. So when Eisenhower and others spoke of foreign economic assistance in 1953, they were speaking about rapidly declining European economic assistance. In contrast, military aid (predominantly grants for military equipment) to Europe—and increasingly Asia—which increased dramatically in the final years of the Truman administration, would continue to receive extensive support.[1] But the new administration promised it would scrutinize expenditures carefully.[2]

Economic assistance, made up primarily of loans and technical aid, would have a small role. Assistance in the form of credits (loans) by the Export-Import Bank of the United States (Eximbank) to finance the purchase of American exports would be continued, although administration officials also wanted to reduce Eximbank's activities (and costs). Its role in financing of large overseas development projects would hopefully be taken over by the International Bank for Reconstruction and Development (IBRD, or World Bank), the multilateral, international organization created after the end of World War II for such purposes. In turn, then, Eximbank could focus on much lower levels of shorter-term lending.

Eisenhower believed in the value of trade liberalization, both to American prosperity at home but, just as importantly, to the creation of economic conditions overseas that would facilitate US Cold War strategy. He was, however, quite willing to compromise in pursuit of those long-term objectives—as in other elements of his economic policy. He had a keen sense of the political, ideological, and economic flexibility he needed to pursue his trade liberalization goals during a decade characterized by increasing protectionist agitation.[3]

Other issues also arose that required new thinking. The immediate postwar "dollar gap"—the inability of the United States' Cold War trading partners to earn dollars—had largely ended in Western Europe and eventually eased in Japan but continued to be a factor in much of the noncommunist, developing world. Now, the new administration had to address the policy implications of a persistent American balance of payments deficit. The difficulties increased dramatically when this deficit ballooned after 1957. But the administration was attentive to long-run problems that might threaten the gold-backed, dollar-based, fixed-rate exchange system established at Bretton Woods. Addressing these problems reinforced Eisenhower's commitment to conservative domestic macroeconomic policy.

In a nutshell, Eisenhower's view of foreign aid, export credit, trade liberalization, and the defense of the dollar reflected his fiscal conservatism and his goal of promoting free economic institutions. Eisenhower's foreign economic policy goals were all quickly challenged; major shifts in the international economic and political environment came about as the nature of the Cold War changed. These included the sudden end of the Korean War; the need to integrate Japan into the international trade regime; the spread of the Cold War to Latin America and Africa, as well as its deepening in Asia and the Middle East; and the onset of economic "competition" between the Soviet Union and the United States in the developing world.

Eisenhower had to respond to such challenges and modify his administration's initial approaches to foreign economic and military assistance, export finance, and foreign trade. Most of the reorientation occurred during his first term. As in other areas of economic policy, Eisenhower promoted early studies of important issues to help guide and build support for his new administration, and foreign economic policy was no different. In spring 1953, he established the Commission on Foreign Economic Policy (CFEP) headed by Clarence Randall of Inland Steel, a firm believer in the virtues of trade liberalization. The commission held hearings during late 1953 and presented its recommendations in early 1954. The CFEP generally endorsed (1) the phaseout of economic aid; (2) the encouragement of private investment abroad; (3) the goal of full currency convertibility; and (4) the promotion of trade liberalization.[4]

EISENHOWER LOOKS AT FOREIGN ASSISTANCE, 1953–1954

Eisenhower outlined his approach to foreign economic assistance in his 1953 inaugural address. Support for the promotion of international trade and private investment and the elimination of most forms of American foreign economic aid received special emphasis. A few weeks later, in his first State of the Union message, he spoke about the balance that needed to be struck between the United States' mutual security (foreign aid) policies and the imperatives of fiscal restraint: "As a matter of common sense and national interest, we shall give help to other nations in the measure that they strive earnestly to do their full share of the common task. No wealth of aid could compensate for poverty of the spirit. The heart of every free nation must be honestly dedicated to the preserving of its own independence and security."[5]

Clearly, Eisenhower thought about the foreign assistance programs in military and largely Eurocentric terms in 1953, since almost 80 percent of the nearly $6 billion in US foreign assistance was for military aid, and less than 20 percent for economic. When discussing a House Appropriations Committee reduction of Mutual Security Agency (MSA) funds at a July 1953 press conference, Eisenhower said, "I have never looked upon what we now call MSA as giveaway programs. Everything I do in my present office, and what I did before, was approached basically from this viewpoint: where lies the enlightened self-interest of the United States? . . . To my mind—and this is the way I approached the determination of the amount of money in that MSA appropriation—I put it right square alongside our own security program, because I think that it belongs there."[6] Somewhat later, in 1957, Eisenhower defended military aid to Western Europe by arguing that if the region came "under the control of Moscow and International Communism, we would have to transform ourselves into an armed camp. The first result of this would be vastly increased military expenditures—possibly 80 to 100 billion dollars per year. We should have a strictly controlled economy—all power centralized in Washington."[7]

Nevertheless, the president had to face frequent and intense political opposition to spending on military assistance. In a letter to General Alfred Gruenther in mid-1953, he characterized foreign military aid programs as a "natural" for members of Congress to attack. When pressed to cut budgets, the aid programs proved an easy target, since cuts probably would not undermine the chances of congressional reelection. According to Eisenhower, "In cutting this item they can shout and scream [about] their own concern for the individual voter and taxpayer and, of course, show how they are helping to protect the value of the dollar. In this particular case, we can be very penny-wise and pound-foolish, as you and I both know. Nevertheless, it is going to be a hard fight to avoid excessive cuts in a field where it is entirely possible—even probable—that the United States is getting more for its money than in any other." Eisenhower added that he thought that nations close to the Soviet Union that received military aid were essential to our "unified strength and collective security." He added that "we should not really kick about taxes until we know that we have made ourselves reasonably secure against any possible move by the Soviets."[8]

A year later in his 1954 State of the Union address, the president spelled out his initial priorities clearly: "Military assistance must be continued. Technical assistance must be maintained. Economic assistance can be reduced. However, our economic programs in Korea and in a few other critical places of the world are especially important, and I shall ask Congress to continue them in the next fiscal year. The fact that we can now reduce our foreign economic assistance in many areas is gratifying evidence that its objectives are being achieved."[9] With such views, there seemed little place for a substantial program of foreign economic assistance, except as an adjunct of large military equipment programs to states like South Korea, Taiwan, and (later) South Vietnam and Pakistan.

Soon after Randall's CFEP issued its report in March 1954, the president announced his own program. Eisenhower affirmed

> the principle that economic aid on a grant basis should be terminated as soon as possible consistent with our national interest. In cases where support is needed to establish and equip military forces of other governments in the interest of our mutual defense, and where this is beyond the economic capacity of another country, our aid should be in the form of grants. As recognized by the Commission, there may be some cases in which modest amounts of grant aid to underdeveloped countries will importantly serve the interests of security. I further agree that in other situations where the interest of the United States requires that dollars not otherwise available to a country should be provided such support to the maximum extent appropriate should be in the form of loans rather than grants.[10]

Such language presupposed little in the way of a program of foreign economic aid. In an interview published in the June 12, 1953, issue of *U.S. News & World Report,* Treasury Secretary Humphrey spoke bluntly. Almost as an afterthought, after lengthy budget questions, the interviewer asked him, "What about foreign aid?" Humphrey's response was, "Foreign economic aid is pretty well gone—well on its way out right now." When asked about foreign military aid, he responded, "Well, when you are spending for military purposes, it is for military purposes."[11]

Beginning in 1953, however, international developments led to reconsideration and then significant refocus of foreign aid policies. While there might have been a thaw in the relations between the United States and the USSR after the end of the Korean War and following the death of Stalin in 1953, Eisenhower could not ignore the new Soviet leadership's avowed policy of peaceful competition with the United States to influence "Third World" or nonaligned countries. He and other officials perceived increasing evidence of Soviet influence in nationalistic movements in Asia, the Middle East, and even Latin America. These included the election and policies of the Mosaddeq government in Iran, Jacobo Arbenz in Guatemala, and the stoking of nationalist sentiments by Egypt's Gamal Abdel Nasser. In Asia, Soviet leaders courted Indonesia's Sukarno and India's Jawaharlal Nehru, both masters of sharp anticolonial, anti-Western rhetoric. In Southeast Asia there were worrisome communist insurgencies in Malaya and the Philippines. Above all the triumph of the communist Viet Minh in French Indochina in 1954, in the view of the administration, increased the prospect of a communist Southeast Asia and indirectly threatened Japan's postwar markets. Finally, developments in Japan itself increased apprehension in the administration.

Following the sudden end of the Korean War, the Japanese economy slipped into a precarious position, which the White House feared strengthened the prospects of that country's communist and socialist parties.[12]

In fact, the USSR's own aid effort was not large in absolute terms. Symbolically, though, it represented a major Cold War strategic initiative. Aid was limited to a few countries such as Egypt, Syria, India, Afghanistan, and Indonesia. It focused on a variety of major, high-profile projects, including steel mills, but also included substantial military aid. Soviet economic and technical assistance accelerated after 1956, approaching $1 billion a year, and included the diplomatic coup of providing aid and technical assistance for the construction of Egypt's Aswan Dam in 1958.

Particularly worrisome to American observers was the apparent attractiveness of Soviet economic, technical, and military assistance to nonaligned nations. Even in democratic countries like India, the historic example offered by the USSR of rapid economic growth through the use of government ownership and state economic planning proved attractive. Many aspects of the Soviet economic model were copied, even if its totalitarian political model was ignored. And though the United States and USSR had aid programs similar in size in only a few nations in Asia and the Middle East, the Soviet Union was willing to accept soft currencies in repayment of loans. The United States, however, usually only extended such concessions to portions of its developmental assistance. The difficulty administration officials had convincing Congress that the Soviet initiatives in the developing world posed a threat was also troubling.

Furthermore, Congress often resisted administration entreaties to support foreign economic aid to governments that aid opponents saw as "socialists," or at least aggressive proponents of state planning. And to make matters more difficult for Eisenhower, many of the proposed recipient nations were outspoken critics of US Cold War diplomacy. Establishing a framework for American economic aid to such places would be a hard sell in Congress and indeed for some within the administration itself.[13] Military aid was also subject to congressional attacks, and as the decade progressed critics shifted their focus from European to Asian countries. The most prominent recipients of military and economic aid during the 1950s were South Korea, Taiwan, South Vietnam, and Pakistan, countries less familiar to most members of Congress than those in Europe.[14]

Eisenhower's views about the importance of foreign economic assistance shifted in late 1954. Eventually economic aid was integrated into his stalwart defense of military assistance. During administration internal debates, Eisenhower over time increasingly challenged the insistence of those like Secretary Humphrey that economic aid to nonaligned nations encouraged socialism and should not be considered an appropriate substitute for direct foreign investment. During the first two years of his administration, the president increasingly came to accept Secretary of State John Foster Dulles's more nuanced views about the rationales for American foreign aid in view of the scope of Latin American, Asian, and Middle Eastern nationalism and an aggressive and opportunistic Soviet Union and its aid program.

EVOLVING VIEWS ON FOREIGN ECONOMIC ASSISTANCE, 1955–1957

The debates in Congress in 1955 over fiscal 1956 Mutual Aid legislation represented something of a turning point for Eisenhower's foreign aid policies. It certainly influenced the president's thinking. Before the 1954 midterm elections Taft-wing Republican legislators, who were hostile to foreign aid, controlled the relevant congressional committees. Even after 1955, when the new Democratic majorities in Congress assumed control of the legislative apparatus, the administration's problems with foreign aid legislation continued. Democrats, especially southern Democrats, increased their opposition to foreign aid as the program "took on an air of permanence." In particular, Democrat Otto Passman of Louisiana, who served on the House Appropriations Committee and later served as chair of the Foreign Operations Subcommittee, seemed to relish eviscerating foreign aid legislation. At times his public opposition seemed to border on the pathological.[15] Eisenhower viewed Passman as a menace to the nation's best interest, a man who "made a career" out of "irresponsibly cutting" foreign aid.[16]

Eisenhower's $3.5 billion request for fiscal 1956 Mutual Aid would be the lowest of his eight years in office. It was less than half of Truman's fiscal 1952 request. Military grants made up the bulk of the program, including over $1 billion for "defense support," that is, nonhardware, which was classified as "economic assistance." Even so, such assistance was usually entwined with military equipment and defense purposes. Only $183 million was sought for economic development aid. The president also proposed $459 million for UN agencies and $200 million to establish the President's Fund for Asian Economic Development. Though the Congress authorized $3.29 billion, it ultimately appropriated only $2.8 billion, including just $100 million for the Asian fund.[17]

Eisenhower's 1955 State of the Union message in January echoed old themes. In it the president continued to endorse military assistance and struck familiar chords about reducing barriers to trade and investment to promote economic

progress. Nothing was said about foreign economic assistance.[18] But presidential thinking on this matter continued to evolve over the year. In November 1955,
during discussions of the fiscal 1957 foreign aid budget at meetings of the National Security Council, the president was clearly annoyed by the continued hostility of Humphrey and Defense Secretary Charles Wilson toward increasing
foreign economic aid. He was seriously concerned that the rapid development of
the Soviet Union "had an enormous impact upon the underdeveloped nations
who sought an equally rapid change in their society." Eisenhower repeatedly
rejected the arguments of Humphrey and Wilson that American foreign economic
aid promoted socialism in recipient countries. He had had enough of such observations about foreign assistance, such as Humphrey's comment that "the Russians had not done 10% as much socializing in the world as the United States,"
referring to aid to countries with central planning and state-run industries. The
president challenged the treasury secretary's arguments, noting that the economic systems of good friends like Denmark, Norway, and Sweden "did not
mean that these countries were inimical to the United States." The president
said, "The fact of the matter was that every country could develop a government
which, while more socialized than we might like, nevertheless succeeded in
avoiding dictatorship and totalitarian methods." Eisenhower finally dismissed
Humphrey's tiresome observations by saying that they were simply no longer
relevant to a discussion of foreign aid matters.[19]

By the time Humphrey left the cabinet in July 1957, Eisenhower had fully
linked support for economic assistance into Dulles's concerns about growing
nationalism and Soviet opportunism abroad. Writing to Humphrey in May 1957,
the president responded to a letter the secretary had copied to him on the subject
of the cultural prerequisites necessary for underdeveloped countries to attract
private capital and make good use of foreign economic assistance.[20]

Eisenhower's reply reflected how much his ideas had evolved, with little of the
implicit racism found in Humphrey's point of view. The president's new thinking
had also been influenced by his experience in the Philippines, where he had
been stationed before World War II. He recalled that many shrewd local Philip-
pine politicians "falsely and corruptly" linked independence and prosperity to the
long-term detriment of their fellow citizens. From this experience Eisenhower
analogized that "few individuals understand the intensity and force of the spirit
of nationalism that is gripping all peoples of the world today. They obtain, from
a realization of their ambitions for national independence, fierce pride and personal satisfaction regardless of the individual's status within his own government. It is my personal conviction that almost any one of the newborn states of

the world would far rather embrace Communism or any other form of dictatorship than to acknowledge the political dominion of another government even though it brought to each citizen a far higher standard of living."

He went on to say that looking at the world through the American historical experience alone was out of date and relevant only to a time and a society of relative peace and isolation, nothing like the challenges that "Afro-Asian areas" faced today. Challenging Humphrey's views, he noted that "education alone will not be enough," for a "country that has reached the saturation point in population long before its people understand or, indeed, even hear of the terms 'personal rights' and 'personal freedom' presents far different challenges from [what] Americans faced in the first half of this century." The combination of nationalism "coupled with a deep hunger for some betterment in physical conditions and living standards, creates a critical situation in the under-developed world." Protection of American interests and the American way of life required that the United States (helped in some minor extent by other Western countries) "face up to the critical phase through which the world is passing and do our duty like men." In this context, foreign aid and some fiscal pain were required to fulfill the United States' role. Eisenhower argued that political opportunism in the undeveloped world had created a situation where the United States was required by history and the Soviet threat to stand up and increase its Mutual Aid expenditures, including funds for economic assistance.[21] The course would be all the more difficult, since the domestic political situation led to demagogy of the foreign aid issue.

As Eisenhower drove toward balanced budgets for fiscal 1956 and 1957, and again after the 1957–58 recession, annual Mutual Aid program requests of approximately $4 billion became inviting congressional targets. This was especially true of the economic aid portion of the requests, which was increasing and also more focused on Asia and avowedly nonaligned nations. In response to the hostile political climate, Eisenhower's aid requests increasingly relied on loans, not grants. Often these were "soft" loans with concessionary interest and repayment terms that could be paid back partially or fully with local currency, which was not freely convertible. The administration hoped that the movement away from grants would mollify opposition in Congress.

The intensity of the 1955 debates over the fiscal 1956 Mutual Aid legislation in Congress surprised the administration. Nevertheless, in 1956 it requested almost $4.7 billion for fiscal 1957, an increase of over $1 billion above Eisenhower's fiscal 1956 request and almost $2 billion more than what Congress appropriated the year before. It included increased special funding for Asia and a new special fund for Africa and the Middle East. Eisenhower publicly argued

192 MICROECONOMIC POLICIES

that the enhanced Soviet economic aid program was forcing the United States to review its foreign economic policy, and he fully embraced the arguments for increased economic assistance hammered home by Dulles in administration counsels since 1953.[22]

The size of the fiscal 1957 foreign aid budget emboldened its opponents. Eventually, Congress appropriated $3.8 billion for military and economic assistance; most of the cuts, surprisingly, came in military aid. Administration arguments about the need for increased economic assistance seemed to gain traction because of the increasing visibility of the Soviet economic aid effort. Furthermore, though Congress denied the request for a special African and Middle Eastern fund and ended the Asian fund, it transferred these to another category and allowed prior years' funding to be carried over into fiscal 1957, so that the net effect was largely to continue these efforts at existing levels.[23]

Eisenhower took many cues from this result when he crafted his fiscal 1958 foreign aid requests during 1957. First, he trimmed the package to $3.87 billion. Almost all of the $800 million reduction was made from military aid; economic aid was not cut, but was actually increased by $104 million. Even the $3.87 billion figure had already been trimmed from initial budget estimates by $535 million, largely in response to the fallout over Secretary Humphrey's "deficit and depression remarks" in January 1957.[24] Eisenhower sought to separate defense (military) assistance from economic development assistance. The latter would be increased and tied more closely to technical assistance programs, and the shift to long-term concessionary aid (also repayable, in part in soft currency) would be accelerated with a Development Loan Fund (DLF).

Eisenhower addressed the nation twice on national television in May 1957. His first message focused on overall budget issues, but in his second address he spent a full half hour outlining his foreign aid program. His public lockstep support for both programs—"the source," he said, "of military and economic strength for our alliances throughout the free world"—marked a substantial change from his views when he took office. In his address he sought broad support by essentially militarizing the economic aid program, juxtaposing its role as a response to Soviet efforts and the politically explosive needs of the underdeveloped world. In his view both military and economic aid were "truly defense programs . . . for the freedom of nations can be menaced not only by guns—but by the poverty that Communism can exploit." The president proposed that the military portion (including "defense support") of his request ($3 billion of the $4 billion sought) subsequently be included as part of the Defense Department appropriation. He observed that most of the nineteen countries slated to receive foreign economic aid were "on the frontier of the Communist world." But he now added Jordan—with its recent elimination of "pro-communist elements in the government"—and especially South Vietnam, to what he saw as briefs for foreign economic assistance, along with the overthrow of governments "inclined" toward communism in Guatemala and Iran earlier in his first term. He sought to promote long-range development in places like India and Pakistan, through a DLF funded with $500 million already in the budget and $750 million for each of the succeeding two years.[25]

Not three years earlier Eisenhower and most of his advisers believed that growth in such areas of the world could largely be achieved through direct foreign investment, not aid. Now things had changed. Since nations' "inherited poverty leaves these people so little for saving" and few resources for long-range investment in infrastructure, there's little for "the sinews of economic growth." He added, "At this critical moment in their economic growth a relatively small amount of outside capital can fatefully decide the difference between success and failure. What is critical now is to start and to maintain momentum." Eisenhower told his audience that the cost of the Mutual Aid program was high—5 percent of the budget—but "to cripple our programs for Mutual Security in the name of false 'economy' can [be] nothing less than a weakening of our nation."[26]

Congress nevertheless savaged Eisenhower's foreign aid request. The administration's mixed and confusing signals on the budget, and the anger of many southern Democrats over administration support for the first civil rights legislation enacted in the century, was more than enough to outweigh the growing support for economic aid fueled by aggressive Soviet outreach to the developing world. The authorization process, normally a less antagonistic affair, reduced Eisenhower's request by $500 million. The congressional appropriations committees reduced it further to just $2.77 billion, more than $1 billion below Eisenhower's request. Only $300 million was appropriated for the DLF.[27]

Battles over Eisenhower's fiscal 1958 foreign aid request was the most serious challenge the program would face in Congress during his tenure, but things got better. Cuts in future years would not be as deep as the over $1 billion lopped off the fiscal 1958 request. Despite his budget missteps in 1957, Eisenhower could point to some successes, such as the establishment of the DLF on a revolving basis and the increasing popularity of Cold War rationales for economic aid. Subsequently, a gradual shift occurred from military to economic aid; from grants to loans; and from European toward Asian, Middle Eastern, African, and Latin American recipients. Later cuts made in the president's requests would become less severe, as congressional support gradually grew.

In 1958 Eisenhower asked for $3.9 billion for fiscal 1959. For the first time since the outbreak of the Korean War, the request for all forms of economic assistance, including defense support ($2.1 billion), exceeded the request for military equipment ($1.8 billion). In the end, Congress appropriated $3.3 billion, $600 million less than Eisenhower had requested. It included $1.5 billion for military assistance (hardware) and $1.8 billion for economic assistance, including $750 million for defense (nonhardware) support and $400 million for the DLF. Congress had increased the nonmilitary equipment part of the package more than $500 million over the prior year.[28]

The results were better than anticipated in 1959. Eisenhower sought $3.9 billion from Congress for fiscal 1960, including $1.6 billion for military assistance (hardware) and $2.1 billion for economic aid, including $835 million for defense support and $700 million for the DLF. Except for the $500 million more for the DLF, most categories were little changed from what Congress had appropriated for fiscal 1959. Ultimately, Congress appropriated $3.3 billion, almost one-third of a billion more than the administration anticipated, including $1.3 billion for military aid (hardware), $0.7 billion for defense support, $0.55 billion for the DLF, and $0.25 billion for technical assistance. The shift to economic aid continued. The authorization level for the DLF for fiscal 1961 was $1.1 billion and, though it would probably not be appropriated at that level based on past patterns, it reflected a growing congressional commitment to long-term economic assistance. Other trends were promising as well. With administration blessing and support, Democratic senator William Fulbright, chairman of the Foreign Relations Committee, included language in legislation directing coordination of military and economic aid to ensure that military assistance be used "to encourage the use of foreign military forces in underdeveloped countries in the construction of public works and other activities helpful to economic development."[29]

During his last year in office, Eisenhower aggressively pursued his foreign aid program despite his administration's preoccupation with balance of payments problems and the political maneuvering of a presidential election year. Energized by his goodwill trip to the Middle East and South Asia in December 1959, the president requested an aid budget of $4.175 billion. Apparently, the administration believed that new requirements in October 1959, which made DLF loans subject to domestic procurement, would temper the use of that program, so Eisenhower only sought $700 million. As in prior years his arguments for the program emphasized Soviet competitiveness and expansionism. The final appropriation was $3.78 billion, which included $1.8 billion for military assistance (hardware); $675 million for defense support, now more closely linked to eco-

nomic developmental objectives; $550 million for the DLF; $230 million for special (technical) assistance; and $250 for the president's Contingency Fund. The
cuts amounted to less than $400 million from Eisenhower's request, the small-
est percentage since he took office in 1953.[30]

In summer 1960, after his fiscal 1961 foreign aid request had been submitted
to Congress, Eisenhower proposed a $600 million social development fund to
aid Latin America. The legislation was announced shortly before an Organization of American States meeting scheduled for Bogotá in September, where the
United States sought to mobilize the hemisphere against Cuba's Fidel Castro.
Prior to this time very little US foreign economic aid had been directed toward
Latin America—just $118 million in fiscal 1958. Over the years the United States
had used Eximbank, and more recently coupled it with World Bank lending, to
address the region's needs. Congress, however, quickly approved the measure in
August 1960, as relations with Castro's Cuba deteriorated.[31]

FOREIGN ECONOMIC ASSISTANCE:
THE EXIMBANK BATTLE, 1953–1954

During the Eisenhower administration, Eximbank's foreign trade credit operations were a significant part of its foreign economic assistance policy, especially
for Latin America. Its export financing activities in dollar terms, however, were
considerably smaller than American military assistance and foreign economic
assistance (foreign aid) under the Mutual Security Act. Nevertheless, the early
battles over the role and scope of Eximbank's operations underscored shifts that
eventually led to important changes in the broader foreign aid program. In the
end, the administration, which had first attempted to circumscribe Eximbank
activities, revitalized and greatly expanded them by the conclusion of Eisenhower's second term as the Cold War spread to the historic focus of its operations—
Latin America.

Secretary of the treasury Humphrey targeted Eximbank, initially because
its foreign trade financing operations were a substantial drain on the budget.
Chartered in 1934, Eximbank operated as the United States' official export credit
agency. It made hard currency loans in US dollars, to be paid back in dollars. All
Eximbank credits had to be used to purchase products made in the United States
to be exported overseas, with very minor exceptions. Congress had also instructed
the bank that "in the exercise of its functions [it] should supplement and encourage [but] not compete with private capital."[32] The bank's stated policy was to
extend credit selectively for those foreign projects that increased a recipient's

"trade base," that is, improved the economy of the borrowing country so that the project made a present and long-term future contribution to American exports.[33]

Since 1945 Eximbank had been an independent agency, managed by a board of four members and a chairman appointed by the president, subject to Senate confirmation. Its loans were subject to approval of the National Advisory Council (NAC) on International Monetary and Financial Problems, headed by the secretary of the treasury. Established in 1945, the NAC existed, in large part, to coordinate the activities of Eximbank with the postwar multilateral lending organizations—the International Monetary Fund (IMF) and the IBRD (World Bank).[34] Unlike Eximbank, the World Bank was an international multilateral agency whose lending operations were funded by income from its existing capital and periodic member capital contributions. Furthermore, countries receiving IBRD credits could make purchases anywhere, not just in the United States. In the years prior to and during World War II, Eximbank focused primarily on loans to Latin America. Usually, these were credits to foreign, sovereign (that is, government) purchasers of American products used in major development initiatives, such as infrastructure projects: roads, railroads, mines, municipal utilities, and power projects. When Congress rechartered Eximbank in 1945, its outstanding loans exceeded $200 million, and its statutory lending authority (ceiling) of $700 million was raised to $3.5 billion.[35]

Before the initiation of the Marshall Plan in 1948, Eximbank was involved in funding postwar aid to Western Europe.[36] But subsequently, from 1948 to 1953, it returned its focus to Latin American lending, often for large sovereign development projects, which included steel mills in Chile and Brazil, dams and irrigation works in Mexico, and mining projects in Peru. Such undertakings created tensions with the World Bank. As the IBRD's activities expanded in the early 1950s, its president, Eugene Black, believed that much of Eximbank's long-term development project lending usurped business that rightfully belonged to the World Bank. Eximbank's operations were not confined to traditional borrowers in Latin America but expanded, albeit modestly, in Asia and Africa, often in the form of loans for infrastructure and the development of strategic materials necessary for the deepening Cold War. Congress increased the bank's lending authority to $4.5 billion in 1951, spurred on by concerns about such strategic materials and the Korean War.

Increased bank lending had an immediate impact on federal expenditures and thus became the target of Secretary Humphrey. Eximbank loans, including substantial long-term project lending, neared or exceeded $400 million annually in fiscal 1948, 1950, and 1951, and was well above $500 million for fiscal 1952 and 1953. When credits were advanced to borrowers, they were treated as federal budget expenditures, under budget concepts in force at the time. Loan repayments were treated as budget receipts. Thus, when lending was accelerating, there were substantial draws on the Treasury with adverse budget impacts.[37]

By 1953 accelerating Eximbank loan activity and its net draw on the Treasury created an inviting target for the incoming administration as it looked for budget savings. Federal budget costs for multilateral organizations like the World Bank, on the other hand, were much more manageable and predictable. The cost to the US Treasury was limited to periodic (multiyear interval) capital infusions by member countries. In the immediate postwar period, American wishes significantly influenced when these occurred and the timing of payments. Eximbank funding was much less flexible and predictable.

To policymakers in 1953, the operations of the Eximbank looked quite different than the Marshall Plan, which had always been envisioned as a temporary program, undertaken because of slow postwar European economic recovery and the attendant political peril posed by the Soviet Union. American foreign policy leaders in the 1940s and early 1950s believed that no such political crisis existed in Latin America. As such, the predominant view was that the region's development needs could be addressed by market rate lending by Eximbank and multilateral agencies like the IBRD and IMF, not grants or "concessionary" loans. Eximbank lending to Latin America also represented "hard" loans, made in dollars and payable in dollars, not "soft" loans repayable in local currencies, which were not freely convertible. Between 1948 and 1953 many Latin American governments bristled as the US foreign economic assistance largely bypassed them while American foreign policy directed billions of dollars of grants for Western Europe under the Marshall Plan.[38]

Nevertheless, Eximbank loans were also often made for political purposes and had been since 1934. The State Department championed Eximbank for its ability to be used (even over its own objections) in "special cases of over-riding national interest." Critics of the bank like Humphrey cited large, postwar, emergency long-term reconstruction credits to France, where repayment looked shaky in 1953, as well as loans to the new state of Israel and others, as just such political loans. Furthermore, Humphrey thought that Eximbank's focus on long-term developmental lending had strayed greatly from its original mission (as defined by Humphrey) of making short-term loans to promote American exports. Humphrey also believed that Eximbank credits to private overseas investment schemes unfairly subsidized competitive American enterprises or "socialist" government-owned enterprises. As previously discussed, he thought administration efforts could be better, and more cheaply, directed to using American influence and power to promote political stability, currency convertibility, and the elimination of discrimination to promote private American investment overseas. In Humphrey's view, lending for overseas, sovereign long-term development investment should be left to the World Bank, especially given the immediate impacts on the US Treasury of Eximbank's operations.[39]

Thus, Humphrey wanted to circumscribe Eximbank for budgetary and philosophical reasons, similar to his position on foreign economic assistance. Though vigorously opposed by the State Department and Secretary Dulles, within its first few months the administration put in place a series of changes that subordinated Eximbank lending to the desires of the Treasury Department and limited the scope of its future lending activities vis-à-vis the World Bank.[40]

Eisenhower initially sided with Humphrey in the decision to reduce the size and scope of Eximbank lending. A fact-finding trip by Milton Eisenhower to Latin America a few months after his brother's inauguration, however, helped create an environment for reconsideration. At a July 1953 cabinet meeting, the younger Eisenhower reported that governments in Latin America were dissatisfied with the United States' seeming preoccupation with Europe and more recently with its attention to Asia. The administration's efforts to scale back Eximbank lending dismayed Latin Americans, who were, after all, the bank's most important customers. Milton Eisenhower's report, however, had little immediate impact.[41]

In the final analysis Dulles and the State Department's views proved much more important in changing attitudes in the administration, including that of the president. Throughout 1953 Dulles argued that Eximbank loans played a crucial part in development, especially private development in the region, and that economic development was the best bulwark against the growth of communist sentiment in Latin America. Such arguments gained traction with what the administration saw as the increasing leftist leanings of the Arbenz government in Guatemala after 1952—a government whose overthrow Eisenhower subsequently engineered in June 1954. Despite heavy-handed responses like this, Dulles was much more attuned than most in the administration to the forces of nationalism, the needs of development, and the resources that were necessary to channel development away from communism.[42]

Dulles believed that an empowered Eximbank, with a flexible mandate and its long-established relationships in Latin America, could play an important role as the Cold War spread to the region. Humphrey's budgetary and philosophical concerns needed to take a back seat. Dulles realized that making such a case to the president, however, was going to take time. During its initial months the working relationship between Dulles and Eisenhower was in a formative stage. According to Roderic O'Connor, Dulles's special assistant, the secretary was nervous about his standing with Eisenhower. Rather quickly their relationship would deepen, but initially it was certainly not the close, intimate one that came later.[43] George Humphrey at Treasury had the advantage early, since Eisenhower's own fiscal conservatism, as well as his party's similar fiscal views, dominated discussions and decisions about funding for Eximbank and foreign aid programs.

But the president's brother and his secretary of state were not the only ones pressing the administration to reexamine its initial restrictions on the Eximbank. Congress injected itself into the dispute by summer 1953. American corporate exporters and export organizations were deeply concerned about the new administration's limitations on Eximbank activities, and they turned to Congress for help. Capital goods exporters like Westinghouse, which led the effort to gain congressional support, had recently encountered increased foreign competition from Western European (especially West German) companies in making foreign sales. The end of immediate postwar reconstruction and the Korean War accelerated a return to more normal prewar trade patterns. Additionally, while the Korean War was not a global affair, its sudden end turned sellers' markets into buyers' markets for many commodities and industrial products exported by American firms. Furthermore, Western European exporters were finally receiving the benefits of their government's 1949 currency devaluations.[44]

Major American exporters, under these circumstances, believed that Eximbank lending should be increasing, not disappearing. In Congress, they enlisted a seemingly unlikely champion in their fight. Indiana Republican senator Homer E. Capehart, an eight-year veteran of the Senate initially associated with the Taft wing of the party, was the chairman of the Senate Banking and Currency Committee. Indiana, however, was also in the center of the machinery and equipment manufacturing belt in the Midwest. It was home to many businesses that relied to varying degrees on Eximbank assistance to establish and maintain overseas markets, especially in Latin America. Capehart enlisted bipartisan support and, beginning in June 1953, his committee investigated the operations of Eximbank and World Bank and "their relation to the expansion of international trade." A two-month trip and review of operations and projects in Latin America in late 1953 was followed by extensive Senate hearings in January and February 1954. Capehart's orchestrations allowed concerned exporters and their organizations to dominate the hearings. While often critical of Eximbank's bureaucratic procedures, most witnesses supported the need for it to make a wide variety of loans, including long-term development loans.[45]

The approaching Inter-American Conference in Caracas in March 1954, deepening administration concern about the Arbenz government in Guatemala, and mounting exporter pressure aided Dulles's efforts to relax the restrictions on Eximbank. The secretary wanted to be able to announce resumption of unrestricted Eximbank lending in Caracas to assist in mobilizing support against Arbenz and what he saw as Soviet interference in the Western Hemisphere. During fiscal year 1954 (July 1953–June 1954), Eximbank lending declined to the lowest level since 1949, as the pressures and policies of the new administration began to have an effect.[46] Ultimately, Dulles was able to announce the resumption of long-term Eximbank lending at Caracas. That news was helpful in obtaining a conference resolution denouncing communist subversion in the Western Hemisphere, although no specific action against Arbenz was approved.[47]

These pressures culminated in April and May 1954, when representatives of the State and Treasury Departments negotiated compromise legislation while closely consulting with Capehart and other legislators. The August 1954 law undid many of the earlier restrictions on Eximbank's activities. The bank's lending authority (ceiling) was increased from $4.5 billion to $5 billion, to allow it to initiate a simplified exporter credit program. In reporting out the legislation, the Senate Banking and Currency Committee stated that "your committee finds no legislative limitation upon the loan authority of the Export-Import Bank [that] would exclude it from making long-term, medium term, or development loans."[48]

It is far from clear exactly how much Eisenhower was personally involved in these disputes and their ultimate resolution. After all, during his first eighteen months in office Eisenhower was overwhelmingly focused on foreign affairs, defense spending, balancing the budget, and the first Republican recession in a quarter of a century. Subsequently, however, Eisenhower upgraded the importance of export credit to foreign economic policy, and Eximbank's activities greatly expanded during his second term. Symbolically, Eisenhower attended the bank's twenty-fifth anniversary celebration in 1959. He remains the only sitting president to visit the Eximbank, which is just two blocks from the White House.[49]

Eximbank lending soon rebounded after mid-1954. Within a year it reached 1947–52 levels, and observers noted a softening of Treasury's attitude toward the bank after 1954. The battle over the role of the Eximbank in the administration's foreign economic policy and its relationship to lending by multilateral organizations like the World Bank and the IMF was largely settled by the end of Eisenhower's first term in 1956. By that time a new Eximbank president negotiated the termination of a Treasury-brokered 1953 agreement between his predecessor and the World Bank president that had dramatically circumscribed Eximbank's long-term lending. As discussed earlier in this chapter, increased Cold War tensions caused the administration to strengthen its other economic, technical, and military assistance programs after 1954–55. The apparent drift to the left in Latin America was of special concern, and it became the impetus for dramatically increased levels of Eximbank loan activity to its traditional customers in the region. The bank also expanded into new markets, such as India. To facilitate these activities, the administration proposed and Congress overwhelmingly extended Eximbank's charter and increased its lending authority from $5 billion to $7 billion in May 1958.[50] The loan activity of the Eximbank during the second term of the Eisenhower administration (fiscal years 1957–61) averaged almost $900 million a year, roughly double the levels of fiscal years 1950–56.[51]

Increasing foreign competition in domestic and overseas markets in Eisenhower's second term increased the use of Eximbank credit by American exporters. When the United States began to incur substantial balance of payments deficits after 1957, a vital export sector became crucial to paying for US overseas Cold War commitments. By the end of Eisenhower's second term, foreign economic aid to Latin America (other than Eximbank loans) was increasing rapidly. Eximbank's Latin American credits, however, had been and continued to be the dominant face of foreign economic assistance to an increasingly volatile region, even as the bank expanded its operations to Asia, and to a lesser extent Africa.

TRADE POLICY IN THE 1950S

American trade policy in the 1950s, as in the decade before and after, was Eurocentric. The greatest challenge to maintenance of the president's liberal trade policy, however, came from increasing Japanese exports. These were the result of Eisenhower's deliberate decision, impelled by Cold War strategic imperatives, to aggressively promote the integration of Japan into the postwar trade system. Dramatic increases in Japanese imports threatened to intensify already significant domestic opposition to trade liberalization in the early and mid-1950s. During the decade Eisenhower largely succeeded in striking a balance between the need for expanded overseas markets for Japanese products and domestic opposition to aggressive Japanese competition largely through the use of voluntary export restraints (VERs). Subsequent presidential administrations would be much less successful than Eisenhower as imports, especially from Japan, increased rapidly after 1960.[52]

Between 1953 and 1961 the United States enjoyed a huge merchandise trade surplus that showed no outward signs of deterioration.[53] (See fig. 6.1.) Careful

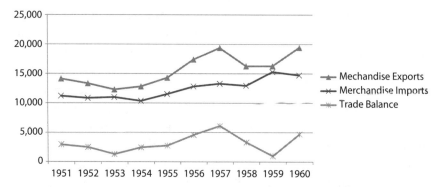

Fig. 6.1. United States Trade Balance, 1951–1960 (in millions of dollars). *Source:* Harold G. Vatter, *The U.S. Economy in the 1950's* (New York: Norton, 1963), p. 262.

analysis, however, revealed that the nature of American trade was shifting and the United States' international competitive position had begun to erode, albeit gradually. Imports of foreign, finished manufactured goods were growing rapidly. As a percentage of total American exports, finished manufactures remained relatively constant during the decade, but foreign, especially European, imports of such items increased dramatically above 1946–50 levels. Also, American exports of semimanufactures (finished somewhere else) declined as a percentage of US exports, while imports of such items remained at higher levels. Trends in imported nonfood consumer goods presented to the American public the face of increasing foreign competition in the 1950s. The United States exported twice what it imported in this category in 1949. By 1955–56 exports and imports were roughly equal, at about $1.3 billion a year. By 1959, however, imports had more than doubled, while American exports remained flat.[54] These figures reflected, in part, the dramatic differences between American manufacturing costs and those of foreign competitors during the decade, much of it associated with significant differences in wage rates, a political lightning rod during the 1950s and 1960s.

While the administration's legislative record on trade liberalization proved to be significant, Eisenhower began cautiously. First came two, one-year extensions of the 1934 Trade Agreements Act (TAA), or the Reciprocal Trade Agreements Act (RTAA), as it was also known. Presidential authority to conduct trade negotiations—originally granted to Congress by the Constitution—grew out of the 1934 legislation enacted in a period of high American tariffs and significant worldwide barriers to international trade. Congress periodically renewed and extended it thereafter, allowing the executive branch to enter into negotiations and agreements with other nations for mutual tariff reductions. These negotia-tions were conducted on a bilateral basis before 1945; after that on a multilateral basis, under the General Agreement on Tariffs and Trade (GATT) in Geneva.[55] The approaches employed by the State Department in these negotiations had not been radical and would not be under Eisenhower. The United States, for exam-ple, did not negotiate "across the board" reductions in tariffs but instead gener-ally proceeded item by item, a practice that continued through 1962. Since the 1920s the United States had also followed "unconditional most-favored nation principles": any reduction in tariffs with one country was "generalized" to other nations that also exported that item to the United States. As a rule, however, the State Department only negotiated reductions with nations that were the princi-pal suppliers of an imported product to limit the competitive impact of such "generalizations" on American imports from other countries.

American tariffs in the early 1930s averaged over 50 percent of the value of dutiable imports. Successful bilateral and later multilateral negotiations be-tween the mid-1930s and the late 1940s significantly lowered these levels.[56] By 1946–50, the comparable percentage had been reduced to about 19 percent and, by the time Eisenhower took office in 1953, to 12 percent. It remained at approxi-mately that figure throughout his two terms.[57] So by the beginning of the Eisen-hower administration, tariffs in many cases did not provide American manufac-turers with much protection against foreign imports.

Of course, by the early 1950s these dramatic reductions in levels of tariff pro-tection had only just begun to impact American manufacturers. Trade, both exports and imports, was a little over 6 percent of gross national product during the 1950s, much lower than in recent decades or today. American tariff levels had always been established with European competition in mind. World War II and the postwar reconstruction dramatically reduced exports to the United States, though that began to change with European recovery, the Marshall Plan, and the devaluations of the major European currencies in 1949. By the early 1950s some foreign imports were beginning to create economic hardship for certain American industries, but the effects had been limited. Eisenhower's treasury secretary, George Humphrey, summed it up in a 1954 cabinet meeting when he noted, "1954 was the first year since the operation of reciprocal trade practices [in 1934] in which there had been a competitive world economy."[58]

This emerging competitive climate shaped foreign trade debates and Eisen-hower's policies during the 1950s. The reappearance of foreign competition heightened protectionist agitation, especially within Eisenhower's own party. On most trade matters the president was more of an advocate of trade liberalization than Congress.[59] Adding to the controversy over trade, during Eisenhower's second term the United States' balance of payments and gold positions deteriorated. These changes boosted the arguments of those who sought greater restrictions on foreign imports.[60]

The initial extension of the TAA in 1953 allowed time for Randall's CFEP to complete its work and make recommendations to Congress in March 1954. Subsequently, the TAA was extended a second year. Eisenhower clearly wanted to use this delay to relieve the pressures for greater trade protection from Taft-wing Republicans. At one of his first meetings with legislative leaders in 1953, the president was quite disheartened by some in his own party who, he thought, "wanted to return to Smoot-Hawley."[61] No new GATT tariff reduction negotiations were undertaken during 1953–54.

The CFEP ultimately recommended a "moderate" trade agreements program, which Eisenhower sent to Congress in 1955. It called for negotiations and maximum reductions in tariffs of 15 percent from existing levels over three years, which Congress enacted. In doing so it also strengthened the so-called escape clause begun in 1942. Under its provisions American concessions made in trade agreements could be withdrawn or modified if injury to domestic producers were demonstrated in Tariff Commission hearings and approved by the president. The 1955 act also included an additional remedy for domestic producers— the president could impose quotas on domestic imports if he believed they were injuring industries vital to the national defense.[62]

The Trade Agreements Act of 1958 was Eisenhower's most important trade legislation. His initial proposal allowed the State Department to enter into negotiations to cut tariffs up to 25 percent from existing levels over a five-year period. Opponents mounted a vigorous attack. Domestic crude oil producers and coal-mining interests feared that crude oil imports would soar once the 1957–58 recession ended. Also opposing the legislation was a growing, vocal group of domestic manufacturers, who faced resurgent European, and especially Japanese, competition.

The real thrust of Eisenhower's 1958 legislation was, as in the past (and well into the 1960s), trade between Europe and the United States. The negotiating authority Eisenhower sought would deflate the new Common Market's external tariff. In passing the legislation, the president received considerable help from Democrats. This extension of the TAA allowed negotiations and tariff reductions of up to 20 percent over four years—implementation would be spread over four subsequent years. Eisenhower opined to British prime minister Harold Macmillan that "he never worked harder for anything than he has in getting [it] extended for four years." Negotiations under the legislation became the Dillon GATT Round in Geneva in 1960–61. The new TAA, however, also strengthened remedies for domestic producers and expanded the scope of relief available in escape clause and "national security" clause cases, victories for opponents of trade liberalization.[63]

It was the exigencies of the Cold War in Asia, however, that generated Eisenhower's greatest trade policy challenge. How was Japan to be integrated into the GATT and the international trading system? The need for Japan to recover economically was urgent following the termination of the American Occupation in 1952 and the sudden end of the Korean War in July 1953. Both had provided substantial stimulus to Japan's still-fragile postwar economy. Almost from the beginning, as an important goal of Cold War policy, Eisenhower was committed to some type of orderly increase in Japanese exports to the United States. The administration also set out to reduce Japan's dependence on American foreign aid grants and increase that country's exports to Southeast Asia and Europe and away from communist China. Meanwhile, White House officials worried that the United States would have to absorb the lion's share of Japan's increasing exports in the short to intermediate term. Thus, Eisenhower needed to balance Cold War strategy with fierce opposition at home and in Europe to increased Japanese imports. Postwar opposition to Japanese integration into world trade on both sides of the Atlantic was so strong that the administration feared it might severely compromise the already weakening American support for postwar trade liberalization.

Japan's aggressive international competition in textiles and inexpensive consumer goods in worldwide markets, including the United States in the 1930s, had left a bitter legacy among its potential postwar trading partners.[64] This would complicate any expansion of postwar Japanese imports. European nations and their existing and former colonies employed quantitative restrictions (quotas) often in combination with high tariffs to restrict foreign imports during the 1930s. In the United States, however, presidential administrations had always preferred high tariffs instead of quotas to regulate foreign competition in manufactured products. Historically, American policymakers had opposed import quotas. They used tariffs instead in large part to avoid complex domestic regulatory mechanisms that would be needed to administer import quotas. Prewar and postwar presidents, including Eisenhower, followed this policy.[65]

High American tariffs in the 1930s, however, were usually not sufficient to blunt aggressively marketed and priced Japanese imports like cotton textiles, other consumer goods, and fish. So a system developed rapidly in which the State

Department encouraged Japanese exporters and their domestic American competitors to enter into "gentlemen's agreements," or voluntary export restraints (VERs). These arrangements set volume limits on Japanese exports to the United States and were designed to prevent "surges" of exports to the American market and provide for the orderly marketing of Japanese goods. Some of the negotiations leading to the agreements were conducted exclusively between both countries' producers without any assistance from the State Department, or with limited assistance. In others, diplomats intervened when negotiations between the two nations' producers broke down. Neither of these situations raised significant problems under pre-1940 antitrust law. Others were negotiated government-to-government. Eventually, most Japanese exports to the United States, except raw silk, came under some form of voluntary restraint during the mid-1930s.[66]

Japanese products largely disappeared from the international economy during World War II and early in the American Occupation of Japan (1945–52)—exports did not reach prewar levels of about $1 billion until 1951 ($1.4 billion)—then they rapidly accelerated because of the Korean War. (By 1955, they reached $2 billion and by 1960, $4 billion.) During the Occupation cotton textiles, tuna, and fish products had been Japan's major exports, as prewar patterns reemerged. Cotton textiles were 29 percent of Japan's exports by 1950. The American Occupation authorities—Supreme Command for the Allied Powers (SCAP) initially—enforced a complete ban on exports of cotton cloth to the United States. They lifted it in 1948 only because Japan desperately needed foreign exchange. SCAP also maintained a capacity limitation on the Japanese industry until 1950 to assure that cotton textiles would not be a major factor in international postwar markets. Productive capacity, however, doubled during the Korean War. Truman administration officials hoped that postwar Japanese exports would find almost all of their markets in Asia, but the subsequent expansion of the Cold War to Asia after 1948 and the "fall" of China in 1949 severely limited this option.[67] During 1934–36 Asia had absorbed 64 percent of Japan's $1 billion in exports; in 1950 the figure was 46 percent of $1.4 billion; and in 1960 the figure would be just 37 percent of $3 billion. The respective figures for exports to China were 18 percent, 2 percent, and 0.2 percent.[68] These exports would have to go other places—that is, the United States.

During GATT tariff negotiations at Geneva, Annecy, and Torquay between 1947 and 1951, the Truman administration continued policies initiated in the 1930s that limited the benefit to Japan of tariff concessions to other countries under unconditional most-favored-nation principles. Few concessions involved products that Japan exported because of the sensitivity of US producers.[69] The peace treaty officially ending the war in the Pacific and the American Occupation of Japan was effective April 28, 1952. According to the treaty, former allied nations could treat Japanese commerce as they chose, and the United States quickly extended most-favored-nation status to Japan. The effect was limited, however, because few tariff concessions had been "generalized" to Japan in the previous two decades. In June 1952, Japan formally applied for GATT membership and was provisionally admitted in October 1953. Formal membership came in 1955, but many countries (and most Western European nations) declined to extend most-favored-nation status to Japan and instituted quantitative restrictions on its imports.[70]

The extremely difficult issues of how and at what speed Japan would be integrated into the postwar trading regime were left to the incoming Eisenhower administration, which also had to deal with questions about who would absorb the anticipated increased level of very competitive Japanese exports. In view of the policies of the other GATT signatories up to 1953, it appeared that the answer was the United States, and in fact that is what occurred during the 1950s. The United Kingdom and the countries that became the European Economic Community (or Common Market) in 1958 absorbed approximately 8 percent of Japan's exports in 1934–36, and in 1950 and 1960. The respective figures for the United States were 16 percent in 1934–36; 22 percent in 1950 and 1955; and 29 percent in 1960.[71]

A dispute over Japanese tuna fish exports late in Truman's term presented the incoming administration with the question of what would be the role of VERs in increasing postwar Japanese trade. Because of the termination of a bilateral trade agreement with Mexico in 1951, there had been large increases in tariff duties for canned tuna, while fresh or frozen tuna remained duty-free. Tuna consumption in the United States was rising rapidly, and within one year imports of Japanese fresh or frozen tuna quickly grew to about 30 percent of the American market and the price of American-caught tuna dropped about 50 percent. This appeared to be a reemergence of a pattern of prewar Japanese import "surges." Japan's tuna exports to the United States exceeded $11 million and represented about 5 percent of its total exports to the United States in 1951. Legislation in Congress proposed a "temporary tariff" of 20 percent on all Japanese tuna, while the Tariff Commission would examine tuna tariffs. The Japanese industry feared increased tariffs on its first major consumer product to deeply penetrate the postwar American market. Representatives of the domestic American and Japanese industry exchanged visits to discuss among themselves quantitative limitations on Japanese exports. Both sides seemed oblivious to the limitations of the new postwar antitrust climate that made such discussions or agreements illegal and seemed to believe that their respective governments could subsequently endorse a privately negotiated "voluntary" restraint without raising antitrust issues.[72]

While Congress considered and ultimately rejected the temporary tariff, the Japanese government instituted a unilateral limit of tuna exports to the United States, based on the two industries' private (and presumably illegal) negotiations. This was the first postwar VER. Truman's State Department opposed it and hoped to convince the Japanese to follow another course: it feared that other Japanese exporters to the American market would succumb to similar pressure, eventually compromising Japan's hopes of economic self-sufficiency.[73]

Eisenhower's administration rejected such earlier concerns. Instead, it embraced VERs as a tool to manage the growth of Japan's imports and the domestic American political challenge they presented. Quite quickly the change was promoted at the very highest levels of the administration—by Dulles and Eisenhower themselves. Before becoming secretary of state in 1953, Dulles had been a member of the American delegation that negotiated the Japanese peace treaty. In that role he was instrumental in reaching a gentlemen's agreement on Japanese-American fishing rights issues. In testimony supporting the 1953 renewal of the TAA in April 1953, he specifically endorsed the new Japanese tuna VER and the bilateral negotiations that led to the agreement:

> You can often work these things out, you know, informally with the foreign countries if you have the disposition to do it. Reference has been made to tuna-fish. . . . I know when I was working on the Japanese situation before there was a very reasonable disposition on the part of the Japanese, at least, to put voluntary restrictions upon the import of tuna fish into this country. I think they have done so to some extent. . . . Very frequently I have found that there is a disposition on the part of these governments to be appreciative of the disturbance, which their exports cause, and voluntarily to take action to restrict them. . . . *I believe many of these situations could be dealt with on an informal basis like that.*" (Emphasis added)[74]

Dulles rejected the prior position of the Truman administration. He believed that VERs were infinitely more desirable than unilateral American import quotas, which he continued vigorously to oppose. But he was aware of the antitrust problems that could arise. Subsequently, when the first Japanese restraint for tuna terminated in 1953, both Japanese exporters and American producers negotiated a private limitation on imports. Taking a cue from the role of diplomats in the 1930s, they presented it to Dulles in the hope that it would become the basis of a diplomatic agreement between the United States and Japan. Dulles, however, rejected this private understanding as detrimental to Japan and possibly illegal under American antitrust laws. Ultimately, the State Department made clear that only bilateral "understandings" between governments (not private parties) or unilateral acts by the Japanese government would be considered useful. Of course, the United States said that it would accept truly voluntary unilateral restraints under Japanese government supervision so long as they were not applied in a manner that harmed American national interests.[75]

Thus, VERs quickly became an integral part of Eisenhower's thinking about how to expand and manage Japanese trade. In August 1954, while preparing for tariff negotiations leading up to Japan's accession to the GATT, the president emphasized at a cabinet meeting that he wanted to approach Japan's post–Korean War economic predicament from many different directions. But what was crucial to him was that the "U.S. prevent development of a situation in Japan which would result in a communist take-over." Eisenhower endorsed voluntary restraints (VERs) as part of the solution: "The president quickly suggested that rather than formal exclusion [of Japanese imports] the situation might be alleviated by a certain amount of restraint on the part of foreign exporters and domestic American importers."[76] Notes of the meeting clearly show that the president was told that a $600 million increase in Japanese exports meant mostly capital goods and equipment to Asia and the underdeveloped world, but at least a $100 million increase in consumer goods would come to the United States in the near term from the projected 1955 tariff concessions. Others like Treasury Secretary Humphrey expressed more caution and opined, "The emphasis should be put on spreading Japanese exports throughout the world rather than having the United States carry the burden of buying Japanese goods."[77]

Other economic considerations underscored the importance of Japanese exports to US Cold War strategy. In 1953, Japan ran a large trade deficit with the world ($1.135 billion); its deficit with the United States alone ($424 million) was one-third of the total. Japan was also a major customer for American exports (third behind Canada and Britain)—between $600 million and $700 million a year during 1951–55. Japan's exports to the United States were initially anemic—just $182 million in 1951, rising to $279 million in 1954, but surging to $432 million in 1955. Japan's trade deficit with the United States declined to $321 million in 1955, but it remained substantial throughout the 1950s. Before the end of the American Occupation in 1952, these substantial deficits had been largely financed by US GARIOA (Government and Relief in Occupied Areas) funds. Furthermore, after the end of the Korean War American military expenditures in Japan declined from over $800 million in 1952–53 to under $600 million for 1954–56. Additional American military procurement, other aid (agricultural), and American investment in Japan allowed it to finance its huge trade deficit with the United States throughout the decade.[78] But the Eisenhower administration wanted some of this aid burden reduced by increased Japanese exports to the United States. Neither the high levels of aid nor increased imports of products were popular policies, but the administration was determined to reduce Japan's aid dependency.

Eisenhower believed that the real crisis in Japanese trade would come in 1955, when Congress considered his proposals to extend the TAA. Existing trade legislation required that items for negotiation of reduced tariffs with Japan, associated with their accession to the GATT and scheduled for Geneva in 1955, needed to be published shortly before the November 1954 elections. The issue might be injected in the fall political campaign, but Eisenhower scorned "any failure by Congressmen to live up to their responsibilities in a matter as essential to the national interest as this."[79]

The negotiations with Japan in Geneva in 1955 had to be conducted under a strict timetable, since the TAA (and the authority to reduce existing duties 50% from 1945 levels) expired on June 11, 1955. Eisenhower's pending legislative proposals would set a new base period and reduce the cuts available to no more than 15 percent of those new tariff levels. Central to the upcoming Geneva negotiations were large tariff reductions on cotton textile products of interest to Japan. Due to the policies of the previous twenty years of trade liberalization, such duties remained relatively high and the deadline had to be met. The American cotton textile industry and its trade association (the American Cotton Manufacturers Institute, or ACMI) knew what was coming, and industry trade publications decried the inevitability of a "textile Munich" to appease what it saw as Cold War strategic requirements relative to Japan.[80]

A House-Senate conference committee approved Eisenhower's TAA three-year extension on June 8, 1955, and the results of the negotiations with Japan were announced later that day. They included tariff reductions of 25 to 48 percent on many types of cotton cloth, effective in September. The ACMI thought that the impact of the reductions was 0.75 to 1.5 cents per square yard, which, it observed, was the current profit margin of the American cotton textile industry.[81] Japanese imports increased quickly from 48 million square yards in 1954 to 143 million square yards (worth $84 million) in 1956. These totals were not significant in the aggregate—only 0.7 to 1.7 percent of the US domestic market. Japanese imports, however, were concentrated in narrow categories, such as cotton velveteens (where they quickly got half of the domestic market) and ginghams. Japanese cotton clothing appeared for the first time, including the exceedingly popular "dollar blouses," which became a department store staple that captured 28 percent of the American market within a year of their introduction in 1955. Such rapid increases (i.e., "surges") lent credence to arguments by the ACMI about the unique characteristics of Japanese competition, which echoed the rhetoric and experience of the mid-1930s.[82]

Over the next eighteen months maneuvering between the governments and the cotton textile industries of the two countries was constant. Within a few months of the effective date of the tariff reductions, the Japanese industry and government implemented unilateral restraints on various types of cotton textile exports to the United States. These VERs were of limited effectiveness, as imports continued to increase. The ACMI did not believe that any unilateral Japanese restraint would be satisfactory and instead sought American-imposed import quotas. Administration officials adamantly opposed legislated quotas on manufactured products, and even if these passed Congress, Eisenhower would surely veto them. Such congressional action, however, even if only symbolic, would be perceived as a serious blow to postwar trade liberalization efforts and a thorn in US-Japanese relations. It was something that the White House sought to avoid at all costs. Instead, the administration encouraged Japan to strengthen efforts to impose orderly regulation on exports to the United States. In May and September the State Department coordinated Japanese statements about the details of their restraint program (VER) with this objective in mind.[83]

American diplomats, however, maintained that they could not enter into an agreement with Japan's government concerning quantitative limitations on imports unless the Tariff Commission made a finding of injury to the domestic industry in an escape clause proceeding. Here the administration and the ACMI were at loggerheads. Though velveteen producers did file an escape clause action, the ACMI argued that the unique character of Japanese imports was so destructive that even small amounts could "disrupt" markets. Such volumes (compared to industry totals) were just too small for a Tariff Commission finding of injury and relief under the escape clause for the industry as a whole, or even for broad categories of cotton cloth. Furthermore, the ACMI's ideas on any VER negotiated between the United States and Japanese governments seemed to envision limited almost pro forma participation of the US government, reminiscent of the 1930s. In the postwar period, however, such a negotiating framework raised huge antitrust concerns. Finally, while Japanese diplomats understood the limitations of the American antitrust laws on possible solutions, most representatives of the Japanese industry often seemed clueless.[84]

In the United States the politics of this situation were also potentially serious. The American cotton textile industry was concentrated in New England and in the Atlantic Southeast, where many of its leaders were active in a revitalized Republican Party. Former New Hampshire governor Sherman Adams, now Eisenhower's chief of staff, had been head of the New England Governors' Conference. Concern arose among Eisenhower's political advisers about how any apparent reluctance to assist the American industry might impact some states in the fall elections.

The pace of the negotiations quickened following July 1956, after the Senate only narrowly defeated an amendment to the Mutual Security Act that would have limited cotton textile imports by an import quota based on the average imports of the previous three years. Adams took charge of coordinating the negotiations as the administration changed its strategy. It informed the Japanese government of what its "best assessment" was of the maximum level of imports that would defuse the ACMI's drive for quotas. Then the Japanese government could craft a program for its exporters.[85] This approach also seemed to limit antitrust exposure for the industries of the two countries. Japan's government began gradually to respond to the increased pressure. In late September it proposed a much more comprehensive program of restraints on cotton cloth. ACMI still believed such an approach insufficient but finally acquiesced in the Japanese insistence on broad categories of cloth (instead of narrow product descriptions) to allow them flexibility in any "voluntary" restraint program they undertook.[86]

Once this debate ended, the parties moved to a settlement rather quickly. The final VER called for an annual ceiling of 235 million square yards on Japanese imports in relatively broad categories, with special limits for ginghams and velveteens. The VER had a five-year duration, with annual reviews. The administration presented the results of the negotiations to the ACMI soon after, and it "approved." The Japanese government formally announced the VER on January 16, 1957.[87]

The administration had been forced to formalize its reliance on "informal voluntary restraint" of Japanese exports more than it wanted to. Adams had thought the approach "innovative and necessary to advance the overall aims of the President's trade program." He told a skeptical Ezra Taft Benson that "the approach taken with regard to this Japanese textile problem . . . illustrates the flexibility that is needed from time to time if our progress toward an agreed goal is not to be threatened by an eruption of accumulated opposition." Dulles thought that if negotiations had broken down Japan would have moved toward closer relations with communist China. The Japanese were not happy but preferred such informal arrangements to escape clause actions or legislated import quotas. Probably the most satisfactory outcome for the administration was that the politically powerful American cotton textile industry would not be a major opponent of the renewal of the TAA in 1958, and the drive for legislated import quotas on manufactured products had been diffused. The administration, however, reinforced its position that Japanese competition was something sui generis, apart from its European counterpart, for which American tariffs had been historically set. It also continued to think of VERs as something that would not be useful or desirable outside of US-Japanese trade.[88]

The cotton textile VER was the centerpiece of a broader, quasi-voluntary scheme of Japanese restraints on their exports to the United States that arose after 1954. The cotton textile negotiations were qualitatively different because of their more formalized, bilateral nature; the political power of the industry; and the sheer dollar amounts of trade involved. But by 1958 the administration began to refer to a "system" of Japanese export restraint that included quantitative restrictions on the export of tuna, paper hats, stainless steel flatware, plywood, sewing machines, wool textiles, and many other less important consumer products. In many instances these unilateral VERs, administered or supervised to at least some degree by the Japanese government, gave its exporters more flexibility than the rather rigid structures of the bilateral cotton textile VER. The US government, however, was often involved in "fine tuning" these Japanese unilateral restraints when pressured by American industry or on its own initiative. Eisenhower was convinced that this series of VERs, if properly administered by Japan and overseen by the United States, provided a mechanism for the orderly expansion of Japanese exports. The administration hoped that the VERs would allow Japanese exports to simply track or keep pace with the overall growth of all American imports but not be "disorderly."[89] This did not happen. Japanese exports to the United States increased from $0.43 billion in 1955 to $1.15 billion in 1960, and this represented an increase from 4 percent of American imports to 7 percent. (Japan's percentage of American imports of manufactures doubled from 7.6% to 15.6% in the same period.) Even so, the United States continued to enjoy a large trade surplus with Japan throughout the decade, as its exports to Japan roughly doubled from $0.68 billion to $1.45 billion.[90]

In 1960, the assistant secretary of state for economic affairs, Thomas Mann, told Congress that Japanese export controls "are imposed on somewhere around 30 to 35 separate products, starting with cotton textiles and running pretty much through the gamut of their export trade."[91] In his testimony supporting the 1958 TAA, Dulles, who since 1953 had never wavered in his support of such VERs, described them as reliable and in the best interest of the United States and its strategy in Asia.[92] Most importantly, the reliance on VERs found a consistent champion in the president himself. During the 1956 cotton textile negotiations, he referred to Japanese unilateral VERs as "constructive and helpful," while at the same time the administration sought tougher, more rigid controls. And in June 1957, he told Japan's prime minister Nobusuke Kishi that the Japanese system of voluntary restraints had proven satisfactory, a sentiment he reiterated at subsequent meetings.[93]

Within the administration, however, there were dissenters to the evolving policy. Agriculture Secretary Benson feared that encouraging Japan to restrict its exports would compromise the US position as a huge agricultural exporter to Japan.[94] Considerable discussion of the negative aspects of the practice occurred at the State Department, although no minds were changed.[95] In fact, the rapidly crystallizing system of Japanese voluntary restraint was not only guided and shaped by American policymakers, it was also facilitated with US foreign technical assistance funds. Beginning in 1955 the State Department's US International Cooperation Administration conducted a "productivity promotion program" in Japan to foster "a businesslike approach in international trade practice by developing orderly markets abroad instead of killing such markets by flooding them." Program expenditures between fiscal 1955 and 1958 approached $1 million annually. These years coincided with the proliferation of VERs in US-Japanese trade.[96]

American industries facing Japanese competition were generally not happy with the developing scheme of Japanese voluntary restraint. They would have preferred imposition of American import quotas or tariff relief under the escape clause, which was seldom granted and was always in the form of tariffs.[97] Instead, the administration pressed domestic industries to accept Japanese VERs. With good reason, administration officials feared draconian remedies that would produce a long-term impediment to what they saw as the orderly growth of Japanese trade. For reasons of practical flexibility and political symbolism, Japanese government and industry officials often orchestrated a crescendo of activity and hand-wringing as escape clause cases moved through the process. They generally favored any type of voluntary restraint, as opposed to an escape clause restriction.

The administration's willingness to work with Japan on voluntary remedies became a matter of contention during Congress's consideration of the TAA in 1958. A surge in imports of Japanese stainless steel flatware brought the issue to a head. Eisenhower displayed an eagerness to promote unilateral Japanese restraint but also a willingness to take a tough position toward Japan when necessary. The Japanese share of the American stainless steel market increased from 7 percent in 1953 to 36 percent in 1956. In 1957 the American Stainless Steel

Flatware Manufacturers Association filed a petition with the Tariff Commission for relief under the escape clause. The immediate response of the Japanese government was to organize its export trade and then announce a unilateral VER for the American market at existing export levels (5.9 million dozen-piece sets). The State Department followed up with "suggestions" about how the VER could be strengthened.[98] The Tariff Commission subsequently recommended dramatically increased tariffs. Eisenhower, however, rejected this statutory relief and instead deferred action to give the unilateral Japanese VER every possible chance to succeed.[99]

Less than a year later it became clear that the Japanese circumvented the VER on stainless steel flatware by shipping products to the United States via third countries. Eisenhower subsequently agreed with the recommendation of the Tariff Commission in 1959 to impose much higher tariffs on imports in excess of the number set in the Japanese VER—a tariff quota.[100] Eisenhower's response reflected his position that some type of quantitative limitations on Japanese exports was necessary. He usually preferred a flexible system of VERs, but not always. Despite the "voluntary" nature of the scheme, Japan needed to be periodically reminded that meaningful enforcement was crucial.[101]

In April 1959 in an address at Gettysburg College, Eisenhower made one of his most impassioned arguments for Japan's strategic importance; increasing Japanese exports to the United States; and the role of unilateral and bilateral VERs in achieving that goal:

Japan is an essential counterweight to Communist strength in Asia. . . . More than perhaps any other industrial nation, Japan must export to live. Last year she had a trade deficit. At one time she had a thriving trade in Asia, particularly with her nearest neighbors. Much of it is gone. Her problems grow more grave. . . . Japan must have additional trade outlets now. Japanese natural markets in Southeast Asia would reappear only gradually with economic development. These can be provided if each of the industrialized nations of the West does its part in liberalizing trade relations with Japan. . . . One thing we in America can do is to study our existing trade regulations between America and Japan. Quite naturally we must guard against a flooding of our markets by goods, made in other countries, to the point where our own industries would dry up. But the mere imposition of higher and higher tariffs cannot solve trade problems even for us, prosperous though we be. . . . Moreover, unless Japan's exports to us are at least maintained at approximately their present levels, we would risk the free world stake in the whole Pacific.

Without stating it in so many words, Eisenhower promoted VERs as a vehicle for the orderly growth of Japanese exports to the United States and linked it to Cold War imperatives. He emphasized that the importance of the orderly growth of Japan's exports was of as much importance to the prosecution of the Cold War as a resolute stand in Berlin or economic and military support for South Vietnam.[102]

By the time Eisenhower left office, Japanese trade had been reintroduced into the international economy, a goal of the administration's Cold War strategy. During a decade when the momentum of trade liberalization was under stress, the United States had absorbed a disproportionately large share of Japan's increasing exports. Two major extensions of the TAA were enacted. Crucial to this accomplishment was some type of orderly expansion of Japanese imports into the United States. Administration officials believed that on balance the president had successfully managed the quick growth of Japanese imports of manufactured goods into the domestic American market. Though Japanese imports were increasing, they did not undermine the 1958 extension of the TAA and the US commitment to a liberal trade regime. Subsequent administrations were less successful as the situation changed. Japanese imports surged after 1963, and agitation about them was a major factor in Congress's unwillingness to grant the executive branch authority to negotiate trade agreements between 1967 and 1975.[103]

THE BALANCE OF PAYMENTS AND FOREIGN ECONOMIC POLICY, 1958–1961

Coupled with American policymakers' commitments to continue postwar trade liberalization was an effort to strengthen the domestic economies and international liquidity positions of its allies in Western Europe, Japan, and elsewhere. Substantial grants of economic aid to Western Europe and Japan were the early centerpiece of this effort. By 1953, however, these had declined dramatically. Military and economic foreign assistance in the mid- to late 1950s shifted to other regions, though commitments of military aid to Western Europe remained significant throughout the decade. The cost of maintaining large numbers of American forces and bases in Western Europe (NATO), South Korea, and Japan was very high. Additionally, the Eisenhower administration promoted long-term capital investments overseas as a viable substitute for expensive and controversial foreign economic assistance programs. Such investments and long-term movements of capital would be facilitated greatly by the external convertibility of foreign currencies, a postwar goal of American policymakers that most Western European countries achieved by the end of 1958.

To varying degrees such policies required that the US government or private American firms spend dollars outside the United States. In the constricted international capital markets of the immediate postwar period (1945–58), the United States initially liquefied the system to address the dollar gap in reserves of America's allies, who were encouraged to acquire and hold dollars. Under the Bretton Woods Agreement, the dollar became the reserve currency and the system was underwritten by the US commitment to exchange dollar holdings of other governments at a fixed rate with gold ($35 an ounce)—the "gold window."

As a result the United States maintained a balance of payments deficit in dollars with the rest of the world throughout the 1950s. The exception came in 1957, when unusual levels of American oil exports to Europe caused by the closure of the Suez Canal reversed the figures. This was a cash payments account. It included the international "current account"—the trade balance and the balance on income from services and investments. The trade balance (exports over imports) was always positive in the 1950s, averaging about $3 billion a year, but it often fluctuated greatly between $6 billion (in 1957) and $1 billion (in 1959). The account for income and services was positive and remarkably steady, at about $1.5 billion annually throughout the decade. (See Table 3.1).

These huge positive international accounts were offset by consistently large outflows—substantial payments by the US government for military expenditures overseas and foreign loans (net). Largely excluded from this "government" account were other substantial aid programs in military equipment and surplus agricultural commodities, since these were predominantly "spent" in the United States, not overseas.[104] Military expenditures overseas, however, averaged approximately $2.5 to $3 billion annually and increased throughout Eisenhower's administration; grants averaged about $1.7 billion and were steady during much of Eisenhower's term, after declining dramatically early in the decade; and loans (net) averaged just $0.5 billion for the decade. But the increased activities of the Mutual Aid program and the Eximbank during Eisenhower's second term increased this figure to about $1 billion annually. Net private, long-term capital investment was negative and averaged slightly over $1 billion a year between 1951 and 1957. It increased to over $2 billion annually between 1958 and 1960, as the creation of the European Economic Community and its external tariff barriers caused investment in Western Europe to increase. Short-term capital flows were usually an insignificant item in the US balance of payments until 1960, when they exceeded negative $1.3 billion.[105]

Thus, for the years 1951–57 the US balance of payments deficit averaged slightly under $1 billion annually, which was considered manageable at the time, given American Cold War strategy and commitments. It varied from a negative $2.1 billion in 1953 to a positive $0.5 billion in 1957. After 1957 the deficit increased fairly dramatically—for 1958–60 it averaged $3.7 billion annually, never dipping below $3 billion.[106] If the United States' efforts to get other nations to consider their dollar holdings on a par with their gold reserves were successful, the United States could continue to run balance of payments deficits with no impact on American gold reserves. But a variety of factors after 1954, which intensified after 1957, increased the balance of payments deficit and the desire of foreign governments to hold gold in lieu of dollars.[107]

US efforts to liquefy the international system provided the "grease" for an acceleration of international trade that brought prosperity to postwar Europe and Japan by the late 1950s. As a result, these countries again became significant international trade competitors, both in overseas markets long dominated by American exporters and in the American domestic market. By the end of the decade the US trade surplus began a long-term decline, but the trend was not yet pronounced and was generally not a major concern of policymakers. The intensification of the Cold War with large, near-permanent overseas troop deployments and the increasing need for military and economic aid, however, clearly strained the US balance of payments position. Finally, European external currency convertibility and the creation of the Common Market increased long-term capital investment flows to Europe and greatly expanded the market for short-term capital movements, taking advantage of differentials in global interest rates. The Eisenhower administration successfully responded to the changed environment of the 1950s: the fading dollar gap (with Europe and Japan), an overseas dollar surplus position, and increasing strains on the US balance of payments position without seriously compromising its commitment to (1) vigorously waging the Cold War; (2) continuing measured trade liberalization and reduction of barriers; (3) facilitating the international movement of investment capital; and (4) increased economic and military assistance to an expanding, diverse clientele of nations.

Even so, almost from its inception the administration monitored the worsening balance of payments position. As early as 1955 Treasury Secretary Humphrey cautioned Eisenhower about declining US gold reserves and potential short-term claims held by foreign governments against the dollar. He noted that if all of those claims were presented, which he deemed highly unlikely, and liquidated in gold, the US gold balance would be below that legally required for the

Federal Reserve system to support the currency. Humphrey observed that the monetary reserves of other countries had been strengthened and the United States' had been weakened. Though he thought this trend presented no current problems, he believed that "we need to give careful thought to making sure of continued confidence in the U.S. dollar."[108]

On April 20, 1956, a cabinet meeting presentation by Secretary Humphrey on the balance of payments set the tone for subsequent administration policy. Characteristically, Humphrey used the potential increases in foreign government claims on American gold (their dollar holdings) since 1949 as a springboard for complaints about military spending and foreign economic assistance programs. Both had immediate impacts on the US balance of payments position and broader spending issues. He believed that there was a financial limit on the domestic and foreign programs the United States could support and argued that "we can't run any more [budget] deficits." Arthur Burns responded that the country had been "a little profligate" but suggested that we "should watch with the greatest care how we spend our dollars at home and abroad." Burns added, "I can't worry about gold with dollar claims increasing, [it] merely shows we are banker of the world and [the need for] confidence in the dollar." Others like Gabriel Hauge affirmed the common belief that the worldwide redistribution of dollars had been desirable and that no one wanted to go back to the situation that existed in 1949 at the height of the dollar gap.[109]

This cabinet discussion reflected the parameters of Eisenhower's strategy over the next four years. Participants recognized a crucial relationship between foreign expenditures, which had a direct impact on the balance of payments, and domestic spending and deficits, whose impact was indirect but nevertheless crucial. Cabinet members believed that the United States' adherence to policies of fiscal and monetary restraint secured the value of the dollar and steadied the willingness of foreign governments to hold dollar reserves, limiting the appetite for payment of dollar claims in gold. Confidence in the dollar made the system work.[110]

Macro- and microeconomic policy making became more difficult when the balance of payments deficit ballooned in 1958 and remained at roughly those levels through the rest of Eisenhower's second term. With regard to the activities that had a direct impact on the US balance of payments account, the administration was not about to fundamentally alter its military or foreign economic strategies it believed crucial to the prosecution of the Cold War, like trade liberalization and increased foreign aid. Adjustments, however, could be made. Over the objections of the State Department, in October 1959 Eisenhower acted on a National Advisory Council recommendation and required that Development Loan Fund procurement of goods and services be restricted to domestic sources. Estimates at the time were that, except for the DLF, about 80 percent of American foreign military and economic aid was procured in the United States. Indeed, Eximbank loans had been tied by statute to domestic procurement from its inception.[111]

Other steps were taken. Beginning in 1959, the Department of Commerce strengthened its efforts to promote American exports and, as discussed earlier in this chapter, the lending authority and activities of the Eximbank increased. The United States also encouraged its European allies to strengthen their export credit agencies and shift away from cash terms for sale of capital goods overseas. Administration officials hoped that this would reduce the burden on the US balance of payments created by dollar export financing to the developing world made by European export credit agencies. And finally, during Eisenhower's last two years in office, he and Treasury Secretary Robert B. Anderson also pressed Western European allies to reduce the American foreign aid burden by initiating or expanding their own foreign aid programs.[112]

Despite these changes, the balance of payments deficit remained largely intractable through 1960 ($3.5 billion in 1958, $3.8 billion in 1959, and $3.9 billion in 1960). After mid-1960, gold redemptions nearly resumed their 1958 pace, following a dramatic reduction in 1959. This trend was especially pronounced during late 1960, as speculation raged about the willingness of candidate, later president-elect, Kennedy to devalue the dollar or restrict gold sales. The administration also intensified efforts to reduce the cost of maintaining American forces in Western Europe, especially West Germany, or to get Europeans to cover more of the costs of the American military establishment there. Actions included a gradual reduction of military dependents in Western Europe. The impact of these overseas cost-cutting measures was gradually felt, but the cost of maintaining the American military establishment in NATO countries remained large: $2.7 billion in 1960, $2.5 billion in 1961, and a projected $2.0 billion by 1964. It was one of the single largest negatives in the balance of payments.[113]

Finally, the dramatic drop in the United States' favorable trade balance in 1959 emphasized how important the trade surplus was in compensating for the negative impacts of such programs as military expenditures overseas, foreign aid, and foreign direct investment. The trade surplus declined from $3.3 billion in 1958 to $1.0 billion in 1959, only to rise again in 1960 to $4.7 billion.[114] At the time the sudden drop was explained away by unique circumstances like relative prosperity in the United States and recession in Western Europe, which reversed the following year; a surge in foreign steel imports due to a strike in 1959; and the increasing popularity of imported cars. Some of these trends subsequently returned to more normal patterns for the time. American automakers, for example, responded to the foreign challenge with "compact" cars, and the share of imports in the American auto market declined dramatically. Steelmakers, however, never succeeded in countering the foreign penetration of their domestic markets. Foreign steelmakers captured markets and expanded market share, which they never lost. American steel exports, once robust, declined and were increasingly restricted to "tied" programs like foreign aid and Eximbank-financed ventures.

White House economic adviser Don Paarlberg attributed the 1959 trade balance decline to an accelerated loss of American competitiveness, but his view was a distinct minority position. CEA chairman Raymond J. Saulnier believed in 1959 that it was an overstatement to say that "we have priced ourselves out of world markets," but he "thought that the steel dispute and outcome was extremely significant since it was painfully evident that we had lost competitive advantage in this particular industry." And by the end of the decade the United States imported roughly twice the nonfood consumer goods it exported—a harbinger of things to come.[115] Especially during his second term, Eisenhower would occasionally make statements about the loss of American competitiveness. But most in the administration, including the president, assumed that the positive trade balance would remain a feature of American foreign economic policy for the immediate future. The increasing balance of payments deficit was not a reason to substantially reverse postwar trade liberalization policies. Various components of the balance of payments deficit could be addressed by discrete policies, but a substantial deficit could be maintained for the foreseeable future—a so-called equilibrium balance subject to a big "if." Eisenhower and Treasury Secretary Anderson were of one mind that protecting the US gold reserve from foreign redemptions was fundamentally a function of continued adherence to sound American budget, fiscal, monetary, and anti-inflation policies, which Eisenhower had pursued since he had taken office and vowed to continue.

Thus, Eisenhower's fiscal conservatism and his anti-inflation views, which had been reinforced by the experiences of the mid-decade boom and the 1957–58 recession, were intensified by the deterioration of the US balance of payments and the potential threat to US gold reserves after 1957. The balance of payments deficit, to some degree, was here to stay. In the relatively closed international financial system of the late 1950s, conservative macroeconomic management of the economy was vital to protecting American gold reserves and fostering the willingness of foreign governments to hold dollars and not redeem them for gold. If the United States, which exported dollars, incurred significant inflation, the reserve status of the dollar would eventually be compromised and, all too soon, external financing of the Cold War would be impaired.[116]

Eisenhower linked the balance of payments situation with an intensifying domestic anti-inflation drive and the need for a vigorous internationalist position. As discussed in chapter 3, Eisenhower's rapid move from a huge budget deficit in fiscal 1959 to a small surplus in fiscal 1960 can be completely understood only in these terms. In 1959 Anderson summarized the administration's position to the American Finance Association and the American Economic Association:

> The importance of avoiding inflation deserves special emphasis. Surely the rate of economic growth in future—which depends heavily on a high rate of savings and capital formation today—will be stunted if fear of inflation is allowed to impair the will to save in traditional, fixed dollar forms. And surely an unsustainable upsurge in economic activity, based on [an] expectation of inflation, is likely to be followed by a fallback to a lower level of activity and consequent under-utilization of our economic resources. . . . The dollar is the major reserve currency of the world. This function can be served efficiently only if foreign holders of dollar claims, who now have a sizable stake in the way in which we manage our affairs, continue to have confidence in the dollar's basic worth and stability. Under these circumstances, a responsible Government must adopt measures and encourage actions at home and abroad that, over time, reduce the size of the deficit and has [sic] as their long-range objective a satisfactory equilibrium in our over-all payments position. Such steps are essential if we are to maintain a sound basis for providing capital on a large scale to underdeveloped countries and to meet our important national and international obligations. . . . Much more could be said concerning the significance of balance of payments developments for our internal economic policies. *However, the major conclusion is that these developments provide another important reason for maintaining stability in the price level as we pursue our goals relating to growth and employment.*"[117] (Emphasis added)

Devaluation of the dollar was never seriously considered, according to the CEA's Saulnier, who believed that addressing the balance of payments by devaluation "was not only instinctively and intuitively unpalatable to Eisenhower" but was unnecessary, given the price level in the United States vis-à-vis other countries. The macroeconomic policies of the administration described in chapter 3 were beginning to have an impact. Saulnier stated that, though there remained some residual inflationary psychology in the United States in 1959, "price levels were close to flat and there was reason to believe they could be kept that way. And it was reasonable to expect that in the end, and presumably before too long, the experience of living under stable prices would govern psychology."[118] Foreign holders of dollars would not redeem them for gold if the United States did not "export" its inflation to them in the form of depreciating dollars.

In a 1967 interview Saulnier observed that the policies of the administration and the Federal Reserve during the second Eisenhower administration were excessively tight and conservative but "attempting to correct the imbalance of international payments required that kind of policy—anything else would have been ineffective and irresponsible." The ultimate result was that the period between 1959 and 1964 had the lowest five-year inflation in the postwar era. Saulnier thought that this legacy of the Eisenhower administration allowed its successor to follow expansionist fiscal policies, without facing severe balance of payments problems. This changed, however, after 1965, as domestic prices and unit costs began to increase rapidly and the expense of the Vietnam War increased the balance of payments deficit. The Johnson administration was forced into fiscal and budgetary austerity as well as external capital controls.[119] The Bretton Woods dollar reserve system lurched from crisis to crisis from 1966 until 1971, when President Nixon closed the gold window and devalued the dollar. By 1973 a regime of floating currency rates was in place and remains today. Expansionist fiscal and monetary policies dominated after 1964, and Eisenhower's policies began to look prematurely "old-fashioned."

CONCLUSION

In foreign economic policy, Eisenhower at times had to make short-term tactical compromises to achieve the larger goals of his Cold War strategy. When Eisenhower came into office, the US Mutual Aid program had been largely militarized and the face of American foreign assistance comprised grants for military assistance or equipment. Soon, however, world events and economic competition from the Soviet Union in the underdeveloped world convinced Eisenhower to increase a wide range of American economic assistance, largely in the form of loans, to Asia, the Middle East, Africa, and Latin America. Economic development came to be seen as much a security need as military assistance. Furthermore, military assistance itself was increasingly examined in terms of "dual use" by the end of the Eisenhower administration—how it facilitated economic development. Rationalizations for these policy changes were couched in terms of Cold War imperatives, but despite this they were a hard sell to Congress. Nevertheless, by the end of Eisenhower's second term the face of American foreign assistance had changed dramatically.

These changes in American foreign assistance also showed Eisenhower's flexibility, as did his trade policy. Japan needed to increase its exports to remain in the "free world" orbit, but that growth had to be managed so as to not fuel protectionist agitation that could undermine US commitments to trade liberalization. Finally, as Cold War obligations increased American balance of payments deficits, Eisenhower managed the threat these posed to the Bretton Woods system of the gold-backed dollar. In his second term Eisenhower's inherently fiscal conservative policies and his keen interest in keeping inflation in check did double duty. They stabilized both the international economic system launched at Bretton Woods and produced more than half a decade (1959–65) of the lowest domestic inflation in the postwar period.

The Eisenhower Legacy

As Eisenhower's time in office approached its end, he began to reflect on his legacy. On the economic front, there were several achievements of which he was proud. Two decades after President Herbert Hoover left the White House in the midst of the worst economic collapse in American history, Eisenhower had demonstrated that a Republican president could manage economic policy in both recession and boom. During his term the country enjoyed modest economic growth that averaged 2.4 percent. This was a rate lower than that achieved in the Truman and Kennedy-Johnson years, but it was attained with very modest increases in inflation, which decelerated markedly in the late 1950s and early 1960s. During 1953–61, the consumer price index increased from 114.4 to 127.4 (in 1947–49 it had been 100), essentially 13 percent over an eight-year period.[1]

Particularly pleasing to Eisenhower was the administration's success in reducing national security spending (including foreign military assistance and nuclear procurement). At the end of Eisenhower's second term, it was lower than during his first year in office; in real (inflation-adjusted) terms it had declined dramatically. National security spending accounted for about 60 percent of the federal budget in 1960, but that was a significantly lower level than the more than 70 percent proposed by Truman when Eisenhower took office in 1953.[2]

Other positive results satisfied the president. By controlling spending and producing three balanced budgets, Eisenhower made it easier for the White House and the Federal Reserve to work together in coordinating policy. Similarly, informal methods of communication with the White House preserved the independence of the Fed while allowing for policy coordination, if not always complete agreement. In addition, the administration's record of fiscal restraint gained the support of foreign leaders, making it easier for the United States to address its balance of payments problems, which intensified in 1959 and 1960.[3]

But Eisenhower did not dwell on these immediate achievements alone. When he was in a philosophical mood, cabinet meetings afforded the president an opportunity to reflect on the broader meanings of his experience. One occasion in particular, on November 27, 1959, stands out. In large part this session was memorable because of the extensive handwritten notes—in addition to the official version produced by the staff secretary—taken by economic adviser Don Paarlberg. His notes capture well the tone and tenor of the president's thinking about his legacy. At the meeting, Eisenhower returned to the big goals first discussed in 1953, themes that in one form or another the president returned to time and again during his administration.[4]

To Eisenhower, the Cold War struggle with the Soviet Union was not primarily about preserving territory. It was a matter instead—as he said on many occasions—of protecting and fostering a way of life. Paarlberg recorded Eisenhower posing two large questions about the problems that the United States had to confront in preserving a free polity and market-based economic institutions during the deepening Cold War: "Can free government, faced by the threat of a singly-controlled economy [i.e., the USSR's], continue to exist? [And] can free government overcome the many demands made by special interests and the indulgence of selfish motives?" His immediate answer, not surprisingly, focused on the need to keep the economy healthy and to keep the dollar strong. It was important that the government "pay its bills and that the debt . . . be reduced." Its approach should also be a model of "Spartan simplicity."[5]

His discussion highlighted the issues of macroeconomic policy that had taken so much of his attention: controlling spending and inflation, balancing the budget, and paying down the deficit. He believed firmly that long-term debt and deficits distorted capital markets, as government limited—"crowded out" was a common term at the time—private access to capital. In doing so, private enterprise encountered higher costs in getting capital for new businesses or expansion of existing enterprises.

But he also turned to a fundamental point about the threat of big government. Growing government spending, he said, inevitably concentrated greater power in the hands of the executive branch. Congress, buffeted by the entreaties of special interests and the short-term considerations of electoral advantage, could not exercise the necessary control over a government grown large by continued spending on new programs. Such restraint would have to fall, then, to the executive to administer ever larger, more expensive programs. Inevitably, this would lead to growing government bureaucracies that could themselves become highly effective interest groups striving to serve their own narrow interests and those of their constituents. Eisenhower feared that such large bureaucracies would require "heavy spending lead[ing] in the direction of authoritarian government."[6] Fundamentally, he doubted the ability of large organizations and bureaucracies to act democratically, dispassionately, and for the larger public interest.

In addition to limiting the growth of government bureaucracy, controlling spending and avoiding deficits had the other great advantage of fighting inflation. In confronting what was a relatively new problem—that is, the possibility of long-term inflation—the president focused on its wide-ranging effects on all members of society. Nothing in the president's opinion was more destructive to the entire economic system. To Eisenhower it had a pernicious effect across class lines, from workers to retirees to businesses to investors. These effects became clear during the spikes in inflation in the immediate post–World War II period. Between 1946 and 1948, the consumer price index increased 33.6 percent. Not surprisingly, Eisenhower focused on government spending, which he assumed helped produce inflation. But his concern was also based on more subtle understandings of the structural roots of inflation. Of course, the president was not alone in these considerations. Economists, even during the deflation of the 1930s, had been interested in inflationary tendencies in the economy in bad times. They concluded that large-scale businesses in oligopolistic industries—automobiles, steel, petroleum, chemicals, tobacco, and packaged foods—had considerable power to "administer" prices. Later, economists added the power of large unions over wages to the mix of forces that caused inflation.[7]

Concern over these structural issues had caused Eisenhower to focus on how to promote the operation of a market economy over the long term. To him economic freedom was inextricably connected to all other freedoms—political, cultural, civic, and personal.[8] His ideas about the tightly entwined ties among the freedoms Americans enjoyed shaped his understanding of the role of economic policy in conducting the Cold War. Protecting a market economy was a crucial part of what the president thought the Cold War struggle was about. It was not a matter simply of territorial control or spheres of influence. How then to maintain market institutions was a consuming issue for Eisenhower. Everywhere he turned, it seemed, they were under attack. It was not only the centrally controlled economies of the USSR and the People's Republic of China that concerned him. Statist solutions of politically left parties in Great Britain, Western Europe, and

Japan troubled Eisenhower, too, especially as leftist parties gained strength in Italy, France, and Japan in the immediate postwar period.[9]

Eisenhower was not opposed to a government role in the economy. He accepted that the federal government had responsibility to fund programs that localities and the states could not afford.[10] But he also understood that government could help promote the operation and the sustainability of markets over time. This point of view was at the heart of his microeconomic policies. His commitment to promoting market discipline was most obvious in his administration's campaign to reform agricultural policy. Spending on agricultural subsidies (price supports) dwarfed all other federal domestic expenditures. Any administration committed to keeping spending in line would have focused on agriculture policy, if for no other reason than its cost. In view of the power of agricultural interests in both the Republican and Democratic parties, there was no serious thought of totally abandoning the federal government's support of agriculture. Nevertheless, the administration attempted to "rationalize," that is, bring agricultural policy more into line with market forces.

Administration policy toward antitrust provided another example of using government to promote market discipline. The administration shaped a dynamic, multifaceted antitrust policy, building on new initiatives and recent statutory changes. At the same time, it carefully maneuvered to reduce uncertainty concerning antitrust precedents and the bitter partisanship associated with the rhetoric of both political parties about the subject. A president committed to the preservation of market institutions could not fail to take account of the dangers of complex, rapidly shifting, and unpredictable antitrust policies.

Likewise, in foreign economic policy Eisenhower wanted to introduce more private sector market discipline into trade and economic assistance. He aimed to reduce the power of US government agencies in the workings of the world economy, decrease economic assistance, and closely scrutinize military assistance. Only with the intensified struggles of the Cold War, as Soviet influence increased in the Middle East, Africa, and Latin America, did he modify his views on these matters. Economic assistance, now dominated by loans to non-European nations, took on a permanent place in US foreign aid policy. Similarly, Eisenhower had to compromise on trade liberalization with special policies for situations driven by Cold War imperatives. The dramatic reintroduction of Japan into the international trading community was accompanied by a largely successful attempt to manage the growth of its exports while maintaining an overall liberal thrust of American trade policy. So, Eisenhower's macro- and microeconomic policy could be pragmatic and flexible over the short run. In the long run, though, the president was concerned with how the economy was structured and how it functioned. Debt reduction and avoiding deficits were not simply a matter of adhering to the Republican orthodoxy of inspiring business confidence. Eisenhower did not disagree in principle with this goal, but he had broader systemic considerations in mind. In achieving long-term objectives, he departed from the Republican party line.

For example, he jettisoned the party's economic catechisms about taxes. Followers of Ohio senator Robert A. Taft—the leader of the most conservative wing of the party—routinely attacked high taxes. Again, in principle Eisenhower did not disagree about the desirability of lower taxes. But for most of the administration's two terms, the president opposed tax cuts, especially when they would have increased budget deficits, adding to public debt and thereby stoking inflation.[11] Even when there were budget surpluses, Eisenhower preferred to apply these revenues to reducing the national debt. To do so would lessen the debt's impact on the working of capital markets and hence on the damage done to businesses and households that borrowed money.

Taft Republicans, not reconciled to the growth of the state during the Great Depression and World War II, might rail against large government in the hope of drastically reducing its size. But Eisenhower accepted many New Deal and Fair Deal initiatives, especially in the Social Security program. Nor did the administration dismantle the regulatory regime established by his predecessors in the banking, finance, transportation, communications, and energy sectors. Because of its enhanced domestic and international responsibilities, it was inevitable that government would remain larger than it had been the last time a Republican occupied the White House.

To Eisenhower the fundamental issue about the size of the federal government was how to manage large-scale bureaucracy so that it did not undermine his longer-term policy goals. His military career had schooled him well in the dynamics of organizational politics and its relationship to partisan politics. With his leadership role during World War II, he had to shape the allies into a unified fighting force. This had not been easy. Commanders of the various forces invariably thought in terms of their own country's objectives. In particular, Eisenhower had his battles with General Sir Bernard L. Montgomery and British prime minister Winston Churchill. After the war, as army chief of staff (1945–48), and as informal head of the Joint Chiefs of Staff (1949), he became embroiled in a bitter, extended debate over unifying the US military services. Service rivalries and jealousies turned the effort to rationalize the country's fighting forces—to reduce duplication, to increase efficiencies—into nothing less than a high-level, bureaucratic, and political brawl. Proponents from the various services enlisted the support of members of Congress, thus further complicating the situation. Eisenhower took from this conflict lessons about the inherent parochialism of large-scale organizations and the inability of their leaders to see one's organization in a larger perspective. His stint to build a multinational military force for NATO as supreme Allied commander, Europe (1950–52) reinforced these views.

By the time Eisenhower became president, he had a well-developed set of ideas about politics—partisan, organizational, and international—which drove his thinking on economic policy. Indeed, his low opinion of partisan politics was well known at the time of his presidency and has informed the writings about the president in the decades since he left office. What he objected to in the behavior of party politicians was their parochialism, the seeking of short-term political advantage to enhance their power and the inability to take a long view. What Eisenhower had learned in his military career was that leaders of large military organizations could exhibit many of the failings of political partisans. That is, high-ranking officers often focused on narrow interests and short-term advantages. In regard to federal government bureaucracy, Eisenhower feared the power of major departments, like Defense and Agriculture, pursuing their own agendas at the expense of other national objectives. Eisenhower extended these insights to the international system as well. In trying to make NATO effective, he came up against member countries—France was his favorite example—that seemed unable to get beyond their own national interest to the larger goals of creating an effective alliance.[12]

It was in his thinking about the workings of the executive branch of the government that he spoke most forcefully. The Defense and Agriculture Departments—and others like Interior—had their champions in Congress, which compounded the problems of governing by tying together the parochial interests of members of Congress with those of the self-aggrandizing goals of major governmental bureaucracies. The latter, Eisenhower thought, posed the greatest threat, because civil service employees survived changes in the political makeup of Congress following elections every two years. Eisenhower thought the government departments were inherently undemocratic. They could continue to pursue institutional goals—expansion of missions, employees, and budgets—even as the partisan makeup of Congress changed. One of the reasons he sought out corporate executives to run major departments like Defense and Treasury was a hope that they could see the big picture. Because of the focused nature of corporate leadership—at its best an ability to understand the tight relationship between the costs of tactics to achieve strategic goals—Eisenhower hoped to keep the focus on the big picture, but he discovered with several of his cabinet secretaries that this did not always work out the way he had hoped.

What, then, were the lessons that he thought his successors in the White House should gain from his experience? In essence, Eisenhower viewed the president as a leader who operated above the fray. His task was to define long-term objectives and to ensure that government policy, especially economic policy, worked toward those objectives. In some respects, Eisenhower's thinking harked back to eighteenth-century ideas of political virtue, that is, the ability of a leader to put self-interest aside in the interest of the greater good. This was how George Washington defined public virtue. To Eisenhower these ideas were still applicable, except for the fact that in the twentieth century self-interest was more than an individual trait. It also encompassed huge bureaucratic organizations, and hence overcoming the power of their self-interest was extraordinarily difficult.

It might appear that Eisenhower was operating in an undemocratic way. But to him leadership in economic policy, as well as in other areas, was more than developing a long-term perspective. It was also the need to convince others in government to accept and follow his vision. This included the public. Eisenhower's frequent news conferences and prime-time television appearances to talk at length to ordinary citizens about arcane economic subjects such as the budget, agricultural policy, and foreign assistance were a testimony to his belief in the need to discuss with the public not only the details of policy but also the larger visions that propelled it.

Finally, what has to be concluded about Eisenhower's approach to government and the economy was the depth of its conservatism. That term, of course, has many definitions and connotations. Eisenhower would probably find it difficult to put himself in the company of many politicians who portray themselves as conservatives today. Perhaps characterizing the conservative nature of Eisenhower's experience provides another value in having studied his economic policy making. In essence, Eisenhower tried to apply many conventional views of fiscal conservatism to a world dominated by large institutions. Along with many other conservatives, he recognized the dangers of large institutions, governmental as well as private. The conservatism extolled by William F. Buckley Jr. and Barry Goldwater in the 1950s and 1960s, which powerfully influenced the development of conservatism in the Republican Party in the decades to follow, focused singularly on the dangers of large government. Eisenhower understood the dangers of all large organizations and the particular peril of large government and private sector organizations making common cause to promote the interests of each, which he believed were often detrimental to the immediate public interest and the long-term viability of American political and economic institutions.

In discussing the dangers of the military-industrial complex in his justly famous farewell address of January 17, 1961, Eisenhower realistically took the measure of the consequences of large public and private bureaucratic organizations working together to further their own interests at the expense of the greater good. This profound insight was at the heart of his approach to economic policy in the 1950s. Because of the size of military spending in that decade, the president had to rein it in. Not to do so, he feared, would lead to what he often referred to as a garrison state that would threaten both political and economic freedoms. In addition to the budgetary consequences of military spending, what alarmed Eisenhower was the specter of huge military and industrial organizations forming an alliance with each other and with powerful members of both the Republican and the Democratic congressional leadership. Together, they would perpetuate, at the center of the American government—supposedly in the interest of national defense—a threat to the very political and economic institutions that the United States was purportedly fighting the Cold War to defend.

The great irony is that the self-described conservatives on the rise during the 1950s—William F. Buckley Jr. and Barry Goldwater—ignored Eisenhower's concern about how bigger government would grow out of an alliance among the Pentagon, Congress, and large defense industry contractors. In doing so, they fundamentally misunderstood, deliberately or naively, one of the great conservative issues of the last half of the twentieth century. Instead, they railed against large government, statism, and socialism as if it was only a problem of the bureaucratization of social programs and federal spending on domestic initiatives. They failed to embrace Eisenhower's much more sophisticated understanding of where the threat of large government was coming from. Eisenhower's profoundly conservative insights about the dynamics that led to government growth were largely ignored by those who inspired modern Republican conservatism. Buckley and Goldwater replaced his distinctive insights about government with an ideology that failed, as most ideologies do, to come to grips with the complex, often messy realities of the time—the emergence during World War II and the postwar era of large public, private, and international organizations. From its founding, Buckley's *National Review,* perhaps the major intellectual influence in the development of conservatism as a political movement, employed a clever rhetoric that limited its brief to domestic programs, spending, the pervasiveness of liberalism, and the continuing growth of the state. In 1956, Buckley editorialized that Eisenhower compared to Stevenson was "the *less bad* of the two" (emphasis in the original).[13] As Eisenhower was about to leave office in January 1961, an unsigned editorial in the *National Review* concluded that although he was trusted by the American people, "yet it must be said, what a miserable President he was."[14]

Hindsight—and the availability of a huge body of material about the Eisenhower presidency, of course—allows for a much more nuanced view of what the president was trying to accomplish in the 1950s. Even so, his positions on many issues at the time were no secret. By dismissing Eisenhower, modern political conservatism in the 1950s, as now, failed to understand his conservatism. Thus Buckley, Goldwater, and many of those who followed them in later years deprived the discourse about economic policy and "big government" of Eisenhower's frank and incisive analysis grounded in the realities of a burgeoning Cold War economy.

Acknowledgments

We would like to acknowledge the assistance and careful reading of the manuscript by Louis Galambos, the coeditor of *The Papers of Dwight David Eisenhower*.[1] Robert Brugger at the Johns Hopkins University Press has been a dedicated editor, and we benefited also from the comments and suggestions of the press's outside reader. Our research and writing was aided by the Eisenhower Institute's Ann Whitman Committee and the Eisenhower–Thomas A. Pappas Committee, which supported our travel to the Eisenhower Library. We have also benefited from the institute's committee devoted to promoting serious scholarship on the Eisenhower administration. Each of the men on the committee served during the Eisenhower years, and we are grateful for the support and insights of Eugene T. Rossides, H. Roemer McPhee, and Douglas R. Price. At the Eisenhower Library we had the invaluable assistance of archivist Tom Branigar and others during trips to Abilene, Kansas, in July 2006 and August 2007. The interpretation of Eisenhower and economic policy is, of course, our own, but our research profited from the time and attention they have devoted to the project.

Comments at presentations about our work at seminars and conferences have also been very helpful. These include the Institute for Applied Economics and the Study of Business Enterprise at Johns Hopkins University; the Smithsonian Institution Contemporary History Colloquium; the Policy History Conference; and the Dwight D. Eisenhower Academy, Eisenhower National Historic Site, Gettysburg College.

Finally, we take pleasure in acknowledging the influence on our thinking of Raymond J. Saulnier, who was the president's second chairman of the Council of Economic Advisers. Steve (as he was known to friends and colleagues) provided us with invaluable personal insights about the administration. In addition to his published work, we had the benefit through conversations and a formal interview of his thoughts about policy making and the working of the White House, where he served through both terms. Steve was one of the last surviving high-level policy-making members of the administration. At age ninety-eight, when we interviewed him, he proved a gracious host, as well as an informative interviewee. We gratefully dedicate our book to the memory of Steve Saulnier, who passed away in 2009.

Abbreviations

AWAS	Ann Whitman Administrative Series
AWCS	Ann Whitman Cabinet Series
AWDDEDS	Ann Whitman Dwight D. Eisenhower Diary Series
AWIS	Ann Whitman International Series
AWLS	Ann Whitman Legislative Series
CDF	Central Decimal File
CFEP	Council on Foreign Economic Policy
DDEPL	Dwight D. Eisenhower Presidential Library
DOS	Department of State
Eckstein Report	US Congress, Joint Economic Committee, *Staff Report on Employment, Growth and Price Levels*, 86th Cong., 1st Sess. (December 24, 1959)
Eisenhower Papers	Alfred D.Chandler, Louis Galambos, and Dawn van Ee, eds., *The Papers of Dwight D. Eisenhower*, vols. 13, 17, and 19 (Baltimore: Johns Hopkins University Press, 1989–96).
ERP	US President, *Economic Report of the President*, 10 vols. (Washington, DC: GPO, 1952–61)
FRUS	US Department of State, *Foreign Relations of the United States, 1946, 1952–1954, 1955–1957, 1958–1960* (Washington, DC: GPO, 1972–1992)
Online Eisenhower Papers	Louis Galambos, and Daun van Ee, eds., *The Papers of Dwight David Eisenhower*, World Wide Web facsimile of the print edition by the Dwight D. Eisenhower Memorial Commission (Baltimore: Johns Hopkins University Press, 1996), www.eisenhowermemorial.org/presidential-papers/index.htm.
OSSLAM	Office of the Staff Secretary, L. Arthur Minnich
PPP	*Public Papers of the Presidents of the United States: Dwight D. Eisenhower*, 8 vols. (Washington, DC: GPO, 1958–61)
RG	Record Group

Notes

PREFACE

1. *ERP, 1980*, p. 289, and *ERP, 1995*, p. 371. After 1975 federal expenditures for transfer payments have always exceeded expenditures for purchases of goods and services by widely increasing margins. During the Eisenhower administration expenditures for goods and services exceeded transfer payments by margins of between 4:1 and 2.5:1.

2. Iwan Morgan, *Eisenhower versus "The Spenders": The Eisenhower Administration, the Democrats and the Budget, 1953–60* (New York: St. Martin's Press, 1991); John W. Sloan, *Eisenhower and the Management of Prosperity* (Lawrence: University Press of Kansas, 1990); Gerard Clarfield, *Security with Solvency: Dwight D. Eisenhower and the Shaping of the American Military Establishment* (Westport, CT: Praeger, 1999).

3. Raymond J. Saulnier, *Constructive Years: The U.S. Economy under Eisenhower* (New York: University Press of America, 1991), provides a valuable "insider's view" of the administration's economic policy making. Saulnier, a noted Columbia University economist, worked with the Council of Economic Advisers in the first Eisenhower term and served as its chairman during the second.

4. See David L. Stebenne, *Modern Republican: Arthur Larson and the Eisenhower Years* (Bloomington: Indiana University Press, 2006).

PROLOGUE: PREPARING FOR THE PRESIDENCY

1. Michael Edelstein, "War and the American Economy in the Twentieth Century," in Stanley L. Engerman and Robert E. Gallman, eds., *The Cambridge Economic History of the United States*, vol. 3: *The Twentieth Century* (New York: Cambridge University Press, 2000).

2. William B. Pickett, *Eisenhower Decides to Run: Presidential Politics and Cold War Strategy* (Chicago: Dee, 2000).

3. Stephen Ambrose, *Eisenhower: Soldier, General of the Army, President-Elect, 1890–1952* (New York: Simon and Schuster, 1983), p. 513.

4. Gerard Clarfield, *Security with Solvency: Dwight D. Eisenhower and the Shaping of the American Military Establishment* (Westport, CT: Praeger, 1999), p. 9. David Jablonsky in "Eisenhower and Unified Commands," *Joint Force Quarterly* 23 (Autumn/Winter 1999–2000): p. 25, observed that by the end of World War II "no American had ever led a vast

unified body consisting of armies, navies, and air forces; and none had ever directed an allied command. While unified and combined operations were conducted in other theaters, Eisenhower had the largest and most complex responsibilities."

5. Robert H. Ferrell, ed., *The Eisenhower Diaries* (New York: Norton, 1981), Entry of December 15, 1945, p. 136.

6. David Jablonsky, *War by Land, Sea, and Air: Dwight Eisenhower and the Concept of Unified Command* (New Haven, CT: Yale University Press, 2010), pp. 134–35, 175, 209, 252.

7. Kerry E. Irish, "Apt Pupil: Dwight Eisenhower and the 1930 Industrial Mobilization Plan," *Journal of Military History* 70 (January 2006): pp. 31–37.

8. Ibid., pp. 36, 40–41.

9. Carlo D'Este, *Eisenhower: A Soldier's Life* (New York: Holt, 2002) provides an excellent overview of the importance of Eisenhower's staff work in the 1930s and its effect on his later career. See pt. 4: "The Interwar Years, 1920–1939," pp. 161–258.

10. Ibid., pp. 154, 611.

11. Ibid., pp. 189–202.

12. Irish, "Apt Pupil," pp. 42–43; D'Este, *Soldier's Life*, pp. 176–83, 191–92.

13. D'Este, *Soldier's Life*, pp. 214–216, 229.

14. Ibid., pp. 284–316.

15. Jablonsky, *Land, Sea, and Air*, pp. 146–51.

16. Eisenhower to Hazlett, April 27, 1949, in Robert W. Griffith, ed., *Ike's Letters to a Friend, 1941–58* (Lawrence: University of Kansas Press, 1984), pp. 54–55.

17. Clarfield, *Security with Solvency*, p. 38. Reflecting Truman's views was an article he published August 26, 1944, in *Collier's* magazine, entitled, "Our Air Forces Must Be Unified."

18. Clarfield, *Security with Solvency*, p. 32.

19. Ibid., pp. 32–33; Alonzo Hamby, *Man of the People: A Life of Harry S. Truman* (New York: Oxford University Press, 1995), pp. 310–11.

20. Clarfield, *Security with Solvency*, pp. 33–48; Ferrell, *Eisenhower Diaries*, July 24, 1947, pp. 142–43.

21. Clarfield, *Security with Solvency*, pp. 46–47; Hamby, *Man of the People*, pp. 310–11; Ferrell, *Eisenhower Diaries*, July 24, 1947, p. 142.

22. It also authorized the creation of the National Security Council and the Central Intelligence Agency.

23. Clarfield, *Security with Solvency*, p. 48.

24. Ibid.

25. Ibid., p. 58.

26. John Moser, "Principles without Program: Senator Robert A. Taft and American Foreign Policy," *Ohio History* 108 (1999): 177–92.

27. Jablonsky, "Eisenhower and Unified Command," p. 26.

28. Jablonsky, *Land, Sea and Air*, pp. 143–46.

29. Ibid., pp. 171–72.

30. Ferrell, *Eisenhower Diaries*, April 29, 1950, pp. 174–75.

31. Clarfield, *Security with Solvency*, pp. 63–65; Ferrell, *Eisenhower Diaries*, December 13, 1948, December 17, 1948, January 7, 1949, January 27, 1949, February 2, 1949, February 4, 1949, pp. 150–57.

32. Jablonsky, *Land, Sea, and Air*, pp. 172–82.

33. Ferrell, *Eisenhower Diaries*, January 8, 1949, pp. 152–53; January 27, 1949, pp. 154–56.

34. Clarfield, *Security with Solvency*, pp. 66–69, 77–79; Ferrell, *Eisenhower Diaries*, March 19, 1949, p. 158.

35. Ferrell, *Eisenhower Diaries*, March 19, 1949; Clarfield, *Security with Solvency*, p. 78.

36. Clarfield, *Security with Solvency*, pp. 78–79.

37. Ibid., pp. 76–85; Ferrell, *Eisenhower Diaries*, July 17, 1949, p. 162; Aaron L. Friedberg, *In the Shadow of the Garrison State: America's Anti-Statism and the Cold War Grand Strategy* (Princeton: Princeton University Press, 2000), pp. 102–105; Hamby, *Man of the People*, pp. 490–98.

38. Ernest R. May, "NSC 68: The Theory and Politics of Strategy," in May, ed., *American Cold War Strategy: Interpreting NSC 68* (Boston: Bedford Books, 1993), pp. 1–19; Friedberg, *In the Shadow*, pp. 108–9.

39. Friedberg, *In the Shadow*, pp. 107–8; Hamby, *Man of the People*, pp. 527–29; Clarfield, *Security with Solvency*, pp. 85, 91–93; Benjamin Fordham, *Building the Cold War Consensus: The Political Economy of U.S. National Security Policy, 1949–1951* (Ann Arbor: University of Michigan Press, 1998).

40. Friedberg, *In the Shadow*, pp. 121–23.

41. Pickett, *Eisenhower Decides to Run*, pp. 66–67.

42. Ibid., pp. 66–67; Ferrell, *Eisenhower Diaries*, October 28, 1950, pp. 178–80; January 1, 1951, pp. 185–86; March 2, 1951, pp. 187–89; April 23, 1951, pp. 191–92; April 27, 1951, pp. 192–93.

43. Clarfield, *Security with Solvency*, pp. 91–92; Ferrell, *Eisenhower Diaries*, January 22, 1952, pp. 209–16.

44. Clarfield, *Security with Solvency*, pp. 91–92; Ferrell, *Eisenhower Diaries*, January 22, 1952, p. 213.

45. A. E. Holmans, *United States Fiscal Policy, 1945–1960* (New York: Oxford University Press, 1961), pp. 135–40.

46. Friedberg, *In the Shadow*, pp. 116–17.

47. Ibid., pp. 118–19, quote on p. 119; Ferrell, *Eisenhower Diaries*, January 22, 1952, p. 209.

48. Hugh Rockoff, *Drastic Measures: A History of Wage and Price Controls in the United States* (New York: Cambridge University Press, 1984), pp. 176–85; Friedberg, *In the Shadow*, p. 121.

49. Ferrell, *Eisenhower Diaries*, July 6, 1951, pp. 176–77.

50. Ibid., April 27, 1951, pp. 192–93.

51. Ibid., January 10, 1952, p. 209.

52. Pickett, *Eisenhower Decides to Run*, pp. 173–76, 190–91.

53. Ibid., p. 215.

54. Clarfield, *Security with Solvency*, pp. 91–92; Ferrell, *Eisenhower Diaries*, January 22, 1952, p. 213.

55. Stephen E. Ambrose, *Eisenhower: Soldier and President; The Renowned One-Volume Life* (New York: Simon and Schuster, 1990), pp. 268–88.

56. Ibid.

57. Ibid.

58. D'Este, *Soldier's Life*, p. 216. In a ten-page letter of March 20, 1952, to George Sloan he laid out his thinking about the relationship between the economy and the Cold War. Ferrell, *Eisenhower Diaries*, January 14, 1949, p. 153; Letter to George A. Sloan, March 20, 1952, *Eisenhower Papers*, vol. 13, doc. 744, pp. 1097–1104.

59. Letter to George A. Sloan, March 20, 1952, *Eisenhower Papers*, vol. 13, doc. 744, pp. 1097–1104.

60. Pickett, *Eisenhower Decides to Run*, pp. 185 (quote), 194.

61. Ferrell, *Eisenhower Diaries*, January 14, 1949, p. 153; Letter to George A. Sloan, March 20, 1952, *Eisenhower Papers*, vol. 13, doc. 744, pp. 1097–1104.

62. Steven Wagner, *Eisenhower Republicanism: Pursuing the Middle Way* (DeKalb: Northern Illinois University Press, 2006), pp. 7–26; Letter to George A. Sloan, March 20, 1952, *Eisenhower Papers*, vol. 13, doc. 744, pp. 1097–1104.

63. Friedberg, *In the Shadow*, pp. 58–60, 112–14.

64. Ibid., pp. 40–47, 58–61; John Morton Blum, *V Was for Victory: Politics and American Culture* (New York: Mariner Books, 1977), pp. 90–116.

65. Ferrell, *Eisenhower Diaries*, January 22, 1952, pp. 209–16.

66. Pickett, *Eisenhower Decides to Run*, pp. 124–26.

67. Ferrell, *Eisenhower Diaries*, January 21, 1953, p. 225.

CHAPTER 1: SETTING A CONSISTENT COURSE

1. Letter, Secretary Humphrey to Joseph W. Martin, Jr., Speaker, House of Representatives, March 17, 1954, in Nathaniel R. Howard, ed., *The Basic Papers of George M. Humphrey as Secretary of the Treasury, 1953–1957* (Cleveland: Western Reserve Historical Society, 1965), pp. 387–89. On Eisenhower's approach to administration and decision making, see Andrew J. Goodpaster, Oral History Interview, 1967 Columbia Oral History Project, DDEPL, pp. 12–17. General Goodpaster served in the White House as staff secretary and defense liaison officer to the president, 1954–61.

2. Iwan W. Morgan, *Eisenhower versus "The Spenders": The Eisenhower Administration, the Democrats and the Budget, 1953–60* (New York: St. Martin's Press, 1990), pp. 13, 50–51.

3. Arthur F. Burns, Interview, in Erwin C. Hargrove and Samuel A. Morley, eds., *The President and the Council of Economic Advisers: Interviews with CEA Chairmen* (Boulder, CO: Westview Press, 1984), pp. 99–100. The editors provide an overview of the council in a lengthy introduction to the volume. Each oral history interview of a council chairman is also preceded by an introduction about the background and tenure of the interviewee; Gabriel Hauge, "Autobiography," Preface, George Bookman Papers, 1981–93, Box 1, DDEPL. During the years following his time in the White House, Hauge engaged

George B. Bookman, a well-known journalist, to help him write his memoirs, but Hauge died before the project was completed. His family decided not to publish the work. Bookman eventually deposited the manuscript in the Eisenhower Library. John W. Sloan, *Eisenhower and the Management of Prosperity* (Lawrence: University Press of Kansas, 1991), pp. 42–43.

4. Burns, Interview, pp. 95–96. On the thinking of professional economists at the time about the Council of Economic Advisers, see Memorandum, Raymond J. Saulnier to Gabriel Hauge, December 15, 1952, "Economic Policy, Memos on, 1952–1961" folder, Box 6, Raymond Saulnier Papers, DDEPL; Wyatt C. Wells, *Economist in an Uncertain World: Arthur F. Burns and the Federal Reserve, 1970–78* (New York: Columbia University Press, 1994). Wells addresses Burns's work on business cycles and at the NBER before he joined the CEA, pp. 2–14.

5. Burns, Interview, pp. 89–90.

6. Ibid., pp. 98–100. Eisenhower's second chairman of the Council of Economic Advisers was less fulsome in his views of the president's grasp of economic analysis. He thought him diligent and serious in attempting to grasp the intricacies of economic behavior. Raymond J. Saulnier, Oral History Interview, 1957, pp. 20–23, Columbia University Oral History Project, DDEPL.

7. Memorandum, Raymond J. Saulnier to Hauge, December 15, 1952, "Economic Policy, Memos on, 1952–1961" folder, Box 6, Saulnier Papers, DDEPL; Burns, Interview, p. 95.

8. Hargrove and Morley, *President and the Council*, pp. 90–92.

9. Ibid.; Burns, interview, pp. 11–15.

10. Hargrove and Morley, *President and the Council*, pp. 90–91.

11. Ibid., p. 91; Burns, Interview, p. 114; Hauge, "Autobiography," chap. 9, pp. 3–4, 11–14.

12. Hauge, "Autobiography," chap. 9, pp. 11–15; on Eisenhower's views of Wilson, see Gerard Clarfield, *Security with Solvency: Dwight D. Eisenhower and the Shaping of the American Military Establishment* (Westport, CT: Praeger, 1999), pp. 98, 107, 159.

13. Hargrove and Morley, *President and the Council*, p. 92; Wells, *Economist in an Uncertain World*, pp. 15–16.

14. Letter, Dodge to Eisenhower, November 17, 1952, "Joseph Dodge 52–53 (3)" folder, Box 12, AWAS, DDEPL; Memorandum, Dodge to Eisenhower, "Personal and Confidential, Regarding the Budget," November 17, 1952, "Joseph Dodge, 52–53 (5)" folder, Box 12, AWAS, DDEPL; Memorandum, Dodge, "Pre-Inauguration Budgetary Review for Department and Agency Designees," January 9, 1953, "Joseph Dodge 52–53 (4)" folder, Box 12, AWAS, DDEPL; Morgan, *Eisenhower versus "The Spenders,"* p. 50.

15. Memorandum, Hauge to Humphrey, May 25, 1953, "GMH Treasury" folder, Box 1, Gabriel Hauge Records, DDEPL; Dwight D. Eisenhower, *Mandate for Change 1953–1956* (Garden City, NY: Doubleday, 1963), pp. 129–30; Morgan, *Eisenhower versus "The Spenders,"* pp. 50–51.

16. Morgan, *Eisenhower versus "The Spenders,"* p. 51.

17. "Annual State of the Union Message," February 2, 1953, *PPP, 1953*, pp. 12–34.

18. Morgan, *Eisenhower versus "The Spenders,"* pp. 50–51; Eisenhower, *Mandate for Change*, pp. 129–30; Harold G. Vatter, *The U.S. Economy in the 1950's* (New York: Norton,

1963), p. 140; Hauge, "Autobiography," chap. 7, p. 13. For a discussion of administrative versus cash budget, see "Annual Budget Message to the Congress; Fiscal Year 1955," January 21, 1954, *PPP, 1954*, pp. 14–15.

19. "Annual State of the Union Message," February 2, 1953, *PPP, 1953*, p. 17; Morgan, *Eisenhower versus "The Spenders,"* p. 51.

20. Morgan, *Eisenhower versus "The Spenders,"* p. 51.

21. Ibid., pp. 52–53; Robert H. Ferrell, ed., *The Eisenhower Diaries* (New York: Norton, 1981), Entry of January 20, 1952, pp. 209–213.

22. Morgan, *Eisenhower versus "The Spenders,"* p. 53; "Special Message to Congress Transmitting Reorganization Plan 6 of 1953 Concerning Department of Defense," April 30, 1953, "Special Message to Congress Concerning the Mutual Security Program," May 5, 1953, and "Special Message to Congress Recommending Tax Legislation," May 20, 1953, *PPP, 1953*, pp. 225–38, 256–59, 320.

23. Memorandum, "Editorial Comment," May 29, 1953, "Tax Matters 1952–53 (1)" folder, Box 760, AWAS, DDEPL; Memorandum, Eisenhower to Director of the Bureau of the Budget, November 5, 1953, "Joseph Dodge 1955 (1)" folder, Box 12, AWAS, DDEPL.

24. Hauge, "Autobiography," chap. 7, pp. 13–16.

25. Morgan, *Eisenhower versus "The Spenders,"* p. 53; Vatter, *U.S. Economy in the 1950's*, pp. 139–41; Ferrell, *Eisenhower Diaries*, May 1, 1953, pp. 235–36.

26. For an example of one of numerous places where he makes this case, see Letter, Eisenhower to Benjamin F. Caffey, July 27, 1953, "Dec 52–July 53 (1)" folder, Box 3, AWD-DEDS, DDEPL.

27. Hauge, "Autobiography," chap. 12, pp. 4–6; Morgan, *Eisenhower versus "The Spenders,"* pp. 56–57, 59–60.

28. George M. Humphrey, Speech, "The Problem Is to Know the Facts," Cleveland Chamber of Commerce, February 17, 1953, in Howard, *Humphrey Papers*, pp. 37–43.

29. Ibid., pp. 39–41; Morgan, *Eisenhower versus "The Spenders,"* 56–57.

30. See Humphrey, "Testimony before House Ways and Means Committee," June 1, 1953, in Howard, *Humphrey Papers*, p. 71.

31. Morgan, *Eisenhower versus "The Spenders,"* pp. 57–58; "Remarks to the Business Advisory Council," March 18, 1953, and "Special Message Recommending Tax Legislation," *PPP, 1953*, pp. 103, 322–25; for an overview, see Eisenhower, "Radio and Television Address to the American People on the Tax Program," March 15, 1954, *PPP, 1954*, pp. 316–18.

32. *ERP, 1954*, pp. 141–44; Morgan, *Eisenhower versus "The Spenders,"* p. 60.

33. On Rep. Reed, see Humphrey, Remarks by Secretary Humphrey on Man of the Week Television Panel, Washington, June 21, 1953, pp. 90–93, in Howard, *Humphrey Papers*.

34. "Notes on the Administration's Tax Bill [1954]," "White House Correspondence 1954 (1) F" folder, Box 102, Arthur F. Burns Papers, DDEPL; Morgan, *Eisenhower versus "The Spenders,"* pp. 58–59.

35. Morgan, *Eisenhower versus "The Spenders,"* pp. 58–59.

36. See A. E. Holmans, "The Eisenhower Administration and the Recession, 1953–55," *Oxford Economic Papers*, New Series, 10, no. 1 (February 1958): p. 45; "Statement by the President upon Signing Bill Revising the Internal Revenue Code," August 16, 1954, *PPP*,

1954, pp. 715–17; *ERP, 1955*, p. 59. Vatter concludes, however, that "the provision for accelerated depreciation . . . no doubt contributed to the dwindling significance of the corporate net income tax as compared with the personal income tax (and helped encourage the industrial capacity expansion of 1955 and 1956). The evidence on this score shows at the very least that the Federal tax structure relaxed somewhat in its incidence on corporate profitability." Vatter, *U.S. Economy in the 1950's*, pp. 144–45.

37. Memorandum, "Review of Basic National Security Policies," James S. Lay, Executive Secretary, NSC, to NSC, February 6, 1953, and Attachment (no date), "Brief of Approved U.S. National Security Objectives and Program with Respect to USSR," *FRUS*, vol. 2, pt. 1: *National Security Affairs*, pp. 223–25; Memorandum of Discussion at the 131st Meeting of the National Security Council, February 11, 1953, *FRUS, 1952–1954*, vol. 2, pt. 1, pp. 236–37; H. W. Brands, "The Age of Vulnerability: Eisenhower and the National Insecurity State," *American Historical Review* 94 (1989): pp. 963–89.

38. Memorandum, Hauge to Humphrey, March 25, 1953, "Economics 1952/3 (1)" folder, Box 558, Central File, Official File, DDEPL; Sloan, *Management of Prosperity*, pp. 42–43.

39. Robert Roosa, Oral History Interview, no. 2 of 3, November 17, 1972, pp. 59–62, Columbia University Oral History Project, DDEPL.

40. See, e.g., Memorandum, Eisenhower to Director of the Bureau of the Budget [Dodge], December 1, 1953, "Joseph Dodge, 1955 Budget (2)" folder, Box 12, AWAS, DDEPL.

41. Minutes, Meeting at President's Office (with Pentagon and Budget officials), March 29, 1956, "Budget 1957 (2)" folder, Box 9, AWAS, DDEPL.

42. Brands, "Age of Vulnerability," pp. 965–66.

43. Memorandum (enclosure "a") to National Security Council, from James S. Lay, Executive Secretary, NSC, February 6, 1953, *FRUS, 1952–1954*, vol. 2, pt. 1, pp. 224–25.

44. The Truman administration had proposed extension of the temporary individual and corporate income tax increases set to expire in 1954 and other unspecified tax increases to address its proposed fiscal 1954 budget deficit. See US Congress, "Staff Report on Employment, Growth and Price Levels," Joint Economic Committee, 86th Cong., 1st Sess. (1959), p. 239. The report was referred to as *Eckstein Report* at the time for the committee's staff director Otto Eckstein.

45. William B. Pickett, *Eisenhower Decides to Run: Presidential Politics and Cold War Strategy* (Chicago: Dee, 2000), pp. 184–86; Letter to George A. Sloan, March 20, 1952, *Eisenhower Papers*, vol. 13, doc. 744, pp. 1097–1104.

46. Brands, "Age of Vulnerability," p. 965.

47. Memorandum of Discussion at the 138th Meeting of the National Security Council, Wednesday, March 25, 1953, *FRUS, 1952–1954*, vol. 2, pt. 1, pp. 260–61.

48. "Radio Address to the American People on the National Security and Its Costs," May 19, 1953, *PPP, 1953*, pp. 306–25; Brands, "Age of Vulnerability," p. 966.

49. "Radio Address to the American People on the National Security and Its Costs," May 19, 1953, *PPP, 1953*, pp. 306–25; Brands, "Age of Vulnerability," p. 966.

50. Report, "Basic National Security Policies and Programs in Relation to Their Costs," April 28, 1953, *FRUS, 1952–1954*, vol. 2, pt. 1, pp. 307–17.

51. Quoted in Brands, "Age of Vulnerability," p. 972; NSC 162/2, October 30, 1953, "Report to the NSC by Executive Secretary Lay," October 30, 1953, and attached "Statement of

Policy by the National Security Council" (no date), *FRUS, 1952–1954,* vol. 2, pt. 1, pp. 577–97.

52. Donald Alan Carter, "Eisenhower versus the Generals," *Journal of Military History* 71, no. 4 (October 2007): pp. 1169–99.

53. John Foster Dulles, "The Evolution of Foreign Policy," *Department of State Bulletin* 30 (January 25, 1962): pp. 107–10.

54. For a nuanced discussion of the New Look, see chaps. 5 and 6 in John Lewis Gaddis, *Strategies of Containment: A Critical Appraisal of American National Security Policy during the Cold War,* rev. ed. (New York: Oxford University Press, 2005), pp. 125–96.

55. Clarfield, *Security with Solvency,* pp. 167–68.

56. Quoted in ibid., p. 168.

57. Matthew Ridgway, "Keep the Army Out of Politics," *Saturday Evening Post,* January 28, 1956, pp. 34, 73.

58. "Science: Missiles Away," *Time,* January 30, 1956, p. 52.

59. Clarfield, *Security with Solvency,* pp. 170–71; David Jablonsky, *War by Land, Sea, and Air: Dwight Eisenhower and the Concept of Unified Command* (New Haven: Yale University Press, 2010), pp. 242–43, 249, 253–55.

60. Clarfield, *Security with Solvency,* pp. 179–80.

61. Ibid., pp. 180–81.

62. Carter, "Eisenhower versus the Generals," pp. 1184–86.

63. Jablonsky, *Land, Sea, and Air,* pp. 221–41; Carter, "Eisenhower versus the Generals," pp. 1188–92.

64. "Farewell Radio and Television Address to the American People," January 17, 1961, *PPP, 1960–1961,* pp. 1035–40.

65. *ERP, 1954,* pp. 19–23; Burns, Interview, pp. 116–18; Sloan, *Management of Prosperity,* pp. 133–34.

66. On unemployment, see *ERP, 1955,* pp. 88–89, 154; numbers from Holmans, "The Eisenhower Administration," Table 3, pp. 38–40; Vatter, *U.S. Economy in the 1950's,* p. 73; Sloan, *Management of Prosperity,* p. 134.

67. *ERP, 1954,* pp. 77–81; E. Cary Brown, "The Policy Acceptance in the United States of Reliance on Automatic Fiscal Stabilizers," *Journal of Finance* 14 (March 1959): pp. 40–51; Saul Engelbourg, "The Council of Economic Advisers and the Recession of 1953–1954," *Business History Review* 54 (Summer 1980): pp. 192–214; Robert P. Bremner, *Chairman of the Fed: William McChesney Martin Jr. and the Creation of the Modern American Financial System* (New Haven: Yale University Press, 2004), pp. 106–10.

68. Memorandum, Eisenhower to Burns, October 13, 1953, "White House Correspondence with President Eisenhower, 1953" folder, Box 103, Burns Papers, DDEPL; *ERP, 1954,* p. 4.

69. *ERP, 1954,* p. 4.

70. William H. Becker and William M. McClenahan, Jr., *The Market, the State, and the Export-Import Bank of the United States, 1934–2000* (New York: Cambridge University Press, 2003), pp. 64–66.

71. Bremner, *Chairman of the Fed,* chaps. 3–5.

72. On back channels between the Fed and the White House, see Roosa, Interview, no. 2 of 3, p. 44, DDEPL.

73. Bremner, *Chairman of the Fed*, pp. 95–97.

74. Holmans, "The Eisenhower Administration," p. 43; Bremner, *Chairman of the Fed*, pp. 106–10.

75. Bremner, *Chairman of the Fed*, p. 109; Holmans, "The Eisenhower Administration," pp. 41–42; Sloan, *Management of Prosperity*, p. 136.

76. *ERP, 1954*, pp. 49–54; Holmans, "The Eisenhower Administration," pp. 42–43; Bremner, *Chairman of the Fed*, p. 110.

77. Hargrove and Morley, *President and the Council*, p. 26; Wells, *Economist in an Uncertain World*, pp. 9–12. The recession of 1953–54 has received a large amount of scholarly attention. It was, of course, the topic of constant discussion at the time. It was the first recession that a Republican president had to face in an era when the public had come to expect that the chief executive had a prime responsibility for the economy's performance. There has been a tendency in this literature to portray the administration's attempt to cope with the recession in Keynesian terms. This was the view of Herbert Stein in his book *The Fiscal Revolution in America* (Chicago: University of Chicago Press, 1969) and of the *Eckstein Report* of 1959. Stein also portrayed the Truman administration in Keynesian terms, observing that Truman was more proactive in dealing with the recession of 1949–50 than Eisenhower during 1953–54. Such a view overstates the case for both administrations and, in fact, Eisenhower seemed less tolerant of unemployment than Truman.

78. Burns, Interview, p. 122.

79. On building confidence in the recession, see "Annual Message Presenting the Economic Report to the Congress," January 20, 1955, *PPP, 1955*, pp. 201–3.

80. *ERP, 1955*, pp. 22–23.

81. *ERP, 1956*, pp. 73–74, 144–45, 154.

82. Memorandum, Eisenhower to Director of the Bureau of the Budget, November 5, 1953, "Joseph Dodge 1955 (1)" folder, Box 12, AWAS, DDEPL.

83. See, e.g., Minutes, Cabinet Meeting, November 4, 1955, pp. 4–5, Box 2, AWCS, DDEPL.

84. "Remarks on the State of the Union Message, Key West, Florida," January 5, 1956, *PPP, 1956*, pp. 28–29; Minutes, Cabinet Meeting, January 22, 1956, Box 2, AWCS, DDEPL; Burns, Interview, pp. 104–6, 106–9.

85. Bremner, *Chairman of the Fed*, pp. 110–11.

86. On inflation harming those on fixed incomes, see Presidential News Conference, February 23, 1955, *PPP, 1955*, pp. 283–84.

87. Arthur Burns, *Prosperity without Inflation* (New York: Fordham University Press, 1957). Eisenhower greatly admired this book.

88. Speech, American Bankers Association, September 22, 1953, and Speech, Detroit Economic Club, November 9, 1953, in Howard, *Humphrey Papers*, pp. 122–23, 491–93.

89. Presidential News Conference, February 17, 1953, *PPP, 1953*, p. 46, n. 1; Speech, American Bankers Association, October 19, 1954, in Howard, *Humphrey Papers*, pp. 159–61; also see *ERP, 1956*, pp. 28–29.

90. *ERP, 1955*, pp. 18–19.

91. Ibid., p. 49. There were also increases in revenues and benefits in 1956 and 1958. Vatter, *U.S. Economy in the 1950's*, p. 139.

92. Speech, "The Secretary Quizzes Himself," National Canners Association, February 19, 1955, in Howard, *Humphrey Papers*, pp. 183–84; *ERP, 1957*, p. 41. See Vatter, *U.S. Economy in the 1950's*, p. 140, for a succinct table on the subject of the cash and administrative budgets.

93. Christina D. Romer and David H. Romer, "A Rehabilitation of Monetary Policy in the 1950s," *American Economic Association Papers and Proceedings* 92 (May 2002): pp. 122–29.

94. *Eckstein Report*, p. 104.

95. Ibid., pp. 131–36, 199.

CHAPTER 2: ECONOMIC POLICY IN GOOD TIMES

1. *ERP, 1956*, p. 208; *ERP, 1958*, pp. 1–12.

2. GNP (in 1954 prices) rose from $370.1 billion in fourth quarter 1954 to $401.1 billion in fourth quarter 1955—an increase of 8.4%. *ERP, 1958*, pp. 10–26.

3. *ERP, 1956*, pp. 13–28.

4. James L. Clayton, ed., *The Economic Impact of the Cold War: Sources and Readings* (New York: Harcourt, Brace and World, 1970), pp. 51–54.

5. Memorandum, Joseph A. Peckman to Council of Economic Advisers, Notes on Meeting with Representatives of the American Bankers Association on Consumer Credit, June 7, 1955, "Fiscal & Monetary—Consumer and Other Debt, 1955 (2)" folder, Box 105, Arthur F. Burns Papers, DDEPL; Raymond J. Saulnier, *Constructive Years: The U.S. Economy under Eisenhower* (Lanham, MD: University Press of America, 1991), pp. 76–78, 82. Also see *Eckstein Report*, p. 105.

6. The statistics in the *ERP* are seasonally adjusted, but show levels of 1 million to 1.2 million in 1952, peaking at about 1.5 million late 1954 and early 1955. See *ERP, 1956*, p. 46.

7. *ERP, 1959*, p. 39; Harold G. Vatter, *The U.S. Economy in the 1950's* (New York: Norton, 1963), p. 9 (chart). According to Eisenhower's second chairman of the Council of Economic Advisers, Raymond J. Saulnier, the nonresidential construction boom had greater staying power. This was a result of the much more liberal treatment of nonresidential construction depreciation created in 1954 tax legislation. Saulnier, *Constructive Years*, p. 78; Thomas W. Hanchett, "U.S. Tax Policy and the Shopping-Center Boom of the 1950s and 1960s," *American Historical Review* 101 (October 1996): pp. 1092–1100.

8. Board of Governors of the Federal Reserve System, *Consumer Installment Credit*, pt. 4: *Financing New Car Purchases: A National Survey for 1954–55*, "Credit (2)" folder, Box 567, Central Files, Official Files, DDEPL.

9. *ERP, 1956*, pp. 138–39. See also *ERP, 1959*, p. 107, which shows that consumer credit remained strong after 1955 (even into 1958, except for automobiles), though not at the explosive rate of 1955.

10. Saulnier, *Constructive Years*, p. 77.

11. Ibid., p. 78; *ERP, 1958,* graphs, pp. 12–13.

12. Also, see the inventory liquidation that begins late in 1956 and the course of residential construction in Vatter, *U.S. Economy in the 1950's,* chart, p. 147, and tables, pp. 86, 108–9.

13. Saulnier ignores depreciation charges. The *Eckstein Report* noted the theories of Charles Schultze that much of the price increase in the mid- to late 1950s can be attributed to increased corporate depreciation charges.

14. The end of the dramatic decline in farm prices coinciding with the boom of 1955–57 indicates that there were significant inflationary pressures in the 1950s. During the period 1947–58, the CPI (all items) rose 29.3%, while all services rose 50.7%. The services sector of the CPI was relatively small—about 20%—and was diverse. But services and the "rent and home purchase" costs segments rose rapidly, while food costs declined, as did their percentage component of the CPI during the 1950s. After the recession of 1957–58 consumer prices continued to rise through the remainder of the decade, although at a much slower pace. There was a similar pattern after mid-1958, because farm prices declined again, though not as precipitously as before. Thus, for the duration of the entire administration, farm prices only rose from mid-1956 through mid-1958, though "prices paid" to the farmers were under much more pressure than "food prices" paid by consumers, which included processing. *ERP, 1957,* p. 29 (chart); *ERP, 1958,* p. 24. For a good summary, see Statement, "The Increase in Price Level, 1955–1957," George M. Humphrey to Senate Finance Committee, June 25, 1957, "George M. Humphrey 1957/58 (2)" folder, Box 21, AWAS, DDEPL; *Eckstein Report,* p. 105.

15. See *ERP, 1958,* p. 11. Vatter, *U.S. Economy in the 1950's,* p. 124, states that the "investment wave of 1955–56, together with the rise in actual and expected military hard-goods demand in the latter year, go far to explain the concomitant rises in capital goods industries." See Vatter for a discussion of the importance of steel prices between 1954 and 1957 and steel profits. Vatter says the steel industry of the period demonstrated all three theories of inflation.

16. See, e.g., discussion of reducing defense spending, Minutes, Cabinet Meeting, August 5, 1955, Box 5, AWCS, DDEPL.

17. Saulnier, *Constructive Years,* p. 82.

18. Letter, Burns to Eisenhower, August 1, 1955, "Arthur Burns 1956–57 (8)" folder, Box 9, AWAS, DDEPL.

19. Memorandum, Eisenhower, February 19, 1955, *Eisenhower Papers,* vol. 16, doc. 1309, pp. 1579–80.

20. Saulnier, *Constructive Years,* p. 82.

21. See discussion, Cabinet Paper, "Policy Concerning Restrictions on Consumer Instalment [*sic*] Credit," May 24, "Minutes, Cabinet Meeting, May 24, 1957" folder, Box 9, AWCS, DDEPL; Press Release, "Stand-by Authority to Regulate Consumer Instalment [*sic*] Credit," May 25, 1957, Box 9, AWCS, DDEPL.

22. Cabinet Paper, "Policy Concerning Restrictions on Consumer Instalment [*sic*] Credit," May 24, 1957, "Minutes, Cabinet Meeting, May 24, 1957" folder, Box 9, AWCS, DDEPL.

23. Saulnier, *Constructive Years*, p. 83.

24. Telephone calls, Eisenhower to Humphrey, January 16, 1956, and January 31, 1956, "Jan 56 Phone Calls" folder, Box 12, AWDDEDS, DDEPL.

25. Letter, Eisenhower to Burns, March 20, 1958, *Eisenhower Papers*, vol. 19, doc. 615, p. 786.

26. Quoted material in editors' comments about Eisenhower Note to Ann Cook Whitman, December 13, 1956, in *Eisenhower Papers*, vol. 17, doc. 2136, p. 2443.

27. Quoted in John W. Sloan, *Eisenhower and the Management of Prosperity* (Lawrence: University Press of Kansas, 1991), p. 125; *ERP, 1957*, pp. 1–3.

28. Quoted in Sloan, *Management of Prosperity*, p. 125.

29. *ERP, 1957*, p. iii.

30. "Annual Message Presenting the Economic Report to the Congress," January 20, 1958, *PPP, 1953*, p. 112.

31. Robert P. Bremner, *Chairman of the Fed: William McChesney Martin Jr. and the Creation of the Modern American Financial System* (New Haven: Yale University Press, 2004), pp. 4, 99–102, 111.

32. Martin's concern about inflation stemmed from the behavior of financial markets. To him, they were a reliable predictor of future economic developments. Speculative explosions in asset values, especially in the stock market, foreshadowed serious problems. Inflation distorted "proper" economic behavior, leading to extensive borrowing and a decline in savings. These distortions led to speculation, which eventually would lead to a market collapse. Key to Martin's thinking was the distinction between speculative and productive lending, which was not something easily agreed upon. Bremner, *Chairman of the Fed*, pp. 110–11.

33. Ibid., pp. 113–15; "A Steward's Summary of His Service," June 18, 1957, in Nathaniel R. Howard, ed., *The Basic Papers of George M. Humphrey as Secretary of the Treasury, 1953–1957* (Cleveland: Case Western Reserve Historical Society, 1965), pp. 299–329.

34. Minutes, Cabinet Meeting, March 2, 1956, p. 3, Box 7, AWCS, DDEPL. Humphrey brought the issue up again late in April, raising questions about gold reserves and balance of payments problems. See Minutes, Cabinet Meeting, April 20, 1956, pp. 1–3, Box 7, AWCS, DDEPL.

35. Minutes, Cabinet Meeting, March 23, 1956, p. 4, Box 7, AWCS, DDEPL; Saulnier, *Constructive Years*, pp. 85–86.

36. Saulnier, *Constructive Years*, p. 86.

37. Minutes, Cabinet Meeting, April 20, 1956, Box 7, AWCS, DDEPL; Eisenhower Letter to Lewis Williams Douglas, September 30, 1956, in *Eisenhower Papers*, vol. 17, doc. 2005, pp. 2297–98; Saulnier, *Constructive Years*, p. 87; Bremner, *Chairman of the Fed*, pp. 111, 115–16, 118.

38. Bremner, *Chairman of the Fed*, pp. 116–17; Saulnier, *Constructive Years*, p. 87.

39. Quoted in Saulnier, *Constructive Years*, p. 87; Presidential News Conference, April 25, 1956, *PPP, 1956*, pp. 438–39.

40. Notes, Cabinet Meeting, April 20, 1956, Box 4, OSSLAM, DDEPL. These handwritten notes made by the cabinet secretary often provide a different, more nuanced view

of the president's thinking in contrast to the printed formal version of the cabinet minutes.

41. Bremner, *Chairman of the Fed*, p. 118.

42. Saulnier, *Constructive Years*, pp. 88–89.

43. Gabriel Hauge, "Autobiography," chap. 12, pp. 16–18, Box 1, George Bookman Papers, 1981–93, DDEPL; Raymond J. Saulnier, Oral History Interview, 1967, pp. 13–15, Columbia University Oral History Project, DDEPL.

44. John W. Sloan, "Eisenhower, Humphrey and Neustadt: A Note on the Battle of the Budget for FY 1958," *Western Political Quarterly* 42, no. 4 (December 1989): pp. 691–98.

45. Saulnier, *Constructive Years*, p. 90; Memorandum, Eisenhower to Arthur Burns, May 28, 1956, acknowledging reading Burns's paper, "Some Observations on the Problem of Inflation," Address to Federation of Financial Analysts Societies, May 21, 1956, "Arthur Burns, 1956–57 (8)" folder, Box 9, AWAS; Letter, Humphrey to Eisenhower, July 3, 1956, "George Humphrey 1956 (2)" folder, Box 21, AWAS, DDEPL; Saulnier, *Constructive Years*, p. 90.

46. "Annual Budget Message to the Congress for Fiscal Year 1958," January 16, 1957, *PPP, 1957*, p. 40; Saulnier, *Constructive Years*, p. 92.

47. Sloan, *Management of Prosperity*, p. 79.

48. Iwan W. Morgan, *Eisenhower versus "The Spenders": The Eisenhower Administration, the Democrats and the Budget, 1953–60* (New York: St. Martin's Press, 1990), p. 82. For Humphrey's views on future tax cuts, see Letter, Humphrey to Eisenhower, December 6, 1956, "George Humphrey 1956 (1)" folder, Box 21, AWAS, DDEPL.

49. Letter, Humphrey to Eisenhower, September 7, 1956, "George Humphrey 1956 (2)" folder, Box 21, and Notes, Cabinet Meeting, January 9, 1957, Box 4, OSSLAM, DDEPL; Letter, Humphrey to Eisenhower, January 8, 1957, "George Humphrey 1957–58 (5)" folder, Box 21, AWAS, DDEPL.

50. Minutes, Cabinet Meeting, February 27, 1957, Box 8, AWCS, DDEPL.

51. Morgan, *Eisenhower versus "The Spenders,"* p. 81.

52. Ibid., p. 81; David L. Stebenne, *Modern Republican: Arthur Larson and the Eisenhower Years* (Bloomington: Indiana University Press, 2006), pp. 277–79.

53. Hauge, "Autobiography," chap. 14, p. 4; Stebenne, *Modern Republican*, pp. 158–59.

54. Stebenne, *Modern Republican*, pp. 170–71, 189–90, 198.

55. Hauge, "Autobiography," chap. 14, pp. 2–3; chap. 22, p. 1; also see Memorandum, Hauge to Eisenhower, June 22, 1953, "The President (1)" folder, Box 1, Hauge Records, 1952–58, DDEPL.

56. Hauge to Ann Whitman, October 12, 1955; Gabriel Hauge, Speech, "The Economics of Eisenhower Conservatism," Commonwealth Club of California, San Francisco, California, October 14, 1955, "Gabriel Hauge 1952/55 (1)" folder, Box 18, AWAS, DDEPL.

57. Morgan, *Eisenhower versus "The Spenders,"* p. 79; Steven Wagner, *Eisenhower Republicanism: Pursuing the Middle Way* (DeKalb: Northern Illinois University Press, 2006), pp. 7–26.

58. Wagner, *Eisenhower Republicanism*, pp. 16–25.

59. Morgan, *Eisenhower versus "The Spenders,"* pp. 79–80; *ERP, 1961*, pp. 127, 187.

60. Morgan, *Eisenhower versus "The Spenders,"* p. 80.

61. Ibid., pp. 79–80, quote, p. 80; Stebenne, *Modern Republican*, pp. 125–26, on Eisenhower and dealing with conservative party critics.

62. "Annual Budget Message to the Congress for Fiscal Year 1958," January 16, 1957, *PPP, 1957*, pp. 38–44.

63. Morgan, *Eisenhower versus "The Spenders,"* p. 78; Gerard Clarfield, *Security with Solvency: Dwight D. Eisenhower and the Shaping of the American Military Establishment* (Westport, CT: Praeger, 1999), pp. 181–92.

64. Letter, Humphrey to Eisenhower, January 8, 1957, Box 8, AWCS, DDEPL. According to a handwritten note on the document, the letter was read to the cabinet.

65. "Annual Budget Message to the Congress for Fiscal Year 1958," January 16, 1957, *PPP, 1957*, pp. 38–44.

66. Sloan, "Battle of the Budget," pp. 691–98; for Gabriel Hauge's "inside" view of the controversy over the remarks of Eisenhower and Humphrey, see Hauge, "Autobiography," chap. 12, pp. 11–12.

67. For a discussion of the politics of the budget, see Minutes, Legislative Meeting, March 5, 1957, "Legislative Meetings 1957 (2) (March–April)" folder, Box 2, AWLS, DDEPL; Morgan, *Eisenhower versus "The Spenders,"* pp. 84–85.

68. Morgan, *Eisenhower versus "The Spenders,"* p. 86.

69. Ibid., p. 88.

70. Ibid., pp. 88–89; Sloan, "Battle of the Budget," pp. 694–97.

71. Stebenne, *Modern Republican*, pp. 207–8.

72. Arthur Larson, *Eisenhower: The President Nobody Knew* (New York: Scribner's, 1968), p. 141; Sloan, "Battle of the Budget," p. 697.

73. Morgan, *Eisenhower versus "The Spenders,"* pp. 33–35, 84–86.

74. Quoted in ibid., p. 37; Robert Dallek, *Lone Star Rising: Lyndon Johnson and His Times, 1908–1960* (New York: Oxford, 1991), pp. 468–69.

75. Morgan, *Eisenhower versus "The Spenders,"* p. 33.

76. Dallek, *Lone Star Rising*, pp. 427, 459–62, 469.

77. It was not until 1974 that the Budget and Impoundment Control Act authorized the creation of budget committees and the Congressional Budget Office to provide independent analyses of the president's budget.

78. Morgan, *Eisenhower versus "The Spenders,"* p. 33.

79. Campaign speeches, including 1956 Acceptance Speech, "A New America" (August 17, 1956), in Adlai Stevenson, *The New America*, ed. Seymour E. Harris, John Bartlow Martin, and Arthur Schlesinger Jr. (Port Washington, NY: Kennikat Press, 1957).

80. See the 1959 *Eckstein Report*.

81. Morgan, *Eisenhower versus "The Spenders,"* p. 41; Richard Goode, "Gardiner Means on Administered Prices and Administrative Inflation," *Journal of Economic Issues* 28 (1994): pp. 173–87.

82. Dallek, *Lone Star Rising*, pp. 427–32, 438–41, 444–46, 463–64.

83. Morgan, *Eisenhower versus "The Spenders,"* pp. 32, 39–40.

84. Robert M. Collins, *More: The Politics of Economic Growth in Postwar America* (New York: Oxford University Press, 2000), pp. 21, 23, 42–43, 44, 49.

85. For an insight into Keyserling's critique of the administration's economic policies in the mid-1950s, see Letter, Neil H. Jacoby to Gabriel Hauge, June 30, 1955, "Correspondence with WH, 53–56 (1)" folder, Box 121, Burns Papers, DDEPL. Also, for a full account of Keyserling's ideas and career, see Donald K. Pickens, *Leon H. Keyserling: A Progressive Economist* (Lanham, MD: Lexington Books, 2009), pp. 145–63.

86. Pickens, *Leon H. Keyserling*, pp. 156–61; Collins, *More*, pp. 131, 132.

87. John Kenneth Galbraith, *The Affluent Society*, 40th ann. ed. (New York: Houghton Mifflin, 1998), pp. 154–65. Also see John Kenneth Galbraith, *A Life in Our Times—Memoirs* (New York: Houghton Mifflin, 1981), pp. 284–85.

88. Collins, *More*, pp. 49–50.

CHAPTER 3: NARROWING THE COURSE

1. "Annual Message to Congress on the State of the Union," January 10, 1957, *PPP, 1957*, pp. 19 (quote), 21.

2. "The Quiet Crusader," *Time*, November 23, 1959, n.p. (p. 1 of 4).

3. Raymond J. Saulnier, "Appointment to the CEA," in *A Selection of Papers: Personal, Political, and Professional* (privately printed, 2007), pp. 25–27.

4. Gabriel Hauge, "Autobiography," chap. 12, pp. 12–13, Box 1, George Bookman Papers, 1981–93, DDEPL.

5. Ibid.

6. Raymond J. Saulnier, Oral History Interview, 1957, pp. 20–23, Columbia University Oral History Project, DDEPL.

7. Stewart Alsop, "The Unconscious Shift," *New York Herald Tribune*, July 7, 1957, "Scrapbook #1, 1957 (1)" folder, Box 90, Robert B. Anderson Papers, DDEPL.

8. Quote from "The Quiet Crusader," n.p. [p. 3 of 4]; Lawrence Stafford and Herbert Bratter, "The Coming Change at the Treasury," *Banking*, July 1957, pp. 44–45; Edwin L. Dale, Jr., "Tough-Minded Texan in the Treasury," *New York Times Magazine*, July 1957, "Stories about Robert B. Anderson 1957–59 (1)" folder, Box 87, Anderson Papers, DDEPL.

9. Quoted in "The Quiet Crusader," n.p. (p. 1 of 4).

10. Ibid. (pp. 1–2 of 4).

11. Ibid. (p. 2 of 4).

12. David L. Stebenne, *Modern Republican: Arthur Larson and the Eisenhower Years* (Bloomington: Indiana University Press, 2006), pp. 218–19.

13. Obituary, "Don Paarlberg, 94, Agricultural Economics Adviser to Three Presidents, Is Dead," *New York Times*, February 20, 2006.

14. Raymond J. Saulnier, *Constructive Years: The U.S. Economy under Eisenhower* (New York: University Press of America, 1991), pp. 97–98. Also see Saulnier, Interview, pp. 37–43; *ERP, 1959*, pp. 1–4; Iwan W. Morgan, *Eisenhower versus "The Spenders": The Eisenhower Administration, the Democrats and the Budget, 1953–60* (New York: St. Martin's Press, 1990), pp. 99–100.

15. Saulnier, Interview, pp. 15–17.

16. Saulnier, *Constructive Years*, pp. 97–98.

17. Ibid., pp. 93–94; Saulnier, Interview, pp. 37–43; *ERP, 1959*, p. 3; Morgan, *Eisenhower versus "The Spenders,"* pp. 93–94.

18. Saulnier, *Constructive Years*, p. 98; *ERP, 1959*, p. 3.

19. Robert P. Bremner, *Chairman of the Fed: William McChesney Martin Jr. and the Creation of the Modern American Financial System* (New Haven: Yale University Press, 2004), p. 129.

20. Saulnier, *Constructive Years*, pp. 106–7.

21. Ibid., p. 98.

22. Bremner, *Chairman of the Fed*, pp. 122–32; *ERP, 1959*, pp. 33–37.

23. Saulnier, Interview, pp. 12–13.

24. Ibid.; Bremner, *Chairman of the Fed*, pp. 130–31.

25. Bremner, *Chairman of the Fed*, p. 130; Saulnier, Interview, pp. 23–25.

26. Saulnier, *Constructive Years*, pp. 100, 107; Minutes, Cabinet Meeting, February 27, 1957, p. 2, Box 8, AWCS, DDEPL; Bremner, *Chairman of the Fed*, pp. 123, 128–29.

27. Transcript, *Meet the Press* Interview with Robert B. Anderson, January 26, 1958, pp. 3–5, "Speeches and Statements, 1957–58 (3)," Box 76, Anderson Papers, DDEPL.

28. Saulnier, *Constructive Years*, pp. 113, 180; Morgan, *Eisenhower versus "The Spenders,"* pp. 91–93.

29. Bremner, *Chairman of the Fed*, p. 131; Stephen E. Ambrose *Eisenhower: Soldier and President; The Renowned One-Volume Life* (New York: Simon and Schuster, 1991), pp. 450–54, 462.

30. Stebenne, *Modern Republican*, pp. 209–10. For another source on how Eisenhower's stroke impacted his second term, see David Eisenhower with Julie Nixon Eisenhower, *Going Home to Glory: A Memoir of Life with Dwight D. Eisenhower, 1961–1969* (New York: Simon and Schuster, 2010), p. 158.

31. Notes, Presentation, Cabinet Executive Session, December 2, 1957, p. 1, "Cabinet Presentation Notes 56–60 (1)" folder, Box 5, Raymond Saulnier Papers, DDEPL; Minutes, Cabinet Meeting, January 24, 1958, p. 1, Box 10, AWCS, DDEPL.

32. Minutes, Cabinet Meeting, February 28, 1958, p. 1, Box 10, AWCS, DDEPL.

33. Saulnier, *Constructive Years*, pp. 106–7.

34. Minutes, Cabinet Meeting, February 28, 1958, pp. 2–3, Box 10, AWCS, DDEPL.

35. Minutes, Cabinet Meeting, November 15, 1957, Box 9, AWCS, DDEPL.

36. Morgan, *Eisenhower versus "The Spenders,"* pp. 123–26.

37. "Statement by the President on the Economic Situation," February 12, 1958, *PPP, 1958*, p. 151; Morgan, *Eisenhower versus "The Spenders,"* p. 102.

38. Transcript, *Meet the Press* Interview with Robert B. Anderson, February 17, 1958, pp. 1–8, "Speeches and Statements, 1957–58 (4)" folder, Box 77, Anderson Papers, DDEPL; Morgan, *Eisenhower versus "The Spenders,"* p. 102.

39. Minutes, Cabinet Meeting, February 28, 1958, pp. 2–3, Box 10, AWCS, DDEPL.

40. Memorandum, Maxwell M. Rabb to Sherman Adams, February 24, 1958, "February 28, 1958 Cabinet Meeting" folder, Box 10, AWCS, DDEPL; Memorandum, Saulnier to Vice President Nixon, February 27, 1958, "Minutes, Cabinet Meeting, February 28, 1958" folder, Box 10, AWCS, DDEPL.

41. Morgan, *Eisenhower versus "The Spenders,"* pp. 102–3.

42. Minutes, Legislative Meeting, February 25, 1958, "Legislative Meetings 1958 (1), Jan.–Feb." folder, Box 3, AWLS, DDEPL.

43. Minutes, Cabinet Meeting, November 15, 1957, Box 9, AWCS, DDEPL.

44. "Letter to the Minority Leaders of the Senate and the House of Representatives Concerning Measures to Aid Economic Growth," March 8, 1958, *PPP, 1958*, pp. 208–11.

45. Presidential News Conference, May 14, 1958, *PPP, 1958*, p. 402.

46. Bremner, *Chairman of the Fed*, p. 131ff.; Herbert Stein, *The Fiscal Revolution in America* (Chicago: University of Chicago Press, 1969), pp. 238–40.

47. Minutes, Cabinet Meeting, April 18, 1958, p. 2, Box 11, AWCS, DDEPL; Minutes, Cabinet Meeting, August 1, 1958, pp. 2–3, Box 11, AWCS, DDEPL.

48. Presidential News Conference, February 5, 1958, *New York Times*, February 6, 1958, p. 18.

49. Minutes, Legislative Meeting, March 18, 1958, "Legislative Meetings 1958 (2) March–April" folder, Box 3, AWLS, DDEPL.

50. Stein, *Fiscal Revolution*, p. 343.

51. Quoted in ibid., pp. 333–34.

52. Ibid., pp. 323–24, 333.

53. Ibid., p. 335.

54. Letter, Burns to Eisenhower, March 31, 1958, and Eisenhower to Burns, April 2, 1958, "Arthur Burns 1958/59 (1)" folder, Box 9, AWAS, DDEPL.

55. Letter, Eisenhower to Donald S. Kenney, April 14, 1958, "Economics: 1958 (3)" folder, Box 560, White House Central Files: Official Files, DDEPL.

56. Address, Economic Mobilization Conference of the American Management Association, May 20, 1958; John T. Woolley and Gerhard Peters, the American Presidency Project (online), Santa Barbara, CA: University of California (host), Gerhard Peters (database), www.presidency.ucsb.edu/ws/?pid=11064.

57. Burns to Eisenhower, May 12, 1958, and Eisenhower to Burns, June 6, 1958, "Arthur Burns 1958/59 (1)" folder, Box 9, AWAS, DDEPL.

58. Stein, *Fiscal Revolution*, pp. 341–42.

59. Ibid.

60. Bremner, *Chairman of the Fed*, pp. 136–37. In the 1953–54 recession, industrial production declined by 9%; in 1957–58 it fell by 14%. Maximum rates of unemployment were higher in 1957–58 (7.6%) than in the earlier recession (6.1%), and they abated much more slowly in the second recession.

61. Robert H. Ferrell, *The Eisenhower Diaries* (New York: Norton, 1981), Entry of March 17, 1958, pp. 352–53. Also see Memorandum, "The Economic Situation and Certain Policy Suggestions," Saulnier to Eisenhower, August 21, 1958, "George Humphrey 1958/60 (2)" folder, Box 18, AWAS, DDEPL.

62. See table and discussion, *ERP, 1959*, p. 42; Saulnier, *Constructive Years*, pp. 108–10; Morgan, *Eisenhower versus "The Spenders,"* pp. 109–10, 114–17.

63. Saulnier, *Constructive Years*, p. 109.

64. Morgan, *Eisenhower versus "The Spenders,"* p. 93; quote on p. 106.

65. Minutes, Legislative Meeting, March 11, 1958, p. 2, "Legislative Meetings 1958 (2) March–April" folder, Box 3, AWLS, DDEPL.

66. Minutes, Legislative Meeting, April 15, 1958, p. 2, "Legislative Meetings 1958 (2) March–April" folder, Box 3, AWLS, DDEPL.

67. Morgan, *Eisenhower versus "The Spenders,"* p. 112.

68. See *ERP, 1960*, p. 44–47; Bremner, *Chairman of the Fed*, pp. 130–33.

69. *ERP, 1959*, p. 159. *ERP, 1961*, p. 147, takes the series out to the end of 1960. Seasonally adjusted unemployment peaked at 7.5% in April 1958, dipped some in May, but rose in August to 7.6%. A year earlier, in July 1957, the figure had been 4.2%. By December 1958 unemployment had declined to 6.1%, seasonally adjusted. By December 1959 unemployment was 5.5% and it bottomed at 4.8% (February 1960) and 4.9% (May 1960), but increased to 6.8% by December 1960.

70. Morgan, *Eisenhower versus "The Spenders,"* p. 125.

71. Minutes, Cabinet Meeting, August 1, 1958, pp. 2–3, Box 11, AWCS, DDEPL; Harold G. Vatter, *The U.S. Economy in the 1950's* (New York: Norton, 1963), p. 140.

72. *ERP, 1959*, pp. 7–33.

73. *ERP, 1960*, pp. 39–42.

74. Minutes, Cabinet Meeting, April 18, 1958, p. 2, and May 23, 1958, p. 2, Box 11, AWCS, DDEPL.

75. Minutes, Cabinet, Meeting, May 23, 1958, pp. 2–3, Box 10, AWCS, DDEPL.

76. Minutes, Cabinet Meeting, August 1, 1958, p. 3, Box 11, AWCS, DDEPL.

77. For a retrospective view of these efforts, see Eisenhower's comments, Cabinet Meeting, June 3, 1960, p. 2, Box 16, AWCS, DDEPL.

78. Minutes, Cabinet Meeting, April 18, 1958, p. 2, Box 11, AWCS, DDEPL.

79. Morgan, *Eisenhower versus "The Spenders,"* p. 129–30; *ERP, 1960*, pp. 18–23.

80. Morgan, *Eisenhower versus "The Spenders,"* pp. 129–30; Report, "Major Accomplishments of Treasury Department, January 1953–December 1960," pp. 8–11, "Robert Anderson 1960/61 (1)" folder, Box 3, AWAS, DDEPL.

81. Bremner, *Chairman of the Fed*, p. 144ff., also pp. 165–66; Report, "Major Accomplishments of Treasury Department, January 1953–December 1960," pp. 2–4, "Robert Anderson 1960/61 (1)" folder, Box 3, AWAS, DDEPL.

82. Vatter, *U.S. Economy in the 1950's*, pp. 260–61, 265. Only in 1957 was it in balance, mostly because of a short-term impact of the closure of the Suez Canal and increased American crude oil exports and reduced imports.

83. Dwight D. Eisenhower, *Waging Peace: The White House Years* (Garden City, NY: Doubleday, 1965) p. 460. The balance of payments issue had come up before 1958. In 1956, Secretary Humphrey used his concern about the continuing deficits in the balance of payments to make a pitch to cut mutual assistance (foreign aid). This was part of his, by then routine, effort to cut military spending and reduce taxes.

84. Notes, Cabinet Presentation, May 2, 1958, p. 3, Saulnier Papers, Box 5, DDEPL. Eisenhower discussed the problem at the cabinet meeting of November 20, 1958, Minutes, Cabinet Meeting, November 20, 1958, p. 3, Box 12, AWCS, DDEPL.

85. Speech, "Financial Policies for Sustainable Growth," American Finance Association and American Economic Association, December 29, 1959, p. 3, "Robert Anderson 1959 (1)" folder, Box 2, AWAS, DDEPL; Bremner, *Chairman of the Fed*, pp. 144–46.

86. Bremner, *Chairman of the Fed*, pp. 145–46; Vatter, *U.S. Economy in the 1950's*, pp. 260–61. The administration's commitment to balancing the budget and the Fed's tight money policy subsequently affected the rate of US gold sales, which declined in 1959 and by early 1960 were greatly reduced. Foreign confidence in Eisenhower's policies played its part in this turn of events, even though the American balance of payments deficit increased somewhat from $3.5 billion in 1958 to $3.9 billion in 1959. Not surprisingly, at the Federal Reserve, Martin also concluded that the balance of payments was one of the country's preeminent economic problems and increasingly factored it into its interest rate–setting decisions. Bremner, *Chairman of the Fed*, pp. 145–46; Vatter, *U.S. Economy in the 1950's*, pp. 260–61.

87. Morgan, *Eisenhower versus "The Spenders,"* p. 129.

88. Minutes, Legislative Meeting, December 15, 1958, p. 2, "Legislative Meetings 1958 (4), July–Dec." folder, Box 3, AWLS, DDEPL; "Major Accomplishments of Treasury Department, January 1953–December 1960," pp. 2–4, "Robert Anderson 1960/61 (1)" folder, Box 3, AWAS, DDEPL; Speech, "Financial Policies for Sustainable Growth," American Finance Association and American Economic Association, December 29, 1959, pp. 1–4, "Robert Anderson 1959 (1)" folder, Box 2, AWAS, DDEPL; Press Conference, Robert B. Anderson, January 16, 1960, p. 1, "Speeches & Statements, July 1959–Dec. 60 (2)" folder , Box 77, Anderson Papers, DDEPL.

89. *ERP, 1961*, pp. 33–40.

90. The distinguished economist Sumner Slichter argued in the late 1950s that there was little that could be done to stop an "inevitable" slow rate of increase in inflation. Martin sharply disagreed; see Bremner, *Chairman of the Fed*, pp. 127–28.

91. Even before that, in the recession of 1948–49—which was less serious than the recession of 1957–58—prices declined, although not by much. Some economists saw indications of a structural tendency toward inflation even during the 1930s. They believed that it was based on the power of large-scale enterprises to "administer" prices. Stein, *Fiscal Revolution*, pp. 238–40, 342–44; Notes, Cabinet Presentation, May 2, 1958, p. 1, "Notes for 1956/60 (2)" folder, Box 5, Saulnier Papers, DDEPL.

92. Bremner, *Chairman of the Fed*, p. 137.

93. Between July 1957 and the end of 1958, wholesale prices rose just 1%, kept down by the 10% decline in farm product prices from March 1958 to the end of 1959. For 1959–60, wholesale prices were essentially unchanged. Almost all categories of goods remained unchanged, and even steel showed some resistance to price increases—the result of increasing foreign competition and the 1960 recession. Consumer prices increased 3.4% in 1957, slowing toward the end of the year. They increased 1.6% in 1958, almost all of that increase occurred before July. Consumer prices showed similar trends. Inflation was almost 4% in 1957—i.e., when taking into account "all items, less food" for the period. It was under 2% for 1958. For the period 1959–60, the growth of the CPI slowed dramatically. For 1959, it was 1.7%; for 1960 it was 2%. For "all items, less food" it was 3.1% and 1.5% respectively. Almost the entire change in 1960 was attributable to food prices. Food prices declined much less dramatically than farm product prices. But services continued to rise about 4% in 1959 and 3% in 1960. While Eisenhower officials focused on administered

prices and wages, the services and, to a lesser extent, the housing sectors seemed to be all but impervious to the price weaknesses seen elsewhere in the economy. They were the core of a persistent, low- to mid-level inflation, even in the period 1957–60, which was characterized in most quarters by recession and slow growth. See *ERP, 1958*, pp. 159–61; *ERP, 1959*, pp. 168–69, 180–85; *ERP, 1961*, pp. 168–72.

94. Cabinet Presentation: Promoting the Growth of the National Economy, August 1, 1958, "Cabinet Presentation, Notes 1956/60 (2)" folder, Box 5, Saulnier Papers, DDEPL.

95. Minutes, Cabinet Meeting, August 1, 1958, p. 1, Box 11, AWCS, DDEPL.

96. Letter, Eisenhower to Eric Harlow Heckett, October 10, 1958, doc. 897, *Eisenhower Papers*, vol. 19, pp. 1153–56.

97. Cabinet Presentation: Promoting the Growth of the National Economy, August 1, 1958, "Cabinet Presentation, Notes 1956/60 (2)" folder, Box 5, Saulnier Papers, DDEPL; Minutes, Cabinet Meeting, August 1, 1958, pp. 1–2, Box 11, AWCS, DDEPL; Memorandum, "News Treatment of Nixon Committee Statement," Allen Wallis to James Hagerty, August 18, 1959, "Price level—Price Fixing, 1958/60" folder, Box 564, White House Central Files: Official File, DDEPL.

98. Saulnier, Notes, Cabinet Presentation, November 11, 1959, "Cabinet Presentations, 1956/60 (2)" folder, Box 5, Saulnier Papers, DDEPL; Saulnier, *Constructive Years*, pp. 116–19, and for the course of the strike, pp. 138–40, fn. 106. Also see Raymond J. Saulnier, "Policies that Ended Inflation," *Proceedings of the Academy of Political Science* 31 (1975): pp. 110–11.

99. Minutes, Cabinet Meeting, August 1, 1958, p. 3, Box 11, AWCS, DDEPL; Minutes, Cabinet Meeting, November 20, 1958, pp. 2–3, Box 12, AWCS, DDEPL.

100. *ERP, 1959*, p. 45; Bremner, *Chairman of the Fed*, p. 137.

101. Indeed, Martin and Fed economists had begun to focus on inflationary expectations—of consumers, investors, and businesses—as an important source of inflation. See Bremner, *Chairman of the Fed*, pp. 122–24.

102. Memorandum, Saulnier to Eisenhower, "The Economic Situation and Certain Policy Suggestions," August 21, 1958, "G. Hauge 1958/60 (2)" folder, Box 18, AWAS, DDEPL; also see Memorandum (No Subject), Hauge to Eisenhower (commenting on Saulnier's memorandum to Eisenhower), "G. Hauge 1958/60 (2)" folder, Box 18, AWAS, DDEPL.

103. Quoted in Bremner, *Chairman of the Fed*, p. 123; also Draft Article, Henry C. Wallich, "Eisenhower Economics," n.d., p. 2, "G. Hauge 1956–57 (2)" folder, Box 18, AWAS, DDEPL.

104. Minutes, Legislative Meeting, January 13, 1959, p. 4, "Legislative Meetings 1959 (1) Jan." folder, Box 3, AWLS, DDEPL.

105. Morgan, *Eisenhower versus "The Spenders,"* p. 132.

106. Ibid., pp. 132–33, 144–47.

107. Ibid., pp. 135–36.

108. Ibid.

109. Ibid., pp. 131–32, 149–50; quote on p. 131.

110. Minutes, Cabinet Meeting, May 1, 1959, pp. 3–4, Box 13, AWCS, DDEPL.

111. "Statement by the President on the Annual Budget Message," January 19, 1959, *PPP, 1959*, pp. 112, 118–19; Morgan, *Eisenhower versus "The Spenders,"* pp. 134–35.

112. See "Annual Budget Message to the Congress: Fiscal Year 1960," January 19, 1959, *PPP, 1959*, pp. 36ff., for a detailed discussion of items and the president's rationale for the budget decisions he made.

113. Morgan, *Eisenhower versus "The Spenders,"* pp. 134–35.

114. Minutes, Cabinet Meeting, May 1, 1959, p. 4, Box 13, AWCS, DDEPL.

115. Morgan, *Eisenhower versus "The Spenders,"* pp. 135–36.

116. Minutes, Legislative Meeting, June 16, 1959, pp. 3–4, "Legislative Meetings 1959 (5) June" folder, Box 3, AWLS, DDEPL; Minutes, Cabinet Meeting, June 22, 1959, pp. 2–4, Box 14, AWCS, DDEPL.

117. *ERP, 1960*, pp. 5–7; Stein, *Fiscal Revolution*, pp. 350–51; Morgan, *Eisenhower versus "The Spenders,"* pp. 152–53.

118. Stein, *Fiscal Revolution*, pp. 221–28, 355–56; Robert M. Collins, *More: The Politics of Economic Development in Postwar America* (New York: Oxford University Press, 2000), pp. 15, 17, 47.

119. "Record of Action," Cabinet, November 12, 1959, pp. 1–2, Box 14, AWCS, DDEPL; Minutes, Cabinet Meeting, June 3, 1960, pp. 1–4, Box 16, AWCS, DDEPL.

120. Morgan, *Eisenhower versus "The Spenders,"* p. 153.

121. Ibid., pp. 47–48, 153–54.

122. Morgan, *Eisenhower versus "The Spenders,"* pp. 157–60.

123. Ibid., p. 162; *ERP, 1961*, pp. 10–15.

124. *ERP, 1961*, p. 21–28; Bremner, *Chairman of the Fed*, pp. 152–53.

125. *ERP, 1961*, p. 43.

126. Ibid., p. 44.

127. Stein, *Fiscal Revolution*, p. 351.

128. Quoted in Bremner, *Chairman of the Fed*, p. 138.

129. Saulnier, Interview, pp. 47–50.

130. *ERP, 1961*, pp. iii–v.

131. Bremner, *Chairman of the Fed*, p. 147.

CHAPTER 4: AGRICULTURE

1. Presidential News Conference, June 16, 1954, *PPP, 1954*, pp. 568–69.

2. *ERP, 1954*, p. 89.

3. It worked as follows: Assume that the price of corn in 1910–14 was $1.00 a bushel and the current average price of all farm products is 150% of the average price of all farm products received during the 1910–14 base period. The $1.00 corn price is divided by $1.50, to show the parity price of corn in 1909–14 of $0.666. If the current price of things that farmers buy is 2.5 times (250%) the prices of 1910–14, the current parity price of corn is 2.5 times $0.666, or $1.6665. So, if the supported price of corn was "90% of parity," that would yield a support price of $1.50 (90% of $1.66) for purposes federal crop loan programs.

4. US Department of Agriculture, *History of Agricultural Price-Support and Adjustment Programs, 1933–84*, (Washington, DC: USDA, 1984), pp. 2–3, 14–15; Willard W. Cochrane and C. Ford Runge, *Reforming Farm Policy: Toward a National Agenda* (Ames: Iowa

State University Press, 1992), p. 42; Virgil W. Dean, *An Opportunity Lost: The Truman Administration and the Farm Policy Debate* (Columbia: University of Missouri Press, 2006), pp. 11–12.

5. The Agricultural Act of 1949 (and its predecessor the Agricultural Adjustment Act of 1938) was the organic farm law during the 1950s. It authorized price supports for over two hundred nonbasic farm commodities or products. For most of these, price supports were discretionary with the Department of Agriculture, and general guidelines were provided by law as a basis for price support without the use of fixed formulas; instead they looked at a number of market-related factors. But, for those commodities where price supports were mandatory, a rigid fixed formula was prescribed and the USDA was required to set acreage allotments (restrictions on land use) if forecasts for crop yields in the coming year seemed likely to exceed consumption by certain established margins. Farmers then held a referendum on the allotments, and if two-thirds or more voted against them, price supports were withdrawn for nonbasic commodities, where supports were voluntary. Farmers of the basics, for whom price supports were mandatory, had little alternative but to agree to acreage restrictions (allotments) in exchange for supports, since legislation provided that if growers rejected allotments at high percentages of parity, price support would be available at 50% of parity. But they still had to stay within their allotments. See Attached Letter, Benson to Ellender, May 2, 1957, "April 12, 1957 Cabinet Meeting," Box 8, AWCS, DDEPL; Eisenhower Letter to Benson, April 26, 1955, doc. 1409, and Eisenhower Memorandum to Benson, March 27, 1953, doc. 108, fn. 1, Online Eisenhower Papers.

6. *ERP, 1956*, p. 55; *ERP, 1957*, p. 30; USDA, *Price-Support*, p. 45. During the Eisenhower administration farm legislation set the support levels at between 75% and 90% of parity for basic crops, perishable dairy products, and a handful of others (reduced to 65% to 90% after 1958). For nonbasics (essentially the rest) some commodities were set at 60% to 90% and most were set at 0% to 90%. Most of these 200-plus commodities and livestock operated without significant surplus problems or, where storage of the product was impractical, market prices were above support prices and government support programs incurred little cost. See Memorandum, Areeda to Morgan, January 10, 1958, "Agriculture (General) (1)" folder, Box 5, Phillip Areeda Papers, DDEPL.

7. *Eckstein Report*, p. 196; *ERP, 1959*, pp. 102–4.

8. *ERP, 1954*, p. 90.

9. Memorandum, "Accomplishments of the Department of Agriculture 1953–1961," "Benson, 1960–61 (1)" folder, Box 7, AWAS, DDEPL.

10. Ezra Taft Benson, Oral History Interview, p. 11, Columbia University Oral History Project, DDEPL.

11. Prior to the Supreme Court's decision in *Baker v. Carr,* 369 U.S. 186 (1962), US House of Representatives districts and state legislative districts were not required to be equally apportioned by population. By the 1950s almost everyone conceded that this formula (or the lack of one) favored rural areas at the expense of urban constituencies, despite relative, or even absolute, declines in rural population.

12. Memorandum (untitled), Hauge to Eisenhower, April 27, 1954, and attached Memorandum (untitled), Benson to Eisenhower, April 13,1954, both in "Gabriel Hauge 1952–55

(5)" folder, Box 18, AWAS, DDEPL; Memorandum (Arthur Burns), "Notes on the Agricultural Situation and Program," December 6, 1955, "Agriculture-Notes on Farm Situation 1955" folder, Box 104, Arthur F. Burns Papers, DDEPL; *ERP, 1956,* p. 59.

13. Donald Paarlberg, Oral History Interview, pp. 85–90, Columbia University Oral History Project, DDEPL; Gabriel Hauge, "Autobiography," chap. 11, pp. 5–6, Box 1, George Bookman Papers, 1981–93, DDEPL.

14. Hauge, "Autobiography," chap. 11, pp. 5–6, Box 1, Bookman Papers, DDEPL.

15. Dean, *Opportunity Lost,* pp. 2–3; Carolyn Dimitri, Anne B. W. Effland, and Neilson C. Conklin, *The 20th Century Transformation of U.S. Agriculture and Farm Policy,* Economic Information Bulletin No. 3, Economic Research Service, United States Department of Agriculture, June 2005, p. 3. E.g., farm output rose by one-fourth in the 1950s, but farm employment fell from 7.5 million to 5.2 million. See Harold G. Vatter, *The U.S. Economy in the 1950's: An Economic History* (Chicago: University of Chicago Press, 1963), pp. 248–49.

16. Cochrane and Runge, *Reforming Farm Policy,* pp. 39–40; USDA, *Price-Support,* pp. 2–3.

17. USDA, *Price-Support,* p. 11; Cochrane and Runge, *Reforming Farm Policy,* p. 41; Eisenhower Letter to Benson, November 15, 1954, doc. 1152, fn. 1, Online Eisenhower Papers.

18. Cochrane and Runge, *Reforming Farm Policy,* p. 22.

19. Dean, *Opportunity Lost,* pp. 9–10.

20. USDA, *Price-Support,* pp. 16; Cochrane and Runge, *Reforming Farm Policy,* p. 42; Dean, *Opportunity Lost,* pp. 12–14.

21. USDA, *Price-Support,* pp. 16; Cochrane and Runge, *Reforming Farm Policy,* p. 42; Dean, *Opportunity Lost,* pp. 12–14.

22. USDA, *Price-Support,* p. 17.

23. Ibid., p. 17.

24. Cochrane and Runge, *Reforming Farm Policy,* p. 42.

25. Dean, *Opportunity Lost,* pp. 203–4; Cochrane and Runge, *Reforming Farm Policy,* p. 42; *Eckstein Report,* pp. 196–99. Commodities in government storage also declined briefly but dramatically early in the Korean War.

26. Not everyone fell within the parameters of the debate over high fixed versus flexible price supports. Some liberal Democrats wanted to expand government programs; distribute agricultural surpluses to the poor; and rely on a modernized parity formula to pay direct cash "compensatory payments" to farmers based on a "pre-Depression" commodity price, rather than rely on price supports determined by what critics saw as an outdated, historical formula for parity. These ideas became the cornerstone of post-1961 programs, buttressed by lower price supports. Other, still more radical proposals emerged in 1948–49, when the Truman administration moved to the left on farm policy. Such income subsidies—"production flexibility contract payments"—became the centerpiece of federal agricultural programs after 1996, when price supports were finally eliminated. Dean, *Opportunity Lost,* pp. 47, 80–81, 129–30.

27. Ibid., pp. 14, 45–46; Cochrane and Runge, *Reforming Farm Policy,* p. 43.

28. Dean, *Opportunity Lost,* pp. 45–46.

29. Vatter, *U.S. Economy in the 1950's,* p. 249. The surge had begun in roughly 1942. For the period 1942–59, agricultural productivity per hour of farm work increased roughly

5% a year, while consumption of farm products increased less than 2% per year. See *Eckstein Report*, pp. 189–90.

30. See Dean, *Opportunity Lost*, pp. 71–77, for a detailed discussion.

31. Cochrane and Runge, *Reforming Farm Policy*, p. 43.

32. USDA, *Price-Support*, pp. 17–18; *ERP, 1954*, p. 93.

33. Paarlberg, Interview, p. 107, DDEPL.

34. Dean, *Opportunity Lost*, pp. 92–93, 97–108.

35. USDA, *Price-Support*, p. 18; Dean, *Opportunity Lost*, pp. 130–32, 136–40; Steven Wagner, *Eisenhower Republicanism: Pursuing the Middle Way* (DeKalb: Northern Illinois University Press, 2006), pp. 45–47.

36. Vatter, *U.S. Economy in the 1950's*, p. 253; Dean, *Opportunity Lost*, pp. 132–33, 141; Cochrane and Runge, *Reforming Farm Policy*, pp. 44–45.

37. USDA, *Price-Support*, pp. 19–20.

38. Ibid., pp. 20–22; Eisenhower Memorandum to Benson, April 4, 1953, fn. 1, doc. 130, Online Eisenhower Papers. Acreage restrictions (allotments) and marketing orders were restored by Eisenhower's USDA in 1953 for wheat and cotton and for corn in 1954, in an attempt to limit production. Corn production had not been restrained for a decade. It presented peculiar problems and was the only feed grain subject to mandatory price supports in 1953. Corn was marketed commercially from limited areas of the country (commercial corn areas), but about 80% was used as feed for livestock on the farm in most areas of the country.

39. *ERP, 1956*, p. 59.

40. Paarlberg, Interview, p. 107, DDEPL.

41. Wagner, *Eisenhower Republicanism*, pp. 43–45.

42. Quoted in Edward L. Schapsmeier and Frederick H. Schapsmeier, *Ezra Taft Benson and the Politics of Agriculture: The Eisenhower Years, 1953–1961* (Danville, IL: Interstate Printers and Publishers, 1975), pp. 7–8.

43. Minutes, Cabinet Meeting, December 11, 1953, Box 2, AWCS, DDEPL; Benson, Interview, pp. 21–22, DDEPL.

44. Benson, Interview, pp. 10–11, DDEPL; Ezra Taft Benson, *Cross Fire: The Eight Years with Eisenhower* (Garden City, NY: Doubleday, 1962), p. 126.

45. Schapsmeier and Schapsmeier, *Ezra Taft Benson*, pp. 13–14, 20–24; Benson, Interview, pp. 1–7, DDEPL.

46. Schapsmeier and Schapsmeier, *Ezra Taft Benson*, pp. 13, 16; Benson, *Cross Fire*, pp. 11, 23–24.

47. Minutes, Cabinet Meeting, December 11, 1953, Box 12, AWCS, DDEPL; "Special Message to Congress on Agriculture," February 9, 1960, *PPP, 1960*, pp. 162–63.

48. Herbert Brownell with John P. Burke, *Advising Ike: The Memoirs of Attorney General Herbert Brownell* (Lawrence: University of Kansas Press, 1993), pp. 286–88, 297–98.

49. Trudy Huskamp Peterson, *Agricultural Exports, Farm Income, and the Eisenhower Administration* (Lincoln: University of Nebraska Press, 1979), p. 7; Paarlberg, Interview, pp. 14, 24–29, DDEPL.

50. Paarlberg, Interview, pp. 110–11, DDEPL. Paarlberg notes that after 1961 Benson's political views moved closer toward libertarianism and he became associated with Robert

Welch and the John Birch Society, which had at one time described Eisenhower as "a conscious and articulate tool of the international communist conspiracy." See ibid.

51. Benson's views on the proper role of government became more reactionary after he left government, but in 1953 he saw a very limited role for government in the economic regulation of agriculture. On the other hand, he was a partisan of the cooperative movement and expanded government efforts to create more efficient production and marketing of farm products.

52. Schapsmeier and Schapsmeier, *Ezra Taft Benson*, pp. 17–19; Memorandum, Hauge to Eisenhower, November 2, 1953, "Gabriel Hauge, 1952–55 (6)" folder, Box 18, AWAS, DDEPL; Benson, *Cross Fire*, pp. 38–39, 46; Paarlberg, Interview, pp. 6–7, 18, DDEPL.

53. Paarlberg, Interview, pp. 12–13, DDEPL.

54. Hauge, "Autobiography," chap. 11, p. 6, Box 1, Bookman Papers, DDEPL.

55. Letter, Eisenhower to Benson, March 20, 1958, "E. T. Benson 1957–58 (4)" folder, Box 6, AWAS, DDEPL.

56. Ezra Taft Benson, "A General Statement on Agricultural Policy," Speeches, February 1953–July 1953 (1)" folder, Box 1, Ezra Taft Benson Papers, Series I, DDEPL.

57. Memorandum (untitled), Benson to Eisenhower, April 30, 1953, "Price Levels—Price Fixing, 1953 (2)" folder, Box 564, Central Files: Official File, DDEPL.

58. Paarlberg, Interview, pp. 20–22, 119–22, DDEPL. Paarlberg notes that despite the administration's efforts the RDP remained "too small" because of disinterest of agriculture committees in Congress and traditional farm organizations like the American Farm Bureau Federation in the issue of rural poverty. The program was designed to increase farming technical assistance and expand training and health facilities. Paarlberg observes that the RDP nucleus was greatly expanded during the subsequent Kennedy and Johnson administrations. See also Memorandum, E. T. Benson, "Accomplishments of the Department of Agriculture, 1953–1960," "Benson, 1960/61 (1)" folder, Box 7, AWAS, DDEPL; Paarlberg, Interview, pp. 20–21, 119–22, DDEPL; Schapsmeier and Schapsmeier, *Ezra Taft Benson*, pp. 142–44.

59. Schapsmeier and Schapsmeier, *Ezra Taft Benson*, pp. 39–40. On the issue of beef (livestock) price supports, see also Eisenhower Memorandum to Benson, October 20, 1953, fn. 1 and 2, doc. 470, Online Eisenhower Papers. The National Farmers Union generally supported Brannan plan–type solutions to farm problems.

60. For an example of Eisenhower's thinking, see Minutes, Cabinet Meeting, December 9, 1955, p. 5, Box 6, AWCS, DDEPL. For Benson's, see Speech, Young Republican National Convention, Denver, Co., June 19, 1959, "Speeches, June 1959–December 1960 (1)" folder, Box 4, Benson Papers, DDEPL.

61. Speech, "Inherited Problems," April 7, 1953, "Speeches, Feb.–July 53 (1)" folder, Box 1, Benson Papers, DDEPL.

62. Hauge, "Autobiography," chap. 11, pp. 5–6, Box 1, Bookman Papers, DDEPL.

63. Eisenhower Memorandum to Benson, April 4, 1953, doc. 130, Online Eisenhower Papers; Benson, *Cross Fire*, pp. 76–78, 170–72. Furthermore, despite Benson's recommendations to allow him to use his discretionary authority to reduce diary supports from 90% to 75%, in 1953 Eisenhower elected to extend 90% of parity for milk and butterfat for another year. The result was declining butter sales vis-à-vis margarine and increased

CCC stocks. The dairy products support levels subsequently were lowered to 75% parity in 1954.

64. Minutes, Legislative Meeting, December 18, 1953, "Legislative Meetings—1953, A–D (6)" folder, Box 1, AWLS, DDEPL.

65. Memorandum (untitled), Eisenhower to Benson, March 31, 1954, "Benson 1954 (5)" folder, Box 6, AWAS, DDEPL.

66. "Special Message to the Congress on Agriculture," January 11, 1954, *PPP, 1954,* pp. 23–39; Schapsmeier and Schapsmeier, *Ezra Taft Benson,* pp. 70–73.

67. Schapsmeier and Schapsmeier, *Ezra Taft Benson,* pp. 73–86; Benson, *Cross Fire,* pp. 204–10; Paarlberg, Interview, pp. 86–90, DDEPL. The American Farm Bureau supported the administration's drive for lower and more flexible supports, as it would throughout Eisenhower's eight years in office, and the National Farmers Union opposed it. See Paarlberg, Interview, pp. 90–93, DDEPL. What had changed since the last major battle over flexible supports in 1948–49 was that most agricultural economists had moved from near-unanimous support for flexible supports to views "that only strong production controls and high price supports could assure acceptable farm income in a period of growing farm productivity." See USDA, *Price-Support,* p. 21.

68. Memorandum (untitled), Morgan to Areeda, January 10, 1958, "Agriculture (General) (1)" folder, Box 5, Areeda Papers, DDEPL.

69. Memorandum (untitled), Hauge to Benson, September 8, 1954, "Benson 1954 (3)" folder, Box 6, AWAS, DDEPL.

70. "Statement by the President upon Signing the Agricultural Act of 1954," August 28, 1954, *PPP, 1954,* p. 221; "Special Message to the Congress on Agriculture," January 11, 1954, *PPP, 1954,* pp. 29–30.

71. "Special Message to the Congress on Agriculture," January 11, 1954, *PPP, 1954,* pp. 30–31; Eisenhower Letter to Milton S. Eisenhower, November 6, 1953, doc. 525, Online Eisenhower Papers.

72. "Statement by the President upon Signing the Agricultural Trade Development and Assistance Act of 1954," July 10, 1954, *PPP, 1954,* p. 626.

73. *ERP,1956,* pp. 57–58; Schapsmeier and Schapsmeier, *Ezra Taft Benson,* pp. 98–99.

74. Schapsmeier and Schapsmeier, *Ezra Taft Benson,* pp. 99–103; *ERP, 1956,* p. 58.

75. Minutes, Cabinet Meeting, December 9, 1955, p. 5, Box 6, AWCS, DDEPL; Paarlberg, Interview, pp. 80–83, DDEPL; Schapsmeier and Schapsmeier, *Ezra Taft Benson,* pp. 100–101.

76. Minutes, Cabinet Meeting, December 9, 1955, p. 5, Box 6, AWCS, DDEPL.

77. For a discussion of possible sales to communist countries, see "Policy Review of Dollar Sales to the Soviet Bloc of Agricultural Surplus Commodities (December 15, 1954)," attached to Minutes, Cabinet Meeting, December 17, 1954, Box 4, AWCS, DDEPL.

78. Though Eisenhower remained personally very popular, the Republicans narrowly lost control of Congress in 1954.

79. The administration often spoke of a "$6 billion time bomb" left on its doorstep— the CCC carryover stocks accumulated by the prior administration and Congress's enactment of 90% of parity for basics through 1954. E.g., see Minutes, Legislative Meeting, April 28, 1959, "Legislative Meetings 1959 (2)" folder, Box 3, AWLS, DDEPL.

80. *ERP, 1956,* pp. 118–19, 132–33; *Eckstein Report,* p. 198.

81. Memorandum (no date), "Agricultural Legislation," "Agriculture (General) (1)" folder, Box 5, Areeda Papers, DDEPL; *ERP, 1959,* p. 103; *Eckstein Report,* pp. 197–99.

82. *ERP, 1956,* pp. 150–51; *ERP, 1957,* pp. 14–15.

83. Hauge, "Autobiography," chap. 11, pp. 6–7, Box 1, Bookman Papers, DDEPL; Paarlberg quoted in Peterson, *Agricultural Exports,* xii.

84. Hauge, "Autobiography," chap. 11, p. 7, Box 1, Bookman Papers, DDEPL.

85. Quoted in Schapsmeier and Schapsmeier, *Ezra Taft Benson,* p. 129.

86. Letter, Eisenhower to Benson, September 1, 1955, "Benson 1955/56 (4)" folder, Box 6, AWAS, DDEPL.

87. Eisenhower, Letter to Benson, September 23, 1955, doc. 1593, Online Eisenhower Papers.

88. Between 1936 and 1938 the New Deal's Soil Conservation and Domestic Allotment Act had been prefaced on similar rationales. Also, from 1934 to 1942, various federal agencies purchased "submarginal" farmland in Great Plains and Dust Bowl regions and converted it to grazing pastures, recreational areas, wildlife sanctuaries, and Indian reservations. See Eisenhower Memorandum to Benson, November 14, 1954, doc. 1152, Online Eisenhower Papers.

89. "Special Message to Congress on Agriculture," January 9, 1954, *PPP, 1956,* pp. 42–45; Benson, *Cross Fire,* 293–95; Eisenhower Letter to Benson, September 23, 1955, doc. 1593, Online Eisenhower Papers.

90. "Special Message to Congress on Agriculture," January 9, 1954, *PPP, 1956,* pp. 45–48; *ERP, 1956,* pp. 59–60; Benson, *Cross Fire,* 291–92; Eisenhower Letter to Benson, September 23, 1955, doc. 1593, Online Eisenhower Papers.

91. Minutes, Cabinet Meeting, December 9, 1955, Box 6, AWCS, DDEPL.

92. Schapsmeier and Schapsmeier, *Ezra Taft Benson,* pp. 161–66.

93. Eisenhower Diary, February 11, 1956, doc. 1748, Online Eisenhower Papers; Benson, *Cross Fire,* 312–17.

94. Dwight D. Eisenhower, *The White House Years,* vol. 1 (Garden City: Doubleday), p. 633; Paarlberg, Interview, pp. 141–43, DDEPL.

95. "Veto of the Farm Bill," April 16, 1956, *PPP, 1956,* p. 388.

96. Ibid., p. 386.

97. Ibid., pp. 386–87.

98. Benson, Interview, pp. 13–21, DDEPL; Benson, *Cross Fire,* pp. 317–19; Wagner, *Eisenhower Republicanism,* pp. 55–57.

99. "Radio and Television Address to the American People on the Farm Bill Veto," April 16, 1956, *PPP, 1956,* pp. 391–92.

100. "Veto of the Farm Bill," April 16, 1956, *PPP, 1956,* pp. 389–90; Benson, *Cross Fire,* pp. 318–21.

101. Benson, *Cross Fire,* p. 323.

102. If Congress had not provided for a freeze on minimum national acreage allotments for wheat and cotton, existing formulas would have mandated dramatic reductions of about 75% from these set levels. See Draft Letter, Benson to Ellender, May 2, 1957, "Minutes, Cabinet Meeting, April 12, 1957" folder, Box 8, AWCS, DDEPL.

103. USDA, *Price-Support*, p. 22; Schapsmeier and Schapsmeier, *Ezra Taft Benson*, pp. 165–66.

104. Schapsmeier and Schapsmeier, *Ezra Taft Benson*, pp. 169–71; *ERP, 1961*, p. 104.

105. Minutes, Legislative Meeting, March 18, 1958, "Legislative Meetings 1958 (2)" folder, and February 2, 1960, "Legislative Meetings 1960 (1)" folder, Box 3, AWLS, DDEPL.

106. *ERP, 1961*, pp. 19–21, 93–95; *Eckstein Report*, p. 194.

107. *PPP, 1959*, pp. 146–48, January 29, 1958, "Special Message to Congress on Agriculture"; Memorandum, "Agricultural Legislation" (no date), "Agriculture (General) (1)" folder, Box 5, Areeda Papers, DDEPL; *ERP, 1959*, p. 103.

108. *ERP, 1961*, p. 20.

109. Dimitri, Effland, and Conklin, *20th Century Transformation*, p. 8.

110. Benson, Interview, p. 24, DDEPL.

111. Minutes, Cabinet Meeting, April 12, 1957, Box 8, AWCS, DDEPL; Cabinet Paper, "Long-Range Agricultural Policy," May 2, 1957 (revised version of paper presented at April 12, 1957, cabinet meeting), also in "Minutes, Cabinet Meeting, April 12, 1957" folder, Box 8, AWCS, DDEPL.

112. Minutes, Cabinet Meeting, April 12, 1957, Box 8, AWCS, DDEPL; Notes, Cabinet Meeting, April 12, 1957, Box 4, OSSLAM, DDEPL.

113. Benson, *Cross Fire*, pp. 381–82.

114. Schapsmeier and Schapsmeier, *Ezra Taft Benson*, pp. 190–200.

115. Ibid.; Benson, *Cross Fire*, pp. 361–62.

116. Minutes, Legislative Meeting, December 4, 1957, "Legislative Meetings 1957 (5)" folder, Box 3, AWLS, DDEPL. The Soil Bank program also tended to bestow benefits on larger farmers, who were generally more able to take large tracts of farmland out of production. The Acreage Reserve, of course, was designed to address the short-term problems of farmers of basics. See Draft Letter, Benson to Ellender, May 2, 1957, "Minutes, Cabinet Meetings, April 12, 1957" folder, Box 8, AWCS, DDEPL.

117. "Special Message to the Congress on Agriculture," January 16, 1958, *PPP, 1958*, p. 103.

118. Ibid., pp. 103–10; Benson, *Cross Fire*, pp. 383–84.

119. "Special Message to the Congress on Agriculture," January 16, 1958, *PPP, 1958*, pp. 103–6.

120. Ibid.; *ERP, 1961*, pp. 103–4.

121. "Special Message to the Congress on Agriculture," January 16, 1958, *PPP, 1958*, p. 103; Runge and Cochrane, *Reforming Farm Policy*, p. 45; *ERP, 1961*, p. 104. In 1985 the Food Security Act revived the Conservation Reserve, and approximately 34 million acres are currently in this program as of July 2008.

122. Schapsmeier and Schapsmeier, *Ezra Taft Benson*, pp. 192–97; Raymond J. Saulnier, *Constructive Years: The U.S. Economy under Eisenhower* (Lanham, MD: University Press of America, 1991), p. 150.

123. Minutes, Legislative Meeting, March 11, 1958, "Legislative Meetings 1958 (1)" folder, Box 3, AWLS, DDEPL; Letter, Eisenhower to Benson, March 20, 1958, "E. T. Benson 1957–58 (4)" folder, Box 6, AWAS, DDEPL.

124. Schapsmeier and Schapsmeier, *Ezra Taft Benson*, pp. 206–7; "Veto of the Farm Freeze Bill," March 31, 1958, *PPP, 1958*, pp. 250–54; "Radio and Television Remarks on the Veto of the Farm Freeze Bill," March 31, 1958, *PPP, 1958*, pp. 255–56.

125. Schapsmeier and Schapsmeier, *Ezra Taft Benson*, p. 208; Benson, *Cross Fire*, pp. 400–406.

126. Unlike other basics, corn growers outside of the "corn commercial area" could exceed their allotments and still get minimum price support, which the administration considered unfair. It hoped to use the referendum to lower overall support levels for all growers (in the commercial area and outside it), with no allotments. They were successful. See Benson, *Cross Fire*, p. 321.

127. Schapsmeier and Schapsmeier, *Ezra Taft Benson*, pp. 208; Benson, *Cross Fire*, pp. 400–406.

128. Schapsmeier and Schapsmeier, *Ezra Taft Benson*, pp. 215–16.

129. For an example of an influential liberal Democratic view of the failure of traditional price supports to address the postwar agricultural situation and the need for an income based, Brannan plan–like solution, see *Eckstein Report*, p. 201.

130. Both quotes from Minutes, Legislative Meeting, December 15, 1958, pp. 8–9, "Legislative Meetings 1958 (4), July–Dec." folder, Box 3, AWLS, DDEPL.

131. Ibid.

132. USDA, *Price-Support*, p. 22.

133. Benson, *Cross Fire*, pp. 321, 445.

134. "Special Message to the Congress on Agriculture," January 29, 1959, *PPP, 1959*, pp. 146–51.

135. Minutes, Legislative Meeting, April 28, 1959, p. 7, "Legislative Meetings 1959 (3)" folder, Box 3, AWLS, DDEPL.

136. Minutes, Legislative Meeting, April 28, 1959, p. 7, "Legislative Meetings 1959 (3)" folder, Box 3, AWLS, DDEPL; for further discussion of limits on payments, see Minutes, Legislative Meeting, May 19, 1957, p. 4, "Legislative Meetings 1957 (4)" folder, Box 3, AWLS, DDEPL.

137. Minutes, Legislative Meeting, May 19, 1959, "Legislative Meetings 1957 (4)" folder, Box 3, AWLS, DDEPL.

138. Schapsmeier and Schapsmeier, *Ezra Taft Benson*, p. 235; Paarlberg, Interview, pp. 21–22, 119–20, DDEPL.

139. "Veto of Bill Relating to the Wheat Program," June 25, 1959, *PPP, 1959*, p. 477.

140. "Veto of the Tobacco Price Support Bill," June 25, 1959, *PPP, 1959*, p. 458; Schapsmeier and Schapsmeier, pp. 224–29; Benson, *Cross Fire*, pp. 444–53.

141. Minutes, Legislative Meeting, February 2, 1960, pp. 5–8, "Legislative Meetings 1960 (1)" folder, Box 3, AWLS, DDEPL.

142. "Special Message to the Congress on Agriculture," February 9, 1960, *PPP, 1960*, p. 162.

143. Minutes, Legislative Meeting, February 2, 1960, p. 8, "Legislative Meetings 1960 (1)" folder, Box 3, AWLS, DDEPL. During the 1960 election campaign, Nixon supported the agricultural programs of the Eisenhower administration but distanced himself from

Benson personally. The Democratic platform called for a wide range of farm policies, including "production and marketing quotas measured in terms of barrels, bushels, and bales," which was a clear acknowledgment of the failure of acreage controls (allotments). It also called for "loans on basic commodities at not less than 90 percent of parity, production payments, commodity purchases and marketing orders and agreements," and it attacked Benson. John Kennedy, the Democratic nominee, however, had voted against 90% parity during his terms in the Senate.

Benson made a small number of campaign appearances but spent much of the late summer and fall of 1960 on three separate overseas fact-finding and trade missions trips, out of sight, if not mind, of the presidential campaign. In early summer Benson's defense of his tenure as USDA secretary, *Freedom to Farm*, was published. One reviewer noted that a "certain quarrelsomeness of tone, together with an impatient sense of mission, creeps into the discourse." See Schapsmeier and Schapsmeier, *Ezra Taft Benson*, pp. 249–62.

Eisenhower was not above making small political concessions in an election year. In September he signed a bill that temporarily raised price supports for certain classes of milk and butterfat from 77% to 80% of parity. He noted, however, that market prices were only slightly above or below these levels. Benson wanted Eisenhower to veto the legislation (and an accompanying bill freezing tobacco price supports at 1959 levels, which Eisenhower had vetoed the year before), but the president argued that they were passed by overwhelming majorities and that Congress was now out of session and would not have an opportunity to override his veto. He also conceded that a veto "would only serve to engender intensely partisan political charges and counter charges." He averred, however, that he had in no way modified his views of what long-term policies were needed for agriculture: "I wish it to be perfectly clear that for my part I shall continue to support the policy that agricultural production must eventually be controlled by economic law rather than by political maneuvering. Until this has happened, there can be no settlement of the so-called 'farm problem' and no sound prosperity for the family-sized farm." See "Statement by the President upon Signing Bill Raising Support Prices for Butterfat and Manufacturing Milk," September 16, 1960, *PPP, 1960*, p. 701; Schapsmeier and Schapsmeier, *Ezra Taft Benson*, pp. 242–43.

Of course, Nixon narrowly lost the election. Only two farm states narrowly shifted to the Democrats—Missouri and Minnesota. Kennedy generally did not do well in rural areas, and Nixon had many other problems. See Paarlberg, Interview, p. 41, DDEPL.

144. USDA, *Price-Support*, p. 44.

145. Dimitri, Effland, and Conklin, *20th Century Transformation*, p. 9.

146. USDA, *Price-Support*, pp. 29–30.

147. Dimitri, Effland, and Conklin, *20th Century Transformation*, p. 9.

CHAPTER 5: A COALESCING ANTITRUST POLICY

1. Since the 1970s modern antitrust doctrine has moved in the direction of promoting market efficiency as its primary goal under the influence of the Chicago School of Economics. But in 1953 the triumph of the Chicago School was almost three decades in the future; traditional antitrust doctrines grounded in deep distrust of concentrated economic

power and assumptions of its adverse economic, political, and societal impacts dominated. These arguments had a not-so-subtle political implication that the Democrats had
emphasized on many occasions in the twenty years prior to Eisenhower's inauguration
in 1953.

2. This is the conclusion of Theodore P. Kovaleff's *Business and Government during the
Eisenhower Administration: A Study of the Antitrust Policy of the Antitrust Division of the
Justice Department* (Athens: Ohio University Press, 1980).

3. Ibid., p. 55; Herbert Brownell with John P. Burke, *Advising Ike: The Memoirs of
Attorney General Herbert Brownell* (Lawrence: University Press of Kansas, 1993), p. 297.
Eisenhower did take a personal interest in several antitrust cases: Kodak's amateur color
film monopoly (Eisenhower was an avid amateur photographer), the Studebaker-Packard
merger, the Bethlehem Steel–Youngstown Sheet and Tube merger, *U.S. v. Du Pont* (General Motors divestiture) and the so-called Electrical cases. The latter three are discussed
in this chapter. See Kovaleff, *Business and Government*, p. 55.

4. A typical critique of the Eisenhower antitrust policy, which we believe underes-
timates the administration's interest and role in antitrust, can be found in Burton I.
Kaufman, *The Oil Cartel Case: A Documentary Study of Antitrust Activity in the Cold War
Era* (Westport, CT: Greenwood Press, 1978), p. 51: "What emerged from this sustained
interest in antitrust activity was a theoretical commitment to a vigorous antitrust policy
in foreign as well as domestic matters and some remedial efforts, such as the Cellar-Kefauver
Amendment, as well as tightening the antitrust laws. However, in terms of making the
antitrust laws more responsive to the changing domestic and foreign economy. Little of
a substantive nature was accomplished (again with the exception of Cellar-Kefauver
Amendment). In this respect the courts were more responsive to the changing times
than either the executive or legislative branches of government."

5. See Richard Hofstadter, "What Happened to the Antitrust Movement," in *The
Paranoid Style in American Politics and Other Essays* (New York: Knopf, 1965), pp. 188,
196–98. During 1921–33 businesses' voluntary cooperation to achieve efficiencies and
"fair" competition was promoted by Secretary of Commerce, and later President, Hoover.
This period of business "associationalism" culminated in Roosevelt's National Recovery
Administration's Codes of Fair Competition, 1933–1935. See Ellis W. Hawley, *The New Deal
and the Problem of Monopoly* (Princeton: Princeton University Press, 1966), pp. 19–43,
53–71; Thomas K. McCraw, *Prophets of Regulation* (Cambridge: Harvard University Press,
1984), pp. 143–52.

6. Wyatt Wells, *Antitrust and the Formation of the Postwar World* (New York: Columbia
University Press, 2002), pp. 43–136; Alan Brinkley, "The New Deal and the Idea of the
State," in Steve Fraser and Gary Gerstle, eds., *The Rise and Fall of the New Deal State,* (Prince-
ton: Princeton University Press, 1989), pp. 89–92.

7. *Report of the Attorney General's National Committee to Study the Antitrust Laws*
(Washington, DC: GPO, 1955), pp. 149–55; Harold G. Vatter, *The U.S. Economy in the 1950's:
An Economic History* (Chicago: University of Chicago Press, 1963), pp. 210–11. In 1951,
Congress also enacted, over two Truman vetoes, the Reed-Bulwinkle Act, which allowed
regulated transportation associations (rate bureaus) an exemption from the antitrust laws,
for "rates, fares, classifications, divisions, allowances or charges" filed with regulatory

agencies (i.e., the Interstate Commerce Commission), that were the product of collective deliberations of the carriers. It essentially facilitated further cartelization of much of the surface transportation industry, under ICC regulatory supervision.

8. Of course, tension between arguments of large producer efficiency versus desirability of smaller producer units has existed throughout the history of the American antitrust laws. Since the late 1970s the pervasive influence of the Chicago School and the primacy of its arguments about the value of efficiency, have essentially overwhelmed traditional antitrust doctrines that rested on a priori assumptions about the dangers of corporate concentration and certain corporate conduct that dominated antitrust thinking from about 1940 into the 1970s.

9. Between 1914 and 1950, the government used Clayton Section 7 in isolation only four times in challenges to corporate mergers. Instead, it was used in conjunction with Sherman Act Section 2 antimonopoly allegations, which required different, and more rigorous, standards of proof and higher levels of resulting market concentration. Even these combined prosecutions were rare—just 16 in the same time period. *Report, Attorney General's Committee*, pp. 115–19; A. D. Neale, *Antitrust Laws of the United States*, 2nd ed. (New York: Cambridge University Press, 1970), pp. 180–81; Kovaleff, *Business and Government*, pp. 10–11.

10. Neale, *Antitrust Laws*, pp. 181–82.

11. United States v. Socony–Vacuum Oil Company, 310 U.S. 150 (1940). After the demise of the NRA in 1935, and with government encouragement, large refiners of gasoline bought up the "distress production" of smaller refiners, in the hope of keeping these desperate sellers out of the market and eventually raising the price of gasoline from very low levels. The conspiracy was only partially effective, and the combination of the larger refiners meant they would have reduced their own sales of gasoline but gave them "the opportunity of influencing the marketing of petroleum in such a way as to keep retail prices fairly stable." See also, *Report, Attorney General's Committee*, pp. 12–17.

12. Neale, *Antitrust Laws*, pp. 35–39.

13. Edward S. Mason, preface, in Carl Kaysen and Donald F. Turner, *Antitrust Policy: An Economic and Legal Analysis* (Cambridge: Harvard University Press, 1959), xiii–xiv.

14. U.S. v. Aluminum Co. of America, 148 F.2d 416 (2d Cir. 1945). The case was decided by the Second Circuit Court of Appeals, by Act of Congress, because a quorum of the Supreme Court could not be achieved, due to recusals, withdrawals from the case by former Roosevelt administration DOJ officials who were now justices on the Supreme Court. See also Neale, *Antitrust Laws*, pp. 105–12.

15. American Tobacco Co. v. United States, 328 U.S. 781 (1946); Neale, *Antitrust Laws*, pp. 112–13. For a general discussion of these matters, see *Report, Attorney's General's Committee*, pp. 48–60.

16. In court cases the specter of "monopoly power" was raised at various percentage levels of control of relevant product markets. According to Neale, the issue was usually engaged at 50% to 70% and presumed to exist above the latter figure. But, courts also shied away from strict percentage standards and instead looked to fact-based inquiries such as "whether those who might have wanted to enter the industry or increase their share of the market could be prevented from doing so, or whether the suspected monopolist was able

to set his own price on his product without much regard to the competition"—a standard that was viewed by the business community as much more pliable and unsettling than fixed percentages. See Neale, *Antitrust Laws*, pp. 120–21.

17. Marc Allen Eisner, *Antitrust and the Triumph of Economics* (Chapel Hill: University of North Carolina Press, 1991), pp. 84–85.

18. Neale, *Antitrust Laws*, pp. 351–54; Wells, *Antitrust and the Formation of the Postwar World*, pp. 126–29.

19. Timken Roller Bearing Company v. United States, 341 U.S. 593 (1951).

20. *Report, Attorney General's Committee*, pp. 88–90; Neale, *Antitrust Laws*, pp. 346–51; Wells, *Antitrust and the Formation of the Postwar World*, pp. 134–36.

21. Neale, *Antitrust Laws*, p. 355.

22. Wells, *Antitrust and the Formation of the Postwar World*, p. 135.

23. Kovaleff, *Business and Government*, p. 11; United States v. E. I. du Pont de Nemours & Co., 353 U.S. 586, 610 [Du Pont (General Motors)].

24. Kaufman, *Oil Cartel Case*, pp. 27–29.

25. Wells, *Antitrust and the Formation of the Postwar World*, pp. 195–97. The shifts in the sources of crude oil production between 1938 and 1955 were seismic. In 1938, 61% of the world's petroleum was produced in the United States, only about 6% in the Middle East. About 15% was from Latin America, and the remainder (about 18%) was mostly from Romania and Russia, with small amounts from the Far East. By 1955, the distribution of significantly higher world production had changed dramatically. The US share declined to 45% (35% by 1960), while the Middle East accounted for 20% and Latin America 18%. The remaining 17% was largely from the Soviet Union and Canada. See Douglas R. Bohi and Milton Russell, *Limiting Oil Imports: An Economic History and Analysis* (Baltimore: Johns Hopkins University Press, 1978), p. 24.

The "As Is," or "Achnacarry," Agreement from 1928 committed the majors to allocation quotas in world markets and a price system based on prices prevailing at the Gulf Coast of the United States (Texas) adjusted for international transportation, even if the market was supplied from another, closer source, such as Venezuela, Romania, or the Soviet Union, as well as other locales in the United States. It never functioned perfectly, because it was never able to dominate the export of oil from the United States, which during the 1930s represented as much as a third of the oil consumed outside of the United States. The operation of the agreement, which was modified in the 1930s, was suspended with the outbreak of World War II, even as some members gave notice of their intent to terminate their participation. See Daniel Yergin, *The Prize: The Epic Quest for Oil, Money and Power* (New York: Simon and Schuster, 1991), pp. 262–68. Despite the uncertain status of the "As Is" Agreement in the postwar environment, evidence of its prewar operation was the cornerstone of the DOJ antitrust case against the oil companies that began in 1952.

26. Kaufman, *Oil Cartel Case*, pp. 41–43. At the time of the BP boycott of Iranian oil, petroleum represented only about 11% of Western European energy requirements, but about 85% of Western Europe's oil came from the Middle East. According to Kaufman the problem was more rearrangement of international logistics than an absolute shortage.

27. Ibid., pp. 38–47.

28. Quoted in Kovaleff, *Business and Government*, pp. 11–12.

29. Eisenhower Letter to Brownell, June 12, 1957, doc. 194, Online Eisenhower Papers; Brownell, *Advising Ike*, pp. 153–54.

30. See *Eckstein Report*, pp. 431–40, for its exceedingly muted criticism of Eisenhower's antitrust policy, which is discussed in the conclusion of this chapter. The *Eckstein Report*, in many ways, reflected the coalescing Democratic, especially liberal Democratic, criticisms of Eisenhower's economic policies and was the blueprint for their positions on economic issues in the 1960 election and the coming decade. It also should be noted that, by the end of Eisenhower's term, the criticism of the Democratic Party's antitrust "warhorses" had declined. Kefauver had abandoned his presidential ambitions and, though still involved in antitrust matters, was more focused on drug regulation. He died in 1963, and O'Mahoney retired in 1961. Emanuel Cellar, however, remained in the House of Representatives until 1973, and his interest in antitrust matters waned only with the installation of a Democratic president in 1961.

31. E.g., see Notes, Cabinet Meeting, March 25, 1955, Box 5, OSSLAM, DDEPL.

32. Minutes, Cabinet Meeting, March 25, 1955, Box 5, AWCS, DDEPL; Memorandum, "Preview of the Anti-Trust Report," March 16, 1955, "Minutes, Cabinet Meetings, March 18, 1955" folder, Box 5, AWCS, DDEPL. See also, *Report, Attorney General's Committee*, pp., 149–55; Brownell, *Advising Ike*, pp. 296–99.

33. Kovaleff, *Business and Government*, pp. 57–59. Both lawsuits ended with consent decrees in 1956. The AT&T settlement did not require the divestiture of Western Electric but instead focused on conduct remedies and compulsory patent licensing. Kovaleff says it was "not a victory for the government." The settlement with IBM, on the other hand was able to restrict many of the practices of the firm that that had been the focus of the complaint.

34. United States v. E. I. Du Pont de Nemours & Co., 351 U.S. 377 (1956).

35. Kovaleff, *Business and Government*, p. 18, Brownell quote; Brownell, *Advising Ike*, pp. 153–54.

36. Kovaleff, *Business and Government*, p. 49.

37. Ibid., p. 51; Stanley N. Barnes, Oral History Interview, pp. 75–76, Earl Warren Oral History Project, DDEPL.

38. Brownell, *Advising Ike*, pp. 153–54.

39. Kovaleff, *Business and Government*, p. 52.

40. Ibid., pp. 71–72. See also, *Report, Attorney General's Committee*, pp. 361–63.

41. Eisenhower Letter to Brownell, June 12, 1957, doc. 194, fn. 5, Online Eisenhower Papers.

42. See Ibid.

43. Vatter, *U.S. Economy in the 1950's*, pp. 204–6.

44. *ERP, 1957*, pp. 51–53; Kovaleff, *Business and Government*, p. 148.

45. *Report, Attorney General's Committee*, pp. 343–49; "Preview of the Anti-Trust Report," March 16, 1955, "Minutes, Cabinet Meeting, March 18, 1955" folder, Box 5, AWCS, DDEPL; Kovaleff, *Business and Government*, p. 28.

46. *Report, Attorney General's Committee*, pp. 360–61.

47. Kovaleff, *Business and Government*, pp. 52–55.

48. For an example of such a probusiness attack on the administration's antitrust policies, focusing on "forced" consent decrees that "really go far beyond the requirements of the law," and Eisenhower's view that the record on this point needed to be corrected "assuming, as I do, that the whole article is based upon misapprehension and misunderstanding, if not downright prejudice," see Eisenhower Letter to Brownell, June 12, 1957, doc. 194, Online Eisenhower Papers.

49. Kovaleff, *Business and Government*, pp. 53–55; *Report, Attorney General's Committee*, pp. 360–61.

50. *Report, Attorney General's Committee*, iv–vi; Brownell, *Advising Ike*, pp. 153–54. Eisenhower's remarks are found in Notes, Cabinet Meeting, March 18, 1955, Box 5, OS-SLAM, DDEPL. Eisenhower asked if all the members were lawyers and if any businessmen were on the committee. He said, "They didn't have to meet a payroll" and were "lawyers seeking business." His comments show either (1) a lack of understanding of the role of the committee; (2) lack of understanding of the role of private lawyers and the structure of law firms and legal work; or (3) simply a comment to elicit responses from his businessman-dominated cabinet. It is most likely the latter. Of course, in his long military career or his short academic one, Eisenhower never had to meet a payroll.

51. Kovaleff, *Business and Government*, pp. 20–22.

52. Thomas E. Kauper, "The Report of the Attorney General's Committee to Study the Antitrust Laws: A Retrospective," *Michigan Law Review* 100 (June, 2002): pp. 1867–71.

53. Ibid., pp. 1867, 1869–70. For an examination of some of the criticisms of the dissenters (Eugene V. Rostow and Louis B. Schwartz), see *Report, Attorney General's Committee*, pp. 40–42, 54–55, 128, 388–93.

54. *Report, Attorney General's Committee*, pp. 12–30.

55. Ibid., pp. 48–55.

56. "Preview of the Anti-Trust Report," March 16, 1955, "Minutes, Cabinet Meeting, March 18, 1955" folder, Box 5, AWCS, DDEPL. The case cited is United States v. United Shoe Machinery Corp., 110 F. Supp. 295, 342 (D. Mass. 1953), *aff'd per curium*, 347 U.S. 521 (1954). The "thrust upon" exception to Sherman Act Section 2 remained a largely theoretical argument used by the business community to highlight the possible dangers of overzealous antitrust enforcement. Prior litigation showed that in monopolization proceedings the government usually had ample evidence of anticompetitive, exclusionary activities of defendants, which standing alone would constitute a Sherman Act Section 1 violation, as well as evidence of monopolistic intent under Section 2. With no major Section 2 cases decided from the mid-1950s to the mid-1960s, the issue gradually receded. See *Report, Attorney General's Committee*, pp. 55–61; *Antitrust Developments, 1955–1968: A Supplement to the Report of the Attorney General's National Committee to Study the Antitrust Laws, March 31, 1955* (Chicago: Section of Antitrust Law of the American Bar Association, 1968), pp. 36–38; United States v. Grinnell Corp., 236 F. Supp. 244 (D.R.I. 1964), *aff'd*, 384 U.S. 563 (563); United States v. American Tobacco Co., 328 U.S. 781 (1946).

57. "Preview of the Anti-Trust Report," March 16, 1955, "Minutes, Cabinet Meeting, March 18, 1955" folder, Box 5, AWCS, DDEPL; *Report, Attorney General's Committee*, pp. 74–76, 88–90, 108–9.

58. "Preview of the Anti-Trust Report," March 16, 1955, "Minutes, Cabinet Meeting, March 18, 1955" folder, Box 5, AWCS, DDEPL; Kovaleff, *Business and Government*, pp. 26–27, 79–80; *Report, Attorney General's Committee*, pp. 118–28.

59. "Preview of the Anti-Trust Report," March 16, 1955, "Minutes, Cabinet Meeting, March 18, 1955" folder, Box 5, AWCS, DDEPL.

60. Brown Shoe v. United States, 370 U.S. 294 (1962). The Eisenhower administration initiated a challenge to Brown's proposed merger with Kinney Shoes in 1955 under Clayton Section 7. Both were retail shoe chain stores, it was a relatively unconcentrated industry (compared to steel), and these firm's market shares were much less than Bethlehem's and Youngstown's. The *Brown Shoe* case also raised issues concerning reduced competition because of the vertical nature of some of the two firms' operations.

61. Kovaleff, *Business and Government*, pp. 91–93; *Antitrust Developments*, pp. 66–70, 76–78.

62. Initially, the lawsuit also challenged Du Pont's minority stock ownership in U.S. Rubber, but this was considered the weakest portion of the case, and DOJ abandoned it before the case went to the Supreme Court in 1957.

63. United States v. E. I. Du Pont de Nemours & Co., 353 U.S. 586, 610 (1957); Kovaleff, *Business and Government*, pp. 93–99.

64. *Antitrust Developments*, pp. 66–70, 73–83.

65. United States v. E. I. du Pont de Nemours & Co., 353 U.S. 586, 589–608; Kovaleff, *Business and Government*, p. 99. See also Memorandum, Siegel to McCracken, "A Note on the Supreme Court Decision in Du Pont Case," June 17, 1957, Box 7, Subject File "Antitrust," Phillip Areeda Papers, DDEPL.

66. Kovaleff, *Business and Government*, pp. 101–3.

67. Vatter, *U.S. Economy in the 1950's*, pp. 204–6.

68. Memorandum, Kahn to Council, "Merger Developments during 1955," November 10, 1955, "Fiscal & Monetary—Business Mergers 1955" folder, Box 105, Arthur F. Burns Papers, DDEPL.

69. Ibid.

70. Kovaleff, *Business and Government*, pp. 79–80.

71. Ibid., p. 80.

72. Ibid., pp. 79–81.

73. United States v. Bethlehem Steel Corporation, 168 F. Supp. 576, 580 (S.Dist.N.Y, 1958); Kovaleff, *Business and Government*, pp. 80–81; "Staff Notes No. 95," April 9, 1957, "April 1957 Diary—Staff Memos (2)" folder, Box 23, AWDDEDS, DDEPL.

74. United States v. Bethlehem Steel Corporation, 168 F. Supp. (1958) 576, 587–611, 618–19.

75. United States v. Brown Shoe, 179 F. Supp. 721 (E.D. Mo., 1959).

76. *Antitrust Developments*, pp. 66–71.

77. Not until 1968 did DOJ publish quantitative guidelines for mergers under the Clayton Act. These set presumptions of anticompetitive effect based on the market percentages controlled by merging firms by reference to a scale of various levels of industry concentration.

78. Kovaleff, *Business and Government*, pp. 119–21. See also Richard Austin Smith, "The Incredible Electrical Conspiracy," in Henry C. Dethloff and C. Joseph Pusateri, eds., *American Business History Case Studies* (Arlington Heights, IL: Harlan Davidson, 1987), pp. 345–78.

79. Kovaleff, *Business and Government*, pp. 113–14, 122, 157. Bicks was nominated to the position of assistant attorney general for antitrust in 1960 but was never confirmed by the Senate. Brownell's representation of Westinghouse began more than two years after his departure, as required by statute; the cases did not begin until after he had left; and he sought and received DOJ clearance for his representation.

80. Kovaleff, *Business and Government*, pp. 122–25; Kauper, "Report of the Attorney General's Committee," pp. 1870–71; Smith, "Incredible Electrical Conspiracy," pp. 369–70, 373–75.

81. Kovaleff, *Business and Government*, pp. 124–25; *Antitrust Developments*, 274–75; *Report, Attorney General's Committee*, pp. 378–79; Kauper, "Report of the Attorney General's Committee," pp. 1867, 1870.

82. Conspicuously, Kovaleff's flattering study of administration antitrust policy avoided all mention of the litigation, or for that matter, any antitrust issue involving the international petroleum industry. He simply noted in his preface, without comment, Burton Kaufman's highly critical study. Kovaleff, *Business and Government*, ix.

83. John Blair, *The Control of Oil* (New York: Pantheon, 1976), pp. 71–76; Kaufman, *Oil Cartel Case;* Robert Griffith, "Dwight D. Eisenhower and the Corporate Commonwealth," *American Historical Review* 87, no. 1 (February, 1982): pp. 87–122. Griffith cites Kaufman's criticisms with approval and notes that the "oil cartel case well illustrates emphasis on negotiation, and cooperative arrangements as well as the generally low priority it gave to antitrust enforcement." He characterizes the administration policies of "widespread use of pre-filing conferences, consent decrees and pre-merger clearances, all which emphasized cooperation and quiet negotiation" as somehow diametrically opposed to vigorous antitrust enforcement. Griffith's analysis seems to ignore that these administrative devices (such as consent decrees) were part of the standard repertoire of antitrust regulators before and after the Eisenhower administration. The very nature of the devices used was a sign of weakness in Griffith's view, therefore settling the oil cartel case by means of consent decrees was a sign of a weak enforcement policy. See Griffith, "Corporate Commonwealth," pp. 104–5.

84. Yergin, *Prize*, pp. 472–75; Wells, *Antitrust and the Formation of the Postwar World*, pp. 187–201.

85. Minutes, Cabinet Meeting, April 8, 1953, and Minutes, Cabinet Meeting, July 8, 1955, both in Box 5, AWCS, DDEPL; Minutes, Legislative Meeting, November 9, 1956, and Minutes, Legislative Meeting, January 1, 1957, both in Box 2, AWLS, DDEPL.

86. Letter, Eisenhower to Anderson, cited in Kaufman, *Oil Cartel Case*, p. 55.

87. Burton I. Kaufman, "Mideast Multinational Oil, U.S. Foreign Policy, and Antitrust: The 1950s," *Journal of American History* 63, no. 4 (March, 1977): pp. 952–53.

88. Bohi and Russell, *Limiting Oil Imports*, pp. 20–22.

89. Ibid., pp. 22–29. Almost all US petroleum imports were crude oil; product imports were quite small. Most crude oil came from Venezuela and by mid-decade the Middle

East and Canada also. Today the United States imports approximately 65% of its crude oil and has significant product imports as well. Until 1948 the United States was a net exporter of crude petroleum and refined products, and in the 1930s this usually represented at least 10% of domestic American demand. See ibid., pp. 22–23. Yergin, however, notes that in the 1930s as much as a third of the petroleum consumed overseas was imported from the United States and that the majors never dominated this trade. See Yergin, *Prize*, pp. 264–65.

90. Despite the relatively small share of imports of the American market, both parties to the civil lawsuit conceded that the overseas production, refining, and marketing of petroleum by American international oil companies had sufficient "direct and substantial effect on United States commerce" to establish US jurisdiction under the Sherman Act. See Kaufman, *Oil Cartel Case*, Appendix G, pp. 171–77 (Memorandum, William L. Fugate for files, April 12, 1957). But also see Memorandum, Herbert Brownell to Eisenhower, September 18, 1957, "September 1957 Toner Notes" folder, Box 27, AWDDEDS, DDEPL, where Attorney General Brownell refers to the impact of the defendants' exploration, production, pipeline, and refining activities abroad as having an "incidental effect on foreign commerce" (of the United States) and at best being "indirect and more than counter-balanced by the national security, foreign relations, and foreign trade advantages to the United States."

91. Wells, *Antitrust and the Formation of the Postwar World*, p. 200; Memorandum, Herbert Brownell to Eisenhower, September 18, 1957, "September 1957, Toner Notes" folder, Box 27, AWDDEDS, DDEPL.

92. Wells, *Antitrust and the Formation of the Postwar World*, pp. 197–200.

93. Ibid., pp. 197–98.

94. Kaufman, *Oil Cartel Case*, pp. 55–60.

95. Ibid., pp. 58–60, 79–84.

96. Ibid., pp. 82–83, 90, 97.

97. Ibid., pp. 93–95. Each defendant was also "enjoined from agreeing with competitors to restrict the sale or distribution of petroleum products in foreign nations or to exclude third persons from competing in the production, distribution, or sale of crude oil." However, both consent decrees omitted "any injunction against joint production, refining, or transportation arrangements solely within one or more foreign countries."

98. Ibid., pp. 94–95.

99. Ibid., pp. 97–98.

100. Between 1955 and 1959, the administration instituted various schemes in an attempt to get oil importers to "voluntarily" control American imports of foreign crude oil. They were largely unsuccessful, and imports increased. These programs were bedeviled by multiple problems, including potential antitrust liability for those firms involved under post-*Socony* antitrust law concerning "government encouragement" and imports by independents with access to Canadian and Middle Eastern oil. The latter was a result of the Iranian consortium agreement and the gradual opening up of the Middle East to nonmajors. Eisenhower ultimately instituted mandatory oil import controls in March 1959, and they remained in place in various forms through 1973. These "voluntary" import quotas

are also briefly discussed in chapter 6. The best short summary of these is Bohi and Russell, *Limiting Oil Imports*, pp. 1–143.

101. Memorandum, Brownell to Eisenhower, September 18, 1957, "September 1957 Toner Notes" folder, Box 27, AWDDEDS, DDEPL.

102. Brownell, *Advising Ike*, pp. 154–55.

103. Wells, *Antitrust and the Formation of the Postwar World*, p. 199.

104. *Eckstein Report*, pp. 431–40.

105. In many respects antitrust law today looks similar to the 1950s, but in other respects there are, not unexpectedly, major differences. The emphasis today on rule of reason in Sherman Section 1 cases is very similar to where it stood in the 1950s, but how it got there is another matter. Beginning in the 1960s the Supreme Court required use of the "per se rule" in various types of Sherman Act cases such as vertical restraints on distribution and maximum prices, etc. Per se rules have certain advantages, because they eliminate much of the uncertainty of litigation. If you prove the defendant is doing it he is liable, where rule of reason cases require a much more detailed analysis of competitive effect and are less "bright line." Starting in the late 1970s, under the influence of the Chicago School, the Supreme Court began to roll back the per se rules that proliferated in the 1960s. Today, the Supreme Court has even gone so far as to roll back the per se prohibition on minimum vertical price restraints that existed since 1912. Also, in the 1960s and 1970s there was an expansion of Robinson-Patman Act enforcement, later scaled back, that the Eisenhower administration would have abhorred. So, the landscape that exists today does look quite like the 1950s, but it reached it by a circuitous journey. See Kauper, "Report of the Attorney General's Committee," pp. 1867, 1871–75.

In other areas the situation is decidedly mixed. Since the introduction of merger guidelines in 1968 to analyze mergers and market concentration, litigation under Clayton Section 7 has become formulaic. Furthermore, with the integration of the United States into the world economy and technological advances since the 1970s, the measurement of markets has become more complex and challenges to mergers much less frequent. After a period of rigorous examination of vertical and conglomerate mergers in the 1970s, challenges to these are rare today.

Finally, major Sherman Section 2 monopolization cases have been rare. Where they have occurred they have had mixed, often indirect, impacts. DOJ's 1974 lawsuit against AT&T revisited some of the issues raised in the early 1950s and more. Ultimately, it was settled, and the consent decree, over time, changed the landscape of the American telecommunications industry. A major case against IBM, filed in 1969, was dismissed in 1982. Its impact was significant but clearly indirect. The more recent Section 2 action against Microsoft was successful, but the impact of the settlement and its reliance on conduct remedies is still far from certain.

CHAPTER 6: FOREIGN ECONOMIC POLICY

1. In 1951 Congress consolidated the European Recovery Program and other foreign aid programs under the Mutual Security Act and thereafter Truman and later Eisenhower

submitted one budget request to Congress for mutual security (later mutual aid) funds. In 1951 (for fiscal year 1952) Truman requested $8.5 billion for mutual security (all foreign aid, including military and economic assistance). Congress reduced the request by $1 billion. See Steven Wagner, *Eisenhower Republicanism: Pursuing the Middle Way* (DeKalb: Northern Illinois University Press, 2006), pp. 182–83.

2. *ERP, 1954,* p. 222; Harold G. Vatter, *The U.S. Economy in the 1950's: An Economic History* (Chicago: University of Chicago Press, 1963), pp. 270–72. The expenditures for foreign military and economic assistance necessitated long "pipelines." Considerable time passed between funds' appropriation by Congress and when they were actually spent. This was a source of frustration for the Eisenhower administration, and criticisms of the "efficiency and administration" of the program by Congress proliferated, despite administrators' efforts to speed up expenditures. Administration legislative requests, congressional authorizations, and most importantly, appropriations are a better barometer of public support, or lack thereof, for the program than actual fiscal year expenditures.

3. For an earlier view, see Thomas W. Zeiler, *Free Trade, Free World: The Advent of GATT* (Chapel Hill: University of North Carolina Press, 1999). In that work Zeiler characterizes Eisenhower as a "free-trader, even a dogmatist, in the mold of Cordell Hull." He adds: "Wisely playing politics, Eisenhower reserved his support for the RTAA [Reciprocal Trade Agreements Act] out of respect for Robert Taft's forces of protectionism in his party. But he steadfastly determined to encourage trade with all noncommunist nations. Ike pushed for free trade, particularly in the Third World, where he saw international communism at work. As president, he would ensure that global resources did not pass into Soviet hands and that nations friendly to the United States and its very way of life would remain allies. Indeed, in his administration during the 1950s, liberal trade would serve as an instrument of national security in the Cold War." He adds further that "President Eisenhower would subsume trade policy under a national security agenda" but notes that protectionism grew in the 1950s and that "protectionism would have no place in his administration because it undercut containment efforts." Zeiler's analysis, however, obscures some of the more pragmatic and sophisticated approaches of Eisenhower toward trade liberalization.

4. Burton I. Kaufman, *Trade and Aid: Eisenhower's Foreign Economic Policy* (Baltimore: Johns Hopkins University Press, 1982), p. 23.

5. Annual Message to the Congress on the State of the Union, February 2, 1953, *PPP, 1953,* p. 14.

6. Presidential News Conference, July 22, 1953, *PPP, 1953,* pp. 507–8.

7. Letter, Eisenhower to Marsh, February 6, 1957, "Foreign Aid" folder, Box 15, AWAS, DDEPL.

8. Letter, Eisenhower to Gruenther, May 4, 1953, "Dec. 1952–July 1953 (3)" folder, Box 3, AWDDEDS, DDEPL.

9. Annual Message to the Congress on the State of the Union, January 7, 1954, *PPP, 1954,* pp. 9–10. In February 1953 Eisenhower proposed that Congress appropriate approximately $5.5 billion for military weapons and equipment for allies under the Mutual Security Agency program and about $0.6 billion for technical, economic, and developmental

purposes for fiscal 1954. This represented a reduction of $1.8 billion from the amounts originally sought by the Truman administration. He subsequently reduced the total amount ($6.1 billion) by another $0.4 billion, and Congress ultimately appropriated a total of $5.3 billion. Initially, the administration considered possibly reducing the economic assistance portion of the package by 30% to 60%, but the proposal was shelved. See *FRUS, 1952–1954,* vol. 1: *General: Economic and Political Affairs,* pp. 581–82, 625–26; Dwight D. Eisenhower, *Mandate for Change 1953–1956* (Garden City, NY: Doubleday, 1963), pp. 215–16.

10. Special Message to the Congress on Foreign Economic Policy, March 30, 1954, *PPP, 1954,* p. 361.

11. "No 'Quick Checkup' in Government," Humphrey Interview in *U.S. News & World Report,* June 12, 1953, in Nathaniel R. Howard, ed., *The Basic Papers of George M. Humphrey as Secretary of the Treasury, 1953–1957* (Cleveland: Western Reserve Historical Society, 1965), p. 83.

12. Kaufman, *Trade and Aid,* pp. 34–35. For the administration's concern that Japan might be moving toward a neutralist position in 1954–55, see Michael Schaller, *Altered States: The United States and Japan since the Occupation* (New York: Oxford University Press, 1997), pp. 3, 12–13, 113–14.

13. In many respects subsequent battles over foreign aid looked similar to the debate about the role the Eximbank in Latin America fought in 1953–54, a subject we will take up later in chapter 6. There were crucial differences, however, most notably few American exporters rushed to defend foreign economic aid, since until late 1959 such assistance was not generally tied to procurement in the United States. The credits (loans) Eximbank granted to importers of American-made products, however, had strong backing by politically well-connected American exporters.

14. Kaufman, *Trade and Aid,* pp. 58–59, 63–69; Memorandum of Discussion at the 267th Meeting of the National Security Council, November 21, 1955, *FRUS, 1955–1957,* vol. 10: *Foreign Aid and Foreign Defense Policy* (Washington: GPO, 1989), pp. 32–37; Memorandum of Discussion at the 273rd Meeting of the National Security Council, January 18, 1956, *FRUS, 1955–1957,* vol. 10, pp. 64–66. The CIA averred that the Soviets were more than willing to accept soft currencies in payment, because it then used portions to finance internal subversion against their new trading partners. For a comparison of the scope of the programs during calendar 1959 the Soviet Union spent about $1 billion and had 4,675 technicians in "free world countries," while the United States spent approximately $2 billion on economic and technical assistance and had 5,700 technicians in countries receiving assistance. See Memorandum of Discussion at the 427th Meeting of the National Security Council, December 3, 1959, *FRUS, 1958–1960,* vol. 4: *Foreign Economic Policy* (Washington, DC: GPO, 1992), pp. 472–74.

15. Kaufman, *Trade and Aid,* pp. 54–57, 68–69. The administration's foreign aid legislation would first be addressed and acted on by congressional foreign affairs committees in the House and Senate, which authorized a level of spending that usually had to be coordinated in legislative conference. Then funds would have to be appropriated by the relevant subcommittee (Foreign Operations) and the full appropriations committees of the House and Senate. During the 1950s the appropriation process was always the source of the most draconian cuts, especially in the House of Representatives.

16. *Business Week*, May 17, 1958, p. 131, cited in Kaufman, *Trade and Aid*, p. 139; Eisenhower, *Mandate for Change*, pp. 215–16.

17. Kaufman, *Trade and Aid*, pp. 54–55.

18. Annual Message to the Congress on the State of the Union, January 6, 1955, *PPP, 1955*, pp. 10–12.

19. Memorandum of Discussion at the 267th Meeting of the National Security Council, November 21, 1955, *FRUS, 1955–1957*, vol. 10, pp. 32–37; Memorandum of Discussion at the 273rd Meeting of the National Security Council, January 18, 1956, *FRUS, 1955–1957*, vol. 10, pp. 64–66.

20. Letter, Eisenhower to George Humphrey, March 27, 1957, "G. M. Humphrey 1957/58 (4)" folder, Box 21, AWAS, DDEPL.

21. Ibid.

22. Presidential News Conference, March 7, 1956, *PPP, 1956*, pp. 292–93; Kaufman, *Trade and Aid*, pp. 67–68.

23. Kaufman, *Trade and Aid*, pp. 68–71.

24. Ibid., p. 106.

25. Radio and Television Address to the American People on the Need for Mutual Security in Waging the Peace, May 21, 1957, *PPP, 1957*, pp. 385–96.

26. Ibid.

27. Kaufman, *Trade and Aid*, pp. 107–10.

28. Ibid., pp. 135–40.

29. Memorandum from Acting Secretary of State Herter to President Eisenhower, March 19, 1959, *FRUS, 1958–1960*, vol. 4, pp. 449–50; Kaufman, *Trade and Aid*, pp. 169–75, quote from pp. 174–75.

30. Kaufman, *Trade and Aid*, pp. 205–6.

31. Ibid., p. 200.

32. William H. Becker and William M. McClenahan, Jr., *The Market, the State, and the Export-Import Bank of the United States, 1934–2000* (New York: Cambridge University Press, 2003), pp. 64–65.

33. Memorandum, Prepared in the Export-Import Bank of Washington (to National Advisory Council on International Monetary and Financial Problems), June 10, 1953, *FRUS, 1952–1954*, vol. 1, pp. 324–29.

34. Becker and McClenahan, *Export-Import Bank*, pp. 63–65.

35. Ibid., pp. 10–56, 305–6.

36. Between 1945 and 1948 Eximbank extended approximately $2 billion in emergency reconstruction credits and Lend Lease termination credits to Western European nations to purchase coal as well as industrial and agricultural goods. The untraditional terms of these loans raised questions about repayment within the bank, but their long maturities and low interest rates were deemed to be crucial for American foreign policy purposes. Congress's fivefold increase in Eximbank's authorized lending to $3.5 billion in the 1945 legislation paved the way for these unusual loans. See also Becker and McClenahan, *Export-Import Bank*, pp. 66–74; "Formulation of a Foreign Financial Program: Policy to Help War-Devastated and Liberated Countries Meet Their Dollar Requirements Pending the Beginning of Loan Operations by the International Bank for

Reconstruction and Development," *FRUS, 1946,* vol. 1: *General: The United Nations* (Washington, DC: GPO, 1972), pp. 1390–1438.

37. "Using 'Taxpayers Money' Abroad," Remarks by Secretary Humphrey before Senator Homer Capehart's Advisory Group on International Trade, September 15, 1953, in Howard, *Humphrey Papers,* pp. 454–56.

38. Becker and McClenahan, *Export-Import Bank,* pp. 78–79.

39. Kaufman, *Trade and Aid,* pp. 29–31; Becker and McClenahan, *Export-Import Bank,* pp. 93–94, 96; *Eckstein Report,* p. 471.

40. Between 1953 and early 1954, the administration appointed a new president of Eximbank, Glenn Edgerton, who was instrumental in implementing revised policies responsive to Treasury's criticisms of the bank. These included restructuring the largest project credit (to date) in bank history, to address Secretary Humphrey's criticisms; entering into an agreement with his counterpart at the World Bank to dramatically circumscribe Eximbank long-term, sovereign lending and limiting its activities primarily to short and medium trade and commodity credits; and generally lowering the level of its activity. The White House also implemented an executive reorganization of Eximbank that increased its subordination to the Treasury and reduced the role of Congress and the State Department in its governance. See Becker and McClenahan, *Export-Import Bank,* pp. 92–99.

41. Milton S. Eisenhower, *The Wine Is Bitter: The United States and Latin America* (Garden City, NY: Doubleday, 1963), pp. 199–200.

42. Kaufman, *Trade and Aid,* pp. 29–32; Becker and McClenahan, *Export-Import Bank,* pp. 104–6; and Bryce Wood, *The Dismantling of the Good Neighbor Policy* (Austin: University of Texas Press, 1985), pp. 150–85.

43. Townsend Hoopes, *The Devil and John Foster Dulles* (Boston: Little, Brown, 1973), pp. 136–41.

44. Becker and McClenahan, *Export-Import Bank,* pp. 96–98; Notes, Cabinet Meeting, February 14, 1954, Box 1, OSSLAM, DDEPL.

45. Walter Sauer, unpublished manuscript, "Export-Import Bank of the United States: The Years 1953–1969," pp. 4–7, Export-Import Bank Library, Washington, DC; Congress, Senate, Committee on Banking and Currency, "Report on Export-Import Bank Act Amendments of 1954," 83rd Cong., 2nd Sess., 1954, pp. 1–8; Memorandum, Waugh to Dulles, "Policies with Respect to the Export Import Bank," October 28, 1954, CDF 1950–54, Box 377 (103-XMB/5–2154), RG 59, General Records of the DOS, National Archives, Adelphi, MD; Becker and McClenahan, *Export-Import Bank,* pp. 96–98.

46. Kaufman, *Trade and Aid,* pp. 31–32; Becker and McClenahan, *Export-Import Bank,* p. 307.

47. Wood, *Dismantling of the Good Neighbor Policy,* pp. 171–73.

48. Sauer, "Export-Import Bank," pp. 4–7; US Congress, Senate, Committee on Banking and Currency, "Report on Export-Import Bank Act Amendments of 1954," 83rd Cong., 2nd Sess., 1954, pp. 1–8; Becker and McClenahan, *Export-Import Bank,* pp. 98–99. The primary negotiators of the compromise legislation were Assistant Secretary of State for Economic Affairs Samuel C. Waugh, who later became chairman of Eximbank (1955–61), and Undersecretary of the Treasury Randolph Burgess. The legislation also reversed much of the White House's 1953 executive reorganization of Eximbank.

49. Becker and McClenahan, *Export-Import Bank,* pp. 99–109.

50. Ibid., pp. 102–4, 157.

51. Ibid., pp. 157, 305–10. As part of its intensified budget-balancing efforts in 1958–61, the administration pushed Eximbank to "guarantee" loans made by the private sector for export credit. This allowed Eximbank to leverage its resources, while reducing the budget-impacting "draw" on the Treasury of direct US loans and credits. While the initial impacts were modest, under Eisenhower's successors, Eximbank guaranteed more private loans than direct government credits.

52. By 1967 domestic agitation about surging imports led Congress to withdraw executive branch authority to conduct trade liberalization (tariff reduction) negotiations for the first time since 1934. It was only restored in 1975 after sea changes in the international economy, including devaluation of the dollar.

53. The US balance of merchandise trade first ran a postwar deficit in 1971, and it became permanent after 1975.

54. *Eckstein Report,* p. 455; *ERP, 1961,* p. 211.

55. The 1934 Trade Agreements Act was extended in 1937, 1943, 1945, 1948, 1949, 1952, 1953, 1954, 1955, 1958, and 1962 before it lapsed from mid-1967 until the enactment of the Trade Act of 1974 in January 1975.

56. The American tariff structure was dominated by specific duties (in amount of money) per unit of duty rather than ad valorem (a percentage of the price of the imported item) duty. So in periods of significant deflation (e.g., 1930–34), effective duty percentages soared, while in periods of inflation, especially the 1940s and, to a lesser extent the 1950s, the effective dutiable percentages declined. See Vatter, *U.S. Economy in the 1950's,* pp. 272–76.

57. Ibid., p. 275.

58. Minutes, Cabinet Meeting, "August 6, 1954" folder, Box 3, AWCS, DDEPL.

59. Vatter, *U.S. Economy in the 1950's,* p. 272. Eisenhower was exceedingly critical of Republican opposition to trade liberalization, in general, and in particular of the 1951 TAA, in which a Republican Congress placed restrictions on the discretion of executive branch trade negotiations. *Mandate for Change,* pp. 208–10. Here Eisenhower also discusses the pressures associated with the first escape clause case presented to him by the Tariff Commission in early 1953—briar smoking pipes imported from Italy, France, Britain, and Austria. Eisenhower notes that though the dollar amounts were minuscule, as a first indication of the direction of administration trade policy, the case was considered huge. Secretary of Commerce Sinclair Weeks told him, "The whole world, as well as Congress, would be watching the result." Eisenhower ultimately rejected the Tariff Commission's recommendation for higher tariffs to protect American manufacturers. See ibid., pp. 210–11.

60. George W. Ball, *The Past Has Another Pattern* (New York: Norton, 1982), pp. 205–9.

61. Eisenhower to Hazlett, July 24, 1954, in Robert Griffith, ed., *Ike's Letters to a Friend, 1941–1958* (Lawrence: University of Kansas Press, 1984), pp. 128–33. The Smoot-Hawley Tariff Act raised US duties at the onset of the Great Depression in 1930.

62. Kaufman, *Trade and Aid,* pp. 41–43.

63. Ibid., pp. 122–28; *ERP, 1958*, pp. 70–71; Memorandum of Conversation, March 22, 1959, *FRUS, 1958–1960*, vol. 4, pp. 42–43. C. Douglas Dillon was undersecretary of state between 1959 and 1961. After that he became secretary of the treasury under Presidents Kennedy and Johnson (1961–65). He had also served as ambassador to France and later deputy undersecretary of state for economic affairs (1957–59) under Eisenhower.

64. The most concise treatment of Japanese-American trade in the 1930s, focusing on US policy is William McClenahan's "Orderly Competition: American Government, Business and the Role of Voluntary Export Restraints in United States–Japan Trade, 1934–72" (PhD diss., George Washington University, 1993), pp. 1–51. For impacts of Japanese competition on other countries during that decade, see Michiko Ikeda, "Protectionism and Discrimination against Japan's Foreign Trade, 1926–1937" (PhD diss., Harvard University, 1989).

65. McClenahan, "Orderly Competition," pp. 20–25, 327–29. See also US Congress, Joint Economic Committee, Subcommittee on Foreign Economic Policy, *Hearings: Foreign Economic Policy*, 87th Cong., 1st Sess., 1961, pp. 26–35; Henry J. Tasca, *The Reciprocal Trade Policy of the United States* (Philadelphia: University of Pennsylvania Press, 1938), pp. 27, 198–201, 225, 291. Also, throughout the 1930s the United States scrupulously avoided negotiating trade agreements with other countries where tariff reductions under most-favored-nation principles could be "generalized" to Japanese exports. In 1940 the Roosevelt administration told Congress that just 3% of Japanese exports to the United States benefited from generalization of tariff concessions extended to others and that it did not "know of any other country that received as little direct benefit from our trade agreements as Japan." See McClenahan, "Orderly Competition," pp. 7, fn. 6, p. 15, fn. 15, p. 19; US Congress, House, Committee on Ways and Means, *Hearings: Extension of Reciprocal Trade Agreements Act*, 76th Cong., 3rd Sess., 1940, pp. 613–615, 628–37. During the 1950s the United States maintained quotas or absolute prohibitions on imports of certain agricultural commodities receiving price supports under the Agriculture Act of 1949. It also maintained various "voluntary" schemes to limit imports of crude petroleum from 1955 to 1959 and instituted mandatory restrictions on imports in March 1959 that were continued in various forms until 1973.

66. Memorandum, Hawkins to Sayre, "The Most Favored Nation Clause in Relation to Japanese Competition," April 2, 1934, Box 3302 (611.9417/27), CDF 1930–39, RG 59 DOS; McClenahan, "Orderly Competition," pp. 20–51.

67. McClenahan, "Orderly Competition," pp. 112–14. The American and British cotton textile industry monitored the rebuilding of the Japanese industry under the Occupation, and joint Anglo-American delegations to Japan in 1950 discussed the need for Japan to plan for "rational competition" in the future. See Despatch, Tokyo to DOS, Washington, DC, "Transmittal of Memorandum on Visit to Japan of Anglo-American Textile Group," May 19, 1950, Box 1861 (411.9431/5–350), CDF 1950–54, RG 59, DOS; "Concerning the Encouragement of Voluntary Restraints by Foreign Countries over Their Commerce with the United States," January 25, 1957, "CFEP 538 (7)" file, Box 7, Policy Papers Series, Records of CFEP, DDEPL.

68. Warren S. Hunsberger, *Japan and the United States in World Trade* (New York: Harper and Row, 1964), p. 185; McClenahan, "Orderly Competition," p. 74.

69. *FRUS, 1952–1954,* vol. 1, pp. 115–17; Memorandum, DOS, "Comments in support of the recommendations of the Trade Agreements Committee for tariff concessions on the following items: Cotton cloth, paragraph 904," (no date), "State Department, Trade Agreements Negotiations, 1950 [5 of 5]" file, Box 54, White House Central File: Confidential File; Harry S. Truman Presidential Library, Independence, MO.

70. McClenahan, "Orderly Competition," pp. 71–74. Many of these countries already maintained quotas for balance of payments purposes, which were allowed under GATT rules. In many situations these were modified to more effectively exclude Japanese imports.

71. Hunsberger, *Japan and the United States,* p. 185; McClenahan, "Orderly Competition," pp. 74, 77.

72. McClenahan, "Orderly Competition," pp. 90–97. The American antitrust laws, as interpreted in the mid-1930s, did not present a serious obstacle to privately negotiated VERs or those negotiated between governments with substantial industry assistance. By the 1950s, however, a radically different antitrust climate existed. It essentially eliminated the option of negotiation of "voluntary" restraints between the countrys' industries and limited involvement of their industries in diplomatic negotiations between governments. Even in the 1930s, however, some American producers and their lawyers expressed concern and sought American government "approval" of private agreements, usually in the form of officials' signatures after private-party negotiations concluded or by calling in diplomats in the final stages of those negotiations.

As discussed in chapter 5, before the Supreme Court's *United States v. Socony–Vacuum Oil Company* decision in 1940, government "encouragement" of private efforts to limit "destructive competition" was widely practiced in the mid-1930s and was thought or assumed to be a viable defense to prosecution under Section 1 of the Sherman Act. The Supreme Court ruled otherwise in *Socony.* The new decision was not applied to any VERs that remained viable before the outbreak of World War II. See McClenahan, "Orderly Competition," pp. 77–89. On the other hand, VERs in almost any form raised no antitrust-type issues under Japanese law in the prewar period, and few in the postwar period.

73. Memorandum of Conversation, Pending Legislation on Imports of Fresh or Frozen Tuna Fish, January 30, 1952, Box 1862 (411.946/1–305), CDF 1950–54, RG 59, DOS; Memorandum, Young to Allison, "Japanese Government's Export Quotas on Tuna," May 23, 1952, Box 1863 (411.943/8–253), CDF 1950–54, RG 59, DOS; McClenahan, "Orderly Competition," pp. 97–99.

74. US Congress, House, Committee on Ways and Means, *Hearings: Trade Agreements Extension Act of 1953,* 83rd Cong., 1st Sess., 1953, pp. 621–23.

75. Letter, Waugh to Locker, January 7, 1954, Box 1862 (411.948/10–1953), CDF 1950–54, RG 59, DOS; McClenahan, "Orderly Competition," pp. 102–10. Collective restraints on Japanese export to the United States reached and administered by Japanese industry, without the supervision of the Japanese government, were presumed to be in conflict with US antitrust law (as a restraint on American foreign commerce), and therefore illegal.

76. Notes, Cabinet Meeting, August 6, 1954, Box 2, and "The President's Character," August 6, 1954, "The President (2) [January 1954–June 1959]" folder, Box 1, both OSSLAM, DDEPL. Eisenhower's closest advisers had different reactions to the prospect of increased

Japanese exports. Dulles conceded the need and feared that Japan would become over-whelmed with a billion-dollar trade deficit and that communist agitation and economic unrest could destabilize the country. He emphasized that the United States had special responsibilities to Japan based on World War II and the Occupation. The secretary of state, however, thought that Japan's long-term future lay in Southeast Asian markets and that there was little future for Japanese products in the United States: "We do not need or want these products since they are nothing more than cheap imitations of American goods." Throughout 1954 Dulles would maintain this argument about Japanese imports. At one point during a November 1954 meeting with Japanese prime minister Shigeru Yoshida, official minutes indicate Dulles pulled a Japanese cotton flannel shirt out of his bag. It was an exact copy of its American counterpart but made out of cheaper materials. He predicted that it would never appeal to Americans, that it was reminiscent of prewar conduct and increased the possibility of trade restrictions on Japan's exports. However, another source (an oral history interview of John Allison of the State Department's Office of North East Asian Affairs) recounts that Dulles shouted, "This is what you people are doing to us . . . competing with us. You can't do this after all we've done." See McClena-han, "Orderly Competition," pp. 76–77, and quote in Shaller, *Altered States*, p. 102.

77. Minutes, Cabinet Meeting, "August 6, 1954" folder, Box 3, AWCS, DDEPL; Notes, Cabinet Meeting, August 6, 1954, Box 2, OSSLAM, DDEPL.

78. Minutes, Cabinet Meeting, "August 6, 1954" folder, Box 3, AWCS, DDEPL; Mc-Clenahan, "Orderly Competition," pp. 69–74; Shaller, *Altered States*, p. 108. See also Aaron Forsberg, *America and the Japanese Miracle: The Cold War Context of Japan's Post-war Economic Revival* (Chapel Hill: University of North Carolina Press, 2000), pp. 1–15, 140–43. The American trade surplus with Japan declined rapidly in the early 1960s and became a deficit in 1965. It has continued ever since.

79. Minutes, Cabinet Meeting, "August 18, 1954" folder, Box 3, AWCS, DDEPL.

80. Memorandum, "Effect of George Amendment on Tariff Negotiations," April 25, 1955, Box 1324 (394–41/4–2555), CDF-1955–59, RG 59, DOS; *Textile World* 105 (February 1955): p. 65; *Textile World* 105 (April 1955): pp. 99–100; McClenahan, pp. 134–39.

81. McClenahan, "Orderly Competition," pp. 139–40.

82. Hunsberger, *Japan and the United States*, pp. 298–300, 318; McClenahan, "Or-derly Competition," pp. 147–48. The most comprehensive treatment of these negotiations is Forsberg, *America and the Japanese Miracle*, pp. 155–64. In *Patchwork Protectionism: Tex-tile Trade Policy in the United States, Japan and West Germany*, (Ithaca, NY: Cornell Uni-versity Press, 1990), H. Richard Friman is exceedingly critical of the Eisenhower admin-istration's approach to these negotiations and its maneuvering to get them concluded before the authority used to negotiate them expired and was superseded by the much lower reductions allowed under the new 1955 legislation. He blames Eisenhower for the initiation of a special regime of trade protection, using VERs, created by the subsequent firestorm of opposition. We disagree. From the beginning, Eisenhower and Dulles, as their predecessors had, assumed that increased Japanese imports (at any level) would be ac-companied by some type of quantitative restraints. Furthermore, if the administration had only negotiated with Japan based on the limits in the 1955 legislation, it would not have been able to reduce the high tariff levels of American goods of interest to Japan,

286 NOTES TO PAGES 211–213

which had remained largely unchanged over the past twenty years. By timing the release of the results of the Japanese negotiations until after the passage of the 1955 TAA extension, the administration did intensify the uproar over the negotiations. In response, for subsequent trade legislation the Department of Commerce, not the State Department, took the lead in congressional hearings.

83. McClenahan, "Orderly Competition," pp. 172–77, 191–96. McClenahan, pp. 146–208, has the most comprehensive account of these negotiations, but see also Forsberg, *America and the Japanese Miracle,* pp. 204–13, and Sayuri Shimizu, *Creating a People of Plenty: The United States and Japan's Economic Alternatives, 1950–1960* (Kent, OH: Kent State University Press, 2001), pp. 109–21, 148–60.

84. McClenahan, "Orderly Competition," pp. 148–79.

85. US Congress, Senate, 84th Cong., 2nd Sess., *Congressional Record* (June 28, 1956), vol. 102, pt. 8, 11233–11242; "Telephone Call from Gov. Adams," September 13, 1956, "Memoranda of Tel. Conv. W. H. Sept. 4, 1956 to Dec. 31, 1956 (2)" file, Box 11, Telephone Calls Series, Dulles Papers, DDEPL; McClenahan, "Orderly Competition," pp. 176–86.

86. McClenahan, "Orderly Competition," pp. 191–96.

87. Ibid., pp. 197–208; Shimizu, *Creating a People of Plenty,* pp. 155–59. Citing the new VER, Eisenhower then rejected a Tariff Commission recommendation in the velveteen escape clause case for much higher tariffs.

88. Letter, Adams to Benson, February 27, 1957, "Voluntary Agreements" file, Box 24, Areeda Papers, DDEPL; "Minutes, Cabinet Meeting, Jan. 18, 1957" folder, Box 8, AWCS, DDEPL. See also US Congress, House, Committee on Ways and Means, *Hearings: Renewal of the Trade Agreements Act,* 85th Cong., 2nd Sess., 1958, pp. 2663, 2684, 2815–16; Letter, Dillon to Douglas MacArthur II, November 22, 1957, Box 1797 (411.9441/11–1557), CDF 1955–59, RG 59, DOS.

89. Despatch, Thibodeaux to DOS, Washington, DC, "Japan's Regulation of Exports," December 20, 1957, Box 1801 (411.949/12–205), CDF 1955–59, RG 59, DOS; McClenahan, "Orderly Competition," pp. 232–41; Shimizu, *Creating a People of Plenty,* pp. 164–67. Secretary of State Dulles made extensive favorable references to Japan's system of VERs in his testimony for renewal of the 1958 TAA in US Congress, House, Committee on Ways and Means, *Hearing: Renewal of the Trade Agreements Act,* 85th Cong., 2nd Sess., 1958, pp. 397–404. *Business Week* also discussed the Japanese system in spring 1958. See "Japan's Export Policy Stirs Debate," *Business Week* May 3, 1958, 84–85. The Japanese government also maintained control over minimum prices for exports (check prices). This was a much longer list of products than those with which it maintained quantitative controls.

90. Shaller, *Altered States,* pp. 108–9; Forsberg, *America and the Japanese Miracle,* pp. 162–63. These significant increases in Japanese exports to the United States tempered the concern of many at the State Department regarding VERs. In its own 1959 words, "The *potential* for harm [to the principles of liberal American trade policy] *greatly* exceeds the harm thus far" (emphasis in original document). See Memorandum, Beale and Gleason, "Trade Policy and National Security," attached to Memorandum of Discussion at the 409th Meeting of the National Security Council, June 4, 1959, *FRUS, 1958–1960,* vol. 4, pp. 214–21. Japanese exports were increasing rapidly because the Japanese government

and industry sought the maximum flexibility under existing restraints, while Japanese industry eagerly moved into new, uncontrolled (unrestrained) export markets.

91. US Congress, Senate, Subcommittee of the Select Committee on Small Business, *Hearings: Impact of Imports on American Small Business,* 86th Cong., 2nd Sess., 1960, pp. 5–7. Mann seems to be referring to Japanese quantitative controls and minimum price controls. The latter were more numerous.

92. US Congress, House, Committee on Ways and Means, *Hearing: Renewal of the Trade Agreements Act,* 85th Cong., 2nd Sess., 1958, pp. 397–404.

93. Presidential News Conference, September 27, 1956, *PPP, 1956,* p. 814; Memorandum of Conversation, "Kishi Call on President," June 19, 1957, "Japan 1957–59 (4)" folder, Box 31, AWIS, DDEPL.

94. Letter, Benson to Adams, February 21, 1957, "Voluntary Agreements" folder, Box 24, Areeda Papers, DDEPL.

95. Memorandum, "Concerning the Encouragement of Voluntary Restraint by Foreign Countries over Their Commerce with the United States," January 25, 1957, "CFEP (3)" folder, Box 7, Policy Papers Series, CFEP, DDEPL. All of the VERs that were not with Japan itself involved US-Japanese trade. E.g., in 1957 Italy was asked to contribute to the effectiveness of Japan's limitations by reducing its export of cotton velveteens to the United States, and it did so very reluctantly. Also, after 1957, exports of cotton cloth and garments from Hong Kong surged. The US government tried to negotiate a limitation on exports with Hong Kong manufacturers, to try to reduce complaints from Japan and the American cotton textile industry. The negotiations failed, and Hong Kong's exports were not controlled until 1961. See McClenahan, "Orderly Competition," pp. 203–5, 253–74.

96. Letter, Flesher to Evans, February 12, 1958, "Committee—Trade Policy—1958" folder, Box 251, RG 174, Records of the Office of the Secretary, Department of Labor, National Archives, College Park, MD.

97. McClenahan, "Orderly Competition," pp. 61–64. From inception of a statutory escape clause in 1948 through passage of the Trade Expansion Act in late 1962, 169 petitions for relief were filed, and the Tariff Commission recommended remedial action to the president in only 41 cases. The president granted relief, always in the form of higher tariffs, in just 15 cases. Though imports from Japan represented between 4% and 7% of all American imports in the 1950s, their presence in escape clause proceedings was all out of proportion to this small figure. Ten (one-quarter) of the cases in which the Tariff Commission found injury involved Japan as a major supplier. In five of the cases where Eisenhower and Kennedy increased tariffs (one-third of the total), Japan was the major supplier. The products were cotton typewriter cloth ribbon, clinical thermometers, stainless steel table flatware, certain types of carpets and rugs, and sheet glass. Eisenhower imposed the first three. In 1960 these five products accounted for $22 million, or just 2% of Japan's exports to the United States, minuscule compared to those products subject to voluntary restraints.

The "national security" clause (first enacted into law in 1955 and revised in 1958) allowed the president to impose restrictions on imports when their importation "tended to threaten" the national security. Twenty-eight petitions requesting tariff or import quota relief were filed under this provision between 1955 and 1962. Eisenhower's imposition of voluntary controls of crude oil and certain other products in 1957 and the subsequent imposition of mandatory controls in March 1959 were the only times affirmative relief was ever granted under this provision. See McClenahan, "Orderly Competition," p. 61, fn. 9. See also Notes, Cabinet Meeting, March 6, 1959, Box 5, OSSLAM, DDEPL.

98. McClenahan, "Orderly Competition," pp. 242–46.

99. Ibid., pp. 245–49.

100. Ibid., p. 249–53. During consideration of the TAA in 1958, Eisenhower also followed a Tariff Commission recommendation and increased tariffs on Japanese clinical thermometers from 42.5% to 85% in another escape clause proceeding. The Japanese industry had been very late in proposing a unilateral VER in this situation. *Business Week,* at the time, called it the one major failure of the two-year-old Japanese program of voluntary export restraint. See *Business Week,* quoted in ibid., p. 248, fn. 61.

101. Assistant Secretary of State Thomas Mann told a Senate committee in 1960 that the breakdown of the stainless steel flatware VER represented only one of "30-odd" VERs with which "we had trouble in enforcement." See McClenahan, "Orderly Competition," pp. 251–53; US Congress, Senate, Subcommittee of the Select Committee on Small Business, *Hearings: Impact of Imports on American Small Business,* 86th Cong., 2nd Sess., 1960, pp. 29–31. In mid-1959, the original bilateral cotton textile agreement came up for renewal. The close involvement of the ACMI that had characterized the 1956 negotiations did not occur. Nothing was submitted to it for its "approval." After the US government agreed to a Japanese suggestion of small increases in exports, the ACMI repudiated the result. This and the subsequent failure of the US government to get Hong Kong exporters to agree to restraints in 1959–60, pushed the ACMI in the direction of a system of global, importer-imposed quotas under GATT auspices that was initiated in 1961 under the Kennedy administration. The cotton textile VER continued as a unilateral Japanese undertaking into 1961. See McClenahan, "Orderly Competition," pp. 218–31, 246–48.

102. "Address at the Gettysburg College Convocation: The Importance of Understanding," April 4, 1959, *PPP, 1959,* pp. 309–17.

103. In Thomas W. Zeiler's *American Trade and Power in the 1960s* (New York: Columbia University Press, 1992), pp. 44–45, the author argues that by invoking the escape clause "which had little effect, Eisenhower remained entrenched in increasingly obsolete, ineffective, and at times, insensitive methods of dealing with imports." Of course, the escape clause was not the vehicle Eisenhower chose to address agitation for protection against the most politically divisive foreign competition. Instead, VERs were used, and in the 1950s they largely worked. Curiously, Zeiler lauds Kennedy's inclusion of trade adjustment assistance in the 1962 Trade Expansion Act as just the type of forward-looking innovation in pursuit of liberal trade that Eisenhower opposed. Trade adjustment assistance, however, was seldom used between 1963 and 1969, as imports (especially Japanese), and the political agitation concerning them, surged and derailed American trade legislation.

104. Vatter, *U.S. Economy in the 1950's,* pp. 258–63; Memorandum of Discussion at the 465th Meeting of the National Security Council, October 30, 1960, *FRUS, 1958–1960,* vol. 4, pp. 526–27.

105. Vatter, *U.S. Economy in the 1950's,* pp. 258–63; *ERP, 1961,* pp. 40–41.

106. Vatter, *U.S. Economy in the 1950's*, pp. 258–63.

107. Ibid., pp. 260–61; *Eckstein Report*, p. 442; Barry Eichengreen, *Globalizing Capital: A History of the International Monetary System*, 2nd ed. (Princeton: Princeton University Press, 2008), pp. 91–132.

108. Letter, Humphrey to Eisenhower, April 15, 1955, Box 22, AWAS, DDEPL.

109. Notes, Cabinet Meeting, April 20, 1956, Box 4, OSSLAM, DDEPL.

110. Ibid.

111. Presidential News Conference, October 22, 1959, *PPP, 1959*, p. 737; Kaufman, *Trade and Aid*, pp. 180–82.

112. Memorandum, "Financing by European Countries of Their Own Exports," Anderson to Eisenhower, no date, "Robert Anderson 1959 (2)" folder, Box 2, AWAS, DDEPL; *ERP, 1961*, pp. 40–41; Kaufman, *Trade and Aid*, pp. 184–86. Over time the Western Europeans and the Japanese reinvigorated their export credit agencies and coordinated their operations with their own expanded foreign aid programs with great success. By the 1980s American exporters faced stiff competition from European and Japanese exporters, who secured export sales using a combination of export credit and just such "tied aid." See Becker and McClenahan, *Export-Import Bank*, pp. 223–31, 263–66.

113. Memorandum, "The Military Burden," Anderson to Eisenhower, no date, "Robert Anderson 1959 (2)" folder, Box 2, AWAS, DDEPL; Memorandum of Discussion at the 465th Meeting of the National Security Council, October 31, 1960, *FRUS, 1958–1960*, vol. 4, pp. 520–38; Kaufman, *Trade and Aid*, pp. 192–96.

114. Vatter, *U.S. Economy in the 1950's*, p. 262.

115. Donald Paarlberg, Oral History Interview, pp. 153–55, Columbia University Oral History Project, DDEPL; Kaufman, *Trade and Aid*, p. 180; Minutes, Cabinet Meeting, August 7, 1959, Box 14, AWCS, DDEPL; *ERP, 1961*, p. 211.

116. Letter, Eisenhower to Anderson, January 13, 1961, "Robert Anderson 1960–61 (1)" folder, Box 3, AWAS, DDEPL.

117. Remarks, Financial Policies for Sustainable Growth, Robert B. Anderson, December 29, 1959, "Speeches by Robert Anderson (5)" folder, Box 74, Robert B. Anderson Papers, DDEPL. The liberal critique of these policies, embodied in the *Eckstein Report*, in late 1959, largely discussed the post-1957 balance of payments deficit as attributable to unique factors and periodic "gold runs" as being of little long-term consequence. The report, as discussed earlier in this chapter, thought the anti-inflation policies of the Eisenhower administration and the Federal Reserve entailed too much adverse impact on long-term economic growth rates. It espoused more expansive economic policies and optimistically thought that they would not accelerate inflation. See *Eckstein Report*, pp. 486–88.

118. Raymond J. Saulnier, *Constructive Years: The U.S. Economy under Eisenhower* (Lanham, MD: University Press of America, 1991), pp. 120–21.

119. Raymond J. Saulnier, Oral History Interview, 1967, pp. 47–50, Columbia University Oral History Project, DDEPL. Both Saulnier and Clarence B. Randall, Chair of Eisenhower's Council on Foreign Economic Policy believed the incoming Democratic administration placed far less emphasis on balance of payments implications and displayed less concern about inflation. Randall thought that incoming CEA chairman Walter Heller "has never experienced the challenge of economics in the foreign frame of reference."

See "Wednesday, January 4th" entry, "12/60–1/13/61" folder, vol. 18, Clarence Randall Diary, Box 6, CFEP, DDEPL.

EPILOGUE

1. Raymond J. Saulnier, *Constructive Years: The U.S. Economy under Eisenhower* (New York: University Press of America, 1991), pp. 224–25; Report, "Major Accomplishments of Treasury Department, January 1953–December 1960," p. 1, "Robert B. Anderson 1960/61 (1)" folder , Box 3, AWAS, DDEPL.

2. *ERP, 1961*, p. 187. Saulnier makes a strong argument that Eisenhower's restraints on defense-related spending may have reduced economic growth rates by as much as 0.6% a year between 1953 and 1961. See Saulnier, *Constructive Years*, pp. 224–25.

3. Robert P. Bremner, *Chairman of the Fed: William McChesney Martin Jr. and the Creation of the Modern American Financial System* (New Haven: Yale University Press, 2004), p. 147.

4. Notes of administration cabinet meetings were usually taken by Staff Secretary L. Arthur Minnich. He took these by hand and then prepared edited transcripts of the cabinet meetings, which became the official record. The official transcripts and Minnich's handwritten notes are both at the Eisenhower Library in Abilene, Kansas. The official transcripts are in the AWCS, while Minnich's handwritten notes are in the Records of OS-SLAM. It is our view that for this particular meeting Paarlberg's role as White House economic adviser and his recounting of the intensity of Eisenhower's views make these notes much more interesting than those taken or drafted by Minnich.

5. Minutes, Cabinet Meeting, November 27, 1959, p. 5, Box 14, AWCS, DDEPL.

6. Paarlberg Notes, "Minutes, Cabinet Meeting, November 27, 1959," folder, Box 14, AWCS, DDEPL.

7. See Richard Goode, "Gardner Means on Administered Prices and Administered Inflation," *Journal of Economic Issues* (March 21, 1994), pp. 173–86; Alan Brinkley, "The New Deal and the Idea of the State," in Steve Fraser and Gary Gerstle, eds., *The Rise and Fall of the New Deal Order, 1930–1980* (Princeton: Princeton University Press, 1989), pp. 85–121.

8. He had first laid out his views on the connectedness of economic freedom to a free society a decade before in a famous speech to the American Bar Association in 1949: "The Middle of the Road: A Statement of Faith in America," *American Bar Association Journal* 35 (October 1949), pp. 810–80.

9. Raymond J. Saulnier reminisces about the development of the president's economic thinking in papers published in *A Selection of Papers: Personal, Political, and Professional* (Privately Printed, 2007). See "First Meeting with Eisenhower, Summer 1947," pp. 23–24, and "Promoting Growth and Personal Freedom by Creating Conditions Favorable to the Operation of a Market-Based Economy," pp. 49–54. Also see Saulnier, *Constructive Years*, pp. 1–25.

10. Minutes, Cabinet Meeting, June 3, 1960, p. 2, Box 16, AWCS, DDEPL.

11. Eisenhower's chief tax reduction legacy was the Revenue Act of 1954, which was a structural reform of the tax laws, heavily weighted toward business incentives. To "pay"

for this reform, he essentially continued a 5% Korean War corporate income tax rate surcharge (that raised marginal rates to 52%) for his entire term.

12. Robert Griffith has an insightful discussion of Eisenhower's views about the inability of individuals and leaders to see beyond their self-interest to promote the interest of a group. Introduction to Robert Griffith, ed., *Ike's Letters to a Friend, 1941–1958* (Lawrence: University of Kansas Press, 1984), pp. 7–12.

13. William F. Buckley Jr., "Reflections on Election Eve," *National Review*, November 3, 1956, p. 6.

14. "So Long, Ike," *National Review*, January 14, 1961, pp. 8–9; Jeffrey Hart, *The Making of the American Conservative Mind: National Review and Its Times* (Wilmington, DE: Intercollegiate Studies Institute, 2006). Also see George H. Nash, "Jeffrey Hart's History of *National Review*," in George H. Nash, *Reappraising the Right: The Past and Future of American Conservatism* (Wilmington, DE: Intercollegiate Studies Institute, 2009), pp. 158–61.

ACKNOWLEDGMENTS

1. Arthur D. Chandler, Louis Galambos, and Daun Van Ee, eds., *The Papers of Dwight David Eisenhower*, 21 vols. (Baltimore: Johns Hopkins University Press, 1970–2001).

Essay on Primary Sources

In our survey of macroeconomic and microeconomic policy making during the Eisenhower administration, we relied extensively on primary source materials at the Eisenhower Presidential Library in Abilene, Kansas. Crucial to any understanding of the administration is Dwight D. Eisenhower, Papers as President of the United States (1953–1961), also known as the Ann Whitman File. It is composed of various series; the most useful were the Administrative Series, Cabinet Series, DDE Diary Series, Legislative Meeting Series, and Name Series. We gained a fuller appreciation of the Cabinet Series by using the handwritten notes of those meetings contained in records of the Office of the Staff Secretary, L. Arthur Minnich. Of much less value was Dwight D. Eisenhower, Records as President, White House Central Files (1953–1961), General File and Official File.

Others have published select primary materials created by the administration that address economic policies we discuss in our work. These include Alfred D. Chandler, Louis Galambos, and Daun van Ee, eds., *The Papers of Dwight David Eisenhower*, 21 vols. (Baltimore: Johns Hopkins University Press, 1970–2001), and Louis Galambos and Daun van Ee, eds., *The Papers of Dwight David Eisenhower*, World Wide Web facsimile by the Dwight David Eisenhower Memorial Commission, at www.eisenhowermemorial.org/presidential-papers/index.htm; and *Public Papers of the President of the United States: Dwight D. Eisenhower*, 8 vols. (Washington, DC: GPO, 1958–61). Also important is the multivolume *Foreign Relations of the United States* for the years 1946–1960. We found especially useful the single-volume works Robert H. Ferrell, ed., *The Eisenhower Diaries* (New York: Norton, 1981), Robert W. Griffith, ed., *Ike's Letters to a Friend, 1941–58* (Lawrence: University of Kansas Press, 1984), and Daniel D. Holt and James W. Leyerzapf, eds., *Eisenhower: The Prewar Diaries and Selected Papers, 1905–1941* (Baltimore: Johns Hopkins University Press, 1998).

The principal participants in economic policy making during the administration have deposited papers at the Eisenhower Library, which also has records associated with these individuals and their organizations. We made substantial use of the following for our study: Ezra Taft Papers (1952–61), Arthur F. Burns Papers (1930–69), Robert B. Anderson Papers (1937–85), Raymond J. Saulnier Papers (1929–85), Donald Paarlberg Records (1954–61), Phillip Areeda Papers and Records (1952–61), Gabriel Hauge Records (1952–58), and George Bookman Papers (1981–93), which contains Gabriel Hauge's unpublished autobiography. The Eisenhower Library also has an extensive collection of oral histories, as well as those of the Columbia University Oral History Project. We found the interviews with Arthur Burns, Raymond Saulnier, Ezra Taft Benson, Don Paarlberg, Robert Roosa, Randolph Burgess, Robert Anderson, Maurice Stans, Herbert Brownell, and Stanley Barnes informative.

Memoirs of the participants in economic policy making also provided varying degrees of usefulness. They include Dwight D. Eisenhower, *Mandate for Change, 1953–1956* and *Waging Peace, 1957–1961* (Garden City, NY: Doubleday, 1963 and 1965); Ezra Taft Benson, *Cross Fire: The Eight Years with Eisenhower* (Garden City, NY: Doubleday, 1962); Herbert Brownell, *Advising Ike: The Memoirs of Attorney-General Herbert Brownell* (Lawrence: University of Kansas Press, 1993); and Raymond J. Saulnier, *Constructive Years: The U.S. Economy under Eisenhower* (Lanham, MD: University Press of America, 1991).

Crucial to our study was Harry S. Truman (1952–53) and Dwight D. Eisenhower (1954–61) *Economic Report of the President*, 10 vols. (Washington, DC: GPO, 1952–61). Finally, US Congress, Joint Economic Committee, *Staff Report on Employment, Growth, and Price Levels*, 80th Cong., 1st Sess. (December 24, 1959), the so-called *Eckstein Report*, was important to our understanding of the critiques of Eisenhower's economic policies.

Index

Page numbers in *italics* refer to figures.

AAA. *See* Agricultural Adjustment Act

ACMI (American Cotton Manufacturers Institute), 210, 211, 288n101

acreage controls. *See* allotments in agricultural policy

Acreage Reserve Program (ARP), 134–35, 137, 139, 143, 144. *See also* Conservation Reserve Program

Adams, Sherman, 88, 145, 212

administrative budget, 30, 97

Advisory Board on Economic Growth and Stability, 27

Affluent Society, The (Galbraith), 78

Agricultural Act: of 1948, 121–22; of 1949, 123, 260n5; of 1954, 129–31; of 1956, 135–38; of 1958, 139, 143–44

Agricultural Adjustment Act (AAA): of 1933, 119; of 1938, 115, 116, 117, 119, 134

agricultural policy: direction of, 150–51; of Eisenhower, 126, 129–32, 228; Golden Promise, 124, 131; legacies of previous administrations, 118–24; overview of, 113–14, 148–51; reform efforts, 117–18, 124–29, 138–39, 140–41; in second term, 138–48; Soil Bank, 132–38; special message to Congress on, 142–43. *See also* Agricultural Act; Agricultural Adjustment Act; price supports, agricultural

Agricultural Trade Development and Assistance Act of 1954, 131–32, 149

agriculture, history of problems in, 118–24

Agriculture and Consumer Protection Act of 1973, 150

Agriculture Department (USDA), 132. *See also* Benson, Ezra Taft

Agriculture Improvement and Reform Act of 1996, 150

Alcoa (United States v. Aluminum Co. of America), 157–58, 163, 168

allotments in agricultural policy, 115, 117, 134, 136, 142–43

American Cotton Manufacturers Institute (ACMI), 210, 211, 288n101

American Farm Bureau Federation, 263n58, 264n67

Anderson, Clinton, 121, 122

Anderson, Robert B.: appointment of, 73–74, 83; foreign aid and, 220; gold reserve and, 221; inflation and, 98, 222; life and career of, 83–84; on *Meet the Press*, 90; on public works programs, 91; recession and, 90–91; tax cuts and, 91, 92, 93

Antitrust and the Formation of the Postwar World (Wells), 159, 177, 178–79, 181–82

antitrust bar, 167, 175–76

antitrust case law, history of, 156–59

Antitrust Civil Process Act of 1962, 166

antitrust policy: Brownell and, 163–64; DOJ Antitrust Division, 155, 164–66; Eisenhower contemplates, 161–63; National Committee to Study the Antitrust Laws, 167–69; oil cartel case, 176–82; overview of, 152–54; partisanship in enforcement of, 152–53, 159, 161, 162, 164, 167; political realities and, 162–63; Roosevelt and Truman legacies, 155–61; trade policy, VERs, and, 208–9. *See also* Clayton Act; Sherman Act

Arbenz, Jacobo, 187, 198, 200

Arnold, Thurman, 155, 167

ARP (Acreage Reserve Program), 134–35, 137, 139, 143, 144. *See also* Conservation Reserve Program

"As Is" Agreement of 1928, 160, 179

automatic stabilizers, 44, 47, 91, 94, 102–3, 107

automobile industry, 59, 86

Baker v. Carr, 260n11

balance of payments deficits: dollar gap and, 184; export sector and, 201; fiscal restraint and, 110; foreign economic policy and, 216–23; inflation and, 98, 99, 100, 222; recession and, 107

Balderston, C. Canby, 87

Barnes, Stanley N.: as assistant attorney general, 164; consent decrees and, 166; departure of, 173; merger section of report, 168–69; National Committee to Study the Antitrust Laws and, 167

Benson, Ezra Taft: career and appointment of, 125; Eisenhower and, 124, 126–27; "A General Statement on Agricultural Policy," 128–29; politics and, 127–28; on politics of agriculture, 117; in presidential campaign of 1960, 267–68n143; on progress made, 148; as Secretary of Agriculture, 83; Soil Bank and, 134–38; on surpluses, 140; unpopularity of, 126, 143, 149; VERs and, 214; on veto of Agricultural Act of 1956, 136–37; wheat price supports and, 141–42

Berle, Adolph, 76

Bethlehem Steel (United States v. Bethlehem Steel Corporation), 169, 172–74

Bicks, Robert, 175

Bison bomber, 40–42

Black, Eugene, 196

Blair, John M., 176

bomber gap, 40–42

Bradley, Omar, 11

Bragdon, John S., 89

Brannan, Charles, 122, 123

Brannan plan, 122–23

Bretton Woods system, 98, 100, 109, 140, 217, 223

British Petroleum (BP), 159, 160–61, 179

Brownell, Herbert: antitrust policy of, 163–64; as attorney general, 152; committee of, 153, 162, 167–69; consent decrees and, 166, 181; departure of, 175; oil production and, 180; partisanship in antitrust enforcement and, 161

Brown Shoe Co. v. United States, 170, 172

Brundage, Perceval F., 67

Buckley, William F., Jr., 231, 232–33

Budget and Impoundment Control Act of 1974, 252n77

budget deficits: of Eisenhower administration, xiii; increase in, 96–97; of Truman administration, 13–14, 19–20. *See also* debt management

budgets: balanced, 225; of departments, 67; of Eisenhower administration, 29–36, 73; federal spending as percentage of GNP, 69; for fiscal 1957, 192; for fiscal 1958, 65–67, 70–73, 192; for fiscal 1959, 194; for fiscal 1960, 103–5, 194; for fiscal 1961, 105–6, 195; of Truman administration, 8, 23, 29, 31. *See also* administrative budget; budget deficits; cash budget; defense spending

bureaucracy: big, threat of, x, 226–27; management of, 229–31; restraint on growth of, xiv; role of, 18

Bureau of the Budget, 28, 29. *See also* Dodge, Joseph M.

Burns, Arthur F.: balance of payments issue and, 219; as chairman of CEA, 25, 26–28; departure of, 82; Humphrey and, 28; on industrial environment, 62; inflation and, 49; influence of, 29; interest rates and, 63; Keynesian theory and, 46–47; recessions and, 43–44; taxes and, 48, 92, 93

Byrd, Harry, 72

Capehart, Homer E., 199, 200

capital goods boom, 56, 86

cash budget, 30, 32, 49–50, 97

Castro, Fidel, 195

CCC. *See* Commodity Credit Corporation

CEA. *See* Council of Economic Advisers

Cellar, Emanuel, 153, 161, 166

Cellar-Kefauver Amendment to Clayton Act: litigation under, 169, 171–72; purpose of, 155–56, 168; as untested, 153, 165

CFEP (Commission on Foreign Economic Policy), 185, 204

Chicago School of Economics, 268n1, 270n8, 277n105

Churchill, Winston, 229

Civil Investigative Demand (CID), 165–66

Clarfield, Gerard, xiii

Clayton Act: Bethlehem-Youngstown merger and, 173–74; Cellar-Kefauver Amendment to, 153, 155–56, 165, 168, 169, 171–72; civil actions and, 166; litigation under, 277n105; Section 5, 166

Cold War: death of Stalin and, 39; deepening of, 81; Eisenhower view of, 38, 226; Korean War and, 31; NSC 68 view of, 37–38; objectives of, ix; post-World War II military and, 2–14; protection of market economy and, 227–28; Soviet strategy in, xi; strategy for, 1–2, 6–7, 23–24

Columbia University, 2, 9, 14

Commission on Foreign Economic Policy (CFEP), 185, 204

commodities: basic, 114, 116; carryovers, 115–16, 120, 132–33, 146; modernized parity for, 121–22, 130, 131; 90 percent parity for, 117–18, 120, 123, 129, 135; overseas disposal of surpluses, 113–14, 131–32, 133, 139–40, 149–50; price support system for, 114–18; shortages in, 120; storage of, 113, 116, 123, 132–33, 145; surpluses of, 139, 150

Commodity Credit Corporation (CCC): cost of commodities owned by, 132–33, 139, 146; disposal of surpluses by, 131; nonrecourse loans from, 115; warehouses of, 120

Common Market (European Economic Community), 207, 218

Congress: antitrust policy and, 155–56; Benson and, 127–28; budget cutting by, 32; districts for members of, 260n11; elections of 1958, 82, 138, 145; Eximbank and, 195, 196, 199, 201; fiscal 1958 budget and, 72–73; Joint Economic Committee, 50, 76; partisanship in, 70; planning for wars and, 4–5, 6; relationships between Pentagon, military contractors, and, 42, 232

consent decrees, 166, 181

Conservation Reserve Program, 135, 137, 143, 150. See also Acreage Reserve Program

conservatism of Eisenhower, x, 221–22, 231–33

consumer credit, 56, 57, 58–59

consumer durables, 55, 56

consumer prices, 51

Control of Oil (Blair), 176

corn farmers, 146

corporate income tax rates, 33, 34, 36, 48, 93–94

cotton textile industry, 210–13, 283n67, 288n101

Council of Economic Advisers (CEA), 24, 108. See also Burns, Arthur F.; Saulnier, Raymond J.

Cross Fire (Benson), 149

crude oil production, sources of, 271n25

debt management, 61–62, 97–98

Defense Department: creation of, 10; relationships between Congress, military contractors, and, 42, 232; year of "maximum danger," 11, 31. See also defense spending

Defense Production Act: of 1950, 160; of 1951, 14; of 1952, 123

defense spending: budget deficit and, 29–32; challenges to holding line on, 70; Democrats and, 74; in fiscal 1958 budget, 71–72; in fiscal 1960 budget, 104; in fiscal 1961 budget, 106; Humphrey and, 31, 36–37, 67; New Look policy, 24, 40, 42, 74; in 1956–1957, 57; nuclear weapons and, 38–40; as percent of budget, 109–10; recession of 1953–1954 and, 44; reduction in, 225; review of, 36–40; Sputniks and, 87–88, 95; in Truman budget, 23

Democratic Advisory Committee, 77

Democratic Party: "defense wing" of, 41; divisions within, 19, 74, 77, 105; economic policy divide between Republican Party and, 74–79; fiscal 1958 budget and, 72; fiscal 1960 and, 104–5; foreign aid and, 189; hearing on bomber gap held by, 41–42. See also Eckstein Report

Development Loan Fund (DLF), 192, 193, 194, 219–20

Dewey, Thomas E., 16, 25, 122
Dillon, C. Douglas, 283n63
direct subsidies to farmers, 119, 122, 150–51
DLF (Development Loan Fund), 192, 193, 194, 219–20
Dodge, Joseph M.: as advisor, 28; budget cuts and, 30, 31; career of, 25; National Security Council and, 36; Truman administration and, 29
DOJ. See Justice Department
dollar: balance of payments and, 98, 99, 100; devaluation of, 222–23; inflation and, 81–82; world economy and confidence in, 219
dollar gap, 184, 218
Douglas, Paul, 50, 76
dual parity for commodities, 135
Dulles, John Foster: Eximbank and, 198–99, 200; Japanese imports and, 285n76; massive retaliation policy and, 39; negotiations with Japan and, 212; USDA and, 132; VERs and, 208, 213; views of foreign aid of, 189
Du Pont (Cellophane) case, 163, 168, 169–70
Du Pont (General Motors) stock case: Clayton Act and, 174; overview of, 170–71; as vertical acquisition case, 169; viewed as partisan vendetta, 159, 161; Wilson and, 163
"Dwight D. Eisenhower and the Corporate Commonwealth" (Griffith), 176–77

Eckstein, Arthur, 50
Eckstein Report: analysis of economic policy in, 106; on antitrust policy, 182, 272n30; fiscal policy in, 78–79, 108; on inflation policies, 50, 289n117
economic boom times (1954–1957): budgets during, 65–74; Federal Reserve, inflation, and, 60–64; overview of, 53–55, 79–80; policy divide between parties, 74–79; prosperity and, 55–60
economic policy: advisors on, 25–29; Eisenhower views on, ix, 17–18; during first term, 51–52; legacy of, 225–29; microeconomic, xiv–xv, 228–29; overview of, xi–xii. See also agricultural policy; antitrust policy; foreign economic policy; inflation; macroeconomic policy; recessions

Economic Report of the President (ERP): in 1954, 114, 116; in 1955, 47; in 1957, 57, 59–60, 165; in 1958, 57; in 1959, 96; in 1961, 107–8; Burns and, 27
Edgerton, Glenn, 281n40
education, federal spending for, 47–48, 69, 72–73
Eisenhower, Dwight D.: on agricultural policy, 142–43; on antitrust enforcement, 161; Benson and, 124, 126–27; Buckley on, 232–33; Burns and, 26; candidacy of, 15; career of, 4, 5–6, 9; compromises of, 223; conservatism of, x, 221–22, 231–33; on economy, 89, 130; election of, 16; experience of in Philippines, 190–91; on farm problem, 268n143; gradualism of, x, 114, 130; Humphrey and, 28; industrial mobilization and, 3–5; leadership of, x–xi, 231; legacy of, 225–33; management style of, 126, 154, 163, 230–31; Martin and, 45, 63; on military assistance, 186; on Mutual Security Agency, 186; opinions on military and strategic issues, 1–2; political realities and, 63, 92, 104, 268n143; on politicians, 95, 135–36; postwar appointments of, 2–3, 9–11, 12; on price support laws, 124; reelection of, 64, 67–68, 76; Republican Party and, 17–18, 229, 231; stroke suffered by, 88; Taft and, 2, 16; on taxation, 93; on Trade Agreements Act, 204–5; on trade with Japan, 215; Truman and, xi, 1–2, 6, 12–13, 15, 68–69; vacation of, 89–90; on vetoing Agricultural Acts, 136, 137, 144. See also Modern Republicanism; State of the Union messages; vetoes by Eisenhower
Eisenhower, Milton, 125, 198
Eisenhower administration, ix–xi, xiii. See also budgets; Economic Report of the President
elections of 1958, 82, 138, 145. See also presidential campaigns
electrical equipment manufacturers, 174–76
Ellender, Allen J., 140, 141
Employment Act of 1946, 24, 25
ERP. See Economic Report of the President
escape clause, 204, 205, 288n103
European Economic Community (Common Market), 207, 218

European Recovery Program (Marshall Plan), 183, 197

excess profits tax, 34, 44–45

excise taxes, 34–35, 44, 93–94

executive branch, Eisenhower views of, 230–31

Export-Import Bank of the United States (Eximbank), 184, 195–201

exports: of agricultural products, 113, 131–32, 133, 139–40, 149–50; of capital goods, and Eximbank, 199; of cotton textile products from Japan, 210–13; from Japan, and VERs, 205–9; of stainless steel flatware from Japan, 214–15. See also Export-Import Bank of the United States; voluntary export restraints

Fair Deal, xi, xiv, 18, 19, 125, 229

Fair Trade laws, 155

farmers, direct subsidies to, 119, 122, 150–51

farm policy. See agricultural policy

Federal National Mortgage Association (Fannie Mae), 58

Federal Open Market Committee (FOMC), 61, 62

Federal Reserve: "active ease" policy of, 107; communication between White House and, 64, 110; independence of, 24, 45, 63, 64; inflation and, 48–49, 60–64; recessions and, 45–47, 95–96; relationship between White House and, 86–87, 225–26. See also Martin, William McChesney

Finletter, Thomas, 13

Fleming, Arthur, 103

Folsom, Marion, 46, 69

FOMC (Federal Open Market Committee), 61, 62

Food and Agriculture Act of 1965, 149–50

foreign economic policy: balance of payments and, 216–23; criticism of, 188; evolution of views on assistance, 189–95; Eximbank battle, 195–201; expenditures, 183–84; goals for, 183–85; legacy of, 228–29; overview of, 223–24; review of assistance, 185–89; trade policy, 201–16

Forrestal, James V., 8–9, 10

Friedman, Milton, 59–60

Fulbright, William, 194

Galbraith, John Kenneth, 77, 78–79

Gardner, Trevor, 41

General Agreement on Tariffs and Trade (GATT), 132, 203, 207

Golden Promise, 124, 131

Goldfine, Bernard, 145

gold reserve, 221. See also Bretton Woods system

Goldwater, Barry, 231, 232, 233

government. See bureaucracy

gradualism of Eisenhower, x, 114, 130

Great Depression: farm prices in, 119, 130, 135; Hoover and, 54; legacy of, x, 1; Taft Republicans and, 229

Griffith, Robert, 176–77

Gulf settlement, 181

Hand, Learned, 157–58

Hansen, Victor, 173, 175

Harris, Seymour E., 77

Hart-Scott-Rodino Antitrust Improvements Act of 1975, 165

Hauge, Gabriel: balance of payments issue and, 219; on Benson, 127; defense spending and, 36; departure of, 84; education and career of, 25–26; on farm price supports, 134; Federal Reserve and, 64; on inflation psychology, 102; interest rates and, 63; "little four" group and, 87; memoirs of, 242–43n3; Modern Republicanism and, 68, 84; recessions and, 43, 90; role of, 28; on Russell, 118; on Saulnier, 83

Heller, Walter, 77, 108, 289n119

highway system, 69

History of Agricultural Price-Support and Adjustment Programs, 1933–84 (USDA), 148

Hobby, Oveta Culp, 69

Hoover, Herbert, xi, 54

Hoover Commission, 9

horizontal agreements among competitors, 157

horizontal mergers, 172

housing market, 46, 56, 58, 85, 94

Humphrey, George M.: antitrust policy and, 162, 163; balance of payments issue and, 218–19, 256n83; budget issues and, 30, 32; Burns and, 28; cash budget and, 49–50; consumer credit and, 57; defense spending

Humphrey, George M. (*continued*)
    and, 31, 36–37, 67; departure of, 48, 83;
    Eisenhower vacation at estate of, 90;
    Eximbank and, 195, 197–98, 199; fiscal 1958
    budget and, 66–67, 71–72; foreign economic
    aid and, 187, 190; on industrial environment,
    62; inflation and, 49, 59; interest rates and,
    63; on Japanese exports, 209; NSC and, 36;
    price supports and, 141; as secretary of
    Treasury, 25; successor to, 73–74; taxes and,
    33, 48; on world economy, 203
Humphrey, Hubert H., 77
Hurley, Patrick J., 3–4

IBRD. *See* International Bank for Reconstruc-
    tion and Development
import quotas, 205
individual income tax rates, 33, 48
Industrial Mobilization Plan (IMP), 4–5
inflation: between 1959 and 1964, 109, 223;
    balance of payments and, 222; consumer
    prices, 51; during economic boom times,
    53–54, 59–64; Eisenhower view of, 24;
    during first term, 47–51; intractability of,
    100–103; in 1970s, 52; during second term,
    96–103, 99; structural roots of, 227;
    temporary income taxes and, 33–34
installment credit, 56, 57, 58–59
interest rates and economic boom times, 55,
    61, 62–63
International Bank for Reconstruction and
    Development (IBRD, or World Bank), 184,
    195, 196, 197, 199
international cartels, 158–59
international concerns about U.S. balance of
    payments and fiscal situation, 98, 99, 100,
    109
internationalism, 68–69
International Monetary Fund, 100, 104, 196
Iran and British Petroleum, 160–61, 179

Jackson, Henry "Scoop," 41
Jackson, Robert H., 159
Jacoby, Neil, 26
Japan: cotton textile products from, 210–13;
    economy of, 187–88; integration of into

trade system, 201, 205–9, 213–14, 216;
    stainless steel flatware from, 214–15; trade
    deficit of, 209–10; VERs and, 215–16
JCS (Joint Chiefs of Staff), 7, 9–11, 14
Johnson, Louis, 10, 11
Johnson, Lyndon B., 74–75, 84, 90
Joint Chiefs of Staff (JCS), 7, 9–11, 14
Justice Department (DOJ): Antitrust Division,
    155, 164; Civil Investigative Demand,
    165–66; *Du Pont* (Cellophane) case, 169–70;
    Du Pont (General Motors) stock case,
    170–71; oil cartel case, 178–79, 180–81;
    prefiling conferences of, 164–65; review of
    pending antitrust cases by, 153–54. *See also*
    Barnes, Stanley N.; Brownell, Herbert

Kahn, Alfred, 172–73
Kaufman, Burton, 176, 177, 180, 269n4
Kauper, Thomas, 167
Kefauver, Estes, 153, 161
Kennedy, John F., 77, 79, 108, 268n143
Kenney, Donald S., 93
Keynesian economic theory, 46–47, 50
Keyserling, Leon, 26–27, 77–78, 108
Kishi, Nobusuke, 214
Korean War: armistice agreement, 36; farm
    prices and, 120–21, 123; growth of military
    and, 19; productive capacity of Japan during,
    206; recession of 1953–1954 and, 44; Soviet
    Union and, 31; temporary taxes to fund,
    33–34, 47, 93–94; Truman and, 11, 12–14
Kovaleff, Theodore, 167, 171

Larson, Arthur, 73, 84, 88
Latin America: drift to left in, 201; Eximbank
    and, 196, 197, 198, 200; social development
    fund for, 195
leadership of Eisenhower, x–xi, 231
LeMay, Curtis, 42
Lovett, Robert, 13, 163

MacArthur, Douglas, 2, 5, 14–15
macroeconomic policy: budget issues, 29–36;
    criticism of, 106, 107–9; legacy of, 225–29;
    overview of, xii–xiii. *See also* economic

boom times; Federal Reserve; inflation; recessions

management style of Eisenhower, 126, 154, 163, 230–31

Mann, Thomas, 213

Mao Tse-tung, 11

market economy, protection of, 227–28

Marshall, George C., 5–6, 14

Marshall Plan (European Recovery Program), 183, 197

Martin, William McChesney: consumer credit and, 57; inflation and, 48, 61; interest rates and, 62; recession and, 45–47, 86, 95–96, 107; Saulnier and, 87; tax cuts and, 91; views of, 64

massive retaliation, policy of, 39–40

McGuire Act of 1952, 155, 162

Means, Gardiner C., 76

mergers, 168–69, 171–74, 277n105

microeconomic policy, xiv–xv, 228–29. *See also* agricultural policy; antitrust policy; foreign economic policy

Middle East, goodwill trip to, 194

military: cost of establishments in NATO countries, 216, 220; pressures for spending from within, 40; rivalries among armed services, 3, 6, 9, 37; unified command structure for, 3–5, 6–8. *See also* defense spending; Korean War

military aid: criticism of, 188; "dual use" of, 223; expenditures, 184; fiscal 1957 budget for, 192; Humphrey on, 187; to Western Europe, 186

military assistance to other governments, 72

military-industrial complex, 42, 232

Miller-Tydings Act of 1937, 155, 162

Minnich, Arthur, 290n4

Mitchell, Billy, 4–5

Mitchell, Wesley C., 26

Modern Corporation and Private Property, The (Means and Berle), 76

modernized parity for commodities, 121–22, 130, 131

Modern Republicanism, xiii–xiv, 48, 54, 67–70, 84

monetary policy. *See* Federal Reserve

monopolization cases. *See* Sherman Act, Section 2 cases

Montgomery, Bernard L., 229

Morgan, Iwan, xiii

Mosaddeq, Mohammad, 179, 187

Mundt, Karl, 135

Mutual Aid, 189, 191–93

Mutual Security Act, 183

Mutual Security Agency, 185–86

Nasser, Gamal Abdel, 187

National Advisory Council on International Monetary and Financial Problems, 196

National Bureau of Economic Research, 26

National Committee to Study the Antitrust Laws, 162, 167–69

National Defense Act of 1947, 5, 8

National Lead (United States v. National Lead Company), 158, 163, 168

National Recovery Administration, 155

National Review, 232–33

National Security Act of 1947, amendments to, 10

"national security" clause, 205, 287–88n97

National Security Council (NSC): Document Number 68 (NSC 68), 11, 12–13, 37–38; Paper 162/2, 38–39; review of strategic posture, 36

NATO (North Atlantic Treaty Organization), 12, 216, 220

Nehru, Jawaharlal, 187

New Deal: agricultural policy, 119, 265n88; farm programs of, 125; policies inherited from, xi; support for programs of, xiv, 18, 19, 54, 229

new economics, 108, 109

New Look policy, 24, 40, 42, 74

New York Federal Reserve Bank, 61

90 percent parity for basic commodities, 117–18, 120, 123, 129, 135

Nixon, Richard: on agricultural policy, 147; Barnes and, 164; Benson and, 267–68n143; budgets and, 103; Burns and, 28; commodity surpluses and, 150; devaluation of dollar and, 223; inflation and, 109; as presidential candidate, 104, 106; recession and, 90, 102; tax cuts and, 92; wage price spiral and, 101

Non-Obligated Authorizations (NOA), 29–30, 32

North Korea, invasion of South Korea by, 11.
    See also Korean War
Nourse, Edward, 27
NSC. *See* National Security Council
nuclear weapons, discussion of role of, 38–40

O'Connor, Roderic, 199
Oil Cartel Case, The (Burton), 176, 177, 180,
    269n4
oil industry cartel case, 159–61, 176–77
oil production, sources of, 271n25
O'Mahoney, Joseph, 153, 161
Oppenheim, S. Chesterfield, 167
overseas disposal of agricultural surpluses,
    113–14, 131–32, 133, 139–40, 149–50

Paarlberg, Don: appointment of, 84–85; on
    Benson and Eisenhower, 126, 127; on CCC
    carryover stock, 133; notes of, 226; RDP and,
    147; trade balance and, 221
partisanship: after congressional elections of
    1958, 145; in antitrust policy enforcement,
    152–53, 159, 161, 162, 164, 167; Cold War
    military strategy and, 40–42; in Congress,
    70; military career and, 229–30; of
    Republican Party, 18–19; in tax policy, 74;
    in Truman budget cutting, 8
Partridge, Earle E., 41–42
Passman, Otto, 189
Patterson, Robert, 8
Pentagon. *See* Defense Department
Pershing, John J., 5
political realities: antitrust policy and, 162–63;
    Benson and, 127–28; cotton textile industry
    and, 211–13; Eisenhower sensitivity to, 63,
    92, 104, 268n143
political virtue, ideas of, 231
prefiling conferences in cases related to
    Sherman Act, 164–65
presidential campaigns: of 1948, 122; of 1952,
    15, 16, 161; of 1956, 64, 67–68, 75–76, 138; of
    1960, 104, 106, 267–68n143
price controls, 14, 49
price-fixing cases, 174–76
price supports, agricultural: in Agricultural
    Act of 1956, 137–38; Benson and, 128–29; as

budget buster, 133, 139, 141; Eisenhower on,
    124; equity of, 147; for feed grains, 145–46;
    history of, 119–24; mandated by Congress,
    119; overview of, 113, 114–18; progress on, 149;
    reforms to, 133–34; for wheat, 141–42
primary sources, 293–94
private lawsuits for treble damages, 175–76
Prize, The (Yergin), 177
productivity of farms, 121
prosperity, "problem" of, 55–60
Proxmire, William, 143
public works programs, 89, 91, 95

Randall, Clarence, 162, 185, 204, 289–90n119
Rayburn, Sam, 74, 75, 84, 90
RDP (Rural Development Program), 128, 147
recessions: of 1953–1954, 43–47; of 1957–1958,
    85–96, 108, 109; of 1960–1961, 102–3,
    107–8; automatic stabilizers, 44, 47, 91, 94,
    102–3, 107; causes of, 85–86; management
    of, 88–91; tax cuts during, 91–94
Reciprocal Trade Agreements Act. *See* Trade
    Agreements Act
Reed, Daniel A., 33, 35
Reed-Bulwinkle Act of 1951, 269–70n7
refinancing public debt, 97–98
regulatory regime, 18, 229
Republican Party: antitrust plan of 1952
    platform, 161; divisions within, 19; economic
    policy divide between Democratic Party
    and, 74–79; Eisenhower and, 17–18, 229,
    231; focus on future of, 54; New Deal and
    Fair Deal policies and, 18; partisanship of,
    18–19; traditional wing of, 68, 70, 83, 229.
    See also Modern Republicanism; Taft,
    Robert A.
Revenue Act of 1954, 35–36, 290–91n11
Ridgway, Matthew, 41
Rivers, Harbor and Flood Control Act of 1958,
    95
Robinson-Patman Act, 153, 155, 162, 277n105
Rogers, William, 175
Roosa, Robert, 36–37
Roosevelt, Franklin D., xi, 155. *See also* New
    Deal
Rural Development Program (RDP), 128, 147
Russell, Richard, 41, 118

Samuelson, Paul, 108
Saulnier, Raymond J.: appointment of, 82–83;
 on capital goods boom, 56; career of, 239n3;
 consumer credit and, 58–59; on devaluation
 of dollar, 222–23; inflation and, 101, 109;
 Martin and, 87; recession and, 85, 86, 88,
 90; steel strike and, 102; trade balance and,
 221; views of Martin by, 64
Schlesinger, Arthur M., 77
Sherman Act: litigation under, 277n105;
 Miller-Tydings Act compared to, 155; "per se
 rule," 157, 173, 277n105; prefiling confer-
 ences in cases related to, 164–65; "rule of
 reason" arguments, 156–57, 168; Section 1
 cases, 152, 156, 168, 174–76; Section 2 cases,
 152, 157–58, 168, 169–70; "thrust upon"
 exception to, 273n56
Sloan, John W., xiii
SoCal (Standard Oil of California), 159, 181
Social Security, xiv, 30, 69, 229
Socony (Standard Oil of New York), 157, 159
Soil Bank, 134–38
Soil Conservation and Domestic Allotment
 Act of 1936, 119
SONJ (Standard Oil of New Jersey), 159,
 180–81
sources, primary, 293–94
South Asia, goodwill trip to, 194
Soviet Union: atomic bomb testing by, 11;
 Bison bomber of, 40–42; foreign aid effort
 of, 188; nonaligned countries and, 187–89;
 North Korea and, 31; policy of massive
 retaliation and, 39–40; surpluses sold to,
 132. See also Sputniks
speeches of Eisenhower: on agricultural
 policy, 142–43; on economic conditions, 89;
 on Mutual Aid, 192–93. See also State of the
 Union messages
Sputniks, 85, 87–88, 95, 108
stabilizing budget policy, 105–6
stainless steel flatware exports from Japan,
 214–15
Stalin, Joseph, 39
Standard Oil of California (SoCal), 159, 181
Standard Oil of New Jersey (SONJ), 159,
 180–81
Standard Oil of New York (Socony), 157, 159
Stans, Maurice, 91, 97

State Department, 132. See also Dulles, John
 Foster; trade policy
State of the Union messages: in 1953, 30, 185;
 in 1954, 186; in 1955, 189–90; in 1957, 59, 81
steel industry, 59, 66, 101–2, 169, 172–74
Stern, Ken, 125
Stevenson, Adlai E., 16, 54, 75–76, 232–33
Stewart, Walter W., 26
stock market and inflation psychology, 102
Sukarno, 187
Summerfield, Arthur, 126–27
Supreme Command for the Allied Powers,
 206
Symington, Stuart, 13, 41, 77

TAA. See Trade Agreements Act
Taft, Robert A.: Benson and, 125; budget
 issues and, 30, 32; as candidate for
 Republican nomination, 15–16; Eisenhower
 and, 2, 16; followers of, 54, 68, 83, 229;
 Humphrey and, 25; military role and, 8
tariffs, 203, 205, 210–13, 215
tax policy: for Korean War funding, 33–34, 47,
 93–94; partisanship in, 74; postponement
 of reductions, 66, 67; reductions during
 recession, 91–94; of Republican Party, 229
tax system, structural changes to, 32–36
Temporary National Economic Committee, 155
Tennessee Valley Authority, 174
Texaco settlement, 181
Thye, Edward, 135
*Timken Roller Bearing Company v. United
 States*, 158–59, 163, 168
tobacco price support bill, 147
Trade Agreements Act (TAA): of 1934,
 extensions of, 202–3, 204, 210, 282n55; of
 1958, 204–5, 213
trade deficits of Japan, 209–10
trade policy: escape clause, 204, 205, 288n103;
 as Eurocentric, 201; liberalization of, 184,
 203–4, 216, 221; "national security" clause,
 205, 287–88n97; overview of, 201–2; trade
 balance, 1951–1960, 202; unconditional
 most-favored nation principles, 203, 206–7
trade surplus, 220–21
Treasury Department. See Anderson,
 Robert B.; Humphrey, George M.

treble damage civil lawsuits, 175–76

Truman, Harry S.: agricultural policy and, 121–23; antitrust cases of, 158–60; budget deficits of, 13–14, 19–20; budgets of, 8, 23, 29, 31; Council of Economic Advisers, 24, 27; criticism of, 12–13; defense department and, 8–9; Eisenhower and, xi, 1–2, 6, 12–13, 15, 68 69; Iranian concession and, 160–61; Korean conflict and, 11, 12–14; MacArthur and, 14–15; unification of services under, 7–8; wage and price controls of, 14. *See also* Fair Deal

tuna fish exports from Japan, 207–8

Twinning, Nathan, 41, 42

unconditional most-favored nation principles, 203, 206–7

unemployment, 44, 55, 85, 94, 107

unified military command structure, 3–5, 6–8

United States v. Aluminum Co. of America (Alcoa), 157–58, 163, 168

United States v. American Tobacco Co., 168

United States v. Bethlehem Steel Corporation, 169, 172–74

United States v. Brown Shoe, 174

United States v. National Lead Company, 158, 163, 168

United States v. Socony-Vacuum Oil Company, 157, 284n72

United States v. United States Steel Corp., 158

urban renewal, federal spending on, 47–48, 69, 74

USDA (Department of Agriculture). *See* agricultural policy; Benson, Ezra Taft

VERs. *See* voluntary export restraints

vertical acquisitions, 169, 172. *See also Du Pont (General Motors) stock case*

vetoes by Eisenhower, 73, 105, 136–37, 144, 147

voluntary export restraints (VERs), 201, 205–9, 211–16

wage price spiral, 101–2

Wallich, Henry C., 103

Warren, Earl, 164

Watson, Thomas, Sr., 163

Waugh, Samuel C., 281n48

Wells, Wyatt, 159, 177, 178–79, 181–82

wheat price supports, 141–42

Wilson, Charles E., 28, 41, 84, 163, 190

World Bank, 184, 195, 196, 197, 199

World War II, Eisenhower in, 5–6, 7

Yergin, Daniel, 177

Young, Milton, 135